Read this book online today:

With SAP PRESS BooksOnline we offer you online access to knowledge from the leading SAP experts. Whether you use it as a beneficial supplement or as an alternative to the printed book, with SAP PRESS BooksOnline you can:

- Access your book anywhere, at any time. All you need is an Internet connection.
- Perform full text searches on your book and on the entire SAP PRESS library.
- Build your own personalized SAP library.

The SAP PRESS customer advantage:

Register this book today at *www.sap-press.com* and obtain exclusive free trial access to its online version. If you like it (and we think you will), you can choose to purchase permanent, unrestricted access to the online edition at a very special price!

Here's how to get started:

1. Visit *www.sap-press.com*.
2. Click on the link for SAP PRESS BooksOnline and login (or create an account).
3. Enter your free trial license key, shown below in the corner of the page.
4. Try out your online book with full, unrestricted access for a limited time!

Your personal free trial **license key** for this online book is: **hbf6-e4gk-rpjz-2t5n**

SAP® BusinessObjects Planning and Consolidation

 **PRESS**

SAP PRESS is a joint initiative of SAP and Galileo Press. The know-how offered by SAP specialists combined with the expertise of the Galileo Press publishing house offers the reader expert books in the field. SAP PRESS features first-hand information and expert advice, and provides useful skills for professional decision-making.

SAP PRESS offers a variety of books on technical and business related topics for the SAP user. For further information, please visit our website: *www.sap-press.com*.

Naeem Arif, Sheikh Tauseef
Integrating SAP ERP Financials
2011, app. 380 pp.
978-1-59229-300-1

Vincenzo Sopracolle
Quick Reference Guide to Financial Accounting with SAP ERP Financials
2010, app. 650 pp.
978-1-59229-313-1

Paul Theobald
Transitioning to IFRS in SAP ERP Financials
2009, 209 pp.
978-1-59229-319-3

William D. Newman
Understanding SAP BusinessObjects Enterprise Performance Management
2011, 300 pp.
978-1-59229-348-3

Sridhar Srinivasan and Kumar Srinivasan

SAP® BusinessObjects Planning and Consolidation

Bonn • Boston

Galileo Press is named after the Italian physicist, mathematician and philosopher Galileo Galilei (1564–1642). He is known as one of the founders of modern science and an advocate of our contemporary, heliocentric worldview. His words *Eppur se muove* (And yet it moves) have become legendary. The Galileo Press logo depicts Jupiter orbited by the four Galilean moons, which were discovered by Galileo in 1610.

Editor Stephen Solomon
Developmental Editor Kelly Grace Harris
Copyeditor Jutta VanStean
Cover Design Jill Winitzer
Photo Credit iStockphoto.com/enot-poloskun
Layout Design Vera Brauner
Production Editor Kelly O'Callaghan
Assistant Production Editor Graham Geary
Typesetting Publishers' Design and Production Services, Inc.
Printed and bound in Canada

ISBN 978-1-59229-239-4

© 2010 by Galileo Press Inc., Boston (MA)
1st Edition 2010

Library of Congress Cataloging-in-Publication Data
Srinivasan, Sridhar.
  SAP BusinessObjects Planning and Consolidation / Sridhar Srinivasan, Kumar Srinivasan. -- 1st ed.
      p. cm.
  Includes bibliographical references and index.
  ISBN-13: 978-1-59229-239-4 (alk. paper)
  ISBN-10: 1-59229-239-9 (alk. paper)
 1. BusinessObjects. 2. Business planning. 3. Strategic planning. I. Srinivasan, Kumar. II. Title.
  HD30.28S65 2010
  658.4'01028553--dc22
                                                                    2010005755

All rights reserved. Neither this publication nor any part of it may be copied or reproduced in any form or by any means or translated into another language, without the prior consent of Galileo Press GmbH, Rheinwerkallee 4, 53227 Bonn, Germany.

Galileo Press makes no warranties or representations with respect to the content hereof and specifically disclaims any implied warranties of merchantability or fitness for any particular purpose. Galileo Press assumes no responsibility for any errors that may appear in this publication.

"Galileo Press" and the Galileo Press logo are registered trademarks of Galileo Press GmbH, Bonn, Germany. SAP PRESS is an imprint of Galileo Press.

All of the screenshots and graphics reproduced in this book are subject to copyright © SAP AG, Dietmar-Hopp-Allee 16, 69190 Walldorf, Germany.

SAP, the SAP-Logo, mySAP, mySAP.com, mySAP Business Suite, SAP NetWeaver, SAP R/3, SAP R/2, SAP B2B, SAPtronic, SAPscript, SAP BW, SAP CRM, SAP Early Watch, SAP ArchiveLink, SAP GUI, SAP Business Workflow, SAP Business Engineer, SAP Business Navigator, SAP Business Framework, SAP Business Information Warehouse, SAP inter-enterprise solutions, SAP APO, AcceleratedSAP, InterSAP, SAPoffice, SAPfind, SAPfile, SAPtime, SAPmail, SAPaccess, SAP-EDI, R/3 Retail, Accelerated HR, Accelerated HiTech, Accelerated Consumer Products, ABAP, ABAP/4, ALE/WEB, Alloy, BAPI, Business Framework, BW Explorer, Duet, Enjoy-SAP, mySAP.com e-business platform, mySAP Enterprise Portals, RIVA, SAPPHIRE, TeamSAP, Webflow and SAP PRESS are registered or unregistered trademarks of SAP AG, Walldorf, Germany.

All other products mentioned in this book are registered or unregistered trademarks of their respective companies.

Contents at a Glance

1 Overview of Enterprise Performance Management 21

2 Overview of SAP BusinessObjects Planning and Consolidation 39

3 Modeling an Application with SAP BusinessObjects Planning and Consolidation for NetWeaver 67

4 Loading, Scheduling, and Managing Data in SAP BusinessObjects Planning and Consolidation for NetWeaver 129

5 Reporting, Planning, and Analysis in SAP BusinessObjects Planning and Consolidation 183

6 Developing Business Logic in SAP BusinessObjects Planning and Consolidation 233

7 Process Management and Collaboration 279

8 Essential Tools for Building Applications 324

9 Consolidation with SAP BusinessObjects Planning and Consolidation 359

10 Outlook for SAP BusinessObjects Planning and Consolidation 387

Contents

Foreword 13
Acknowledgments 17

1 Overview of Enterprise Performance Management 19

1.1 Enterprise Performance Management 19
1.2 Planning, Budgeting, and Forecasting 22
    1.2.1 Planning Horizon 23
    1.2.2 Planning Types 25
    1.2.3 Planning Areas 26
    1.2.4 Common Scenarios for Planning in Business 29
    1.2.5 Considerations in Planning 30
1.3 Consolidation 33
    1.3.1 Elimination of Intercompany Transactions 33
    1.3.2 Consolidated Net Income 35
    1.3.3 External Minority Interest 35
1.4 Summary 36

2 Overview of SAP BusinessObjects Planning and Consolidation 37

2.1 Business User Owned and Managed 38
    2.1.1 Software Usability and Flexibility to Support Change 38
    2.1.2 SAP BusinessObjects Planning and Consolidation (Microsoft and NetWeaver) 40
    2.1.3 SAP BusinessObjects Planning and Consolidation (for NetWeaver) 44
2.2 Unified Planning and Consolidation 45
    2.2.1 Planning in SAP BusinessObjects Planning and Consolidation 46
    2.2.2 Consolidation in SAP BusinessObjects Planning and Consolidation 46
2.3 SAP BusinessObjects Planning and Consolidation NetWeaver Architecture 49
    2.3.1 Client Interface 50

	2.3.2	Web Server and .NET Application Server	50
	2.3.3	SAP NetWeaver Application Server	50
	2.3.4	Database Server	51
2.4	Introduction to SAP NetWeaver BW		52
	2.4.1	Objects Used in SAP NetWeaver BW	52
	2.4.2	Extraction, Transformation, and Loading Data in SAP NetWeaver BW	55
	2.4.3	Process Chains	58
	2.4.4	SAP Business Content	58
2.5	Terminology and Objects in SAP BusinessObjects Planning and Consolidation		59
	2.5.1	Terminology	59
2.6	Summary		64

3 Modeling an Application with SAP BusinessObjects Planning and Consolidation for NetWeaver ... 65

3.1	Rich Bloom, Inc.		65
	3.1.1	Business	66
	3.1.2	Offices	66
	3.1.3	Products	66
	3.1.4	Currency	67
	3.1.5	Case Study	67
	3.1.6	Decision to Use SAP BusinessObjects Planning and Consolidation for NetWeaver	68
3.2	Building the Data Model in SAP NetWeaver BW		69
	3.2.1	Creating and Activating InfoObjects	72
	3.2.2	Creating an InfoArea	83
	3.2.3	Creating a Sales InfoCube	84
3.3	Building Applications in SAP BusinessObjects Planning and Consolidation		90
	3.3.1	Accessing the BPC System	92
	3.3.2	Application Set	96
	3.3.3	Dimensions	102
	3.3.4	Application	115
3.4	Summary		126

4 Loading, Scheduling, and Managing Data in SAP BusinessObjects Planning and Consolidation for NetWeaver ... 127

- 4.1 Loading Data into an InfoCube in SAP NetWeaver BW ... 128
  - 4.1.1 Creating a DataSource ... 128
  - 4.1.2 Creating Transformations ... 133
  - 4.1.3 Creating the Data Transfer Process (DTP) ... 135
  - 4.1.4 Creating InfoPackages ... 137
  - 4.1.5 Load Data from the PSA to the Data Target ... 141
- 4.2 Loading Data into SAP BusinessObjects Planning and Consolidation ... 142
  - 4.2.1 Transformation and Conversion ... 143
  - 4.2.2 Data Manager Packages ... 152
  - 4.2.3 Process Chains ... 157
  - 4.2.4 Loading Data from a Flat File into a Dimension ... 158
  - 4.2.5 Loading Data from an InfoCube into an SAP BusinessObjects Planning and Consolidation Application ... 165
- 4.3 Copying Data Inside an SAP BusinessObjects Planning and Consolidation Application ... 174
- 4.4 Summary ... 178

5 Reporting, Planning, and Analysis in SAP BusinessObjects Planning and Consolidation ... 181

- 5.1 Reporting and Analysis in SAP BusinessObjects Planning and Consolidation ... 182
  - 5.1.1 SAP BusinessObjects Planning and Consolidation for Excel ... 184
  - 5.1.2 Current View ... 187
  - 5.1.3 Measures Dimension ... 188
  - 5.1.4 Develop Reports Using Dynamic Templates ... 190
  - 5.1.5 Developing Reports Using Ev Functions ... 193
  - 5.1.6 Control Panel ... 205
  - 5.1.7 Developing Reports Using SAP BusinessObjects Planning and Consolidation Web ... 211

		5.1.8	Developing Reports Using Structures and VB Macros	214
	5.2	Planning in SAP BusinessObjects Planning and Consolidation Using Input Schedules		221
		5.2.1	Standard Templates for Input Schedules	222
		5.2.2	Workbook Options	223
		5.2.3	Developing an Input Schedule	225
		5.2.4	Worksheet Dimension Lock Option	228
		5.2.5	Park N Go	228
	5.3	Summary		229

6 Developing Business Logic in SAP BusinessObjects Planning and Consolidation — 231

	6.1	Dimension Logic		232
		6.1.1	Dimension Formulas	232
		6.1.2	Solve Order	234
	6.2	Script Logic		237
		6.2.1	Script Logic Construct	237
		6.2.2	Executing Script Logic	243
		6.2.3	Creating Script Logic to Revalue Plan Data	243
		6.2.4	Script Logic Files Provided by SAP	252
	6.3	Business Rules		253
		6.3.1	Account Transformation	254
		6.3.2	Intercompany Booking	254
		6.3.3	Carry-Forward	254
		6.3.4	Automatic Adjustments	254
		6.3.5	Currency Translation	255
	6.4	Allocations		262
	6.5	Using BAdIs to Code Logic		267
	6.6	Validation		268
	6.7	Summary		275

7 Process Management and Collaboration — 277

	7.1	Work Status		278
	7.2	Comments		286
		7.2.1	Add Comments	287
		7.2.2	Viewing Comments	290
		7.2.3	Report on Comments	294

		7.2.4	Ev Functions for Comments	296
7.3	Distribution and Collection			297
		7.3.1	Creating a Distribution List	299
		7.3.2	Offline Distribution Wizard	302
		7.3.3	Collection	307
7.4	Integrating SAP BusinessObjects Planning and Consolidation Data into Word and PowerPoint			311
7.5	Menus			315
7.6	Summary			322

8 Essential Tools for Building Applications 323

8.1	Transporting SAP BusinessObjects Planning and Consolidation Objects			324
8.2	Concurrency Locking			331
		8.2.1	Approaches to Locking	332
		8.2.2	Locking Features in SAP BusinessObjects Planning and Consolidation for NetWeaver	332
		8.2.3	The Locking Process in SAP BusinessObjects Planning and Consolidation for NetWeaver	333
8.3	Web Administration Parameters			337
8.4	Statistics			341
8.5	Audit			345
8.6	Content Library			346
		8.6.1	Accessing the Content Library	347
		8.6.2	Posting a Document	347
		8.6.3	Editing Document Properties	349
		8.6.4	Add Web Page to Content Library	349
8.7	Security			353
		8.7.1	Users	353
		8.7.2	Team	353
		8.7.3	Task Profile	353
		8.7.4	Member Access Profile	355
		8.7.5	Security Model	355
8.8	Summary			355

9 Consolidation with SAP BusinessObjects Planning and Consolidation ... 357

- 9.1 Business Rules ... 357
  - 9.1.1 Carry Forward ... 359
  - 9.1.2 Intercompany Eliminations (US Eliminations) ... 366
- 9.2 Journals ... 373
  - 9.2.1 Creating a Journal Template ... 374
  - 9.2.2 Managing Journals ... 377
  - 9.2.3 Journal Reports ... 379
- 9.3 Consolidation Logic ... 380
- 9.4 Summary ... 383

10 Outlook for SAP BusinessObjects Planning and Consolidation ... 385

- 10.1 Harmonization ... 385
  - 10.1.1 Authentication and Single Sign-On ... 386
  - 10.1.2 Platform Support ... 386
- 10.2 Integration ... 387
  - 10.2.1 ETL Integration ... 387
  - 10.2.2 Data Replication ... 388
  - 10.2.3 Drill-Through ... 388
  - 10.2.4 Integration with SAP BusinessObjects Process Control ... 389
  - 10.2.5 Integration with Xcelsius ... 389
  - 10.2.6 Integration with SAP BusinessObjects Voyager ... 389
- 10.3 Enhancements ... 390
  - 10.3.1 Audit Enhancement ... 390
  - 10.3.2 SAP BusinessObjects Planning and Consolidation for Excel Enhancement ... 390
  - 10.3.3 Business Process Flow ... 391
  - 10.3.4 Enhancements to Consolidations ... 394
  - 10.3.5 Enhancements to Work Status ... 394
  - 10.3.6 Enhancement to Script Logic ... 394
- 10.4 Summary ... 396
- 10.5 Conclusion ... 397

The Authors ... 399
Index ... 401

Foreword

Solutions around Planning, Budgeting, Forecasting and Consolidation are not new to SAP. After all, the "P" in ERP stands for Planning, which is SAP's forte. A little more than 10 years ago SAP launched the Strategic Enterprise Management (SEM) suite of products. This included Business Planning and Simulation (BPS) and Business Consolidation (BCS) plus a number of other solutions under the SEM umbrella. These solutions were installed as an add-on to the Business Warehouse (BW), which is SAP's data warehouse offering. Fortune 500 companies and other large customers that had an SAP R/3 footprint were the typical consumers of SEM applications. SEM was primarily designed for an IT audience to own and maintain while Finance, as the end user, provided some support in the form of power users. BPS and BCS were separate products and customers were able to integrate the data, but this was not an out of-the-box process. Both products were also shipped about 6 months after a BW release, so customers who had an embedded solution were dependent on the availability of an SEM release in order to upgrade their BW system. Some customers installed standalone systems and moved data between them to provide more flexibility, but this came with a higher Total Cost of Ownership (TCO). They also had to support separate security models, reporting tools, metadata, and so on.

SAP worked closely with various user groups including the Americas SAP User Group (ASUG) to gather requirements and feedback for the future development of planning and consolidation solutions. Customers requested tighter integration with BW and the ability to leverage the same tools, which would reduce implementation time and effort to train end users. About 5 years ago, SAP decided to create a next-generation planning solution called Integrated Planning (BW-IP), which would be the successor to BPS. The solution combined the analytic (OLAP) and planning engines into one, and utilized the same queries, variables, security, etc., as BW. It was designed to be a planning platform upon which other product areas within SAP, as well as ISV's, partners, and customers could build their own planning applications. On the surface, BW-IP looked like it would be a strong solution, and there was strong demand from customers and partners to get their hands on the beta version (Ramp-Up). However impressive, the technical advantages of BW-IP only solved part of the equation; the reality was that many businesses were growing tired of IT departments having to own and maintain planning and consolidation solutions, and they demanded solutions that the business could own and maintain with IT support, not ownership.

In early 2007, SAP formed a new organization focused on the Business User. This was a big departure from the traditional transaction-oriented and task-worker based applications that SAP was traditionally known for. An Enterprise Performance Management (EPM) team was launched under this area to address the needs being expressed by the CFO suite. Strategy Management was the first application in the portfolio and was the result of SAP's acquisition of Pilot. It was a very simple and easy-to-use solution for the business to leverage in defining strategy, initiatives, and results monitoring. In parallel, the EPM development team created planning prototypes on top of the BW-IP platform. The challenges they found were centered mostly around the constraints of Business Explorer (BEx) for Planning and Reporting. Since its first release in 1997, the BEx had moved far from its roots as a power user tool to being more open to the needs of a casual user, but it had not come far enough to deliver a world-class user experience. Although the interfaces were Excel- and web-based, the desired ease-of-use was difficult to achieve at the level customers expected and SAP strived for. So the EPM team evaluated potential acquisitions that had the desired ease-of-use and simplicity, and discovered it with OutlookSoft. The user environment was native Excel, which Finance users live and die by, but it also had another huge advantage. The founders of OutlookSoft came from Hyperion and they had endeavored to build a product that integrated planning and consolidation into one. This was a first in the industry and provided one solution to the customer. While the concept seemed promising, would OutlookSoft solve the problems our customers were telling us were important in their planning and consolidation decision-making processes?

Meanwhile, feedback from one of our BW-IP early adopters indicated that although BW-IP was a big improvement over BPS, the customer decided to the purchase OutlookSoft product so the business could own the solution. This customer validation of the strength of the OutlookSoft solution was important, and prompted internal stakeholders at SAP to divine some proof that OutlookSoft was as strong as the business case stated, and that it could be implemented as easily as claimed.

Members of OutlookSoft and SAP were summoned to SAP headquarters in Walldorf. A business scenario was created and two teams were formed. The first was from SAP, and this included experts from BW, ABAP developers, web application development, and finance. In the other corner was the OutlookSoft team made up of a couple finance users with no data warehousing or development skills. The two teams split up and started building their planning applications using the two different solutions, BW-IP and OutlookSoft. About 30 minutes later the OutlookSoft team came back with a completed application; it took the SAP team over 6 hours to build the same application using BW-IP. This sealed the deal within SAP and through the acquisition of OutlookSoft, SAP now has the best user experience in the industry, planning and consolidation in one product, and a solution that is much faster and easier to implement. This is welcome news to our customers, as you might imagine

Prior to the acquisition, there was only about a 15% overlap between OutlookSoft and SAP customers. The OutlookSoft product was a Microsoft-centric application that leveraged SQL Server, Analysis Services, Reporting Services, and other Microsoft technologies. In order to give customers a choice, part of the agreement to acquire OutlookSoft was to offer the solution in another flavor as part of SAP NetWeaver. There are over 15,000 BW customers and if this solution is to eventually become the strategic planning and consolidation solution at SAP then it needed to have the tight integration not only with BW but also ERP. The development timelines were aggressive; the first version BW-based version was due in one year. What is now known as SAP BusinessObjects Business Planning and Consolidation for SAP NetWeaver was completed in July 2008 as planned, and the first Beta customers started their implementations in August. The rest is history. The adoption of the product has been nothing short of impressive, and BPC is the second-most demonstrated product to customers. In addition, one of the most compelling features of BPC 7.5 is the integration with the SAP BusinessObjects Business Intelligence (BI) tools. This allows customers to leverage the world-class features of the top BI tools in the market with not only BPC but the entire EPM suite, and provides one comprehensive set of reporting, query, analysis, and information management tools. The second version (BPC 7.5 NW) entered ramp-up in December 2009, and prior to the start the customer pipeline was two times greater than our KPI. As of February 2010, we achieved our Key Performance Index (KPI), with many more customers in the pipeline, making this one of the most sought after products in SAP history. This comes with another set of challenges: supporting a product that is in such high demand requires all resources, including development, solution management, and the Regional Implementation Group (RIG), to take an active role. This is a nice problem to have.

The analyst community has also overwhelmingly validated SAP's vision and strategy. Gartner rated SAP as a leader in the CPM Suites Magic Quadrant for 2009/2010, with the strongest vision in the market for the second year in a row. According to Gartner, SAP now occupies the strongest position in the market. The Forrester Business Performance Solutions Wave Report 2009 was published in November and not only did it list SAP as one of four leaders in the market, it awarded SAP with the highest score for current product offering out of all vendors. IDC's 2009 annual analysis of the software markets reported SAP as the market leader in performance management and analytic application with a 20.3 percent market share of that year. Balanced scorecard creators Kaplan and Norton recently announced a software certification program and subsequently announced SAP as the first (and currently only) vendor to be certified in the Kaplan-Norton Balanced Scorecard and the Strategy Management system of which it is a part.

The authors of this book have a strong SAP background and specifically with BW-IP and BW, and were among the early implementers of the BPC NW product. They're able to leverage their deep expertise in planning and consolidation as well as data warehousing to compare and contrast the SAP solutions, and provide in depth knowledge around the BPC NW product. This book should serve as an excellent reference, and an implementation and information source for customers and partners. Whether you are sitting in an airport terminal and have some time to catch up on reading, onsite at a customer and have a question and need to get a quick answer, I hope you enjoy this book and that it will be something that you can utilize over and over whether you are an executive or a member of a project team implementing BPC NW. Enjoy and we hope BPC NW is a huge success for you now or in the future!

Bryan Katis
Global VP, Regional Implementation Group (RIG) & Customer Advisory Office (CAO)
Enterprise Performance Management
SAP BusinessObjects Division

Acknowledgments

This book has been produced with the help of several people who have reviewed the materials and offered invaluable suggestions in the shaping of the book. Their contributions and advice have helped in the realization of this book.

We would like to offer our thanks and special appreciation to the following people for their contributions:

- The editors of this book, Stephen Solomon and Kelly Grace Harris, for guiding us through the book development process.
- The production manager of this book, Kelly O'Callaghan, for managing the production and successful release of the book.
- Carl Satterfield at MWV, who reviewed the initial chapters of the book and provided us with ideas for presentation of topics related to planning and consolidation.
- Lucky Pandit at Halliburton, who reviewed the initial chapters of the book and provided perspective to planning that has been incorporated in the book.
- Buntic Georgian at VIP Consulting, who reviewed the initial chapters of the book and offered several points to consider in the functional areas of planning.
- We would like to thank our families for providing us the motivation and enthusiasm and for their support and patience as we spent long hours writing the book.

Sridhar Srinivasan
Kumar Srinivasan

Additional Information

Additional information on the topics covered in this book can be found in the following places:

- SAP Help Portal: *http://help.sap.com*
- SAP Developer Network: *http://www.sdn.sap.com*
- SAP Service Marketplace: *http://www.service.sap.com*

1 Overview of Enterprise Performance Management

The purpose of this chapter is to provide you with an overview of enterprise performance management (EPM) and to introduce you to concepts in planning, budgeting, forecasting, and consolidation.

In Section 1.1, we will discuss the definition and importance of EPM and its relevance in different areas of business.

In Section 1.2, we will discuss concepts in planning, budgeting, and forecasting, and introduce you to methods and best practices in these areas.

In Section 1.3, we will discuss basic concepts in consolidation and introduce you to the processes involved in consolidation.

1.1 Enterprise Performance Management

The importance of EPM is growing in this era of rapid technology development, global competition, modernization, and ever-changing customer needs. The need to make accurate decisions and at the same time meet regulatory requirements is important to gain a competitive edge, ensure control of business operations, and provide precise business status information to statutory bodies, shareholders, and business partners.

EPM deals with bridging the gap between the strategies set by top management and the execution of the strategy by operational staff. It streamlines the execution of strategy and ensures accountability. Its objective is also to provide timely and compliant reporting, and help companies optimize cost and improve profitability. EPM provides the framework for establishing processes that are needed to meet strategic objectives and for monitoring the execution of these processes.

SAP BusinessObjects EPM solutions provide the following software tools:

- **Strategy Management**
  This software allows you to prioritize and communicate strategic initiatives and effectively monitor, measure, and collaborate on strategy.

- **Planning and Consolidation**
  SAP BusinessObjects Planning and Consolidation software helps you to perform planning, budgeting, and forecasting tasks. It also allows you to perform financial consolidation and reporting. The objective of this book is to discuss the functionality available in this application in detail.

- **Financial Consolidation**
  This software allows companies to perform financial consolidation and reporting.

- **XBRL Publishing**
  The eXtensible business reporting Language (XBRL) is a new global standard for exchanging financial information and allows accounting jurisdictions such as banks, regulators, and agencies to download, codify, and analyze financial data. The XBRL Publishing software allows you to create XBRL documents based on data available in SAP BusinessObjects Planning and Consolidation, SAP BusinessObjects Financial Consolidation, and SAP Business Suite software.

- **Financial Information Management**
  This software lets you access, map, and load data from different source systems to the SAP BusinessObjects Financial Consolidation and SAP BusinessObjects Profitability and Cost Management applications.

- **Inter-company Reconciliation**
  isThis software lets you reconcile intercompany balances in real time via the Web, enabling your organization to close its books more quickly.

- **Profitability and Cost Management**
  This software allows you to accurately and effectively measure product, customer, and channel profitability, and develop and dynamically test ways to improve profitability.

- **Spend Performance Management**
  This software provides you with insight into savings opportunities and compliance by enabling access to aggregated and enriched spend data.

- **Supply Chain Performance Management**
  This software helps you improve the effectiveness of supply chain operations such as lowering costs and improving return on working capital. It also pro-

vides an accurate measure of whether you are meeting your supply chain goals, warns you of potential bottlenecks, and alerts you to new opportunities.

SAP's solution in the area of EPM complements its existing software product offerings; SAP is a leader in the enterprise resource planning software arena, which helps re-engineer business processes and execute them efficiently. SAP's offerings in other areas—such as business intelligence, supplier relationship management, supply chain management, customer relationship management, and industry-focused solutions—help accelerate innovation and improve return on investment (ROI). Continuing this trend, SAP's acquisition of BusinessObjects ensures its ongoing leadership and its ability to help you devise effective business strategies.

Figure 1.1 details how SAP software solutions integrate insight, strategy, and decisions across governance, risk, and compliance (GRC); EPM; and business intelligence platforms. It also shows how these solutions bridge into business applications that can run on any technology platform. This closed-loop business performance optimization allows companies to obtain a complete picture of their business performance.

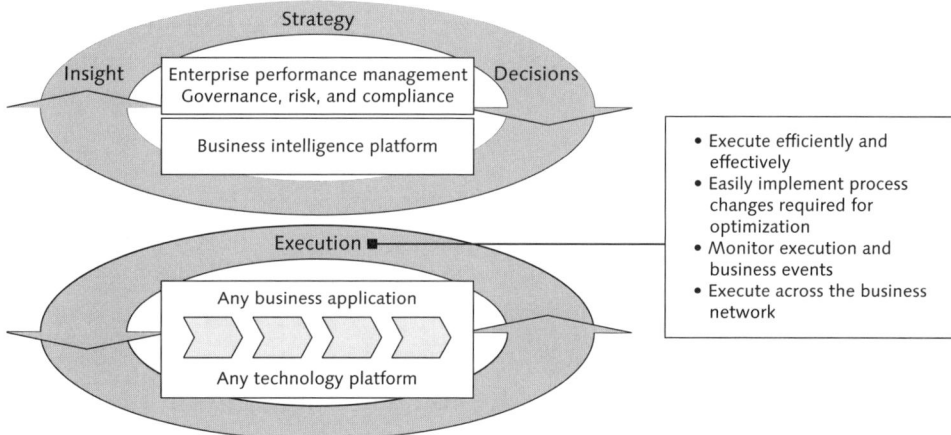

Figure 1.1 Closed-Loop Business Performance Optimization

In the next section, we will review basic concepts used in planning, budgeting, and forecasting.

1.2 Planning, Budgeting, and Forecasting

In simple terms, *planning* involves thinking ahead and formulating a set of activities you will execute in the future; in other words, it is the process of modeling or projecting future business activities. Companies strive for profitability and growth in complex business environments where they have to deal with global competition, rapid technology development, geo-political situations, and ever-changing customer needs, and planning is a key management cycle component that allows companies to position themselves in these complex environments.

The process of planning identifies the individual tasks involved in reaching a goal, provides the time frame for executing the tasks, and determines the resources needed for successful completion of the tasks. It is an iterative activity where the actual performance is measured against set targets and refined accordingly. A business, as part of its existence, has to plan for multiple resources, and to ensure that these activities are undertaken in an optimal manner, a good system of planning should be in place. A good idea or a good product does not necessarily contribute to the success of a company; the company must make decisions to sell the right product at the right time, and through the right channel and more importantly control costs in that process. In order to best achieve the goals of the company, the plan to achieve these goals must be clearly defined and refined during the planning process.

Although strategic planning objectives are set by top management, a company may formulate and carry out multiple plans at lower levels to achieve the targets set at the higher level. Therefore, it is imperative for the company to ensure that there is complete coordination and oneness of objectives among the different plans. This should be taken into account when planning decisions are made.

Microsoft Excel spreadsheets have been used for financial planning by a majority of organizations but their limitations are many: accessibility issues, lack of security, insufficient control mechanisms on who can modify data, and an inability to clearly understand how the planning data was derived. This is one area where SAP software can help, and a topic we will come back to in Chapter 2.

When discussing EPM, it is important to understand the differences between planning, budgeting, and forecasting.

As discussed above, *Planning* is the process of modeling and projecting future business resources. Depending upon the type of planning, the planning horizon can be short, medium or long term.

Budgeting is the process of allocating resources once the planning process is approved and accepted by the company's management. It is the start of the action phase following the planning process. The budgeting process is usually executed before the start of the budget year. In the budgeting process, requisite details are worked out for the implementation of the plan. This is also the period where financial allocations are made to various departments such as finance, sales, information technology, human resources, and son on.

Forecasting deals with the realization of the plan, and is used as a monitoring mechanism to facilitate the success of planning. Business environments do not remain the same—what was planned for yesterday may not be the same today. Forecasting is done during the course of the current budget year with a key objective to provide visibility on the current state of the business in a timely manner so that corrective action can be taken when there is a significant difference between the current state of the future and what was planned for during the planning process.

In the subsections that follow, we will discuss several aspects of the planning process: the planning horizon, planning types, planning areas, common scenarios for planning, and some of the important business elements to be taken into account when planning.

1.2.1 Planning Horizon

The planning horizon determines the time frame for planning. Planning horizons are divided into three separate categories, which are discussed in more detail next.

Short Term Planning

The planning time frame in short term planning is usually a year or less. This type of planning is used when the business has clear-cut short term goals. Examples of short term planning include cutting costs, increasing labor productivity by freezing new hires, and effectively training the workforce. Short term planning is also suitable in situations where the industry in which the business is operating is constantly changing, and wherein it is difficult to make reliable long term projections.

Medium Term Planning

Medium term planning usually covers a period of one to three years and is applicable if the business can reasonably plan the outlook for this time period. You might develop a medium term plan to increase market share in a particular segment of the business, for example.

Long Term Planning

Planning is considered long term when the duration of the plan exceeds three years. This type of planning usually involves the investment of a large amount of capital to achieve company objectives. This is also applicable for businesses where projects have a long gestation period. In these types of industries, there is a long time gap between initial investment and final realization of sales and profits; this is true for companies in the utility, steel, or bio-technology industries, for example.

It should be understood that the level of detail in short term planning is high because it represents the immediate future. In medium term planning, the level of detail is reduced. In long term planning, the level of detail again is very high. Although different time frames can be used for planning, no single formula to decide on the option to be used exists; instead, the period selected depends on the business requirements.

In reality, you may use different terms for different areas of your business. For example, your business may come up with a short term plan to reduce costs in the immediate future. However, at the same time, you may also have a long term plan in place to gain the highest market share in your industry.

In general, routine business operation plans that address the immediate future are good candidates for short term planning. Programs and plans that involve large capital investment and that take more time to mature and yield results are categorized as long term plans.

1.2.2 Planning Types

The planning type provides more clarity to the process by clearly differentiating the objective of the plan. It is based on the planning horizon and the granularity of the planning process. We will discuss each of the planning types next.

Operative Planning

Operative planning is typically used for the short term and is generally conducted at the operational level of a company. This type of planning usually has an immediate objective in mind; for example, to improve productivity by controlling variable costs. With this type of plan, employees at the bottom level of the hierarchy may be part of the planning process to make it successful. The planning method used during the operative planning process is bottom-up planning, where the planners involved in executing the plan are also involved in the creation of the plan. Upon completion of the plan, planners send the plan to their supervisors, and after approval by the supervisors, plan implementation begins.

Using bottom-up planning is very helpful to getting employee commitment for the planning process. Because employees are involved in the planning process, the probability that the plan will be successful is increased.

Tactical Planning

Tactical planning is associated with planning for the medium term and is generally conducted at the division level of a company. It is suitable for projects that can be completed in less than three years. For example, you might start an initiative to improve the quality of a product, which may take two years to realize. Although the tactical plan may be in consonance with the long term plan, it may be developed at the middle management level.

Strategic Planning

Strategic planning is associated with planning for the long term and is generally conducted at the organizational level of a company. Company management usually plays a major role in this type of planning. An example of strategic planning is when a company decides to finance research and development to develop a new line of products. The products may take more than three years to develop, and the company may want to develop a plan to finance the new program.

This type of planning usually begins at the top level of the company and trickles down to lower levels. The planning objective and process are agreed to by the company's top management, and may be split into sub-plans during the implementation process.

In Figure 1.2, you can see how the different types of planning are categorized based on the granularity of the plan (high level vs. detailed level) and the *gestation period* (time) to achieve the plan objectives. Strategic planning has the longest gestation period and the lowest level of granularity. Operational planning has the shortest gestation period and the highest level of granularity.

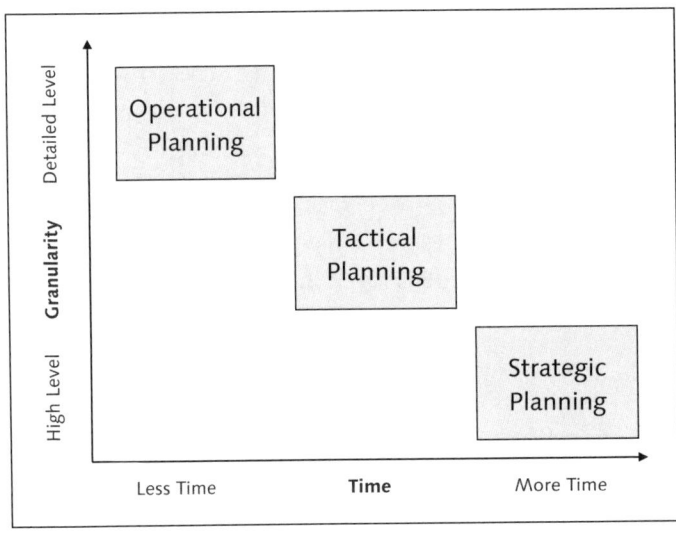

Figure 1.2 Planning Types

1.2.3 Planning Areas

Planning is a generic function applicable to all areas of business. The planning area is the sub-area of the business for which you develop a plan. Next, we will discuss how the relevance of financial planning can be understood in several sub-areas of business.

Finance

The finance department is the control room of any given business; it is responsible for planning, implementing, and directing the financial aspects of the business.

Examples of financial planning include investing in a new venture, maintaining an optimal cash position (*liquidity*), reducing cost, and increasing profits. The focus of this book is to illustrate the development of a financial planning application for a company that has an objective to increase its gross profit margin.

In this context, it may help to discuss certain areas of financial planning:

- **Liquidity planning**
  Liquidity planning focuses on planning for maintaining optimal cash flow to be able to run the business. It involves taking the current cash position of the company into account, estimating the inflow of cash from customers and the outflow of cash to vendors and employees, and planning the liquidity over the next few months.

- **Cost center planning**
  Cost center planning is done for costs that will be incurred by the company at various cost center levels. This includes planning for operational costs, non-operational costs and capital expenditures that will be incurred by the company.

- **Asset planning**
  Asset planning is concerned with planning for the purchase of new assets and the disposal and maintenance of existing assets, based on the company's objective to deliver products to its customers.

- **Profitability planning**
  Profitability planning determines profitability by identifying sales revenue and costs that will be incurred in the future.

Production

You should plan how much to produce and when and where to produce it, with the goal of producing products in the most optimal manner while satisfying customer requirements and maintaining sufficient capacity to fulfill demand. Different variables such as seasonal behavior, geographical demand, and user behavior should be taken into account when planning for this area. The financial implication of your production plan should be consistent with the overall financial plan of the company, and the inventory cost and overhead costs incurred as a result of the production plan should be kept at optimal levels.

Human Resources

Every business should have the workforce required to run the business, and workforce requirements should be planned based on your company's overall growth objectives. When there is a shortage of employees in the industry, you will have to make decisions about whether to hire new employees, train existing employees on new technologies, or bring people in from the outside as consultants to meet requirements. This area of planning is especially important in industries that require large numbers of employees and where specialized skills are required for realizing the objectives of the business. Costs associated with meeting labor requirements have a direct impact on the financial plan.

Marketing

The marketing department provides the necessary information to plan the products that can be sold and the price at which they can be sold. The distribution of products and services to customers should also be taken into account. The sales plan can be formulated based on actual sales in past years, revaluation based on future trends in the industry, the geo-political environment in which your company has sales operations, and the strategic vision of the company.

Maintenance

The maintenance department will typically develop a strategy for maintenance of plant according to equipment strategy and breakdown of the maintenance work into categories. These categories include In Program Work, Functional Failures and Discretionary Work. Based on the overall maintenance strategy, the maintenance plan can be developed to cover different types of maintenance activities within the plant such as turnarounds, preventive maintenance, breakdown maintenance etc.

Proper maintenance of plant equipments can significantly reduce the overall operational costs and also boost the overall productivity of the plant. Costs associated with the maintenance costs have a direct impact on the financial plan.

The above-mentioned areas are critical for the survival of the business and have a direct or indirect effect on the financial plan of the company. Planning for these areas is important to ensure the smooth functioning of business.

1.2.4 Common Scenarios for Planning in Business

You should plan for different scenarios depending on individual requirements at different points in time. This subsection delves into some of the common scenarios used by companies for planning. These planning scenarios are based on the company's targeted objectives.

Gross Profit Margin Planning

The revenue obtained through the sale of a company's products, along with the costs that are incurred to produce/buy the product, is planned under this scenario. This usually starts with gathering external information on product demand. Often, prior year revenue results can indicate a trend for future sales planning. This information, along with management's strategic vision and demand estimates provided by the sales force, helps the company plan its products' quantity and prices.

Expected manufacturing costs can be arrived at using standard costing procedures. This process should take into account any expected increase to material, labor, and overhead costs in the future. Expected revenue and manufacturing costs are used to determine the expected gross profit margin.

Profit and Loss and Balance Sheet Planning

This type of planning is related to the financial area of business. It is the process in which you prepare a profit and loss sheet, along with a balance sheet, to see whether it meets the returns expected by the business. This can also provide clues as to which areas may need corrective action. For example, it may become obvious from the projections that overhead costs are increasing every year; based on this, management may need to take corrective action.

Investment Planning

Investment planning is also associated with the financial aspect of business. It focuses on new investments the company is planning in the future. The expected ROI for the investment is a key metric in this planning.

Labor Planning

Labor planning is the process of planning workforce requirements for your company. It should take both new projects and expected expansion into consideration, which may require additions to the workforce. The plan should take into account expected attrition from the workforce, both from retirement and labor turnover. Human capital is crucial to the business, and labor planning is vital to ensure that the company has the right people with the right skills to operate the business.

Sales Planning

With sales planning, a plan is developed to sell the company's products. The focus is on developing a marketing plan that will be most beneficial to the company and help sell the company's products at the optimal price. The marketing plan should reflect the overall strategic vision of the company—for example, a company may decide to place a lot of emphasis on two specific products. The sales plan will need to reflect this objective. The inputs for developing a sales plan is obtained based on market intelligence and opportunities data collected by sales managers.

Demand Planning

Demand planning presupposes that the process of sales planning is complete. Depending on the sales forecast, production planning is geared to fulfill the expected demand. Assuming that production capacity exists, demand planning uses the existing sales forecast to plan for material, labor, and machinery to produce the products.

1.2.5 Considerations in Planning

You should perform the planning process in a manner that is in tune with the strategic objectives of your company. Consider the following key points:

Importance

Planning is an important component of every business that contributes to the success of the company. There are many examples where good planning and execution have paved the way to the success of a business, as well as many examples where inadequate planning or no planning resulted in the failure of a company. Thus, management needs to understand the importance of planning in helping the company be successful in its business operations.

Skills

Planning is an art and one that requires a lot of foresight. The ability to take all of the factors (internal and external) into account is the key to developing a successful plan. It takes a lot of experience, maturity, and knowledge to develop a plan. The person(s) entrusted with this responsibility should posses these skills.

Internal

The person(s) involved in developing a new plan should understand how the new plan relates to other projects that are currently underway, as well as those that are likely to be undertaken by the company in the future. Also, cross-functional aspects should be taken into account. For example, if a plan is undertaken to improve production capacity, the question of financing should be studied before getting started with the plan.

Data

The data that is used in planning should be reliable. For example, if market research and intelligence is used as the basis for planning, the data used for this purpose should come from a trustworthy source. The possibility of error in the data must also be taken into account.

Governance

A good governance process should be established for planning. The levels of responsibility should be clearly defined so that there is no ambiguity, and the people involved in planning should clearly understand their role in the process.

Communication

Good communication among all company levels is of vital importance at all times during planning. This ensures that the various participants stay well informed of the plan's progress and take actions at the different plan implementation stages.

Monitoring

A sound review process should also be in place to monitor the execution of the planning process. The availability of such a system helps identify any deviations and aids in taking corrective action.

Planning Method

There are two types of planning methods: top down and bottom up. With the *top down planning process*, upper level management decides what is to be done, and the lower levels of the organization implement the process. This type of process is relevant for strategic decision making; for example, when management decides on which areas of the business the company should focus over the next 10 years. The *bottom up planning process* is used more for operational planning, where planning starts at the lower levels of the organization and is approved by upper levels.

Participation

The planning process is more likely to succeed if people who are responsible for the execution of the planning process are consulted when the planning goals are initially set. This helps in participative decision-making and promotes cooperation from everyone involved in implementing the plan. It also provides an opportunity for management to solicit employee feedback regarding the identified planning objectives.

Issue List

If issues come up during the planning process, they should be recorded so that progress towards their resolution can be tracked. There should also be a good system in place for employees to address these issues.

IT Department

The planning process involves collecting information from different sources. This information may come from cross-functional areas in the company (finance, production, marketing, or human resources), or sometimes from external sources. Integrating this information is facilitated by the IT department, with the goal to build a process for planning that can meet business demands in a reliable and timely manner. The success of this process requires an IT department that can handle this responsibility effectively.

Flexibility

The planning process should be flexible so that it can absorb any necessary changes that may occur along the way. This will make the process less rigid and more open.

You should now have an understanding of the basic concepts in planning. In the next section, we will discuss basic concepts in consolidation.

1.3   Consolidation

To better understand consolidation, we will look at an example of relationships between companies. If a company (P) owns more than 50 percent stake of another company (S), then P is a majority investor and is referred to as the parent. S is referred to as the subsidiary. The U.S. Generally Accepted Accounting Principles (GAAP) require the parent company to combine financial statements of subsidiaries with those of the parent; these financial statements are referred to as *consolidated financial statements*. The consolidated financial statements present the financial results of the operations (income statement), financial position (balance sheet), and cash flows (cash flow statement) of the parent and subsidiaries, as if the group of companies is composed of a single entity. In other words, the parent and each subsidiary are legally separate entities, but they operate as one centrally controlled economic entity. The consolidated financial statements provide more useful information to shareholders than do separate financial statements of each legal entity. Consolidation of revenues, expenses, assets, and liabilities provide a clear picture of the operation and financial status of the consolidated single entity.

To understand consolidated financial statements, you need to understand the basic concepts discussed in the subsections that follow.

1.3.1   Elimination of Intercompany Transactions

State laws require that each legal entity prepare its own financial statements to record its financial transactions. The consolidation of financial statements involves summing up the amounts across all separate legal entities and providing a unified view of the operations of the economic entity. In this consolidation process, however, it is important to eliminate double-counting resulting from intercompany transactions. For example, if the parent company sells products to the subsidiary, the consolidated financial statement should eliminate this sale because it is an intercompany transaction. The objective of consolidated financial statements is to report the consolidated entity's transactions to outsiders.

The following inter-company transactions must be eliminated.

Intercompany Sales and Cost of Goods Sold

Consider a case where a parent company sells a product to a subsidiary company, the subsidiary company then sells the product in the same or a different form to an external customer, and the sales revenue for the sale of the product is then counted twice—once in the books of the parent company and once in the books of the subsidiary. This double-counting needs to be eliminated. Similarly, in this scenario, the cost of goods sold (COGS) associated with the product is also counted twice—once in the books of the parent and once in the books of the subsidiary—and thus should also be eliminated from consolidated statements.

Intercompany Receivables/Payables

When a parent company sells a product to a subsidiary company, the amount associated with the sale is recorded as accounts receivable in the books of the parent company. Similarly, the transaction is recorded as accounts payable in the books of the subsidiary. This transaction does not result in the consolidated company to receive or owe any amount to an external customer or supplier. Therefore, the intercompany accounts receivable and payable transactions should be eliminated from the consolidated statements.

Intercompany Investments

Consider a case where a parent company (P) owns 100% of a subsidiary (S). The balance sheet of P shows an asset "Investments in company S." The balance sheet of the subsidiary shows its individual assets. If you were to sum the assets of the parent company and subsidiary to prepare the consolidated statement, you would be double-counting the assets of the subsidiary for the consolidated firm. Therefore, the consolidation process should eliminate the asset "Investment in company S." Because the accounting equation *assets = liabilities + shareholder's equity* needs to be maintained, this amount is also eliminated from the shareholders equity account of the subsidiary company.

1.3.2 Consolidated Net Income

The *consolidated net income* is the sum of the profit or loss of individual entities after eliminating profit or loss arising out of intercompany transactions. The consolidated net income is calculated as follows:

Parent company's net income + parent company's share of subsidiary's net income − profit (or loss) of intercompany transactions

1.3.3 External Minority Interest

Now assume that a parent company does not hold 100% of the subsidiary but only 70%. Even though the parent company owns only 70% stake in the subsidiary, the parent company can show all assets and liabilities of the subsidiary. The consolidated balance sheet and income statement will disclose the interest of the minority shareholders in the consolidated statements. The amount of minority interest appearing in the balance sheet is calculated by multiplying common shareholder equity of the subsidiary by the percentage of the minority interest. The consolidated income statement shows all of the subsidiary's revenue and expenses and subtracts the minority percentage of the subsidiary's income.

In summary, the consolidation process does the following:

- Balance sheet
    - Eliminate investment account and replace with asset/liability of subsidiary
    - Show minority interest in subsidiary's net assets
    - Eliminate intercompany assets and liabilities
- Income statement
    - Sum individual revenue and expenses of parent and subsidiary
    - Eliminate intercompany profit and loss
    - Subtract minority interest in subsidiary net income
- Cash flow from operation
    - Sum individual source and use of cash of parent and subsidiary.
    - Using the indirect method, add minority interest to net income to obtain cash provided by operations

In the following chapters, we will discuss how you can use the SAP BusinessObjects Planning and Consolidation application to perform the discussed tasks.

1.4 Summary

In this chapter, we discussed the importance of EPM software, and introduced you to key concepts in the area of financial planning and consolidation. In Chapter 2, we will discuss an overview of the SAP BusinessObjects Planning and Consolidation application and its use for the purpose of planning and financial consolidation.

2 Overview of SAP BusinessObjects Planning and Consolidation

The purpose of this chapter is to provide you with an overview of the SAP BusinessObjects Planning and Consolidation software application (focusing primarily on the NetWeaver version), and to introduce you to some of its key features. We will discuss the flexibility, control, and ease this application offers in managing and analyzing data, and explain how you can use the software to meet both the planning and consolidation needs of your organization. We will also detail the multifaceted range of applications where you can use it, and expound on how you can use it to support a reliable and effective decision-making process. Finally, we will discuss how you can use the application to perform financial consolidation for a company that is composed of multiple legal entities and generate financial reports that explain the overall performance of the organization.

In Section 2.1, we will introduce you to a key requirement most business users look for when using a software application — the ability to manage and analyze data with less dependence on an IT solutions team — and explain how SAP BusinessObjects Planning and Consolidation satisfies this need.

In Section 2.2, we will explain how you can use the application to meet planning and consolidation requirements, discuss its implementation in different areas of planning, and explain how you can derive competitive advantage by using it. We will also cover how the application provides an environment for performing legal consolidation and management consolidation of an organization. This is especially important for multiple-entity organizations that are required to perform legal consolidation and release financial results of the entire company per statutory requirements.

In Section 2.3, we will discuss the architecture of the NetWeaver version of SAP BusinessObjects Planning and Consolidation and explain how it interfaces with the SAP NetWeaver Business Warehouse (SAP NetWeaver BW) system.

In Section 2.4, we will introduce you to the SAP NetWeaver BW system and explain the process of extracting, transforming, and loading data from a source system to an SAP NetWeaver BW system. The section also highlights the usage of SAP Business Content to expedite the development of data warehouse applications.

In Section 2.5, we will introduce you to objects configured in the SAP BusinessObjects Planning and Consolidation and explain the relationship between these objects and the objects created in SAP NetWeaver BW.

2.1 Business User Owned and Managed

The needs of a business are sometimes predictable, but at other times, they are not clearly defined, or are even unpredictable. This element of unpredictability has a direct bearing on the IT applications that are developed for business users. The model of an application should be free form and must be flexible enough to meet the needs of the business users. A model that is rigid and that cannot satisfy the needs of the business will not be accepted by users. In these cases, the application will not be used and will not meet the objectives for which it was developed.

The cost of retooling an application to support additional business requirements is something that should be considered when the application is initially designed. A clear process should be in place for how the data model fits the current scope and how it will support the business if the design requires changes during the life of the application. We have seen how organizations have spent increasing amounts of money to redesign their applications to meet user needs; some of this money could have been saved if good design principles had been followed in the first place.

In addition to the design element, the software that is used for building the application should be flexible enough to support changes. Because not every business change can be anticipated, a good software tool should be able to accommodate changes in a fashion that does not involve too much cost or time.

2.1.1 Software Usability and Flexibility to Support Change

The following are some software tool aspects that ensure usability and flexibility to support changes:

- **Reporting**
  You must be able to design custom reports on your own to support any analyses that may not be supported by standard reports delivered by the IT solutions team.

- **Control of data**
  Data is owned by users, and it is only right that you have the ability to control how this data is loaded into the system. The software tool should let you load data into the application so that it can be used for analysis later. This is particularly important for users of planning applications, where you have the discretion to decide what data to use, when to use it, and how to use it. This applies to consolidation applications as well, regarding how you want to use your data for statutory reporting. The options in the software tool such as the ability to schedule the loading of data and to replace existing data, enable you to make more efficient use of the application.

- **Business rules**
  Business rules are used when you want to transform data that is loaded into an application. You should be able to configure and view these rules so that there is no ambiguity in how the rules are being used in the application.

- **Out of the box functions**
  Depending on the application, the software should provide you with all of the functions that are used to meet the principal requirement of the application. These functions should be made available as part of the software tool. This not only reduces the total cost of ownership (TCO) but also helps you make real use of the application without relying on other tools to perform these functions.

- **Custom settings**
  The software should enable you to see report descriptions in your own language (e.g., if you are in France, you should be able to see the application user interface in French).

- **Customization**
  You should be able to customize the application without having to rely on the help of your IT solutions team. Customizations may involve a change to the data load process, or reporting logic, for example.

- **Collaboration**
  Some applications require collaboration to ensure that all members of the business team are in sync and have the latest information. For these applications, it is essential that the software provides features that allow collaboration. Col-

laboration may assume different forms. For example, you may post a document to get input from another user, or you may post a document for others to read and use in their decision making.

- **Distribution and collection**
  As a corollary to collaboration, it may be necessary to disseminate data to other business users who may in turn modify the data and may want to retract the modified data back to the application. The software tool will need to allow you to distribute and modify information as well as retract modified information back to the application.

- **Programming interface**
  You may need to develop scripts that allow you to perform specific functions within an application. The software tool should provide an easy-to-use programming interface that enables this.

2.1.2 SAP BusinessObjects Planning and Consolidation (Microsoft and NetWeaver)

How does SAP BusinessObjects Planning and Consolidation measure up against the need to support usability and flexibility to support change? The application provides an environment that satisfies all of these requirements, in a manner that grants you sufficient flexibility in using your applications. Next, we will discuss some of the features of the application, as well as some of the disadvantages of relying solely on Microsoft Excel for planning purposes.

Features of SAP BusinessObjects Planning and Consolidation

SAP BusinessObjects Planning and Consolidation lets you develop your own reports, enabling you to decide how you view your data. Although the data you can view is governed by your security access, you can customize your reports in a fashion that suits your decision-making requirements.

The application also allows you to load data yourself. This has two benefits: first, it removes your dependence on the IT solutions team, and second, it allows you to load data at any time, which in turn provides more control.

SAP BusinessObjects Planning and Consolidation supports the creation of business rules that dictate how data is transformed in the application. For example, you can set up business rules for performing currency conversions.

The application also provides out-of-the-box functions for performing planning and consolidation. These functions can be used as-is or in combination with additional business rules to support specific application requirements. The following are some of the out-of-the-box functions:

- **Currency translation**
  You can use this function if your organization has its place of business in more than one country and does business in different currencies. Statutory requirements specify that financial information must be reported in one currency, and the currency translation function provides this ability.

- **Intercompany elimination**
  If your organization is composed of a group of companies and transactions occur between the different companies, you may need to eliminate intercompany transactions for purposes of financial reporting. This is accomplished by using the intercompany elimination logic.

- **Allocations**
  Planning may take place at a high level and you may later allocate the plan to lower levels. For example, you may need to allocate planned expenses incurred by the corporate office to each of its divisions based on some ratio, perhaps allocating corporate expenses to divisions based on the planned revenues of each division. The logic to perform this allocation is available in SAP BusinessObjects Planning and Consolidation.

- **Account transformation**
  In some cases, you may need to change the account information for data loaded into a planning application. For example, for cash flow planning, you may need to group different accounts into one account. This is accomplished using account transformation logic.

- **Validations**
  Validation logic enables you to validate data loaded or entered into the application. For example, you can run the validation logic that ensures that corporate expenses are posted only to a corporate entity.

- **Carry forward opening balances**
  You run the carry forward opening balance when you need to close a particular year and carry forward that year's closing balance to the opening balance for the subsequent year. For example, you can carry over the inventory closing bal-

ance from the last period of the calendar year to the inventory opening balance of the first period of the subsequent year.

▶ **Automatic adjustments**
You can execute the automatic adjustments logic during the course of consolidation and generate adjustments for intercompany transactions between the group's companies. The automatic adjustments logic supports the process of generating a consolidated financial statement.

SAP BusinessObjects Planning and Consolidation allows you to view and store information in multiple languages. It also includes a feature to augment collaboration by enabling you to enter comments about your data. This provides context information to the data (making it more understandable), and aids in decision making. For example, you can enter a comment to explain a reduction in overhead expenses from last year to the current year. This is clearly a better solution than storing this information in a different location that may or may not be accessible to the user making the decision.

Another feature of the application, Work Status, lets you lock data so that it cannot be changed in the application. Using this feature, you can define the range of data that can be modified or locked. For example, if a sales plan was created by a sales representative and has been sent to his manager for approval, during the approval time frame, the data can be locked from being changed.

SAP BusinessObjects Planning and Consolidation also enables the distribution and collection of financial data. The application allows you to send plan information to other people, even people who do not use the application. The recipient can then make modifications to the data, and the changes can be retracted back to the system. This facilitates the exchange of data and truly supports collaboration between and participation of all people involved in fulfilling the organization's planning objectives.

Another important feature of this application is its easy-to-use programming interface, which allows you to create and execute logic that may be used for planning and consolidation. For example, you can develop a script to perform revaluation of a plan by a certain percentage. The application lets you implement logic using a variety of methods to manage the data, and it lets you include logic than can be categorized into three broad areas. We will discuss this at length in Chapter 6; for now, we will only offer a brief description of each area.

- **Dimension logic**
  You configure this via simple mathematic formulas. For example, a formula could be set in the application to subtract the cost of goods sold from the gross sales to obtain the gross profit.

- **Business rules**
  You can develop rules to perform a certain function in planning or consolidation. For example, custom business rules can be defined for currency translations, intercompany transactions elimination, account transformations, and so on to tailor the application to the needs of the business.

- **Script Logic (or K2 Script Logic)**
  You can develop scripts that perform certain functions. This feature is generally used to apply detailed business rules to achieve a specific function, especially when out-of-the-box functionality cannot satisfy the business requirement. The script logic is a fully developed language for this application and can meet any special requirements not available in the standard application. For example, you may require script logic when you want to determine the depreciation of a certain group of assets based on some logic; if the logic is not readily available, it will need to be created in SAP BusinessObjects Planning and Consolidation.

The application frontend for planning, consolidation, and reporting runs on top of Microsoft Excel, which is widely used by planners and accountants all over the world. This lets you perform planning functions in the familiar Excel environment and helps you avoid spending time learning new software. Creating graphical data in Excel provides an intuitive display of the data that can be easily understood, interpreted, and analyzed.

Microsoft Excel versus SAP BusinessObjects Planning and Consolidation

Some organizations solely use Excel for planning, but there are many disadvantages to this approach:

- **Managing Excel spreadsheets**
  In Excel, planning data is stored in spreadsheets, which can be an issue from a security perspective; the only option to control access is to keep the files on a shared network drive and provide access only to select users. This in turn creates additional work for the IT solutions team. SAP BusinessObjects Planning and Consolidation alleviates this issue by storing the data in a database and enforcing security on the data.

- **Versions**
  When a new version of data is required, SAP BusinessObjects Planning and Consolidation can store the data in a separate version while maintaining the current data. In Excel, the data file has to be saved under a new name as the new version, which leaves room for user error when naming files.

- **Floating files**
  In Excel, it is possible for different users to maintain the same file on their respective computers, which makes it difficult to track whose file is the latest and most reliable version. SAP BusinessObjects Planning and Consolidation is a central repository for financial data and can be accessed by several users at the same time.

- **Collaboration**
  Excel does not support true collaboration, whereas SAP BusinessObjects Planning and Consolidation allows you to store comments that can serve to inform other users of important information.

SAP BusinessObjects Planning and Consolidation also lets you integrate data into Microsoft Word and Microsoft PowerPoint for reporting purposes.

2.1.3 SAP BusinessObjects Planning and Consolidation (for NetWeaver)

The NetWeaver version of SAP BusinessObjects Planning and Consolidation provides additional advantages. Because it is integrated into the SAP Business Warehouse (BW) system, the data is stored in SAP NetWeaver BW InfoCubes and enjoys all of the advantages of this system. Some advantages specific to the NetWeaver version are as follows:

- **Star schema**
  The technical architecture of an SAP NetWeaver BW InfoCube consists of a central fact table surrounded by a number of dimension tables, all grouped in the form of a star schema. The NetWeaver version of SAP BusinessObjects Planning and Consolidation makes use of the extended star-schema for storing data, which makes it a superior choice for reporting.

- **Database independent**
  The NetWeaver version runs independent of the database and can run on major databases such as Oracle, DB2, SQL Server, and Informix.

- **BW Accelerator**
  BW Accelerator is an optional tool that can be used in the NetWeaver version, to improve reporting performance. BW Accelerator provides enhanced reporting performance, even with a large data set. The investment in BW Accelerator not only helps with providing an enhanced reporting experience but also contributes to considerable cost savings by minimizing troubleshooting issues related to reporting performance.

- **ABAP language support**
  The K2 script logic, which we mentioned earlier, is the programming language used for developing script logic. The NetWeaver version of SAP BusinessObjects Planning and Consolidation also allows you to use ABAP to develop this logic. You can develop a business add-in (BAdI) interface in the backend SAP system using ABAP, which can then be called from the script logic that is developed in SAP BusinessObjects Planning and Consolidation. Scripts coded using ABAP can be used to handle complex business requirements and simultaneously leverage the experience and expertise of the IT solutions team. This feature helps reduce development time for organizations that have been using SAP for a long time, because developers will be familiar with the ABAP programming language and can use it to deliver customizations.

From the previous discussion, you now have an idea of the many features SAP BusinessObjects Planning and Consolidation offers. Most of the features discussed require less assistance from the IT solutions team on an on-going basis (although they will of course be involved in both the initial stages of the development of the applications and their on-going support). The features that are built into this application allow you to automatically assume ownership of the application, and then partner with the IT solutions team in fulfilling specific business needs.

In the next section, you will see how the application can be used for performing both planning and consolidation functions.

2.2 Unified Planning and Consolidation

SAP BusinessObjects Planning and Consolidation provides a full-fledged environment for organizations to create flexible and powerful applications for different types of planning. It can also be used for consolidating and reporting financial data to satisfy the legal requirements of your organization.

2.2.1 Planning in SAP BusinessObjects Planning and Consolidation

In today's world of intense competition, it is necessary for organizations to plan and stay ahead. Planning is the life-blood of business and the ability to spot opportunities and prepare for various courses of action has become imperative because the fast-changing needs of consumers require them to be vigilant and act with vision. To meet this objective, organizations are looking for software that can provide an enabling environment to handle planning needs.

As we have discussed, SAP BusinessObjects Planning and Consolidation has many features that make it an ideal tool for planning, designed to maximize your ability to manage and take ownership of data. Its robust interface allows for customization and collaboration and makes it a compelling choice for planning. Unlike most software, this application reduces the dependence on the IT solutions team while also providing more time for the team to handle the portions of application development and maintenance they best serve (i.e., system configuration and performance).

2.2.2 Consolidation in SAP BusinessObjects Planning and Consolidation

The consolidation functionality of SAP BusinessObjects Planning and Consolidation provides an environment to report the financial results of your entire organization. You can use it to determine the financial health of the company as a whole, after taking into account the currency translations, elimination of intercompany transactions, and other necessary adjustments. When the consolidation report is prepared, the application considers different types of investments among organizational units.

Consolidation provides the means for internal and external enterprise reporting of a company's financial data. When the reporting is external, it serves the objective of statutory compliance, also known as *legal consolidation*. This is classified as formal reporting and must satisfy the acceptable accounting practice that is applicable to the country where the consolidation is done.

Internal reporting is also called *management consolidation*. This provides more latitude and flexibility in defining the methods used for consolidating data. The objective of this type of consolidation is to provide you with the necessary tools for decision making. You can consolidate based on customer-defined consolidation units, which can represent, for example, companies, plants, business areas, profit centers, or cost centers. You can also portray matrix organizations; for example, by using a combination of companies and profit centers.

The first step you perform in consolidation is to standardize the financial data reported by individual consolidation units to adhere to the accounting standards of the group. You then translate the standardized financial data from the various local currencies into the group currencies (if the local and group currencies are different). Finally, you eliminate the effects of intercompany transactions. Thus, you calculate the consolidated financial statements as if the group were a single entity. You can use the reporting functions of SAP BusinessObjects Planning and Consolidation to analyze and report on your consolidated financial statement data. You can use SAP's XBRL publishing software to create XBRL documents based on data in the application SAP BusinessObjects Planning and Consolidation to exchange financial data with accounting jurisdictions such as banks, regulators, and agencies.

Next, we will discuss the features and advantages of performing consolidation in SAP BusinessObjects Planning and Consolidation.

Features

SAP BusinessObjects Planning and Consolidation allows you to use different charts of accounts for consolidation, enabling you to generate several consolidated financial statements in parallel to accommodate different accounting principles.

You can collect data for consolidation in the NetWeaver version using the following methods:

- Online data entry
- Flexible upload from a data file
- Loading from an InfoProvider

The application allows you to execute the following tasks:

- Currency translation
- Intercompany eliminations
- Consolidation of investments
- Automatic posting of adjustments

- Reclassification
- Allocation
- Balance carry forward
- Validation

These tasks can be executed independently or as part of the script logic.

Advantages of Performing Consolidation in SAP BusinessObjects Planning and Consolidation

Performing consolidation with SAP BusinessObjects Planning and Consolidation has the following advantages:

- **Legal and management consolidation**
  The application provides a systematic process to perform legal consolidation. You can also perform management consolidation using different sets of data to highlight different scenarios for management, as well as parallel consolidations with different categories of data and using different accounting principles.

- **Accuracy**
  The design of the application's system for consolidation enables the consolidation process to run in a controlled manner, with the ability to perform checks and balances along the way. This mitigates any errors during the process and ensures the completeness and accuracy of the data.

- **Multiple source systems**
  You can compile financial data from various source systems into a single system for the purpose of consolidation.

- **Reporting**
  You can generate reports based on consolidated data, which you can then use as a tool for measuring the organization's performance. The reports allow you to view key metrics such as return on equity, ROI, and so on.

- **Validation of data**
  You can analyze different sources of data used to generate the consolidated data to ensure that the data is valid and reliable. You can also reconcile the data in the application with the source system, facilitating reliability.

- **Collaboration**
  The application supports extensive collaboration needed to gather data from multiple sources. This helps with the consolidation of data from diverse sources.

You should now have an understanding of how SAP BusinessObjects Planning and Consolidation can be used by organizations to meet both their planning and consolidation requirements. In the next section, we will discuss the architecture of SAP BusinessObjects Planning and Consolidation for NetWeaver and explain how it interfaces with the SAP NetWeaver BW system.

2.3　SAP BusinessObjects Planning and Consolidation NetWeaver Architecture

The architecture of SAP BusinessObjects Planning and Consolidation for NetWeaver (Figure 2.1) is designed to leverage the capabilities of the planning and consolidation application and SAP NetWeaver BW. You can use the planning application frontend tool to configure planning and consolidation features. The data that is entered or loaded through this frontend application is then stored in the SAP NetWeaver BW system. The SAP NetWeaver BW system is based on the extended star schema, and is designed to provide high performance reporting.

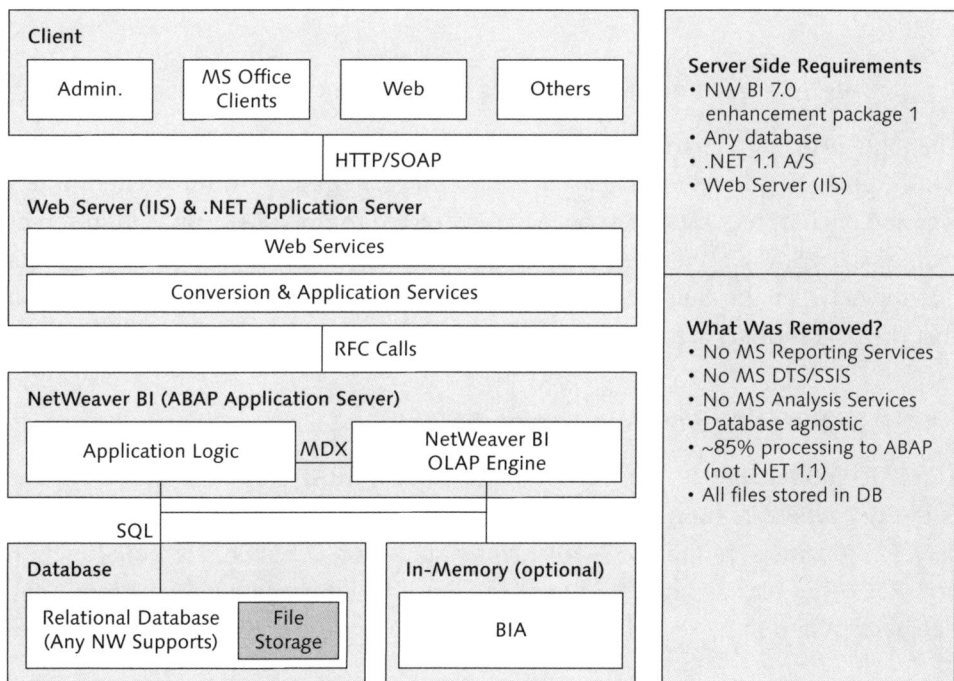

Figure 2.1　SAP BusinessObjects Planning and Consolidation for NetWeaver Architecture

Figure 2.1 shows the architecture of the system for NetWeaver. The architecture consists of four tiers, discussed in more detail next.

2.3.1 Client Interface

The client interface comprises the Microsoft Excel-based Admin Client, Microsoft Office Client, and a web-based tool for configuring and reporting. You can use the Excel Admin Client tool to configure the application; the tool includes a robust and intuitive interface for defining the configuration and managing the development process. All aspects of the development, including setting up security, are performed using this interface. In addition to using Excel, you can also use other Microsoft tools such as Word and PowerPoint to report data in SAP BusinessObjects Planning and Consolidation.

You can use the Excel-based Office Client to plan and consolidate data in the application and to create and execute reports. The Web Interface is a zero footprint option available to create web-based reports, manage unstructured documents, monitor the status of a planning application, and set certain custom parameters for an application.

2.3.2 Web Server and .NET Application Server

The tools available as part of the client interface use web services to connect to the .NET Application Server tier. This server manages requests from the client interface and enables requests for service to be directed to the ABAP application server that is part of SAP NetWeaver BW. The main purpose of this layer is to convert data flowing between the client interface and the SAP NetWeaver Application Server so that the data formats are understood by the two servers.

2.3.3 SAP NetWeaver Application Server

The SAP NetWeaver Application Server is also the ABAP Application Server. This is the tier where requests are processed. The request from the .NET application server is processed in the SAP NetWeaver Application Server as a remote function call (RFC). The requests may be to either report data or update information in the database. When the SAP NetWeaver Application Server receives a request, it processes it and sends the results back to the .NET Application Server. The .NET Application Server then receives the result and sends it back to the client interface.

2.3.4 Database Server

The database server is the tier where data is stored. The SAP NetWeaver BW system is the backend system where objects are created and the data is stored for SAP BusinessObjects Planning and Consolidation. The NetWeaver version is database-agnostic and supports all popular databases including Oracle, Informix, SQL Server, and DB2.

The client interface interacts with SAP NetWeaver BW system to manage objects and data. When you create, read, update, or delete objects or data using the client interface, the system performs these tasks on the SAP NetWeaver BW system.

Although a majority of the development tasks related to SAP BusinessObjects Planning and Consolidation are accomplished using the client interface, a few tasks are performed directly in the SAP NetWeaver BW system. These include activities related to improving performance, setting locks, setting validation rules, and creating custom ABAP programs. Process chains, which are used to schedule data loads, are also created directly in the SAP NetWeaver BW system.

You may sometimes extract master, text, hierarchy, and transaction data from a source system into the SAP NetWeaver BW system before loading the data to an SAP BusinessObjects Planning and Consolidation system. In this case, the SAP NetWeaver BW system is used as a staging system for data before being loaded to the planning and consolidation application. The objects related to setting up the staging environment are created directly in the SAP NetWeaver BW system.

> **Note**
>
> It is recommended to *not* perform any manual configuration for SAP BusinessObjects Planning and Consolidation directly in the SAP NetWeaver BW system, except for the few tasks mentioned. The application should be configured using the frontend tools (Admin Console, Office Client, and Web Interface).

As you can see, the integration of SAP BusinessObjects Planning and Consolidation with NetWeaver provides many benefits to leverage the power of Excel and SAP NetWeaver BW systems.

In the next section, we will introduce you to objects created in the SAP NetWeaver BW system.

2.4 Introduction to SAP NetWeaver BW

When you create an object using the SAP BusinessObjects Planning and Consolidation frontend, the system creates equivalent objects in the SAP NetWeaver BW system. In addition, the SAP NetWeaver BW system may sometimes be used to stage data coming from various source systems before being loaded to the planning and consolidation application. In the subsections that follow, we will discuss the objects in SAP NetWeaver BW, the data flow process the system utilizes, process chains, and SAP Business Content.

2.4.1 Objects Used in SAP NetWeaver BW

In this section, we will introduce you to the objects used in SAP NetWeaver BW.

InfoObject

An *InfoObject* is the basic object for building a data model in SAP NetWeaver BW. There are several different types of InfoObjects:

- **Characteristics**
  - A characteristic InfoObject represents an entity of a business or an attribute related to an entity. Examples of business entities include customers, materials, and employees.
  - An InfoObject that provides additional information about an entity is called an attribute. Attributes are InfoObjects themselves but are used in conjunction with the parent InfoObject. Examples of attributes are customer address and phone number. (These InfoObjects are included as attributes in the Customer InfoObject.)
  - You can configure an InfoObject to store master, text, and hierarchy data.
  - When you define an InfoObject to store master data, it contains the master data table with the InfoObject and the attributes associated to it. For example, the customer number, along with city, state, zip and country, can be stored as master data.

- When you design an InfoObject to store text data, it contains the text values of the InfoObject. For example, the names of customers can be stored as text values.
- When there is an inherent parent-child relationship in data, you can define the InfoObject as a hierarchy InfoObject. This is useful for analysis where there is a relationship in data. For example, the reporting relationships between manager and employees can be defined as a hierarchy.

- **Time characteristics**
  - The time characteristic InfoObject is used to set the value for the time-related characteristic of a transaction. Examples of time characteristics are calendar month, calendar year, fiscal year, and so on.

- **Unit characteristics**
  - The unit characteristic InfoObject provides meaning to quantitative data. Currency and units of measure are examples of unit characteristics. For example, the sales amount for a transaction can be recorded as a currency. The quantity sold can be recorded as a unit (kg and lbs).

- **Key figures**
  - The key figure InfoObject represents the quantitative measure associated with a transaction. Examples of key figures are the quantity and amount associated with a sales transaction.

InfoProvider

An InfoProvider is the object provided for storing data in SAP NetWeaver BW; it is comprised of a collection of InfoObjects. InfoProviders can contain characteristic, time characteristic, unit characteristic, and key figure InfoObjects.

There are two types of InfoProviders:

- **Physical InfoProviders**
  - Physical InfoProviders are used to store data, and can be InfoObjects, InfoCubes, and DataStore objects. They are also referred to as *data targets*, because they physically contain the data.
  - An InfoCube is a collection of InfoObjects, and represents the extended star schema architecture in SAP NetWeaver BW. It is made up of a fact table and a number of dimension tables. Related characteristics in an InfoCube are

grouped together under dimensions. When you load data to an InfoCube, a dimension ID is created by the system for each unique combination of characteristics in a dimension. A record in a fact table is made up of the individual key figures and the dimension IDs associated with a transaction. The individual characteristics in a dimension, and the corresponding attributes of a characteristic, are related using surrogate IDs (SIDS). The InfoCube is the recommended approach for reporting in SAP NetWeaver BW, because it provides the full advantage of the star schema architecture.

- A DataStore object is a transparent table that usually serves as the first layer of extracting data from a source system. The data loaded in a DataStore is often used for detailed analysis, because it contains raw data extracted from the source system. The data extracted into the DataStore can be further loaded into another InfoProvider, depending on the particular requirements of analysis.

- **Logical InfoProviders**

  - Logical InfoProviders do not physically contain data but are used for providing views of data. They are InfoSets, MultiProviders, and virtual InfoProviders.

  - An InfoSet lets you join objects that store data. For example, two DataStore objects can be joined together to create an InfoSet. The joins created in an InfoSet are database joins. There is considerable flexibility when you define an InfoSet using inner and outer joins. Using an outer join, you can view all of the data defined in the left object of the InfoSet—for example, you can view the sales of all customers, including customers who did not have any sales reported in a particular period. InfoSets can also be used to combine data from an InfoCube and another InfoProvider.

  - A MultiProvider provides a powerful feature to view data contained in more than one InfoProvider. For example, a MultiProvider can be used to view data from an InfoCube and a DataStore. The MultiProvider provides a union of data in the underlying InfoProviders. This helps to combine the data available in more than one InfoProvider.

  - A virtual InfoProvider enables remote access of data from a source system connected to the SAP NetWeaver BW system.

2.4.2 Extraction, Transformation, and Loading Data in SAP NetWeaver BW

This section explains the process of extracting, transforming, and loading data into data targets in SAP NetWeaver BW.

DataSource

The DataSource is the source of data used for extracting data into SAP NetWeaver BW. DataSources can be configured to extract data from a variety of source systems:

- **SAP systems**
  Data can be extracted from SAP systems (SAP R/3, SAP CRM, and other new dimension products offered by SAP) into SAP NetWeaver BW. There is a tight connection between SAP systems and the SAP NetWeaver BW system. The Service application programming interface (API) provides the interface to extract data from these systems.

- **Flat files**
  In this case, data is extracted from a standard file into SAP NetWeaver BW (e.g., an Excel file). A DataSource is defined in the SAP NetWeaver BW system corresponding to the file layout for extracting data.

- **Web applications**
  An XML interface can be used to extract data from a Web application using the simple object access protocol (SOAP).

- **DB Connect**
  A direct connection to a variety of external databases systems such as Oracle, Informix, and so on can be established using DB Connect.

- **Universal Data Connect**
  This connection provides access to external relational databases and multidimensional databases via the J2EE server.

- **Third-party systems**
  In this case, a business application programming interface (BAPI) is used in conjunction with third-party tools to extract data into the SAP NetWeaver BW system. Some examples of third-party systems are Informatica and Ascential.

DataSources can be configured for each of these source systems.

Flow of Data in SAP NetWeaver BW (Extraction, Transformation, and Loading)

The data transfer process in SAP NetWeaver BW provides a flexible and improved process of extracting data from a source system, transforming the extracted data, and subsequently loading the transformed data into a data target.

The following are the components of the data transfer process in SAP NetWeaver BW:

- **Persistent staging area (PSA)**
  - A PSA table is generated when a DataSource is activated in SAP NetWeaver BW. The PSA is a transparent table and is the first layer for storing data.
  - When data is requested for a DataSource from a source system, the data is initially loaded into the corresponding PSA table of the DataSource.

- **Transformations**
  - A transformation process is defined between a source and target object in SAP NetWeaver BW. The objective of the transformation is to map data coming from a source to a target using specific rules. It also lets you apply changes to data coming from a DataSource.
  - You can use the DataSource (PSA), InfoSource, DataStore object, InfoCube, InfoObject, and InfoSet as source objects in the transformation.
  - The InfoSource, DataStore object, InfoCube, and InfoObject can be used as target objects in the transformation.
  - The transformation rule allows mapping fields and InfoObjects to a target InfoObject, setting a constant value to a target InfoObject, developing a routine in ABAP to perform the mapping, creating a formula, looking up master data attributes to determine the value of a target InfoObject, and performing time determinations.
  - An InfoSource acts as an additional layer of transformation before data reaches a data target. It can be used as an optional process when two or more transformations are required before data is transferred from a DataSource to a data target.

- **Data transfer process**
  - The data transfer process facilitates the flow of data in SAP NetWeaver BW from one persistent object to another; for example, after data is transferred

from a source system into the PSA, the DTP is used to load from the PSA to a data target.

- PSA, InfoObject, InfoCube, and DataStore objects are examples of persistent objects in the SAP NetWeaver BW system.

- The data transfer process may encompass one or many transformations. A transformation process is defined to provide the rules to map data between a source object and a target object. Transformation rules provide the ability to apply changes to the data coming from a source to a target. The data transfer process moves data from the source to the target using the rules specified in the transformation

- **InfoPackage**

    - An InfoPackage is the object used to request data for a DataSource from the source system. After data is requested by the InfoPackage, the data for a DataSource is transferred from the source system to the PSA table.

In Figure 2.2, you can see the flow of data in SAP NetWeaver BW. Transformation rules are created between the source and target objects, and a data transfer process is used to load data from one persistent object to another.

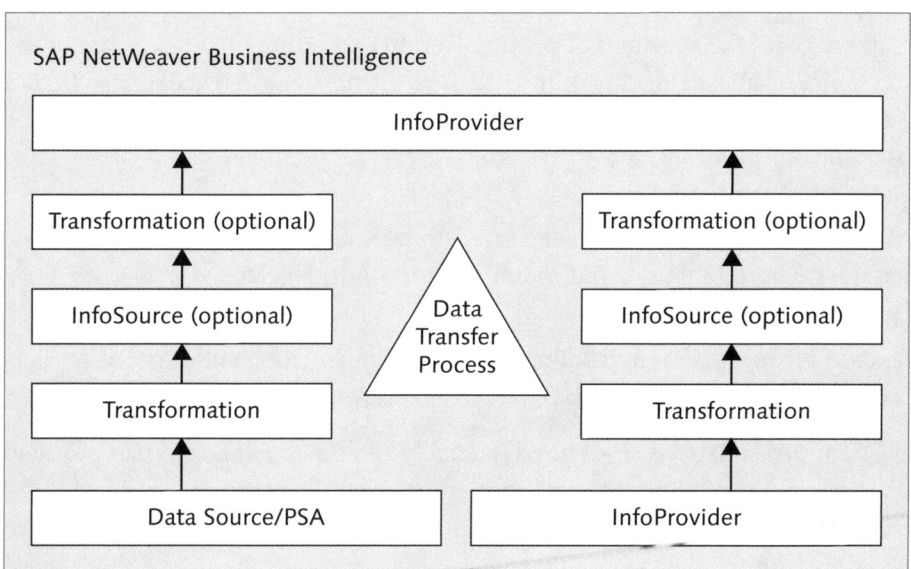

Figure 2.2 Data Transfer Process in SAP NetWeaver BW

2.4.3 Process Chains

A *process chain* provides different types of processes to manage data within the SAP NetWeaver BW system. You use process chains to automate the process of extracting, transforming, and loading data, as well as to more effectively administer data. For example, the InfoPackage that is executed to request data from the source system, and the DTP process that is used for moving data within SAP NetWeaver BW, can be automatically scheduled in a process chain.

2.4.4 SAP Business Content

In the previous section, we mentioned that you can use SAP NetWeaver BW as a staging environment before loading data into SAP BusinessObjects Planning and Consolidation. SAP Business Content is what allows you to build this staging environment; it consists of preconfigured objects that help accelerate the process of development of an SAP NetWeaver BW application. SAP Business Content is available in the following areas:

- **DataSources**
  SAP supplies DataSources to bring data from R/3 to SAP NetWeaver BW systems. The logic for extracting the data is supplied with the DataSource. This greatly reduces the time and effort involved in extracting the data. Some of the DataSources have delta capabilities for extracting data. A DataSource that is delta-enabled brings over only the data that was created or modified since the last extraction from the source system.

- **InfoObjects**
  SAP supplies standard InfoObjects used in business applications, for example Customer, Plant, Material, and Material Group InfoObjects.

- **InfoProviders**
  Standard business content InfoProviders are available for a wide area of applications. These include InfoCube, DataStores, and MultiProviders.

In addition, SAP Business Content is available for objects that are used to load data, for example InfoSources, transformations, and data transfer processes. The processes to control data loading using InfoPackages and process chains are also delivered by SAP.

From this, you can see that the process of setting up the SAP NetWeaver BW system is greatly facilitated through SAP Business Content. Although SAP Business Content may not be able to provide a solution for all of the analysis requirements of a business, it can be used as the starting point to prototype a solution. SAP Business Content can subsequently be enhanced to meet the analysis requirements of specific users.

In the next section, we will introduce you to objects created in the SAP BusinessObjects Planning and Consolidation system.

2.5 Terminology and Objects in SAP BusinessObjects Planning and Consolidation

In this section, we will discuss some of the terminology used and some of the objects created in SAP BusinessObjects Planning and Consolidation for NetWeaver. We will also explain how a request to create an object in the planning and consolidation application translates into creating an equivalent object in the SAP NetWeaver BW system.

2.5.1 Terminology

Application Set

An *application set* is the starting point for creating any application in SAP BusinessObjects Planning and Consolidation. It can be described as a functional area designed to include the applications associated with a segment of the business. For example, you can create an application set for sales applications and another application set for head-count planning.

Although the general objective of creating application sets is to support a business requirement (such as sales planning, production planning, head-count planning, etc.), there are no rules on what applications can be contained in an application set. It is left for you to decide how you want to structure applications within an application set.

The application set is created via the Admin Console in the planning and consolidation application. A new application set can only be created using another application set as the basis. When the system is initially installed, an application set with the technical name "AppShell" is available. This serves as a reference for creating other application sets in the system. We recommend that you do *not* make any changes to AppShell; instead, use it to create a new application set and customize that application set for the application. You should have system administrator access to create an application set.

Dimensions

Dimensions represent the entities of a business (e.g., accounts, company codes, and categories); they represent the master, text, and hierarchy data for each of the business entities. Dimensions belong to the application set in which they are configured. It is very important to note that dimensions cannot be used or shared across application sets.

Secured Dimension

A dimension can be marked as secure for an application. When a dimension is marked as secure, specific read and write access has to be granted to users who use the application so they can access the data.

Properties

A dimension is designed to include *properties*, which provide additional meaning to the dimension. For example, an account dimension can include an *account type property* to indicate the type of account (whether it is an income account or an expense account). Property values can be used as a selection criterion for reporting.

Dimension Members

The data points associated with a dimension are referred to as *dimension members*. Each dimension member record represents master, text, and hierarchy data associated with the key of a dimension. A dimension member can store hierarchical relationships with another dimension member in the same dimension, which is very useful for reporting hierarchical relationships between data. There is no restriction on the number of hierarchies that can be created.

Application

An application is a repository that consists of a number of dimensions, and is used to meet your planning, consolidation, and reporting needs. The application is configured based on the specific needs of the business. It is where you interface to plan, consolidate, and report data.

Data Package

SAP BusinessObjects Planning and Consolidation provides standard out-of-the-box functionality to execute common tasks required for planning and consolidation such as currency translation, intercompany profit elimination, and so on. These tasks are executed via a data manager package.

User

A user is an individual who can use the applications in an application set.

Team

A team is a group of users and is created based on the users' roles. For example, all of the developers can be grouped together and identified as a team.

Tasks

There a number of activities that you can perform in SAP BusinessObjects Planning and Consolidation that are known as *tasks*. Examples of tasks are creating an application set, running a report, configuring security, and so on. Users are granted access to specific tasks based on their role in the organization.

Task Profile

A number of tasks can be grouped together and included in a task profile. Task profiles can be assigned to a user or to a group of users in a team.

Member Access Profile

The member access profile identifies data-level access to an application and is relevant only for dimensions that were identified as secured dimensions in the application. For each application that includes dimensions marked as secured dimensions, the member access profile is configured to identify the read and write access available to users for each of the secured dimensions.

Business Rules

SAP BusinessObjects Planning and Consolidation includes a rule-based table for defining certain common requirements for planning and consolidation. A company that has business operations in different countries may have a need to translate their data to one common reporting currency for financial reporting. The rules-based table provides a method for defining how local currencies should be translated to a group currency.

Business rules can be set up for account transformations, converting period balances, validation of data, elimination of intercompany sales, and setting up methods and rules for the consolidation of data.

Script Logic

Script logic is designed to provide greater flexibility in managing data for an application and includes SQL- and MDX-based programming structures for custom programming. Business rules do not require the use of script logic and provide a convenient table-based approach to define the rules for different conversions. However, there may be business scenarios that cannot be satisfied using business rules; in these cases, script logic provides the means to achieve that objective.

Relationship Between Objects Created in SAP BusinessObjects Planning and Consolidation and SAP NetWeaver BW

When objects are created in the SAP BusinessObjects Planning and Consolidation system, the system creates equivalent objects in the SAP NetWeaver BW system. The corresponding objects created in the SAP NetWeaver BW system are shown in Table 2.1.

Terminology and Objects in SAP BusinessObjects Planning and Consolidation | 2.5

Object Ceated in SAP BusinessObjects Planning and Consolidation	Object Created in SAP NetWeaver BW
Application Set	InfoArea An application set in SAP BusinessObjects Planning and Consolidation is equivalent to an InfoArea in SAP NetWeaver BW. When a request for an application set is initiated in the SAP BusinessObjects Planning and Consolidation frontend, an InfoArea is created in SAP NetWeaver BW with InfoObjects and InfoCubes under it. In SAP BusinessObjects Planning and Consolidation, objects added under an application set are not shared across oher application sets. In SAP NetWeaver BW, objects created under an InfoArea can be shared by objects in other InfoAreas.
Application	InfoCube An application in SAP BusinessObjects Planning and Consolidation is created with respect to an application set and is used for storing transaction data. When a request for creating an application is initiated in SAP BusinessObjects Planning and Consolidation, an InfoCube is created in SAP NetWeaver BW.
Dimension	InfoObject A dimension in SAP BusinessObjects Planning and Consolidation is equivalent to an InfoObject in SAP NetWeaver BW. It is created under an application set, and is used for storing master data. Examples include account, product, and customer dimensions.
Property	Attribute A property is equivalent to an attribute included in an InfoObject, and is dependent on the dimension under which it is created. Example. A customer dimension may include a property called "customer group."

Table 2.1 Relationship Between Objects Created in SAP BusinessObjects Planning and Consolidation and SAP NetWeaver BW

Object Ceated in SAP BusinessObjects Planning and Consolidation	Object Created in SAP NetWeaver BW
Dimension Member	Master data record
	The dimension member is equivalent to master, text, and hierarchy data in SAP NetWeaver BW.
Master data to store text and hierarchy data	In SAP NetWeaver BW, an InfoObject should be enabled to store text and hierarchy data for an InfoObject.
	In SAP BusinessObjects Planning and Consolidation, a property with the technical name DESCRIPTION is automatically created as a property when creating a dimension to store text data.
	In SAP BusinessObjects Planning and Consolidation, you can create a hierarchy when entering data for a dimension in the Excel worksheet by including a column "PARENT(Hn)," where n is the number of hierarchy for the dimension.
Unsigned Data	Key figure
	Only one type of object is used for recording quantitative values for transaction data in SAP BusinessObjects Planning and Consolidation: unsigned data. This object is equivalent to a key figure in SAP NetWeaver BW.

Table 2.1 Relationship Between Objects Created in SAP BusinessObjects Planning and Consolidation and SAP NetWeaver BW (Cont.)

2.6 Summary

In this chapter, we introduced you to the concepts and terminology used in SAP BusinessObjects Planning and Consolidation and you learned how the SAP BusinessObjects Planning and Consolidation application can be used by organizations to meet both their planning and consolidation requirements. You also studied the architecture of SAP BusinessObjects Planning and Consolidation for NetWeaver, and were introduced to some of the advantages of staging a SAP BusinessObjects Planning and Consolidation application on a NetWeaver platform. Furthermore, you learned about certain objects that are configured in the SAP BusinessObjects Planning and Consolidation and SAP NetWeaver BW systems. In the next chapter, we will discuss the details of configuring an application using the SAP BusinessObjects Planning and Consolidation software tool.

3   Modeling an Application with SAP BusinessObjects Planning and Consolidation for NetWeaver

In this chapter, we will introduce you to a case study of a model company that has decided to plan its gross margin by implementing the NetWeaver version of SAP BusinessObjects Planning and Consolidation. The details of the company and how it wants to use the software for planning are explained in this chapter. The case study is also used as the basis for all planning and consolidation examples presented in subsequent chapters.

Section 3.1 will introduce you to a case study that is used to illustrate the key features of the NetWeaver version of SAP BusinessObjects Planning and Consolidation. This case study explains the details of an organization, Rich Bloom, Inc., which uses the software for planning its gross margin.

Section 3.2 will explain the steps involved in modeling objects in SAP NetWeaver BW to meet the requirements of the case study. The objects created in SAP NetWeaver BW are used in this case as a staging environment to store data coming from a transactional source system, before being loaded into SAP BusinessObjects Planning and Consolidation.

Section 3.3 will explain the steps involved in modeling objects in SAP BusinessObjects Planning and Consolidation for NetWeaver to meet the requirements of the case study. This section serves as a solid foundation to understand the features of the tool.

3.1   Rich Bloom, Inc.

Throughout this book, we will use a sample company called Rich Bloom, Inc. to explain the features of SAP BusinessObjects Planning and Consolidation for NetWeaver. In this section, we will discuss the case study to better understand the model company and the objectives the company is trying to meet using SAP BusinessObjects Planning and Consolidation for NetWeaver.

3.1.1 Business

Rich Bloom, Inc. is a clothing retailer headquartered in the U.S. with a presence in Germany and England. The company began its operations in the year 2000 and has seen its growth and profit increase rapidly due to its excellent management and operation of its business. It has been able to vary its mix of products and consistently exceed customer expectations.

In a recent survey, the company determined that the ongoing worldwide recession has caused a reduction in the amount spent on clothing. This has energized the company to further strengthen its planning process so that it can continue to grow and thrive under difficult business conditions.

3.1.2 Offices

The company's business is incorporated as follows:

- 20 – Rich Bloom, Inc., San Diego, CA, USA
- 22 – Rich Bloom Corporate, Inc., Philadelphia, PA, USA
- 23 – Rich Bloom New Markets, Inc., Houston, TX, USA
- 25 – Rich Bloom Ltd, London, UK
- 30 – Rich Bloom AG, Frankfurt, Germany

3.1.3 Products

The company sells clothing for teenagers and pre-teenagers, including the following products:

- RB T-shirts
- RB shirts
- RB jackets
- RB designer jeans
- RB Apollo shirts

The company has partnerships with large wholesalers involved in the clothing business, through which it sells its products. Rich Bloom, Inc. also has a few retail outlets in several key locations, through which it sells products directly to customers. It introduced the RB Apollo shirt in 2008, and this product has been very successful. It has found wide acceptance among teenagers and pre-teens, which has considerably increased profit forecasts.

The company is facing stiff competition to some of its products. Increased competition has stalled growth of sales of these products, and the company is looking to increase returns by improving the efficiency of its operations and by introducing product innovations to grow sales momentum.

3.1.4 Currency

The company operates in more than one country and has business transactions in multiple currencies. The currencies used for its operations are as follows:

- US Dollar
- British Pound
- Euro

The company reports the financial transactions in one currency, USD, because the company is headquartered in the U.S.

3.1.5 Case Study

Rich Bloom, Inc. has been using the SAP ECC system for recording its business transactions. It has also been using the SAP NetWeaver BW system as its data warehousing system to analyze information and make decisions. Using these systems has helped the company manage its business quite efficiently.

However, Rich Bloom, Inc. would like to streamline the planning function of the business. The company currently does not have a systematic planning process. The global recession and stiff competition have made management look into improving its efficiency of operations and creating a sound planning system. Management recognizes that having a good planning tool will help the company face competition and retain leadership in the market.

Rich Bloom, Inc. wants to be able to compare plan data with actual data to see if it is able to meet what it set out to accomplish in the first place. The company has been using Excel spreadsheets to manage its planning process, but this has proved wanting in several respects. First, the Excel spreadsheet does not provide a unified tool for entering plans and monitoring the planning process, which has resulted in multiple versions of plans created on user desktops, making it difficult for the company to distinguish between the latest and older versions. Second, the process of consolidating plan data from different Excel spreadsheets takes considerable time, making the entire process inefficient. Third, Excel lacks security controls. All of this has prompted Rich Bloom, Inc. to look at other tools for planning. Although users have become accustomed to planning using Excel, Rich Bloom, Inc. is grappling with its limitations and with using it exclusively for planning.

Rich Bloom, Inc. has now decided that it will use the recently introduced SAP BusinessObjects Planning and Consolidation for NetWeaver for planning. First, this tool has an Excel-based frontend for planning, with which users are familiar. Second, Rich Bloom, Inc. wants to leverage the SAP NetWeaver BW environment, which uses an enhanced star schema architecture to provide a superior user experience. Rich Bloom, Inc. also believes that SAP BusinessObjects Planning and Consolidation for NetWeaver is an advanced tool for planning that will provide a much needed edge in the difficult and competitive market place.

The company will use SAP BusinessObjects Planning and Consolidation for NetWeaver to plan its gross margin for 2010, using the actual sales and cost data for 2009 as the basis to plan for 2010. It will maintain an InfoCube in SAP NetWeaver BW that contains actual sales and cost data, and the initial plan data for 2010 will be created by copying the actual sales and cost data for 2009 into the plan version for 2010. Subsequently, users will be able to manually change the sales and cost data to reflect current market conditions.

The plan data will be consolidated, reviewed, and approved by management. After the plan data is approved, no further changes will be allowed.

3.1.6 Decision to Use SAP BusinessObjects Planning and Consolidation for NetWeaver

Rich Bloom, Inc. has decided to use SAP BusinessObjects Planning and Consolidation for NetWeaver for the following reasons:

- It wants to reduce the cycle time required to complete the planning process.
- It wants to overcome the limitations of Excel as a stand-alone tool for planning. When using Excel, data cannot be stored in a database, and the tool does not provide a robust method of securing the data.
- Users are familiar with Excel for planning and analysis. The SAP BusinessObjects Planning and Consolidation for NetWeaver frontend is based on Excel; therefore, the company can tap this existing skillset to successfully manage its planning process.
- SAP BusinessObjects Planning and Consolidation for NetWeaver provides role-based access to the data for users. This enables you to provide the appropriate level of access to users, based on their role in the planning process.
- Rich Bloom, Inc. believes that it can leverage existing actual sales and cost data currently available in SAP NetWeaver BW as the basis for planning. Actual data can be directly loaded into SAP BusinessObjects Planning and Consolidation, and can be used for planning.
- The company would like to leverage the already existing SAP NetWeaver BW environment to provide enhanced reporting to SAP BusinessObjects Planning and Consolidation users.

You should now have an understanding of Rich Bloom, Inc.'s requirement to develop a planning application to project gross margin using SAP BusinessObjects Planning and Consolidation for NetWeaver. In the next section, we will develop objects in the SAP NetWeaver BW environment that will be used to stage actual sales and cost data coming from the SAP ECC system before being loaded into SAP BusinessObjects Planning and Consolidation for NetWeaver.

3.2 Building the Data Model in SAP NetWeaver BW

As previously discussed, Rich Bloom, Inc. wants to plan its gross margin for 2010 using actual sales and cost data from 2009. In this section, we will discuss the development of the staging environment in SAP NetWeaver BW that will house the actual sales and cost data. This data will eventually be loaded into SAP BusinessObjects Planning and Consolidation for NetWeaver to be used for planning.

3 | Modeling an Application with SAP BusinessObjects Planning and Consolidation for NetWeaver

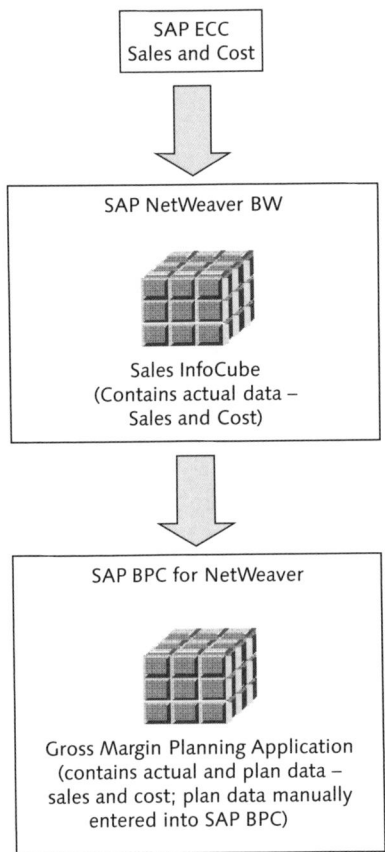

Figure 3.1 Flow of Data from SAP ECC to SAP BusinessObjects Planning and Consolidation

Figure 3.1 displays the flow of data from SAP ECC to SAP NetWeaver BW, and subsequently to SAP BusinessObjects Planning and Consolidation for NetWeaver. An InfoCube called Sales that will be used as one of the sources of data for the purpose of planning for the future will be created in SAP NetWeaver BW to store the actual sales and cost data for the last four years. Market research will also be used to forecast future demand, and the necessary adjustments will be made for future sales and cost. The data in the Sales InfoCube will be loaded with data from the SAP ECC system on a daily basis.

We will now build the objects necessary for storing the actual sales and cost data in SAP NetWeaver BW. The InfoObjects to be included in the Sales InfoCube are listed in the following tables, and are SAP-delivered unless indicated by the words *custom InfoObject*:

3.2 Building the Data Model in SAP NetWeaver BW

- **Characteristics**
  The characteristics and their values are listed in Table 3.1.
- **Time characteristics**
  The time characteristics and their values are listed in Table 3.2.
- **Unit characteristics**
  The unit characteristics required are listed in Table 3.3.
- **Key figures**
  The key figures (quantitative measures) required for reporting are listed in Table 3.4.

Characteristics	Values
0COMP_CODE	20,22,23,25 AND 30
	20 — Rich Bloom, Inc., San Diego, CA, USA
	22 — Rich Bloom Corporate Inc, Philadelphia, PA, USA
	23 — Rich Bloom New Markets Inc, Houston, TX, USA
	25 — Rich Bloom Ltd, London, UK
	30 — Rich Bloom AG, Frankfurt, Germany
0MATERIAL	CK2000,CK2001,CK2002, CY7000
	CK2000 — T-Shirts
	CK2001 — Shirts
	CK2002 — Jackets
	CK2003 — Apollo Shirt
	CY7000 — Jeans
0CUSTOMER	C1-C4, C20-21, C30-31
	C1-C4 — Customers in the U.S.
	C20-C21 — Customers in the UK
	C30-C31 — Customers in Germany
ZACCOUNT (Custom Characteristic)	Revenue, COGS, SG&A
	Revenue — Sales Revenue
	COGS — Cost of Goods Sold
	SGA — Sales, General and Administrative Expenses
	Overhead — Corporate Expenses

Table 3.1 Characteristics and Values

Characteristics	Values
0CALMONTH	Calendar period for actual data
0CALYEAR	Calendar year for actual data

Table 3.2 Time Characteristics

Characteristics	Values
0CURRENCY	Used to store the currency associated with the amount value; is used in key figure ZAMOUNT

Table 3.3 Unit Characteristics

Characteristics	Values
ZAMOUNT (Custom Key Figure)	Amount in local currency (key figure of type currency—associated with 0CURRENCY currency measure)

Table 3.4 Key Figures

3.2.1 Creating and Activating InfoObjects

Based on the requirements listed in the case study, we will now start building the necessary objects. The InfoObjects listed in the previous tables are required for building the data model; most of them have a technical name that starts with 0. These are SAP-supplied InfoObjects. Before an InfoObject that is delivered by SAP can be used, however, it must be activated. We will start by checking the status of InfoObjects and learn how to activate them if they are not yet active.

Checking the Status of an SAP-Supplied InfoObject

As illustrated in Figure 3.2, the following are the steps to check the status of an SAP-supplied InfoObject:

1. Open the Edit InfoObjects: Start window using Transaction RSD1.
2. Under Type, select Characteristic and next to Version, select Active/Revised (Figure 3.2, ❶ and ❷).

3. In the text field next to InfoObject, enter the name of the InfoObject to check (Figure 3.2, ❸).
4. Click on the Display button (Figure 3.2, ❹).

If the InfoObject is not yet active, the following message is displayed in the status bar of the window: "Enter valid Characteristic...."

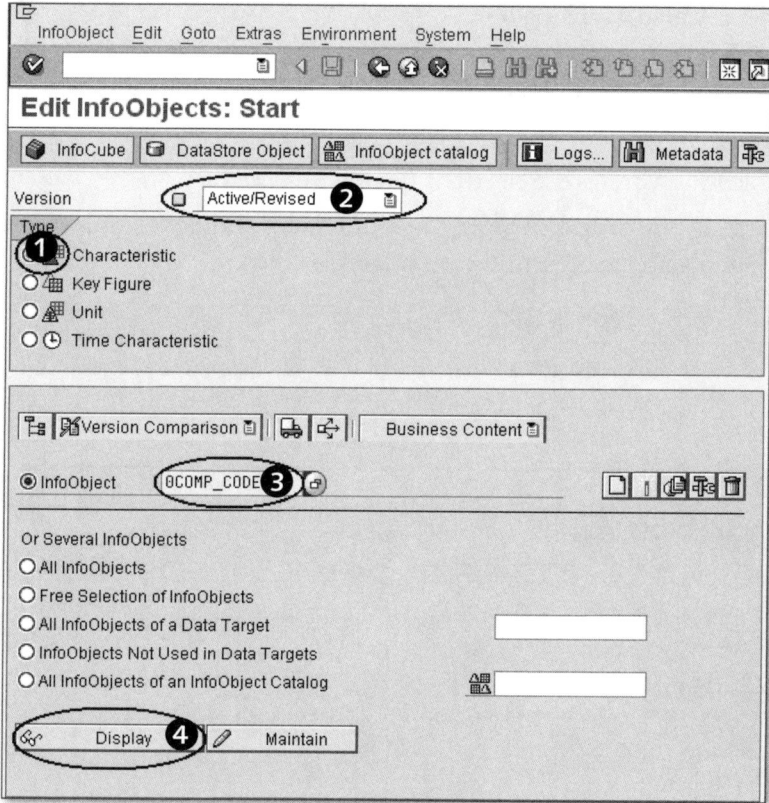

Figure 3.2 Checking the Status of an InfoObject

Activating an SAP-Supplied InfoObject

By default, none of the SAP-supplied InfoObjects are active, so we will start by activating them. The process, illustrated in Figures 3.3, 3.4, and 3.5, is as follows:

3 | Modeling an Application with SAP BusinessObjects Planning and Consolidation for NetWeaver

1. Open the Data Warehousing Workbench: BI Content window using Transaction RSA1.
2. In the left pane, select Object Types (Figure 3.3, ❶).
3. In the right pane, under Grouping, select Only Necessary Objects. For Collection Mode, select Collect Automatically (Figure 3.3, ❷ and ❸).
4. Under InfoObject, double-click on Select Objects (Figure 3.3, ❹). This opens the Input Help for Metadata dialog box.
5. In the Input help for Metadata dialog box, select all of the SAP-delivered InfoObjects required for the case study that need to be activated, as outlined in Tables 3.1, 3.2, and 3.3.
6. When finished, click on Transfer Selections (Figure 3.4, ❺).
7. In the Data Warehousing Workbench: BI Content window, under Install, select the Install option to activate the InfoObject (Figure 3.5, ❻).

> **Note**
> Activating an InfoObject also activates all inactive InfoObjects that are dependent on this InfoObject.

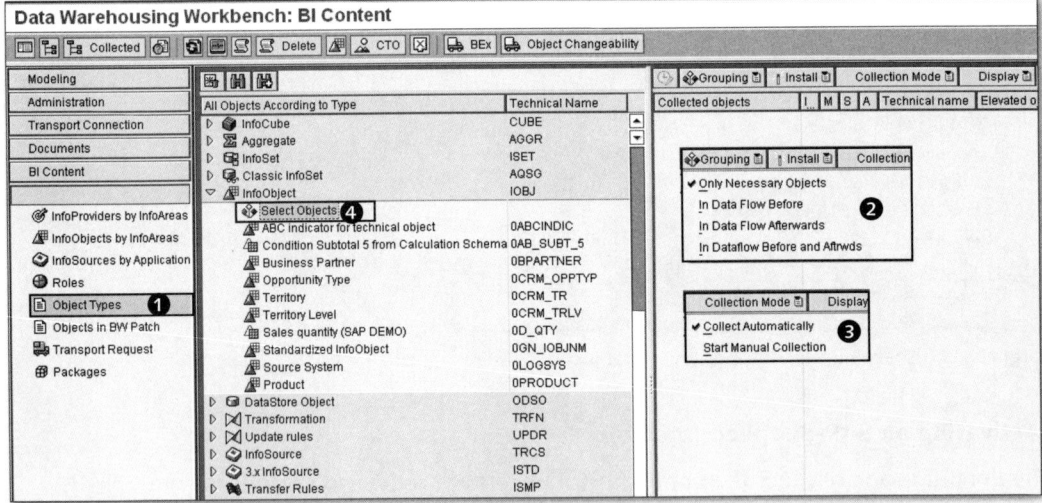

Figure 3.3 Settings to Activate an InfoObject

3.2 Building the Data Model in SAP NetWeaver BW

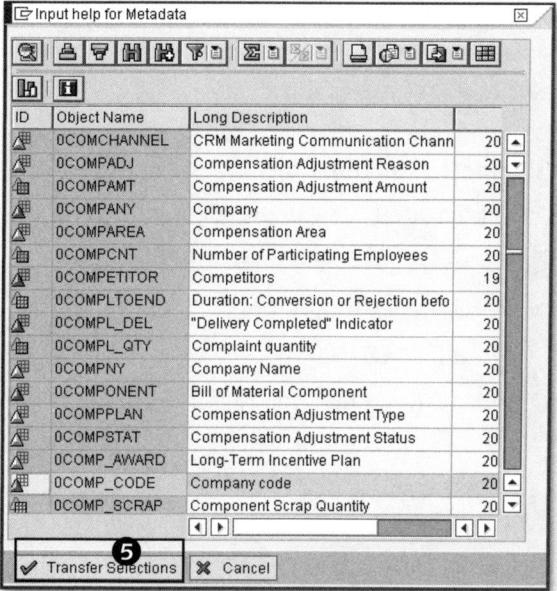

Figure 3.4 Selecting the InfoObject(s) to Activate

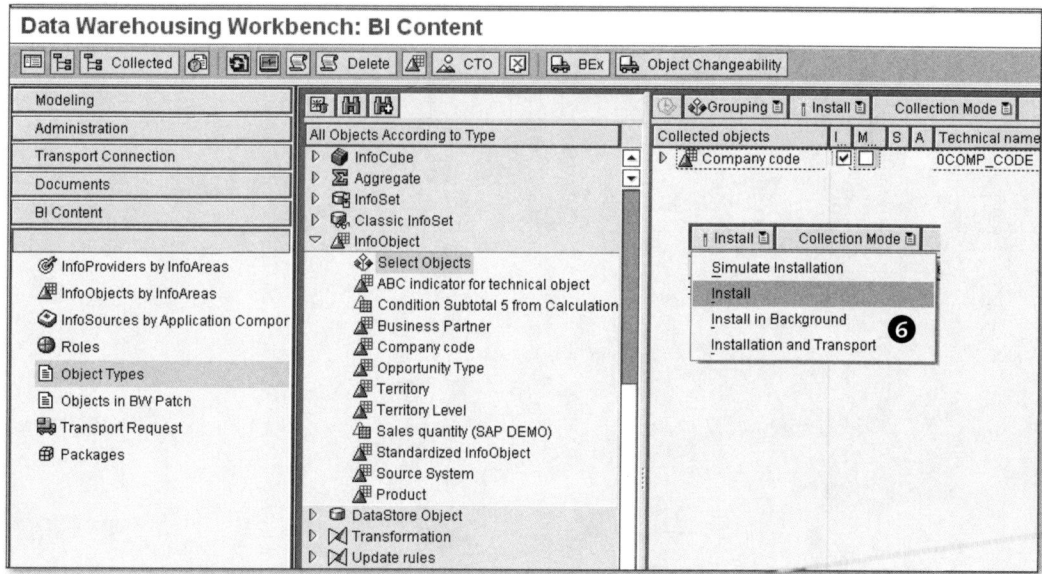

Figure 3.5 Activating an InfoObject

3 | Modeling an Application with SAP BusinessObjects Planning and Consolidation for NetWeaver

After you are done activating the SAP-supplied InfoObjects, you will need to create and activate the custom InfoObjects needed for the case study, as outlined in Tables 3.1 and 3.4. Let us take a closer look at how to do this.

Creating and Activating a Custom Characteristic InfoObject

We will start by creating the InfoObject ZACCOUNT (Account), as illustrated in Figures 3.5 and 3.6. This InfoObject should be a characteristic InfoObject.

1. Open the Edit InfoObjects: Start window using Transaction RSD1.
2. Under Type, select Characteristic (Figure 3.6, ❶).
3. In the text field next to the InfoObject option, enter the technical name of the InfoObject ("Account") and click on the Create button (Figure 3.6, ❷ and ❸).

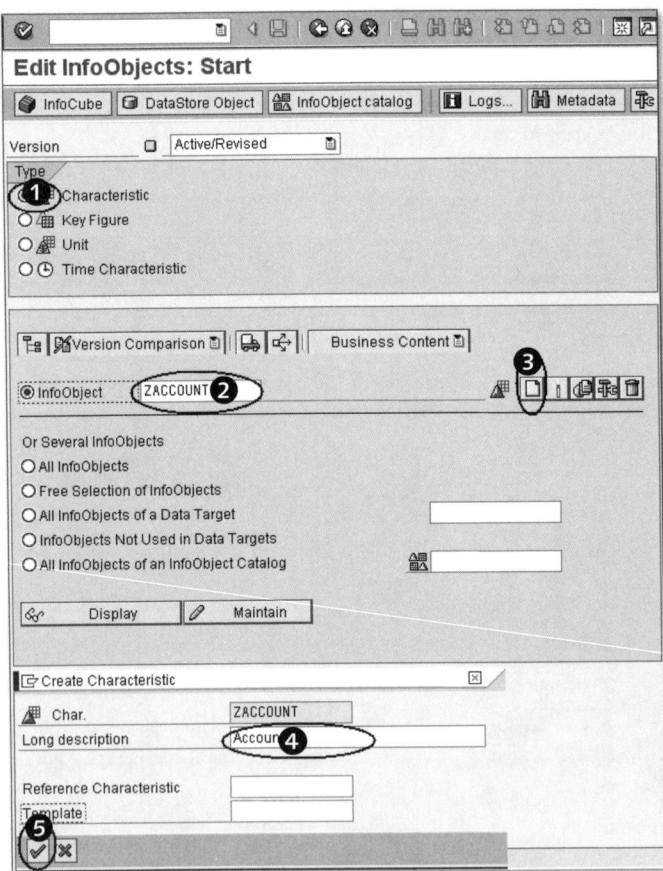

Figure 3.6 Settings to Create a New Characteristic InfoObject

3.2 Building the Data Model in SAP NetWeaver BW

4. In the Create Characteristic dialog box, in the Long Description text field, enter a description ("Account"), and then click on the Enter button (Figure 3.6, ❹ and ❺).

5. On the General tab of the Create Characteristic <InfoObject_Name>: Details window, specify the Short Description ("Account"), Data Type ("CHAR"), and Length ("13") (Figure 3.7, ❻, ❼, and ❽).

6. No attributes are required for this InfoObject; therefore, you can click on Activate (Figure 3.7, ❾).

The ZACCOUNT InfoObject is now saved and activated.

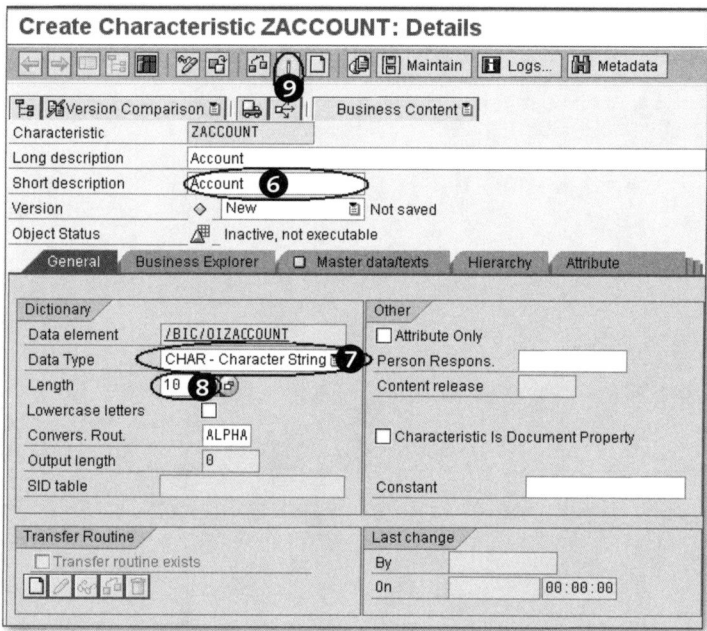

Figure 3.7 Activating a Custom InfoObject

Using a similar process, you will now need to create and activate the remaining required custom InfoObjects, ZAMOUNT. Let us get started.

Creating a Custom Key Figure InfoObject

> **Note**
> The SAP-delivered unit currency InfoObject, 0CURRENCY, should have been activated before creating the custom Key Figure.

77

3 | Modeling an Application with SAP BusinessObjects Planning and Consolidation for NetWeaver

We will now create a custom key figure InfoObject, as illustrated in Figures 3.7 and 3.8. The technical name of the InfoObject is ZAMOUNT.

1. Open the Edit InfoObjects: Start window using Transaction RSD1.
2. Under Type, select Key Figure (Figure 3.8, ❶).
3. In the text field next to the InfoObject option, enter the technical name of the InfoObject ("ZAMOUNT") and click on the Create button (Figure 3.8, ❷ and ❸).
4. In the Create KeyFigure dialog box, in the Long Description text field, enter a description ("Amount") and then click on the Enter button (Figure 3.8, ❹ and ❺).

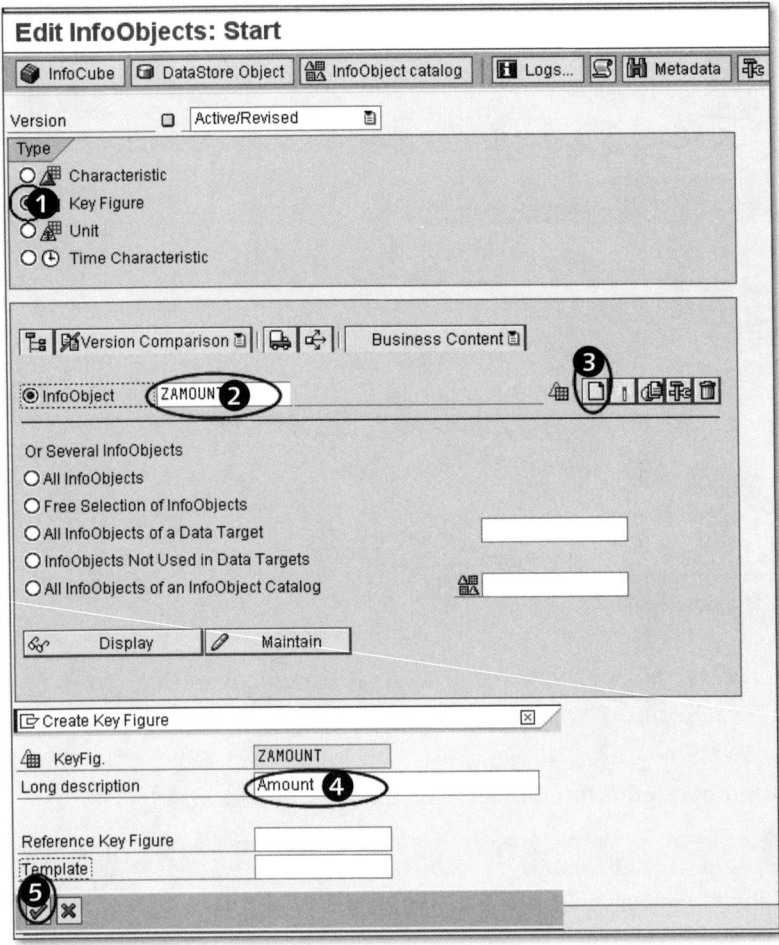

Figure 3.8 Settings to Create a New Custom KeyFigure InfoObject

3.2 Building the Data Model in SAP NetWeaver BW

5. In the Create Key Figure <InfoObject_Name>: Details window, enter a Short Description ("Amount") (Figure 3.9, ❻).

6. On the Type/Unit tab, select Amount and then select CURR – Currency Field, Stored as DEC. (Figure 3.9, ❼ and ❽).

7. Per the requirements, the ZAMOUNT InfoObject should be attached to the 0CURRENCY InfoObject. Thus, under Currency/Unit of Measure, select 0CURRENCY (Figure 3.9, ❾).

8. Click on Activate (Figure 3.9, ❿). The ZAMOUNT InfoObject is now saved and activated.

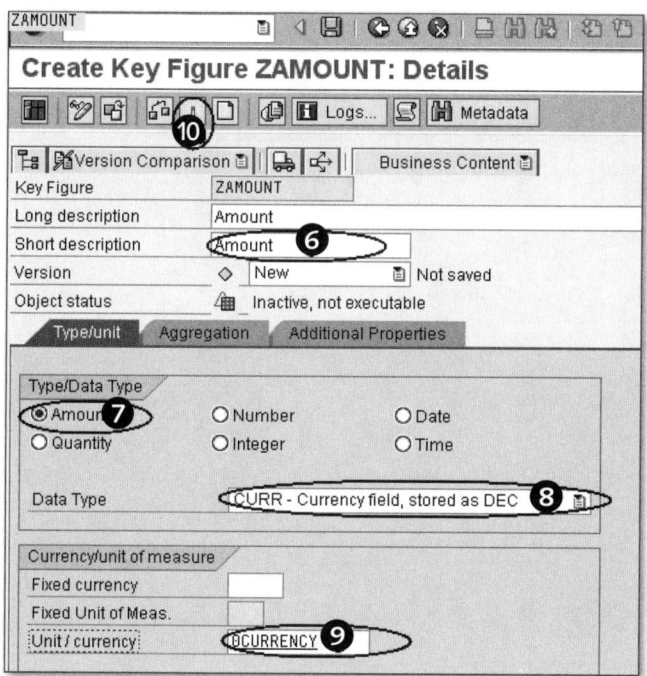

Figure 3.9 Settings to Create a New Custom KeyFigure InfoObject (ZAMOUNT)

Populating Master Data

The next step in the process is to load master data for InfoObjects with the values listed in the reference table for the characteristic values (Table 3.1). As we have mentioned before, master data can be populated from a variety of sources: an SAP R/3 system, a flat-file system, an Oracle Database system using DB Connect, and so on.

In this example, because there are only a few records in the master data table, we will manually enter the values for the characteristics. Normally, however, the master data would be populated from a source system.

We now manually enter the data for the Company Code InfoObject (0COMP_CODE), as illustrated in Figures 3.10 and 3.11:

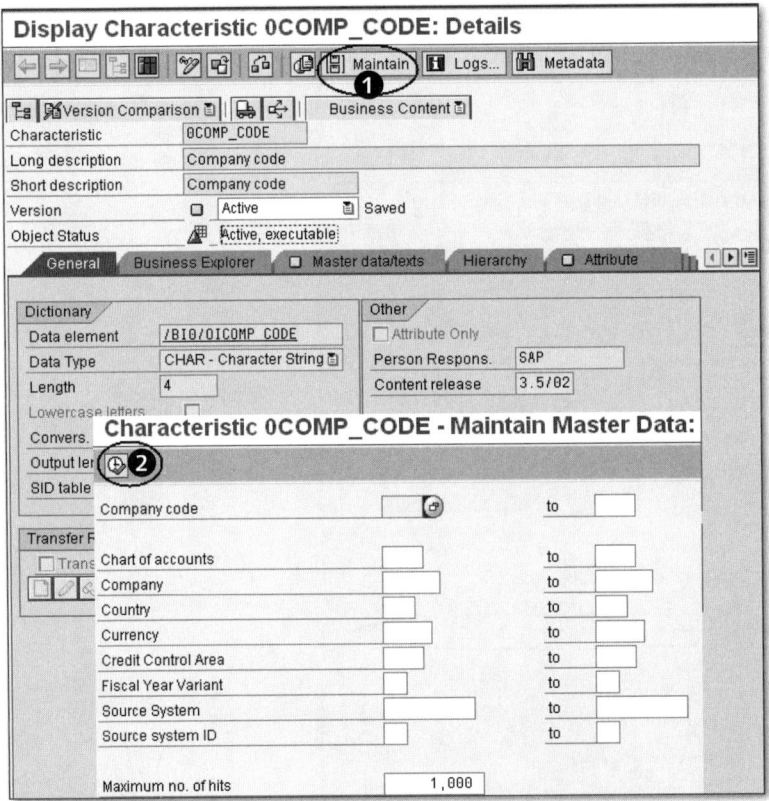

Figure 3.10 Manually Entering Data for a Characteristic InfoObject

1. Open the Edit InfoObjects: Start window using Transaction RSD1.
2. Specify the InfoObject by entering its name ("0COMP_CODE") or selecting it from the dropdown list. Then click on the Display button.
3. In the Display Characteristic <InfoObject_Name>: Details window, click on Maintain to create or modify data for this InfoObject (Figure 3.10, ❶).

4. In the Characteristic *<InfoObject_Name>* - Maintain Master Data: List window, click on the Execute button (Figure 3.10, ❷).

5. In the Characteristic *<InfoObject_Name>* - Maintain Master Data: List window, click on Create to create a new record (Figure 3.11, ❸). Enter a value for the Company Code InfoObject ("20"), as listed in Table 3.1.

6. Click on the Enter button (Figure 3.11, ❹) and then click on the Save button (Figure 3.11, ❺).

7. Use steps 1 through 6 outlined here to insert master data for the other characteristics listed in Table 3.1.

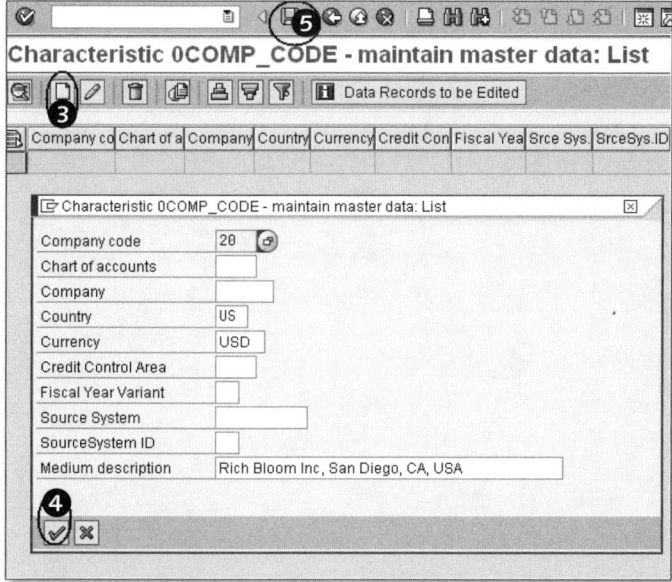

Figure 3.11 Manually Inserting a New Record for an InfoObject

Applying the Hierarchy/Attribute Change Process

When you create a new record in the master data table, no action is necessary for the changes to become effective. Any changes to an existing record, however, require that you run the Apply Hierarchy/Attribute Change process, as follows, and as illustrated in Figure 3.12.

1. Open the Data Warehousing Workbench using Transaction RSA1.

2. Select TOOLS • APPLY HIERARCHY/ATTRIBUTE CHANGE from the menu.

3. In the Execute Hierarchy/Attribute Changes for Reporting window, click on InfoObject List to identify the characteristic InfoObjects that have undergone a change since the last change run (Figure 3.12, ❶).

4. Select the InfoObjects for which the changes to data should apply and click on Save (Figure 3.12, ❷ and ❸). InfoObjects that are displayed here but are not selected for the change run will not reflect the latest changes made to the data when reporting.

5. After you click on Save, a job name is automatically assigned by the system, and you are taken back to the Execute Hierarchy/Attribute Changes for Reporting window.

6. Click on the Execute button (Figure 3.12, ❹).

7. Click on the Refresh button to confirm that the changes have been activated. The Change Status is displayed at the top of the table (Figure 3.12, ❺).

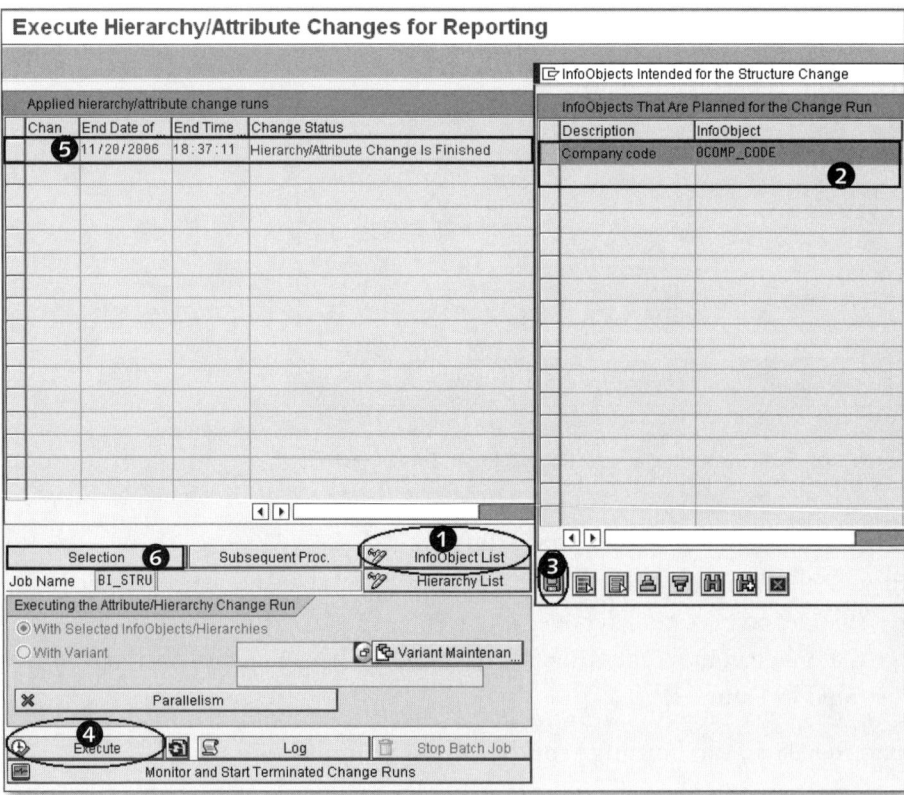

Figure 3.12 Manually Executing the Attribute Change Run Process

The Apply Hierarchy/Attribute Change process can be scheduled from this location to run at selected time periods. It can also be scheduled based on an event by clicking on the Selection button (Figure 3.12, ❻) in the Execute Hierarchy/Attribute Changes for Reporting window and then making the appropriate selections.

Subsequent events can be triggered following successful or unsuccessful completions of the change run.

3.2.2 Creating an InfoArea

Now that you have created the InfoObjects, the next step is to create an InfoArea that will later contain InfoCubes. An InfoArea lets you group InfoProviders together.

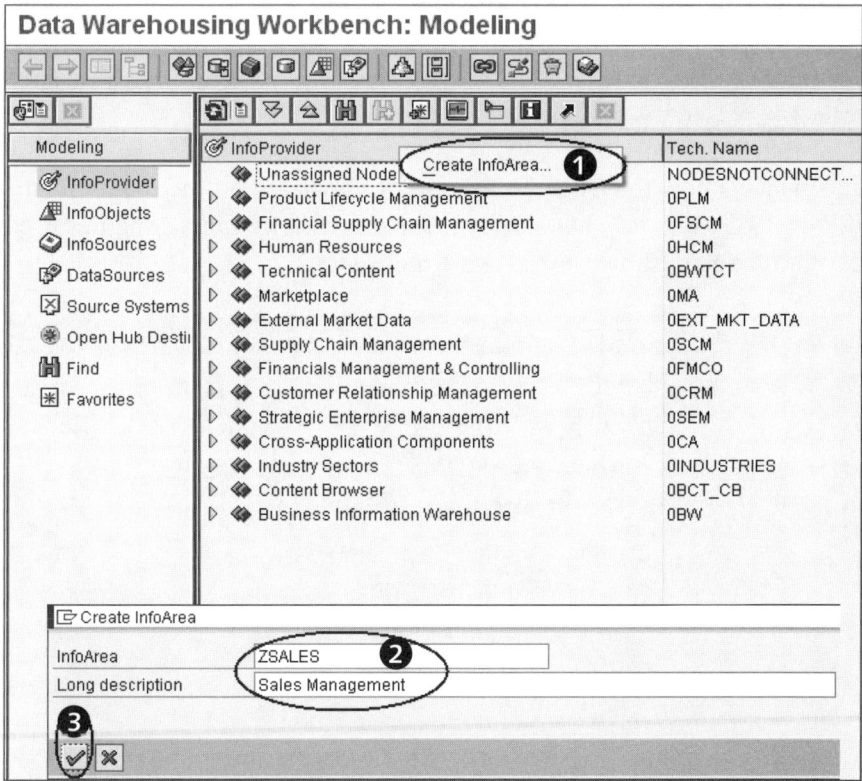

Figure 3.13 Create InfoArea

The following are the steps to create an InfoArea, as illustrated in Figure 3.13:

1. Open the Data Warehousing Workbench using Transaction RSA1.
2. Select MODELING • INFOPROVIDER.
3. Right-click on InfoProvider and select Create InfoArea (Figure 3.13, ❶).
4. In the Create InfoArea section, in the InfoArea text field, enter the technical name for the InfoArea ("ZSALES"). In the Long Description field, enter a description ("Sales Management") (Figure 3.13, ❷).
5. Click on Enter (Figure 3.13, ❸).

3.2.3 Creating a Sales InfoCube

Now that you've created an InfoArea, the next step is to create the Sales InfoCubes under it, as shown in Table 3.5.

InfoCube	Description
ZSLS_ACT	Sales Actual InfoCube

Table 3.5 InfoCube for Storing Actual Sales Data

This section explains how to create the Sales InfoCube based on the requirements listed earlier in Tables 3.1, 3.2, 3.3, and 3.4. The dimensions and key figures used in the Sales InfoCube are shown in Table 3.6 and Table 3.7.

Dimensions	Characteristics
Company	Company Code (0COMP_CODE)
Material	Material (0MATERIAL)
Customer	Customer (0CUSTOMER)
Account	Account (ZACCOUNT)
Time	Calendar Month (0CALMONTH)
	Calendar Year (0CALYEAR)
Unit	Currency (0CURRENCY)

Table 3.6 Dimensions for the Sales InfoCube

Key Figures	Description
ZAMOUNT	Amount in Local Currency

Table 3.7 Key Figures for the Sales InfoCube

Building the Data Model in SAP NetWeaver BW | **3.2**

The following are the steps and concepts you should follow to create the Sales InfoCube. The discussion includes creating dimensions as well as assigning characteristic InfoObjects to dimensions and assigning key figures to the key figure folder. This process is illustrated in Figures 3.14, 3.15, 3.16, 3.17, and 3.18. Let us get started:

1. Open the Data Warehousing Workbench using Transaction RSA1.
2. Select MODELING • INFOPROVIDER.
3. Right-click on the Sales Management InfoArea you created earlier and select Create InfoCube from the context menu (see Figure 3.14, ❶).

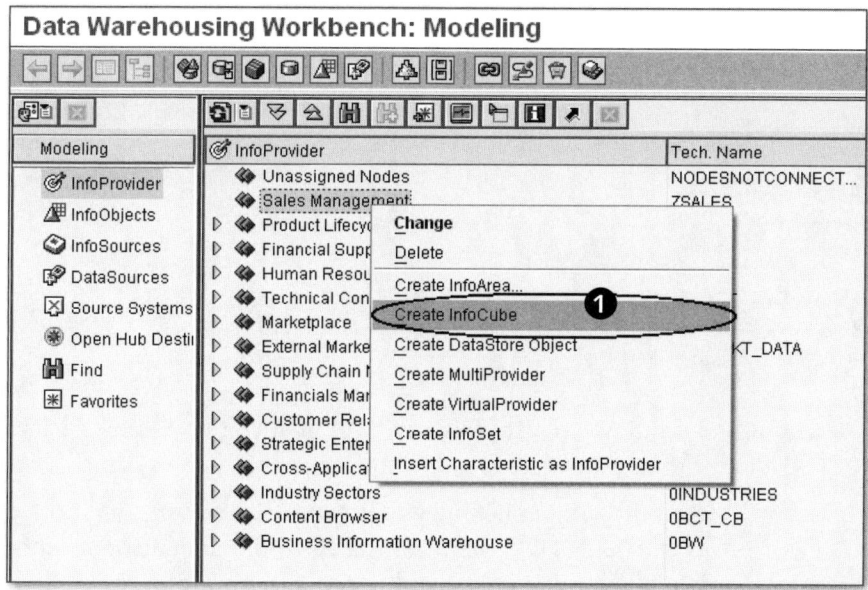

Figure 3.14 Creating an InfoCube—Part A

4. The Edit InfoCube window appears (Figure 3.15). Enter the technical name of the InfoCube ("ZSLS_ACT"), and the long description ("Sales actual") into the text field next to InfoCube. Make sure Standard InfoCube is selected under InfoProvider Type. Then click on Enter (Figure 3.15, ❷, ❸, and ❹).

3 | Modeling an Application with SAP BusinessObjects Planning and Consolidation for NetWeaver

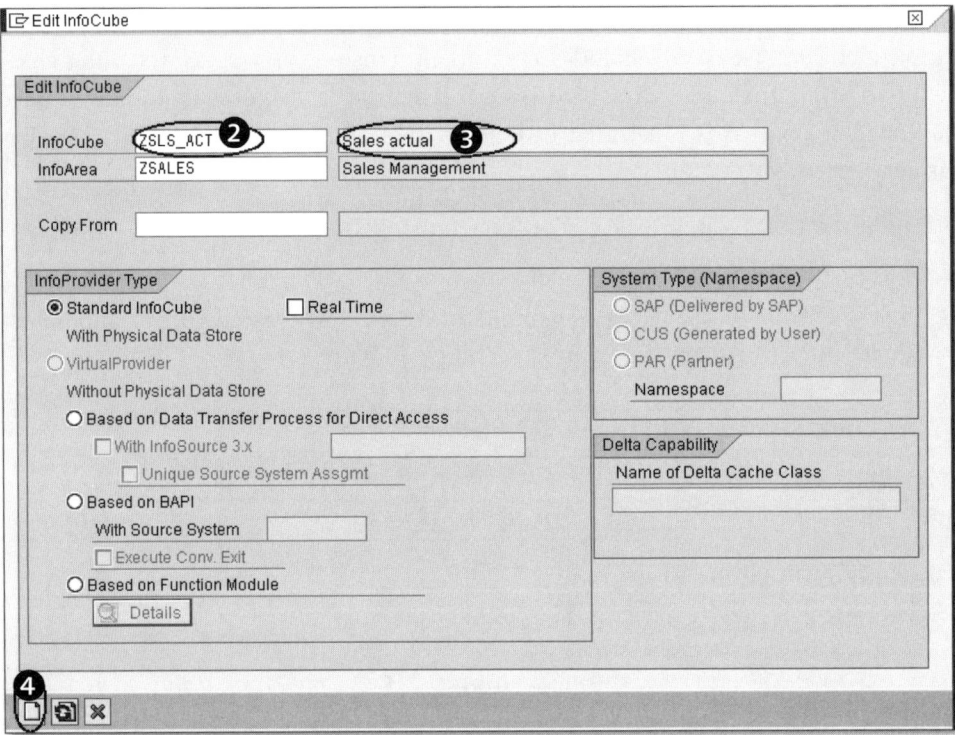

Figure 3.15 Create InfoCube—Part B

5. The Edit InfoCube window appears (Figure 3.16). Notice that the data package, time, and unit dimensions are created automatically by the system.

6. Create a new dimension by right-clicking on Dimensions and selecting Create New Dimensions (Figure 3.16, ❺). The technical ID of the dimension is automatically assigned and cannot be changed, but the description of the dimension *can* be changed.

7. In the Create Dimensions window, enter a description for the dimension ("Account") (see Figure 3.16, ❻).

8. Click on the Create button (Figure 3.16, ❼). This creates the dimension and then opens the Create Dimensions window again.

9. Enter the description for the next dimension ("Financial Organization").

10. Repeat steps 8 and 9 to create the remaining dimensions for the Sales InfoCube that are specified in Table 3.6. They are:

- Material
- Customer
- Account

11. Click on Enter when you are finished (Figure 3.16, ❽).

> **Note**
> You can create up to 13 user-defined dimensions in an InfoCube.

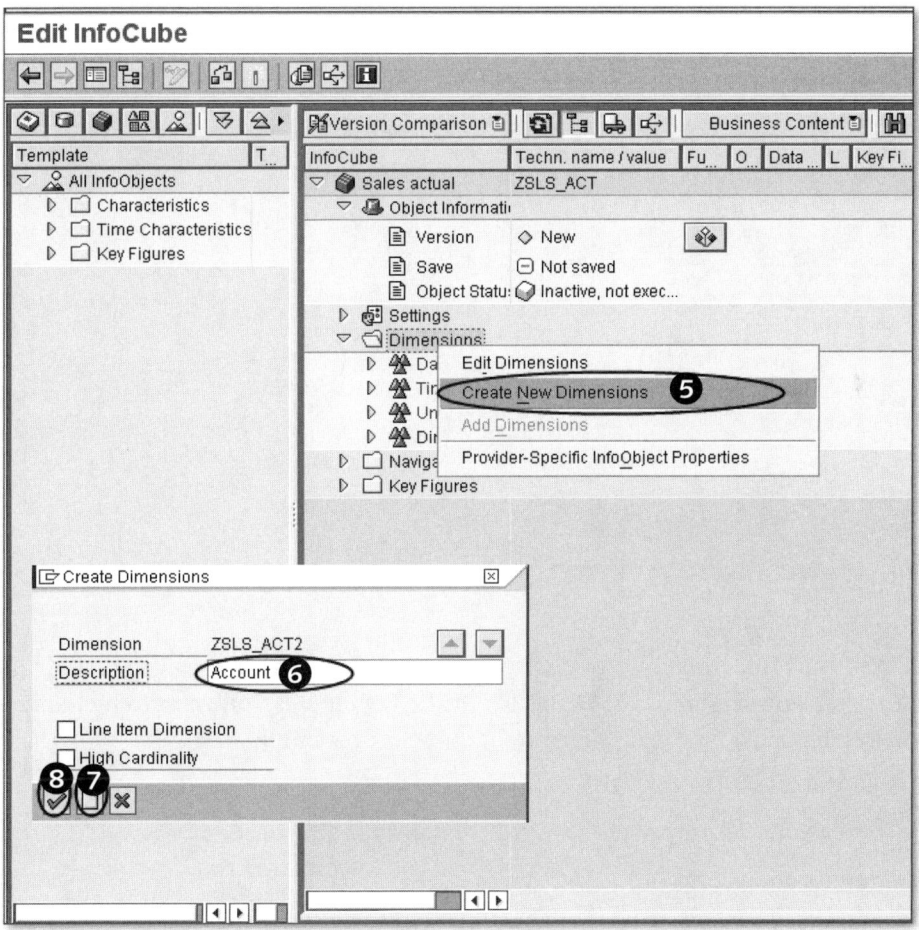

Figure 3.16 Create InfoCube—Part C

You have now created the dimensions needed for the Sales InfoCube. The next task is to assign characteristic InfoObjects to dimensions and key figure InfoObjects to the Key Figures folder. Similar characteristics are grouped under one dimension. An InfoObject can be directly assigned to a dimension or the Key Figures folder (using the InfoObject Direct Input option), as we will show in the following steps:

1. Right-click on the Dimensions or Key Figures folder, and select InfoObject Direct Input (Figure 3.17, ❾).

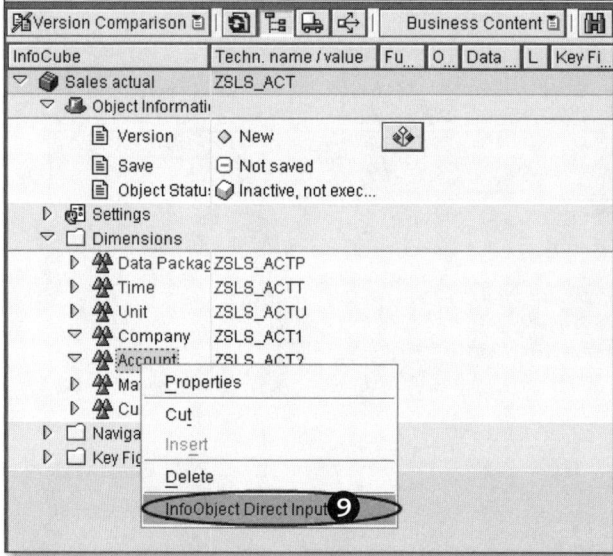

Figure 3.17 Create InfoCube—Part D

2. In the Insert InfoObjects window, select the InfoObjects you want to include in the dimension (Figure 3.18, ❿ and ⓫) or the key figures you want to include in the Key Figures folder (not illustrated) and click on Enter.

   Assign the following InfoObjects to the dimensions:
   - Dimension 1 (Company)—0COMP_CODE
   - Dimension 2 (Account)—ZACCOUNT
   - Dimension 3 (Material)—0MATERIAL
   - Dimension 4 (Customer)—0CUSTOMER
   - Time Dimension—0CALYEAR and 0CALMONTH.

Assign the following key figure to the Key Figures folder:

▶ ZAMOUNT

For key figures that are of the data types Quantity or Currency, the corresponding unit/currency measure associated with the key figure is automatically added to the unit dimension.

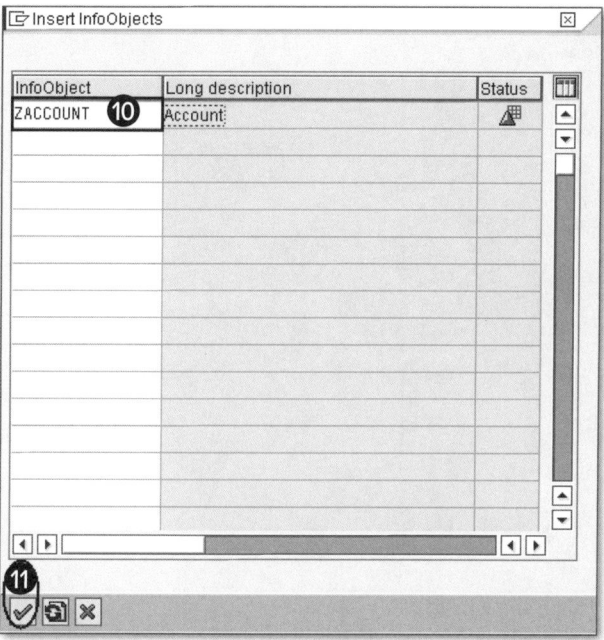

Figure 3.18 Create InfoCube—Part E

> **Note**
>
> An alternative way exists to include InfoObjects in a Dimensions or Key Figures folder. If the InfoObjects required for the InfoCube are in an InfoSource, DataStore, InfoCube, or InfoObject Catalog, select the corresponding template in the left pane of the Edit InfoCube window. Here, you can also select the InfoObjects All template. This option lets you display all characteristic and key figure InfoObjects. Drag an InfoObject from the template to the desired Dimensions or Key Figures folder.

The InfoCube is now ready to be saved and activated. Click on Activate to activate the InfoCube (Figure 3.19, ⓬).

3 | Modeling an Application with SAP BusinessObjects Planning and Consolidation for NetWeaver

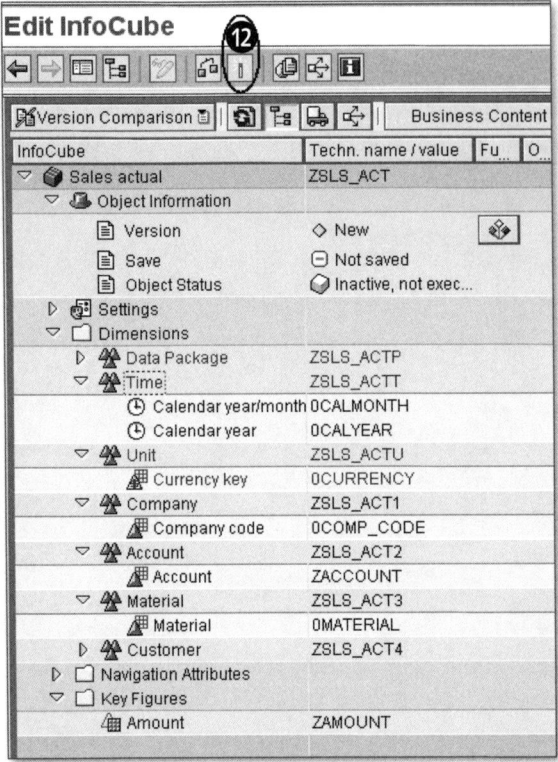

Figure 3.19 Activating the InfoCube

We have now created the InfoCube to store actual sales and cost data in the SAP NetWeaver BW system. We will discuss how to load data into this InfoCube in Chapter 4. In the next section, we will configure the objects required for this case study in the SAP BusinessObjects Planning and Consolidation system.

3.3 Building Applications in SAP BusinessObjects Planning and Consolidation

In this section, we will teach you how to configure an application in SAP BusinessObjects Planning and Consolidation. This application contains actual and plan data related to sales and cost. Rich Bloom, Inc. requires the following pieces of data in the application to be able to plan effectively:

- Account
  - Account ID
  - Description
  - Account type (income account, expense account, etc.)
  - Rate type (average, year end, etc., to indicate the rate to use for currency translation)
- Entity
  - Entity ID (the company ID)
  - Description
  - Currency (the currency used by the company)
- Category
  - Category ID (denotes the nature of data—actual, budget, etc.)
  - Description
  - Year
- Time
  - Time ID
  - Description
- Currency
  - Currency ID (the currency associated with the transaction)
  - Description
  - Reporting (indicator used for currency translation)
- Product
  - Product ID
  - Description
- Customer
  - Customer ID
  - Description
- Data Source
- Quantitative measure (amount/quantity)—also called SIGNEDDATA

We must create dimensions for all of the characteristics listed. A *dimension* is a type of object that is used to build an application. It represents the master data associated with any characteristic. For example, the Entity dimension represents the different company codes and their descriptions. The key to any dimension is referred to as an ID, and each record that is identified by the ID in a dimension is called a *dimension member*. In addition, *properties* can be described to provide meaning to the dimension member.

The SIGNEDDATA field is automatically available in all applications to store quantitative information. This field contains either quantity or amount information. An application has only this field to store quantitative data; the Account dimension qualifies the data in the SIGNEDDATA field. Therefore, you can see how SAP BusinessObjects Planning and Consolidation uses the account-based data model, where there is only one key figure in an application that is qualified by the information in the Account dimension.

For this case study, we make use of two applications, one to store actual and plan data, and the other to maintain currency exchange rates. Because Rich Bloom, Inc. does business in more than one country and uses different currencies, we use a rate application that can be used to convert amounts from the local currency to the reporting currency.

We will now review the steps of creating an application in SAP BusinessObjects Planning and Consolidation.

3.3.1 Accessing the BPC System

Recall the discussion from the last chapter about the architecture of SAP BusinessObjects Planning and Consolidation for NetWeaver. The SAP BusinessObjects Planning and Consolidation client interface must be installed on every developer's computer. The Admin Console is the central interface for building applications in SAP BusinessObjects Planning and Consolidation. This tool is used by developers to configure and maintain applications.

Let us see how to access the SAP BusinessObjects Planning and Consolidation system from the Admin Console. The following steps explain the process for logging in to the SAP BusinessObjects Planning and Consolidation system from the Admin Console:

1. When the client interface for SAP BusinessObjects Planning and Consolidation is installed on your computer, you can see the Admin Console icon. Double-click on it (Figure 3.20, ❶).

2. Click on Connection Wizard to connect to the SAP BusinessObjects Planning and Consolidation application server (Figure 3.20, ❷).

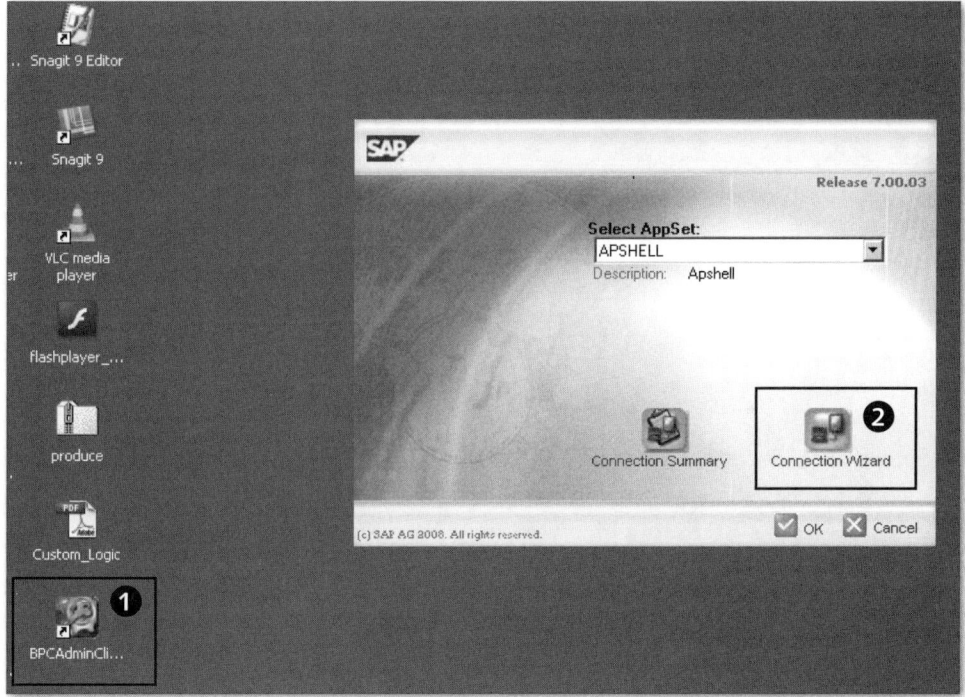

Figure 3.20 Accessing the BPC Admin Console—Part A

3. Enter the name of the server to connect to under BPC Server Name (Figure 3.21, ❸). Under Connection Options, select the option that is applicable for your installation, and then click on Next (Figure 3.21, ❹ and ❺).

3 | Modeling an Application with SAP BusinessObjects Planning and Consolidation for NetWeaver

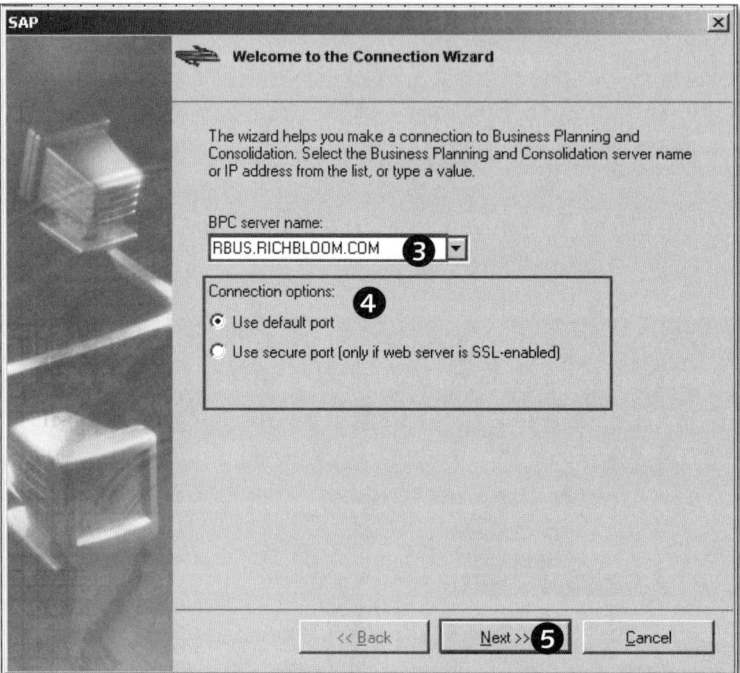

Figure 3.21 Accessing the BPC Admin Console—Part B

4. Select Use a Different User ID and Password (Figure 3.22, ❻). Then, enter your user ID, password, and domain name for the SAP BusinessObjects Planning and Consolidation system to which you are connecting. Click on Next (Figure 3.22, ❼, ❽, ❾, and ❿).

5. The BPC server, user name, password, and domain name is authenticated, and you are prompted to select an application set from the dropdown list. In Figure 3.23, ⓫, the APSHELL application set has been selected. Click on Next to access the selected application set (Figure 3.23, ⓬).

The application sets you see in the dropdown list are governed by your security access to the application set. If you do not see an application set, you do not have authorization to access it.

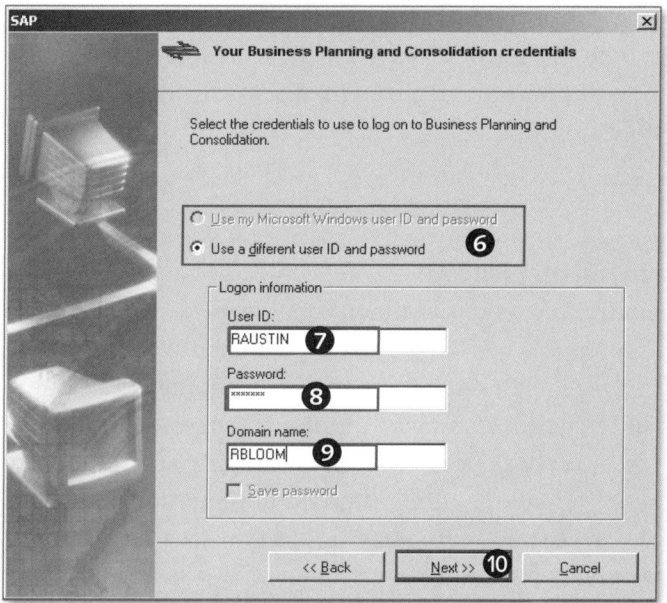

Figure 3.22 Accessing the BPC Admin Console—Part C

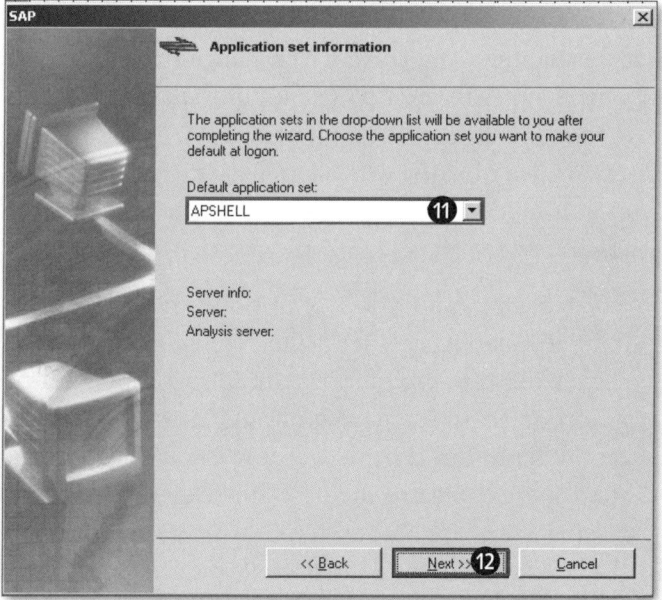

Figure 3.23 Accessing the BPC Admin Console—Part D

You have now seen how to log into the SAP BusinessObjects Planning and Consolidation system from the Admin Console, as well as how to access an application set. Before we create new application sets, we will discuss the key features of application sets and how they are used.

3.3.2 Application Set

The first step in building an application in SAP BusinessObjects Planning and Consolidation is creating an application set (also known as an *appset*). An *application set* is designed to contain the applications for a given functional area; for example, one application set can be created exclusively for sales planning applications; another can be created for head-count planning applications. A new application set cannot be built from scratch; it is always copied from an existing application set. In this context, it is important to note that dimensions and dimensions members within an application set are not shared with other application sets.

One of the steps in the installation of a SAP BusinessObjects Planning and Consolidation system is the installation of an application set with the technical name *ApShell*. This is also the only application set that is available when the system is first created. This special application set comes with the standard dimensions and includes sample applications for planning and currency exchange translation. We do not recommend making any changes to the ApShell application set; it should only be used as a reference or basis to create a new application set. The dimensions and applications included in ApShell are loaded with sample data, and it therefore serves as a good reference point to understand how applications are built in SAP BusinessObjects Planning and Consolidation.

When an application set is created, the application definitions are copied from the source application set to the new application set. When copying one application set to another, a flag is available that provides the option to copy application data from the source application set to the new application set. If this flag is not checked, only the application definition is copied. If this flag is checked, the data from the source application set is copied to the new application set. Several options are available when creating a new application set; they are used to indicate the type of data you would like to copy from the source application set to the new application set, and they are:

- Database records
- Content library
- Live reports
- Journals

> **Note**
> When an application set is created, the dimension members are automatically copied from the source application set.

Only a user with system administrator access can create and maintain application sets. When a request for the creation of a new application set is initiated in the SAP BusinessObjects Planning and Consolidation system, a background job is scheduled in the SAP NetWeaver BW system. The background job creates all of the necessary objects, including InfoObjects and InfoCubes, based on the options selected in SAP BusinessObjects Planning and Consolidation when initiating this request. You can also choose to have the data copied from the source application set to the new application set. Certain parameters can be set for an application set; these will be discussed in Chapter 7 when we discuss the web interface for SAP BusinessObjects Planning and Consolidation.

So far, you have seen how to access the Admin Console and log into the SAP BusinessObjects Planning and Consolidation system to access an application set. We will now discuss the process of creating a new application set.

Creating an Application Set

Our case study requires us to build an application for gross margin planning, which we do by using ApShell as the source. To create a new application set, proceed as follows:

1. Follow the steps listed in Section 3.3.1 to log into the SAP BusinessObjects Planning and Consolidation system and to access the ApShell application set (Figure 3.24). The left pane lists the available options for maintaining and managing an application set. We will discuss some of these options in this chapter, and others in following chapters. The options displayed in the middle right pane display context-sensitive menus based on the option selected in the left pane. For example, APSHELL is selected in the left pane (see Figure 3.24, ❶); therefore, the action menu associated with an application set is displayed in the

right pane. The lower right pane (Figure 3.24), under Available Interfaces, lists the additional tools used in SAP BusinessObjects Planning and Consolidation for development and reporting. We discuss each of these tools later.

2. Click on the APSHELL application set, as shown in Figure 3.24, ❶).

3. The context-sensitive middle right pane displays the various options for managing an application set. Click on Add a New Application Set (see Figure 3.24, ❷).

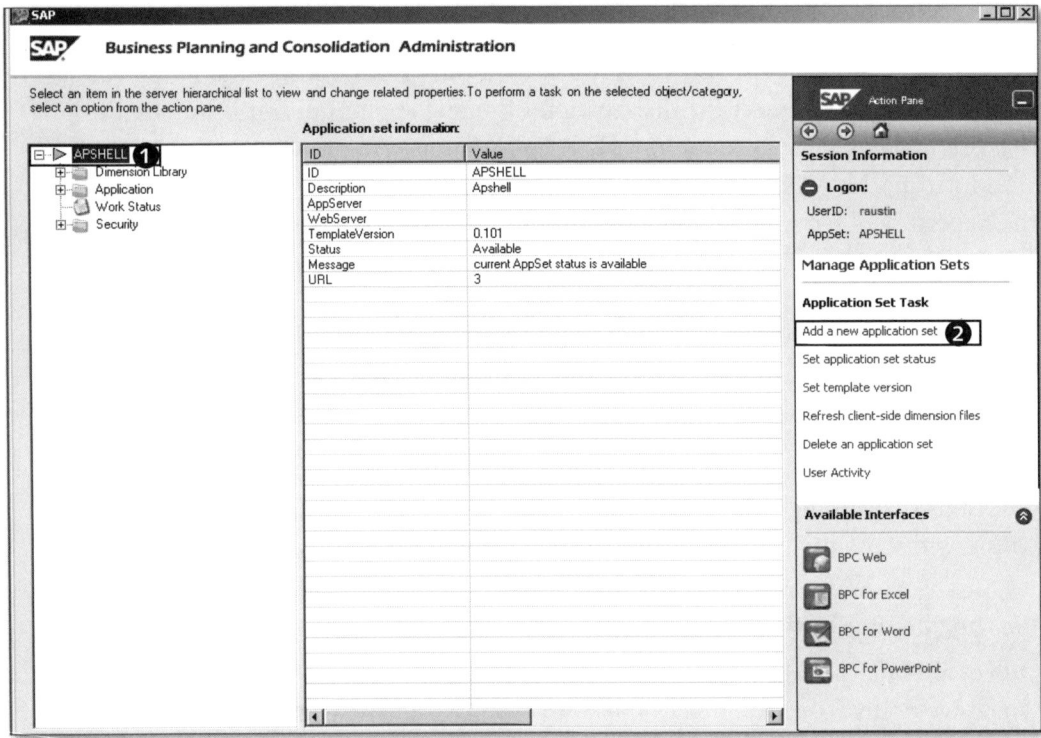

Figure 3.24 Creating an Application Set—Part A

4. Enter the technical name ("ZRB_GM_PLAN") and description ("Gross Margin Planning") for the new application set (Figure 3.25, ❸ and ❹). Select the appli-

cation set you want to use as the source for creating the new application set; in this case, select APSHELL from the dropdown list (Figure 3.25, ❺). Then click on Go to Next Step 2 of 2 (Figure 3.25, ❻).

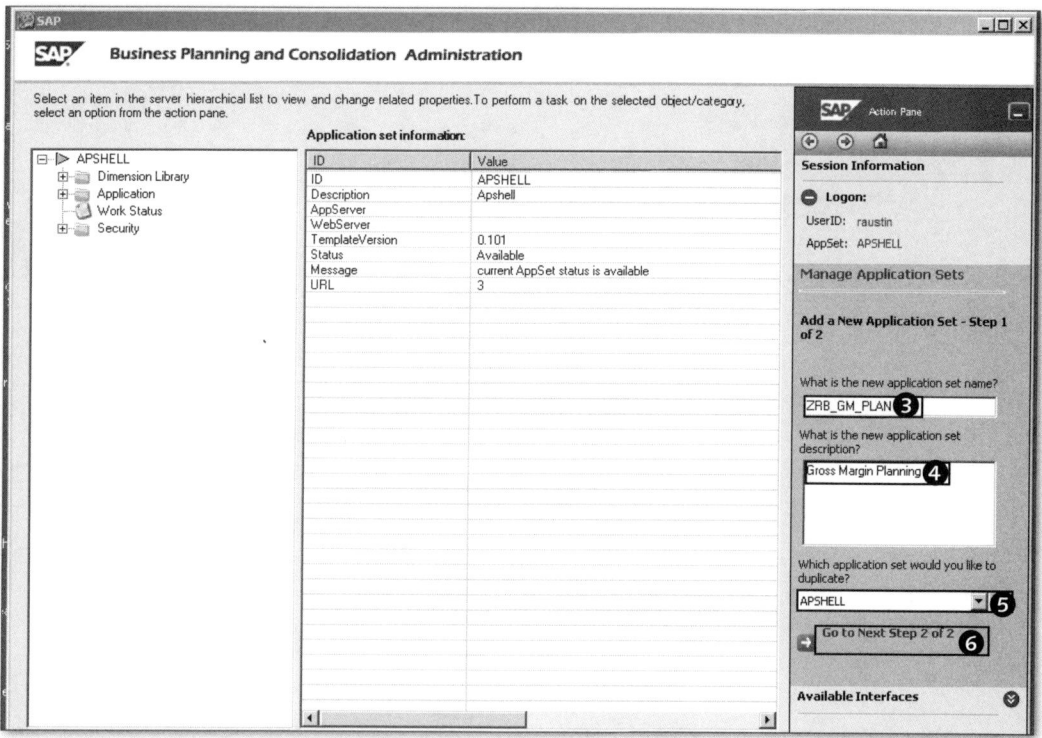

Figure 3.25 Creating an Application Set—Part B

5. Select the options you want to use for copying data from the source application set (Figure 3.26, ❼). When Database Records is checked, the application data is also copied to the new application set. For our case study, we will uncheck this option. Click on Add a New Application Set (Figure 3.26, ❽). The SAP BusinessObjects Planning and Consolidation system schedules a background job in the SAP NetWeaver BW system to create the objects and displays a status message to indicate that the new application set has been created successfully (Figure 3.26, ❾).

3 | Modeling an Application with SAP BusinessObjects Planning and Consolidation for NetWeaver

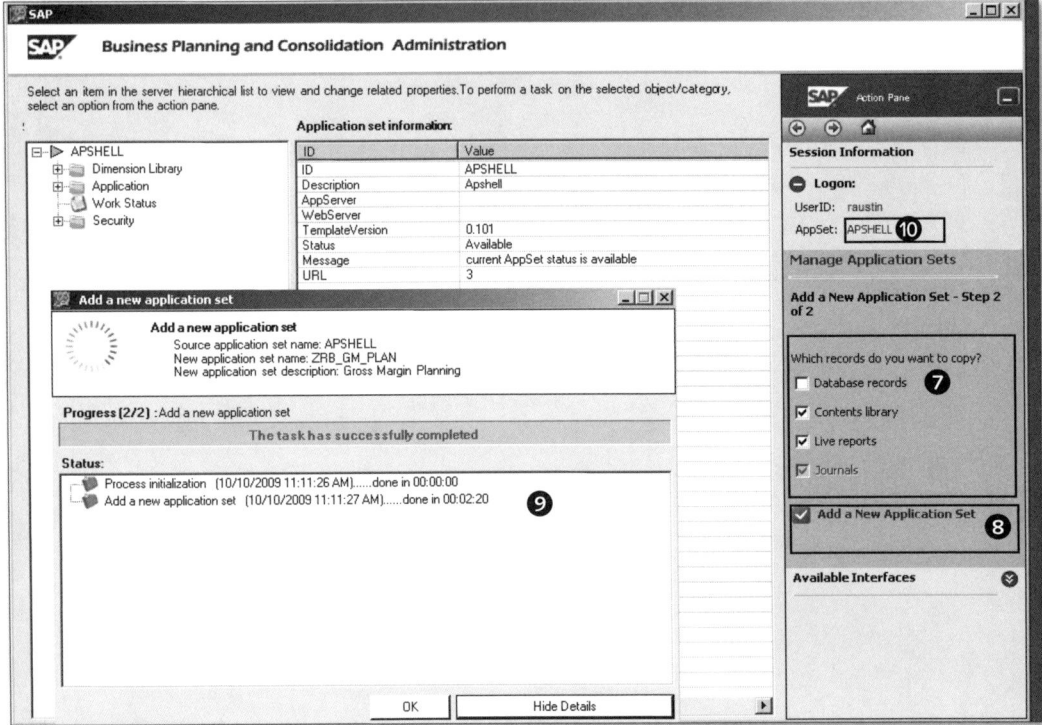

Figure 3.26 Creating an Application Set—Part C

Even though you have created a new application set, the session information continues to show the APSHELL application set, because you are signed on to this application set. To access the new application set, ZB_GMPLAN, click on APSHELL, as shown in Figure 3.26, ❿. This brings you to the SAP BusinessObjects Planning and Consolidation connection screen. However, at this point, the new application set is still not available in the dropdown list for you to select; first, you must connect to the new application set using the Connection Wizard. After you have been able to successfully connect to the new application set, it will be available in the dropdown box for subsequent logons. Refer to Figure 3.27, ⓫.

3.3 Building Applications in SAP BusinessObjects Planning and Consolidation

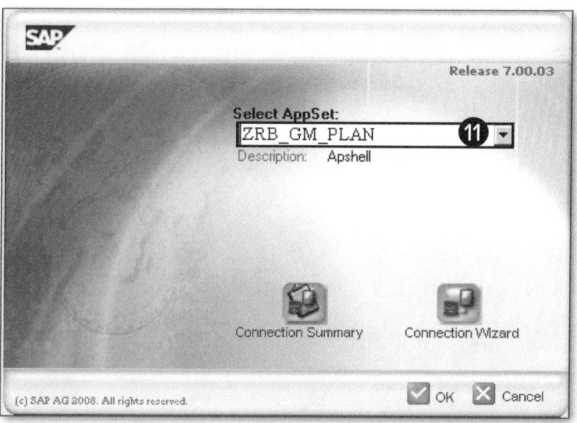

Figure 3.27 Creating an Application Set—Part D

You should now understand how to create a new application set. We will use the new application set we created for building the dimensions and applications for our case study.

Application Set Tasks

The following actions can be executed for a given application set:

- **Set availability of application set**
  An application set can be set to Not Available by choosing the Set Application Status option in the action pane. A user who is not a system administrator in SAP BusinessObjects Planning and Consolidation cannot access any application in the application set when the status of an application set is set to Not Available. An information message can be added to provide more information to users about this status, which is particularly useful when maintenance on the application set is in progress. The message can provide an estimate on when the application set will be back, and when users can log back on.

- **Set template version**
  SAP BusinessObjects Planning and Consolidation lets you create and maintain standard templates specific to application sets for reporting. When changes are made to the standard templates, you can refresh them immediately. To do this, update the client cache and set a higher version by choosing Set Template Version from the action pane.

- **Refresh client-side dimension files**
  When you log into the application set, the dimension data is automatically updated and refreshed in the client cache. When dimension members or properties are updated, you can immediately refresh them by selecting Refresh Client Side Dimension Files in the action pane.

- **Delete application set**
  An application set can be deleted by selecting Delete an Application Set from the action pane. When an application set is deleted, all of the objects under the application set are also deleted. Exercise caution when deleting an application set—it cannot be recovered.

- **Monitor user activity**
  The activity associated with an application set can be monitored by selecting the User Activity option in the action pane.

You should now have an understanding of how to create an application set, as well as of the different tasks associated with application sets. Next, we will discuss how dimensions are used in SAP BusinessObjects Planning and Consolidation.

3.3.3 Dimensions

Dimensions are the building blocks used in creating an SAP BusinessObjects Planning and Consolidation application; they describe the different elements of the business. Examples of dimensions are Account, Entity, Time, Customer, and Product. Note the following points related to dimensions:

- Dimensions are always created within an application set and can only be used in that application set. A dimension created in an application set cannot be shared or used in another application set.

- The name for a dimension can be a maximum of 16 characters.

- Dimensions can include properties. For example, the Account dimension can include a property called *account type*. Properties can be used as filter criteria for selections in reports. The length of a property can be set to any number. When the length of a property exceeds 60 characters, it is not available for selection when creating reports.

- The properties for a dimension can be classified under three distinct types:
  - User-defined: These are properties defined for a dimension by the user. For example, the Customer dimension can include a property called "country" that indicates the customer's country.
  - Reserved property: These are system-defined properties that are delivered with dimensions. The EvDescription property is automatically created for every dimension and stores the description for each of the IDs associated with a dimension. The scaling and format properties are system-supplied properties for the Account dimension.
  - Hidden property: These are properties that are not visible but are used internally by the SAP BusinessObjects Planning and Consolidation system.
- SAP BusinessObjects Planning and Consolidation provides standard dimensions used for planning and consolidation functions. Table 3.8 lists the different types of dimensions available in SAP BusinessObjects Planning and Consolidation.

Dimension Type	Example
Category	Plan Version, Actual, and so on
Account	GL Account or Statistical Codes
Time	Calendar Months or Fiscal Periods
Entity	Company Code
Currency	Local or Reporting Currency
Data Source	Manual, Automatic
Inter Company	Trading Partner
Sub Tables	Flow Dimension—Opening Balance
User Defined	Customer, Product

Table 3.8 Dimension Types

- The Account, Category, Entity, and Time dimensions are required in all applications. A dimension type cannot be used more than once in an application; for example, an application cannot include more than one Entity dimension.
- When a new dimension is created, the dimension type is associated with it. The default properties of the dimension type are available in the new dimension. Custom properties can then be added to the dimension.

- A new dimension can be copied from an existing dimension. When a dimension is copied, all of the dimension members from the source dimension, along with its properties, are also copied to the new dimension.
- A dimension can be modified to either include new properties or delete existing properties.
- A dimension can be deleted, provided it is not included in any of the applications in the application set.
- In SAP BusinessObjects Planning and Consolidation, when you create a dimension, the system creates an equivalent InfoObject with corresponding attributes.
- Security can be set to restrict users' read and write access, based on specific values of a dimension. The security is set for each application. We will explain how this is done when we discuss the security features in SAP BusinessObjects Planning and Consolidation.
- Data in dimensions is referred to as *dimension members*. The key for the dimension is called the ID. The maximum length of the ID can be 20 characters and it is case-sensitive. The ID member value of a dimension cannot be renamed once it is saved.
- Dimension data can be added into a dimension via the Admin Console. A member sheet is available to enter data for a dimension.
- When dimension members are maintained, you must run the Process dimension to make the modified data available. When the Process dimension option is requested, the SAP BusinessObjects Planning and Consolidation system schedules an *attribute change run* for the corresponding InfoObject in the SAP NetWeaver BW system. This process activates the data and makes the modified data available in the SAP BusinessObjects Planning and Consolidation application.
- A set of selected dimensions constitute an application. The dimensions required for an application can be selected when creating the application.

Reference Dimensions

The purpose of *reference dimensions* is to support the validation of member values that can be entered in the property of a dimension. Table 3.9 details the properties of dimensions belonging to a particular type that are validated based on values of members in the reference dimension.

Dimension Type	Property Name in Dimension	Reference Dimension	Reference Attribute Name
A - Account	Rate Type	A - ACCOUNT	ID
C - Category	Year	T - Time	Year
E - Entity	Currency	R - Currency	ID
I - Inter Company	Entity	E - Entity	ID

Table 3.9 Reference Dimension

Hierarchies in Dimensions

There are certain applications that require the use of a hierarchy. For example, consider a situation where you want to group the accounts of a particular type, say Revenues, into one bucket. This can be satisfied using a hierarchy, and SAP BusinessObjects Planning and Consolidation lets you create any number of hierarchies for a dimension. A hierarchy can be created by adding a new column, called ParentH(n), where n represents the hierarchy in the Excel member sheet.

There are certain rules when using hierarchies. They are as follows:

- The Excel member sheet is available for maintaining dimension member data. The system does not allow a hierarchy with ParentH3 to be created if ParentH1 and ParentH2 do not exist.
- The values in the hierarchy column should be valid dimension members as well.
- A parent in SAP BusinessObjects Planning and Consolidation must have the same children if it is reused across multiple hierarchies.

> **Note**
> Currently, time-dependent hierarchies are not supported in the SAP BusinessObjects Planning and Consolidation NetWeaver version.

Dimension Formulas

Dimension formulas automate the process of calculations in SAP BusinessObjects Planning and Consolidation. A dimension can include a special property called a formula. This is used in particular in the Account dimension. Let us, for example, consider a scenario where you have entered the quantity and price for a product independently. You may want to calculate the revenue as *quantity × price*. This is possible using dimension formulas. To achieve this, a reserved property called "formula" should be included in the dimension.

When a formula is created, the calculation is automatically effected for all applications in the application set that contains the dimension. When this formula is used in reports, situations could occur with conflicts in the calculation of the formula. In this case, SOLVEORDER determines the sequence of how the formula should be calculated.

Displaying Dimension Properties and Member Data

We will now explain how to review the properties of a dimension and display the members of a dimension. First, let us review the properties and members for the P_Acct dimension.

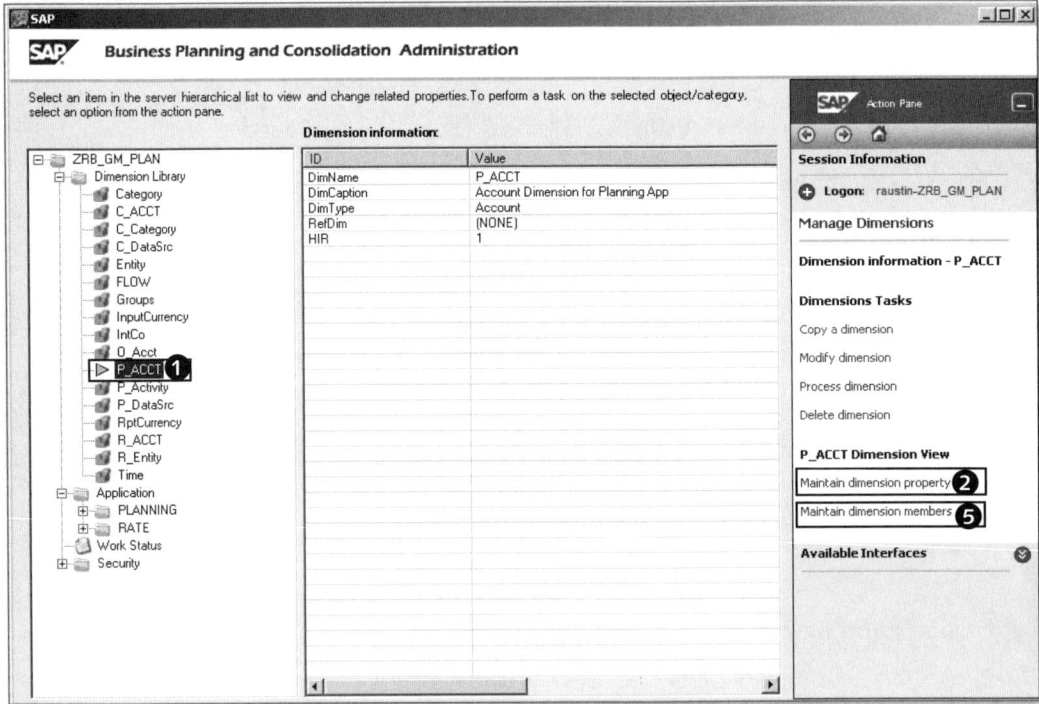

Figure 3.28 Displaying Dimension Properties and Member Data—Part A

1. Under Dimension Library in the left pane, click on the P_ACCT dimension (Figure 3.28, ❶). The middle right pane lists the tasks associated with a dimension. Click on Maintain Dimension Property (Figure 3.28, ❷) to view the properties. After reviewing the properties, click on the P_Acct dimension again to return to the previous screen.

2. The properties for the P_ACCT dimension are displayed (Figure 3.29, ❸). Click on the P_ACCT dimension to go back to the previous screen (Figure 3.29, ❹).

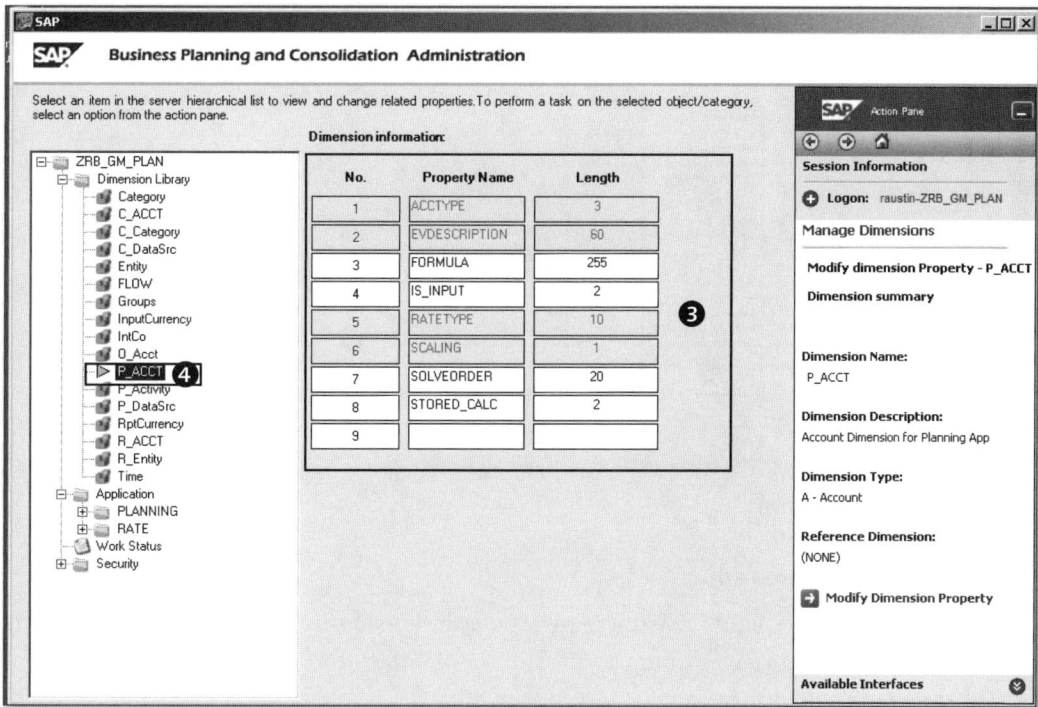

Figure 3.29 Displaying Dimension Properties and Member Data—Part B

3. Click on Maintain Dimension Members in the right pane (Figure 3.28, ❺ to display the Dimension Elements (Figure 3.30). The member IDs and their descriptions are displayed (Figure 3.30, ❻ and ❼). Member IDs are case-sensitive. Hierarchies can be defined by using the convention ParentH(n) in the column headings, where n is the hierarchy number. The hierarchy for P_ACCT is displayed (Figure 3.30, ❽).

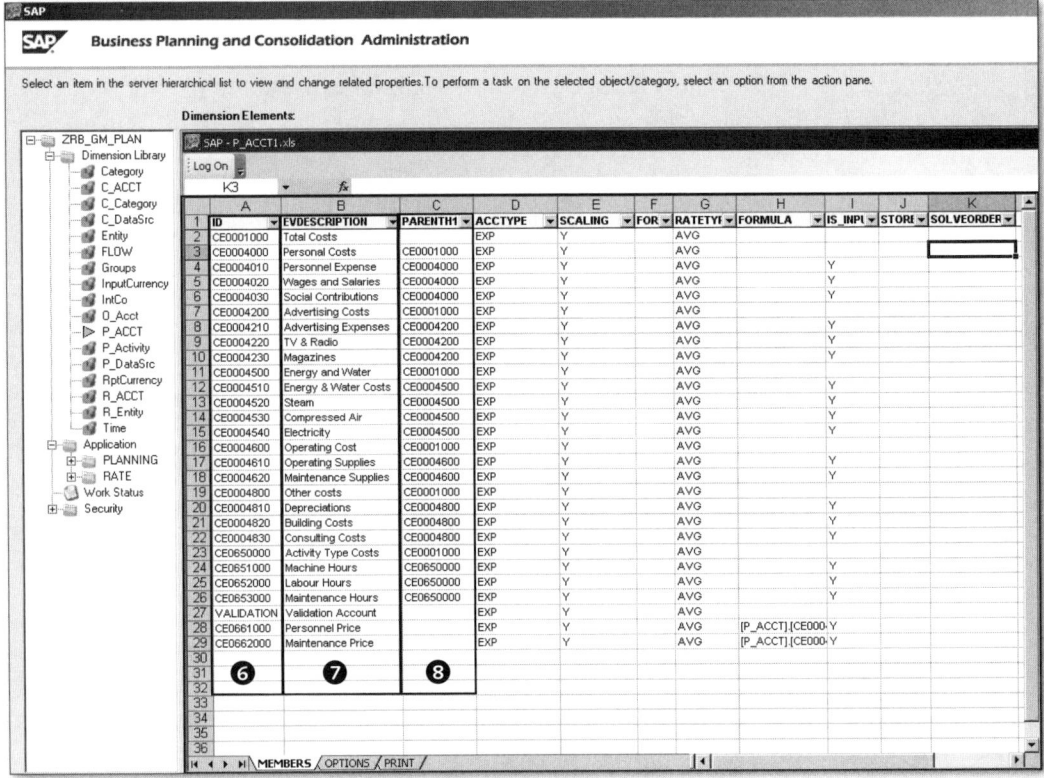

Figure 3.30 Displaying Dimension Properties and Member Data—Part C

Copying a Dimension

We will now explain how to create a new dimension by copying from an existing dimension. Our case study requires us to maintain the following dimensions for the planning application:

- RB_ACCOUNT
- RB_CATEGORY
- RB_ENTITY
- RB_PRODUCT
- RB_CUTOMER
- RB_DATASRC

▶ RPTCURRENCY

▶ Time

We will start by creating the RB_ACCOUNT dimension by copying it from the P_ACCT dimension. When a dimension is copied, the members of the source dimension are copied to the new target dimension.

1. To copy a dimension, click on Dimension Library in the left pane and then select Copy a Dimension (Figure 3.31, ❶ and ❷).

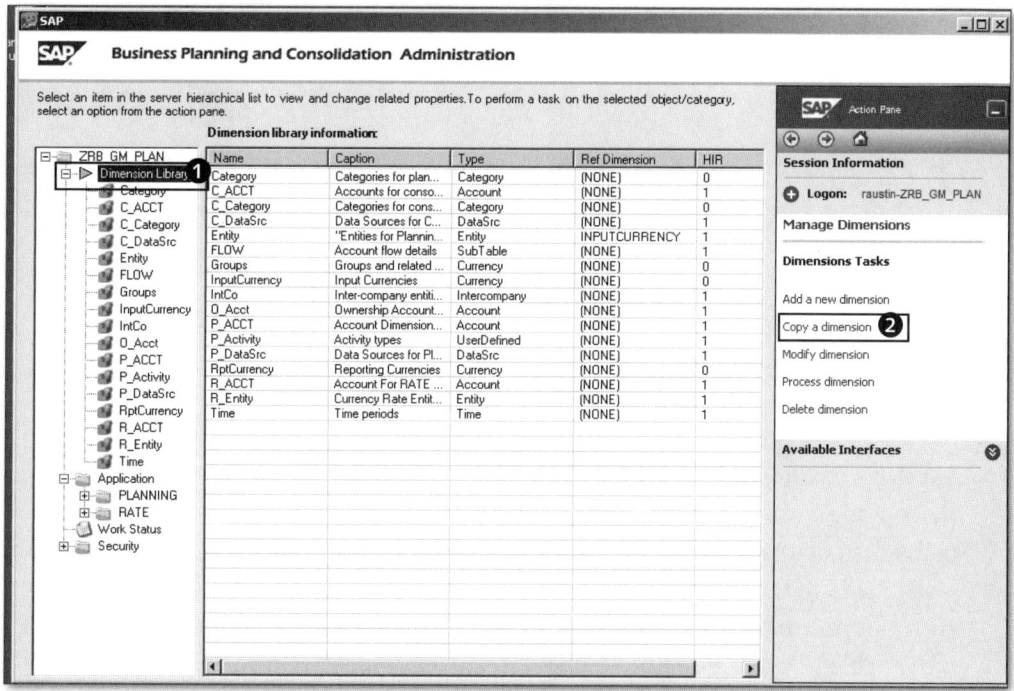

Figure 3.31 Copying a Dimension—Part A

2. Select the dimension you want to use to copy to the new dimension. We will select the P_ACCT dimension from the dropdown as the source dimension (Figure 3.32, ❸). Enter "RB_ACCT" as the technical name of the dimension (Figure 3.32, ❹). Enter "RB Accounts" as the description for the dimension (Figure 3.32, ❺). Click on Save as Dimension (Figure 3.32, ❻).

3. A status message box indicates the dimension was successfully created, and the newly created dimension is shown under the dimension library in the left pane.

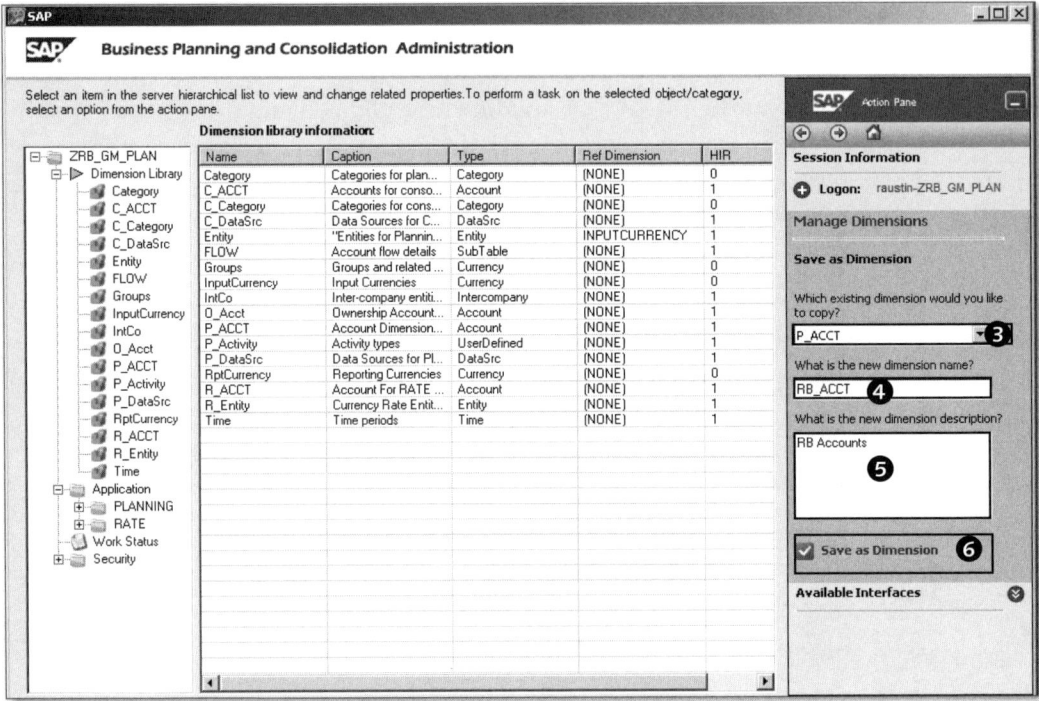

Figure 3.32 Copying a Dimension– Part B

Similarly, create the RB_CATEGORY, RB_DATASRC, and RB_ENTITY dimensions by copying from the Category, P_DataSrc, and Entity dimensions. Because we are using the copy task, all of the dimension members from the source dimension are also copied to the new dimension. If you want to create a new dimension without copying from an existing dimension, you can use the Add a Dimension task, which is available in the right pane.

Creating a Custom Dimension

Our sample company requires product and customer data for planning. These dimensions are not standard dimensions provided by SAP BusinessObjects Planning and Consolidation; instead, they must be created as custom dimensions. We will now create the product dimension as a custom dimension using the following steps:

1. Click on the Dimension Library and select Add a New Dimension from the right pane.

2. You are now prompted to enter the technical name and description of the dimension. Enter "RB_PRODUCT" for the technical name and "RB PRODUCTS" as the description (Figure 3.33, ❶ and ❷). Select Go to Step 2 of 3 (Figure 3.33, ❸).

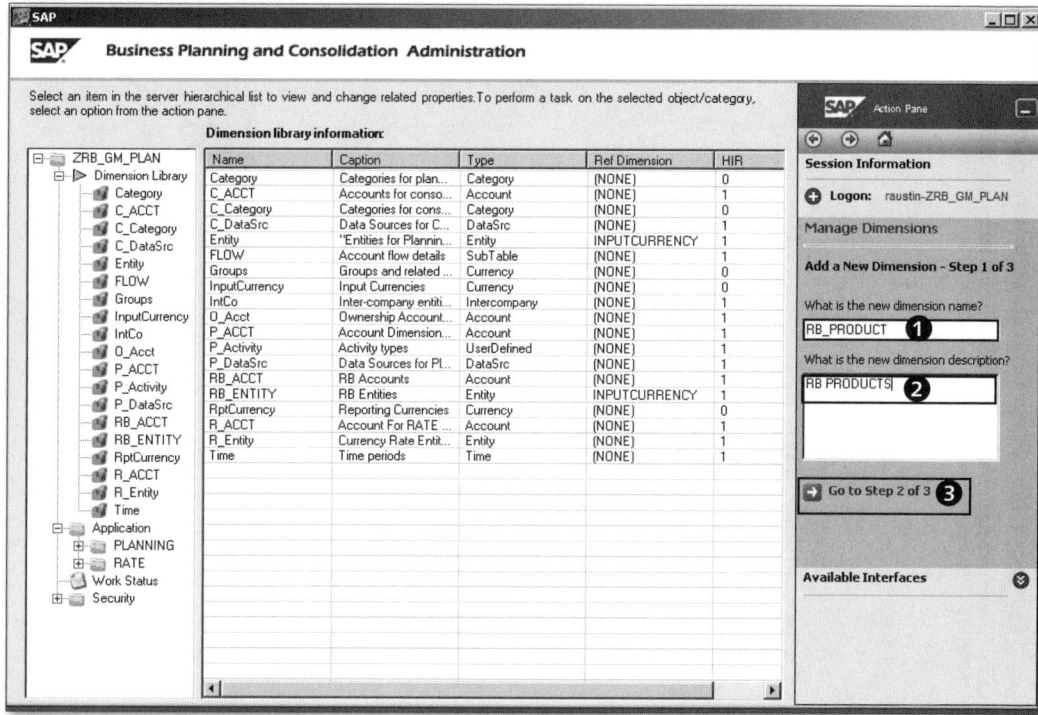

Figure 3.33 Creating a Custom Dimension—Part B

3. You are now prompted to select the dimension type from the dropdown list: U – User Defined (Figure 3.34, ❹). Click on Go to Step 3 of 3 (Figure 3.34, ❺).

3 | Modeling an Application with SAP BusinessObjects Planning and Consolidation for NetWeaver

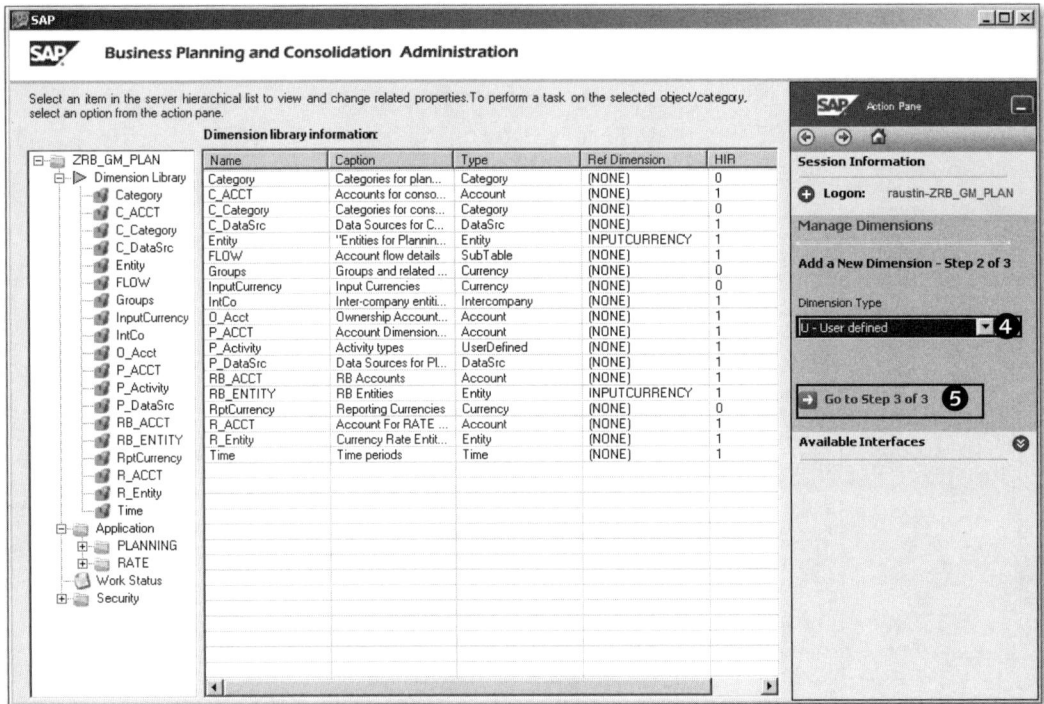

Figure 3.34 Creating a Custom Dimension—Part B

4. The standard properties are automatically added for the dimension type (Figure 3.35, ❻). You can now add new properties as needed, although we do not need to add any new properties to this dimension for our case study. Click on Add a New Dimension (Figure 3.35, ❼). A status message indicates that the dimension has been created successfully (Figure 3.35, ❽).

Similarly, add a property called PRD_GRP to the Product dimension, and create another custom dimension with the technical name "RB_CUSTOMER" and description "RB CUSTOMERS." Add the PARENTH1 property to this dimension to maintain hierarchy information for customers.

Building Applications in SAP BusinessObjects Planning and Consolidation | 3.3

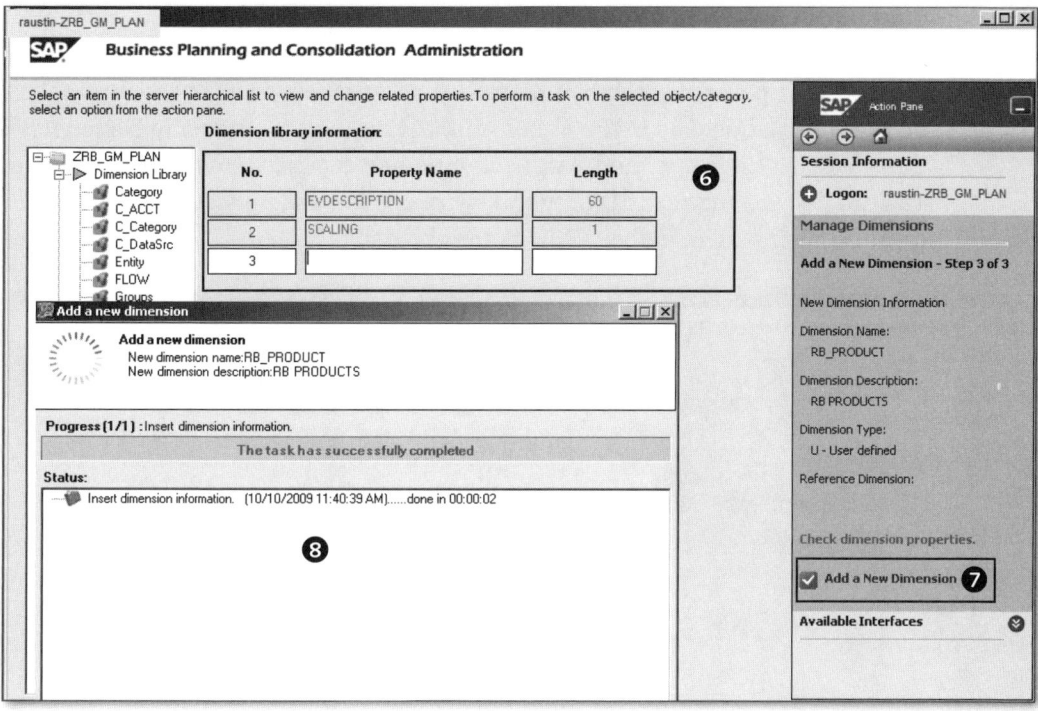

Figure 3.35 Creating a Custom Dimension—Part C

Manually Entering Data into a Dimension

Two options are available when entering data into a dimension in SAP BusinessObjects Planning and Consolidation: it can be loaded from a flat file, or entered manually. We will discuss the option of loading data from a file in Chapter 4, when we discuss the process of loading master and transaction data. The option to enter data manually into a dimension can be used when there are limited records of data in the dimension.

Next, we will explain how to manually enter data into the RB_ACCT dimension for our case study.

1. To add data manually, click on the RB_ACCT dimension in the left pane, under the Dimension Library, and select Maintain Dimension Information in the right pane. This displays the member, hierarchy, and property data of the dimension. Delete the existing data in the dimension, because it was originally copied from the P_ACCT dimension, and enter the member data as shown in Figure 3.36. You can delete a member ID only if it is not used in an application. If any application contains the member ID, it cannot be deleted.

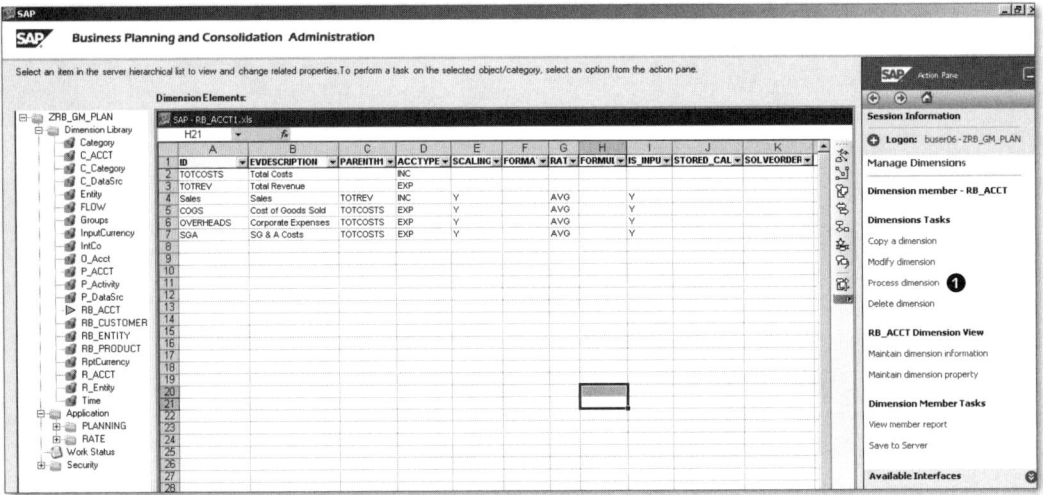

Figure 3.36 Manually Entering Data into a Dimension

2. The data entered into the dimension has to be processed in SAP BusinessObjects Planning and Consolidation to take effect. Select Process Dimension (Figure 3.36, ❶).

3. This opens the Process Dimensions dialog box (Figure 3.37). Processing a dimension causes a corresponding attribute change run for the InfoObject in SAP NetWeaver BW. Deselect the option to Take System Offline. Select the option Process Members from Member Sheet. Confirm that RB_ACCT is selected in the dimensions. You can select more than one dimension. Click on OK to process the data for the dimension(s) selected.

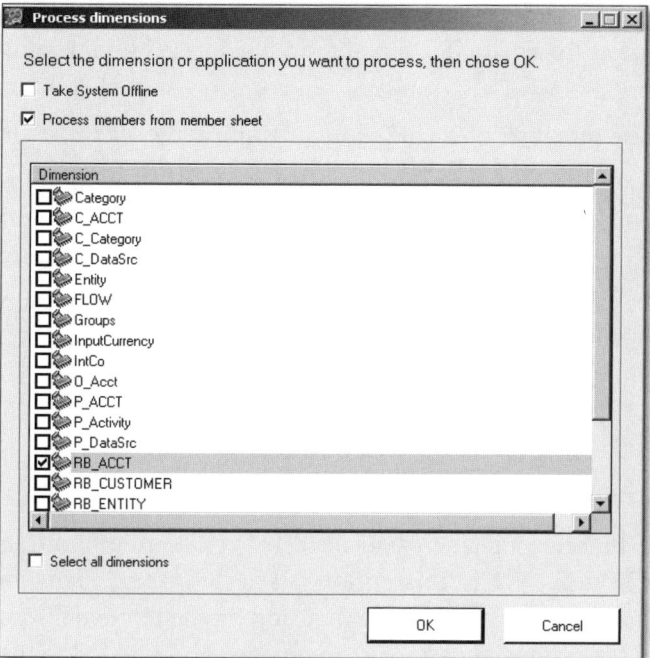

Figure 3.37 Processing a Dimension

You have now seen how dimensions are created and maintained in SAP BusinessObjects Planning and Consolidation. We displayed properties associated to dimensions and discussed how hierarchies are used in dimensions. We also created a dimension by copying from an existing dimension and created a custom dimension. We will now discuss applications, and how they are created.

3.3.4 Application

An application in SAP BusinessObjects Planning and Consolidation meets a particular functional business requirement. It is used for storing transaction data and is available for reporting. Examples of applications are sales planning, gross profit planning, and head-count planning. The following are a few basic but important facts about applications:

- An application is created with respect to an application set and is a collection of dimensions. The dimensions for an application are modeled based on business requirements.
- An application can use any dimensions included in an application set.
- There are no restrictions on the number of dimensions included in an application, but it is recommended that the number is limited to maintain good performance.
- A number of objects and tables are created in the background, depending on the type of application created. Some of these include comment tables, journals, work status tables, audit tables, script logic files, file service folders, Web Admin parameters, and default packages to load and manage data for applications.
- Two options are available when creating an application:
  - Add: This option can be selected when you need to create an application based on another application. When this option is selected, the dimension assignments can be changed. For example, a dimension can be removed from what was provided by the template, or a new dimension can be added to the application.
  - Copy: This option can be selected when it is necessary to copy records from a source application to a target application.

There are two main types of applications:

- **Reporting**
  These applications are used for reporting; examples of reporting applications are sales planning and consolidation applications. The following sub-types are available under reporting applications:
  - Financial: This type of application is used primarily for planning.
  - Consolidation: This type of application is used for reporting financial data if an organization is comprised of a group of companies. It is necessary to report the financial data of the group companies as a whole.
  - Generic: A reporting application that is neither a financial nor a consolidation application is categorized as a generic application.

- **Non-reporting**
  This type of application is used to support a reporting application. The following sub-types are available under non-reporting applications:
  - Rate: This application is used for storing exchange rates and to enable currency translation for reporting applications. When a company does business in more than one currency, it may need to translate the business transactions into one reporting currency. In these cases, the rate application is used to perform currency translations to one reporting currency.
  - Ownership: The ownership application is used for consolidating financial information. An organization may be composed of a group of companies with a different ownership mix; for example, it may hold a 50% stake in one company and have also made a significant investment in another company. In such cases, it may be necessary for legal reporting to consolidate the financial data of all of the companies in the group as a whole. The ownership application stores the percentage ownership in different companies and helps with performing legal consolidation.
  - Generic: This type of application is used to support a reporting application. An application containing the price of products is an example of a non-reporting generic application.

All applications, whether reporting or non-reporting, must include the four basic dimensions: category, account, entity, and time.

When a request for creating an application is initiated in SAP BusinessObjects Planning and Consolidation, a corresponding InfoCube and MultiProvider is created in the SAP NetWeaver BW system. A table, UJA_APPL, stores the technical name of the InfoCube and MultiProvider. The naming convention when creating the InfoCube and MultiProvider is as follows:

- InfoCube:
  /CPMB/<Application SetPrefix>I<ApplicationPrefix><1GeneratedChar>
- MultiProvider:
  /CPMB/<Application SetPrefix>M<ApplicationPrefix><1GeneratedChar>

It is easy to delete or add dimensions to an application in SAP BusinessObjects Planning and Consolidation. When dimension data is deleted from an application, the SAP NetWeaver BW system creates a shadow InfoCube in the background and moves the data from the original InfoCube to the shadow InfoCube. After successfully loading the data to the shadow InfoCube, the system updates the database for the application to point to the shadow InfoCube and deletes the original InfoCube because it is no longer required.

> **Note**
> Do not change any application objects directly in the SAP NetWeaver BW system. Always use the SAP BusinessObjects Planning and Consolidation frontend to make changes to an application.

Application Optimization

SAP BusinessObjects Planning and Consolidation lets you optimize applications. Two options are available for this, as follows:

- **Lite Optimize**
  When data is loaded into an application, an open request is created for the InfoCube associated with the application in the SAP NetWeaver BW system. This request is open (shown with a yellow status) until a particular threshold of records is updated. When the threshold is reached, the request is closed (shown with a green status). When Lite Optimize is selected, all open requests are closed and set to green. The cube is compressed, and all of the indexes are built. The statistics for the InfoCube are also updated during this process.

- **Full Optimize**
  Full Optimize works the same as Lite Optimize. However, it also reviews the data model for scope for additional optimization. If, during the course of the check it is determined that the data model of the InfoCube requires changing, the necessary changes to the data model will be made. This process can take some time to complete, depending on the volume of data in the InfoCube.

Parameters for an Application

A number of parameters can be set for an application. One of these is YTDINPUT. YTDINPUT determines how quantitative data is stored in an application. By default, the value of this parameter is 0. This implies that the quantitative data for each record in the application is stored for the period for which it is entered. When the value of this parameter is set to 1, the quantitative data is year-to-date and up to the period for which it is entered.

We will use an example to illustrate the functionality of this parameter. Consider a situation where YTDINPUT is set to 1, with two records entered into an application. The first is for an amount of $200—entered for January 2009—and the second is for an amount of $500—entered for February 2009. In this case, the entries for these two months represent YTD values. Therefore, the periodic value for January 2009 is $200, and the periodic value for February 2009 is $300 ($500 - $200).

We will discuss other application-specific parameters in Chapter 7.

Create Application

We will now explain how to create an application for Rich Bloom, Inc. to use for planning gross margins. The dimensions required for our planning application are as follows:

- RB_ACCT
- RB_CATEGORY
- RB_ENTITY
- RB_CUSTOMER
- RB_PRODUCT
- RB_DATASRC
- RPTCURRENCY
- Time

We will create a new planning application that includes these dimensions. Proceed as follows:

1. Access the ZRB_GM_PLAN application set.
2. Click on the application option in the left pane and select Add a New Application (Figure 3.38, ❶ and ❷).

3 | Modeling an Application with SAP BusinessObjects Planning and Consolidation for NetWeaver

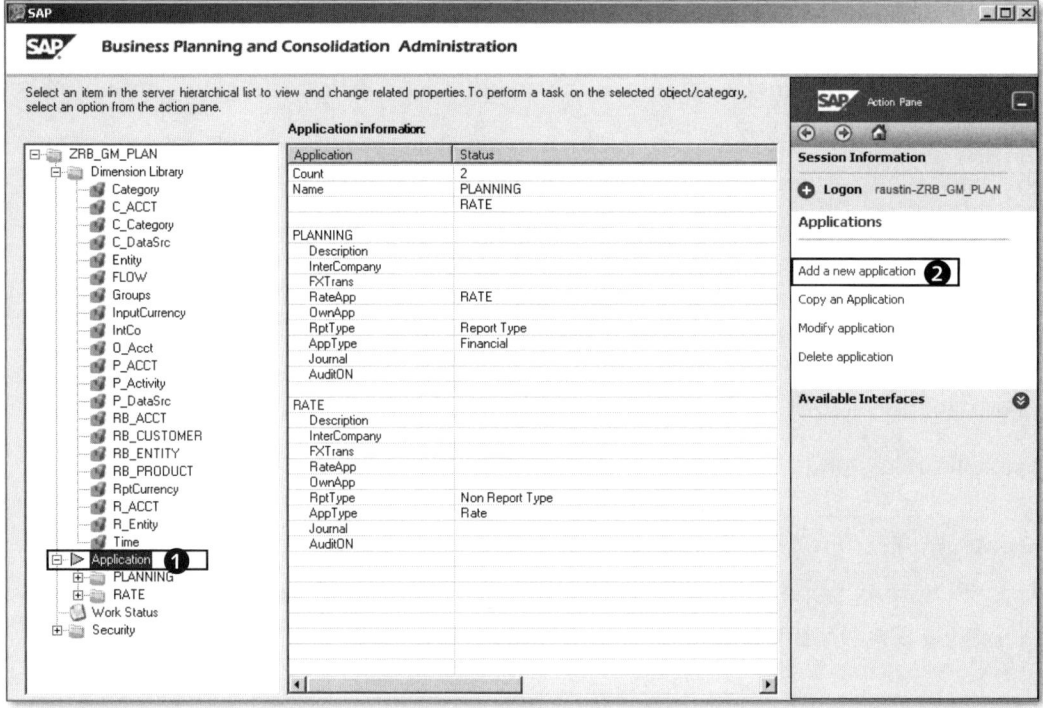

Figure 3.38 Creating an Application — Part A

3. You are now prompted to enter the new application name and description. Enter "RB_GM_ PLAN" as the technical name and "Gross Margin Planning" as the description for the application (Figure 3.39, ❸ and ❹). Select Go to Step 2 of 4 (Figure 3.39, ❺).

4. You are prompted to select the application type. We want to create a financial application that can be reported. Under Reporting Type, select Financial (Figure 3.40, ❻). Select Go to Step 3 of 4 (Figure 3.40, ❼).

Building Applications in SAP BusinessObjects Planning and Consolidation | 3.3

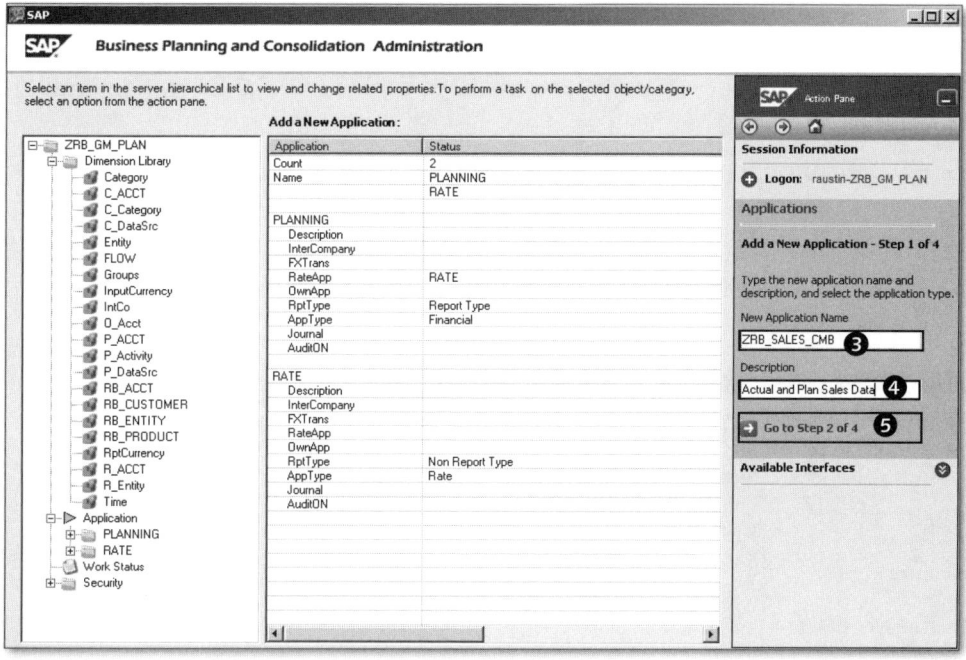

Figure 3.39 Creating an Application—Part B

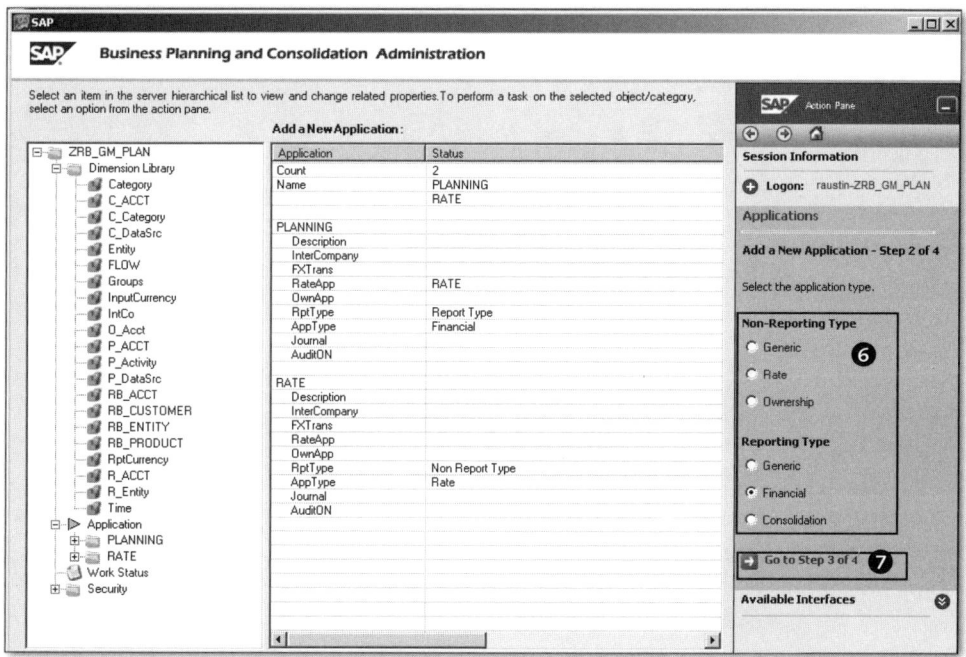

Figure 3.40 Creating an Application—Part C

3 | Modeling an Application with SAP BusinessObjects Planning and Consolidation for NetWeaver

5. In this step, select the source application you want to use as the template for creating the new application. Select PLANNING, which is an application that is delivered as part of APSHELL, and has been copied into the current application set (Figure 3.41, ❽).

6. Every finance application must be associated to a rate application; this is the application that is accessed for performing currency translations. An application called "RATE" is delivered as part of APSHELL and has been copied into the current application. Associate the RATE application to the current application (Figure 3.41, ❾).

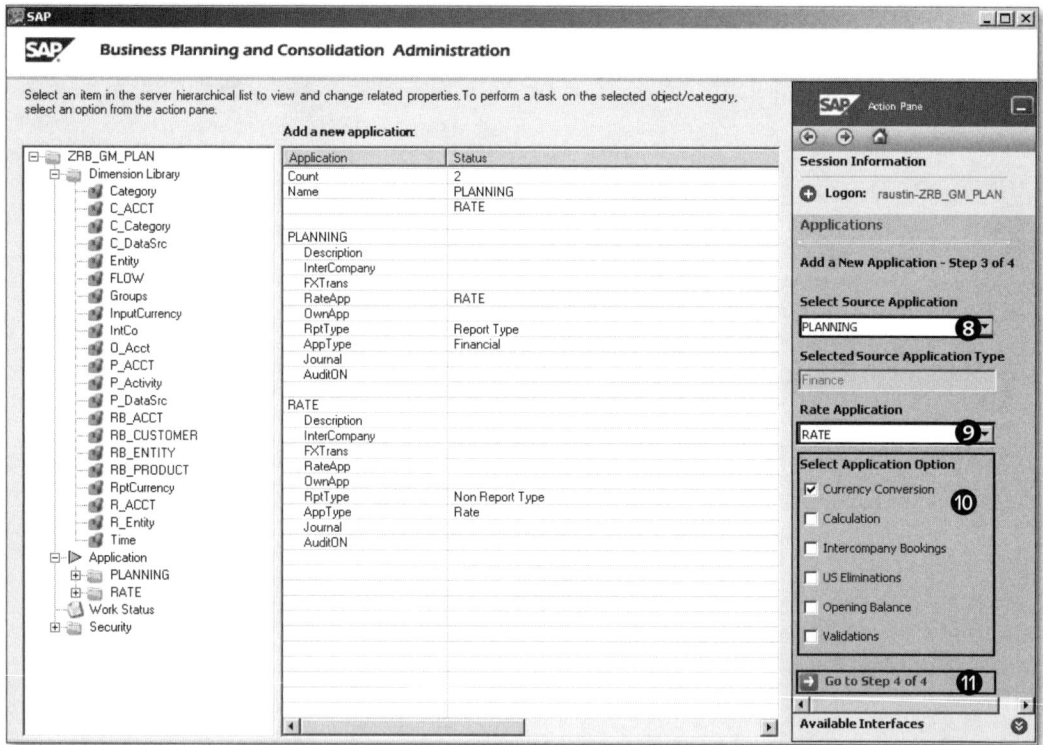

Figure 3.41 Creating an Application — Part D

3.3 | Building Applications in SAP BusinessObjects Planning and Consolidation

7. Select the application options you want to use with this application (Figure 3.41, ❿). These options can be used for configuring currency conversions, intercompany bookings, and so on. For this application, select Currency Conversion. Select Go to Step 4 of 4 (Figure 3.41, ⓫).

8. In the next screen, uncheck Dimensions (Figure 3.42, ⓬). This enables you to change the dimensions that have been copied from the source application. Also uncheck Journals, because you will not be using it in our application (Figure 3.42, ⓭). Click on Add a New Application (Figure 3.42, ⓮).

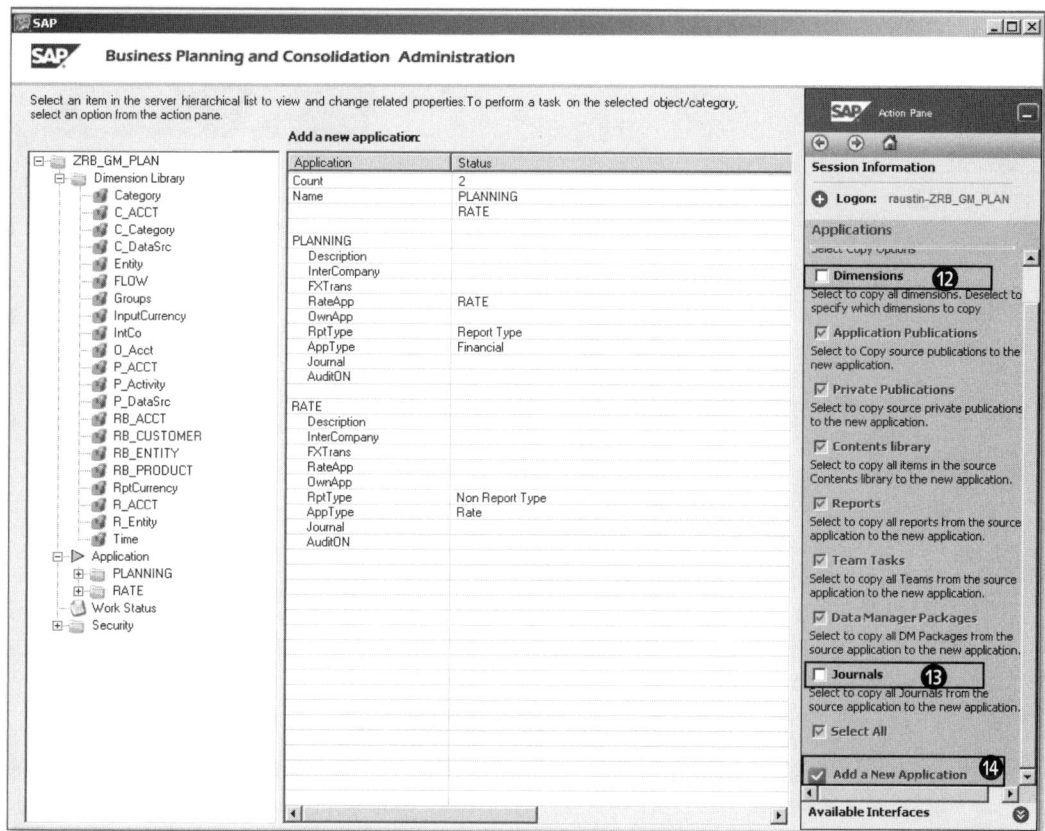

Figure 3.42 Creating an Application — Part E

123

3 | Modeling an Application with SAP BusinessObjects Planning and Consolidation for NetWeaver

9. In the next screen, use the arrows to remove and include dimensions to your application. Our application will not need the dimensions shown in Figure 3.43, ⓯. Click on the arrow as shown in Figure 3.43, ⓰, to remove them from the application.

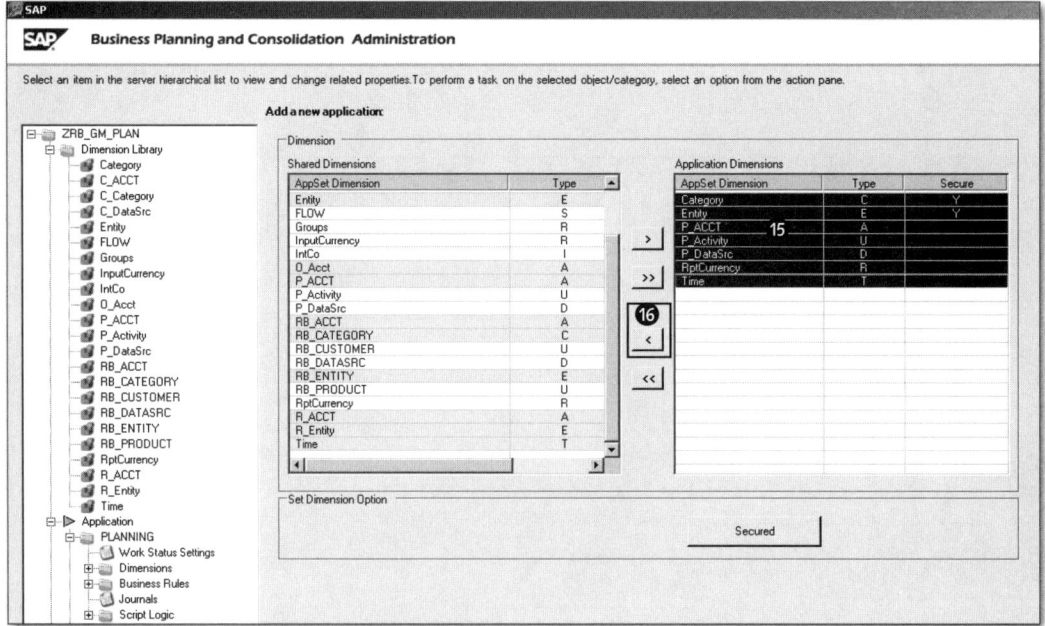

Figure 3.43 Creating an Application—Part F

10. Add the RB_ACCT, RB_CATEGORY, RB_CUSTOMER, RB_DATASRC, RB_ENTITY, RB_PRODUCT, RptCurrency, and Time dimensions (Figure 3.44, ⓱) from the list of available dimensions in the left area to the new application in the right area using the right-facing arrow (Figure 3.44, ⓲).

11. Mark RB_ENTITY as a secured dimension. Marking a dimension in this way assists with restricting data access for users based on values in that dimension. To do so, select the RB_ENTITY dimension (Figure 3.45, ⓳) and click on Secured (Figure 3.45, ⓴).

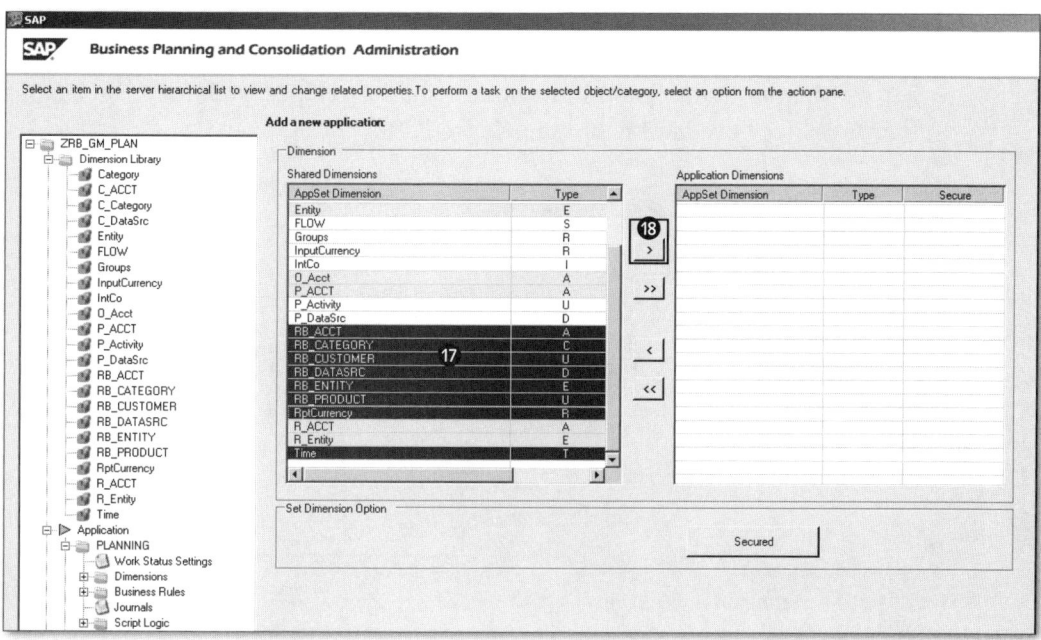

Figure 3.44 Creating an Application—Part G

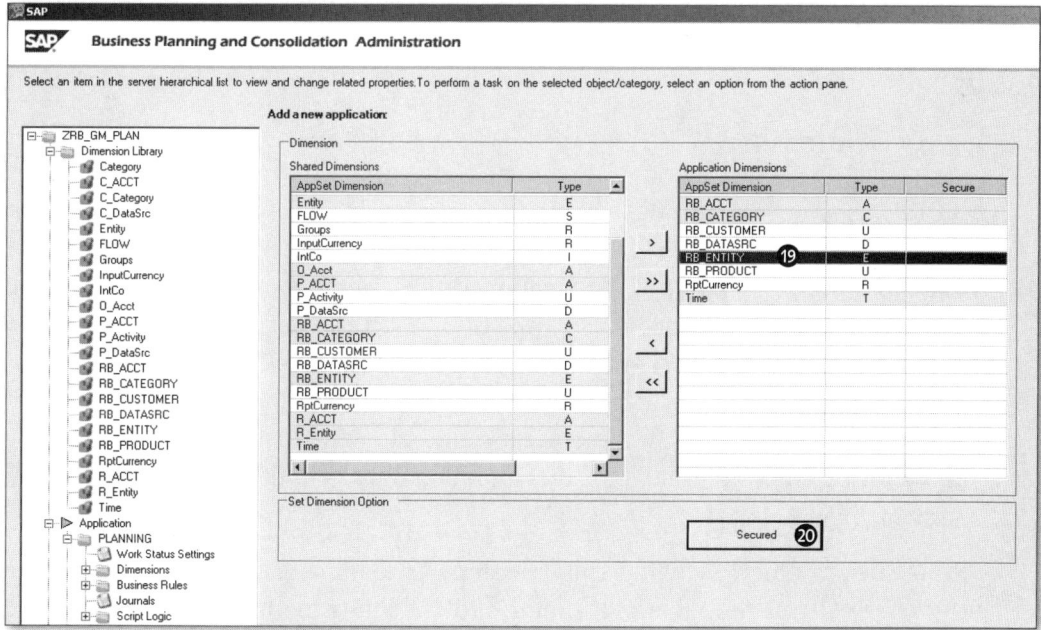

Figure 3.45 Creating an Application—Part H

12. Click on Add a New Application in the right pane to add the new application. A status message indicates that the new application has been created. The Gross Margin Planning application is created and displayed under the Application folder in the left pane (see Figure 3.46).

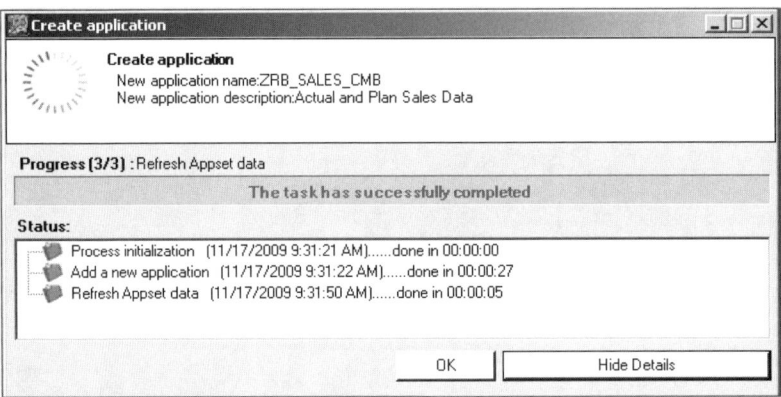

Figure 3.46 Creating an Application—Part I

We have now configured a planning application Rich Bloom, Inc. will use for planning gross margins. We included all of the necessary dimensions in the application that will be used to develop a plan and compute the gross margin.

3.4 Summary

In this chapter, we introduced you to a case study of a sample company, Rich Bloom, Inc., who uses the SAP BusinessObjects Planning and Consolidation tool for gross margin planning. We developed the staging environment in the SAP NetWeaver BW system that will be used to store actual sales and cost data. We also discussed the building blocks of creating the planning application in SAP BusinessObjects Planning and Consolidation. We discussed application sets, dimensions, and applications, and saw how the objects created in SAP BusinessObjects Planning and Consolidation translated to corresponding objects in the SAP NetWeaver BW system.

In the next chapter, we will discuss the steps for loading data into SAP NetWeaver BW and SAP BusinessObjects Planning and Consolidation for NetWeaver.

4 Loading, Scheduling, and Managing Data in SAP BusinessObjects Planning and Consolidation for NetWeaver

In the last chapter, we discussed a case study for our model company, Rich Bloom, Inc. To meet the requirements of the case study, we built an InfoCube in SAP NetWeaver BW and an application in SAP BusinessObjects Planning and Consolidation to store actual sales and cost data. In this chapter, we will discuss how to load data in the SAP NetWeaver BW and SAP BusinessObjects Planning and Consolidation environments.

Section 4.1 discusses the steps of loading data from a flat file to an InfoCube in SAP NetWeaver BW. If you are new to SAP NetWeaver BW, this section will help you understand the process of loading transaction data into an InfoCube.

Section 4.2 explains the options available to load master and transaction data into SAP BusinessObjects Planning and Consolidation. You will see how transformations and conversions are used when loading data to dimensions and applications. This section also explains the importance of data manager packages and discusses how to create and maintain them. Data manager packages enable you to perform different tasks regarding loading and managing data in SAP BusinessObjects Planning and Consolidation. In this section, we will discuss the use of process chains in a data manager package and you will be introduced to the process types available for use in a process chain inside an SAP BusinessObjects Planning and Consolidation application.

Section 4.3 discusses how to use 2009 actual sales and cost data to create a base line plan data for 2010. We will copy actual sales and cost data for 2009 to a plan version for 2010.

4.1 Loading Data into an InfoCube in SAP NetWeaver BW

In this section, we will discuss the steps of loading data from a flat file into an InfoCube in SAP NetWeaver BW.

4.1.1 Creating a DataSource

A *DataSource* is an object that provides data to load into an InfoProvider in SAP NetWeaver BW. The actual source of the sales and cost data for our sample company, Rich Bloom, Inc., is in an SAP ECC system. The daily sales and cost data created in the SAP ECC system is brought into the SAP NetWeaver BW system on a nightly basis. However, for the purposes of our case study, we will assume that the sales and cost data for the year 2009 exists in a flat file. We will load the sales and cost data from this flat file into the Sales InfoCube in the SAP NetWeaver BW system.

Before you start creating the DataSource, you must create a flat file that contains the sales and cost data for the year 2009. We use a CSV (comma separated) format containing the following columns:

- Account
- Company Code
- Calendar Month
- Calendar Year
- Material
- Customer
- Amount in Local Currency
- Currency

Then, enter data as shown in Figure 4.1. Name the file "us_salesdata.csv" and save it to a directory called *C:\Planning*.

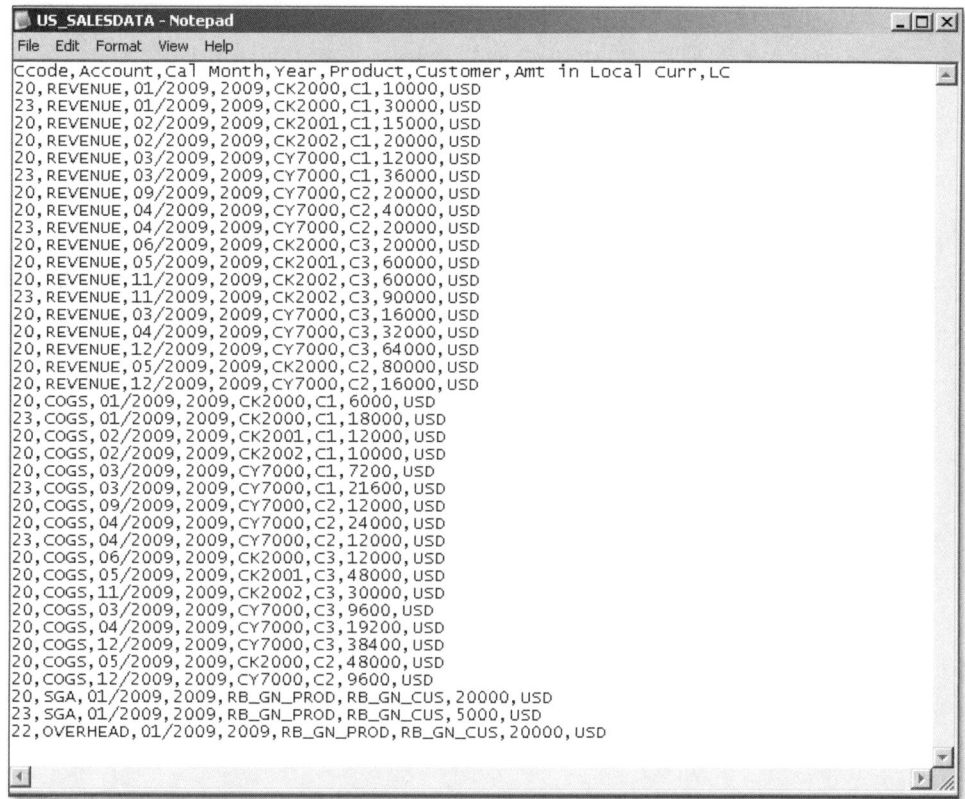

Figure 4.1 Sales and Cost Data for 2009 in a Flat File

Next, perform the following steps to create the DataSource, as illustrated in Figures 4.2, 4.3, and 4.4:

1. Open the Data Warehousing Workbench using Transaction RSA1.
2. Select MODELING • SOURCE SYSTEMS.
3. Select and double-click on a flat file source system for creating the DataSource. We used the PC File System (Figure 4.2, ❶).
4. The DataSource for <File System> dialog box displays (in this case, PC_FILE PC File System). Select any application component area (for example, Non-SAP_Sources), right-click, and choose Create DataSource from the context menu (Figure 4.2, ❷).

4 | Loading, Scheduling, and Managing Data

5. In the Create DataSource window, enter the name of the DataSource ("ZSLS_FILE") (Figure 4.2, ❸), and then select Transaction Data from the Data Type DataSource dropdown list (Figure 4.2, ❹).

6. Click on Enter (Figure 4.2, ❺).

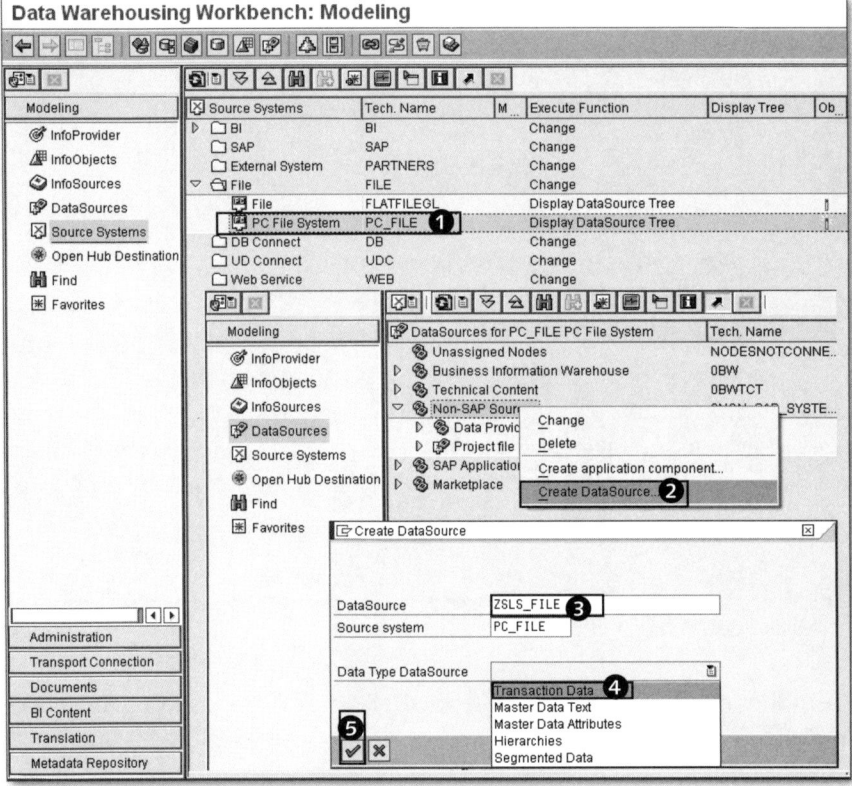

Figure 4.2 Create a Flat File DataSource for Sales Data—Part A

7. On the General Info tab in the Change DataSource *<File Name>* window, enter the short ("Sales actual file"), medium ("Sales actual file"), and long descriptions ("Sales actual file") for the DataSource. We will be using this DataSource to load sales and cost data for the year 2009 from a flat file.

8. On the Fields tab, enter the list of fields for which data exists in the flat file. The sequence you use is the same as that used for the data in the flat file. Instead of entering a field name, you can also enter the name of an InfoObject in the

first row of the Template InfoObject column (Figure 4.3, ❻) that represents the field.

9. After you enter the first InfoObject (0COMP_CODE) and click on Enter, the Default from InfoObjects dialog box displays (Figure 4.3). Select Do Not Show This Question Again in This Session, and click on Copy (Figure 4.3, ❼ and ❽). This transfers all of the properties from the InfoObject to the corresponding field in the Field column (Figure 4.4, ❾).

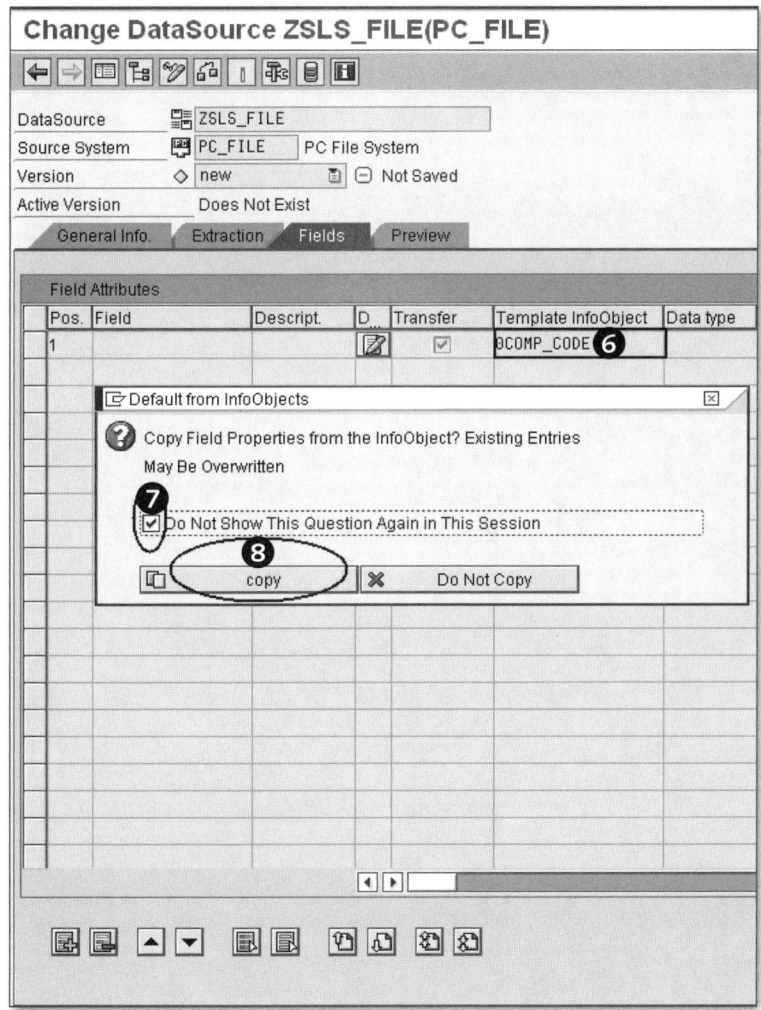

Figure 4.3 Create a Flat File DataSource for Sales Data—Part B

10. Continue to enter InfoObjects into the Template InfoObject column (Figure 4.4, ❿) by clicking on the Insert button (Figure 4.4, ⓫), following the sequence of data coming from the flat file that contains the sales and cost data for 2009.

11. Click on the Activate button to save and activate the DataSource (Figure 4.4, ⓬).

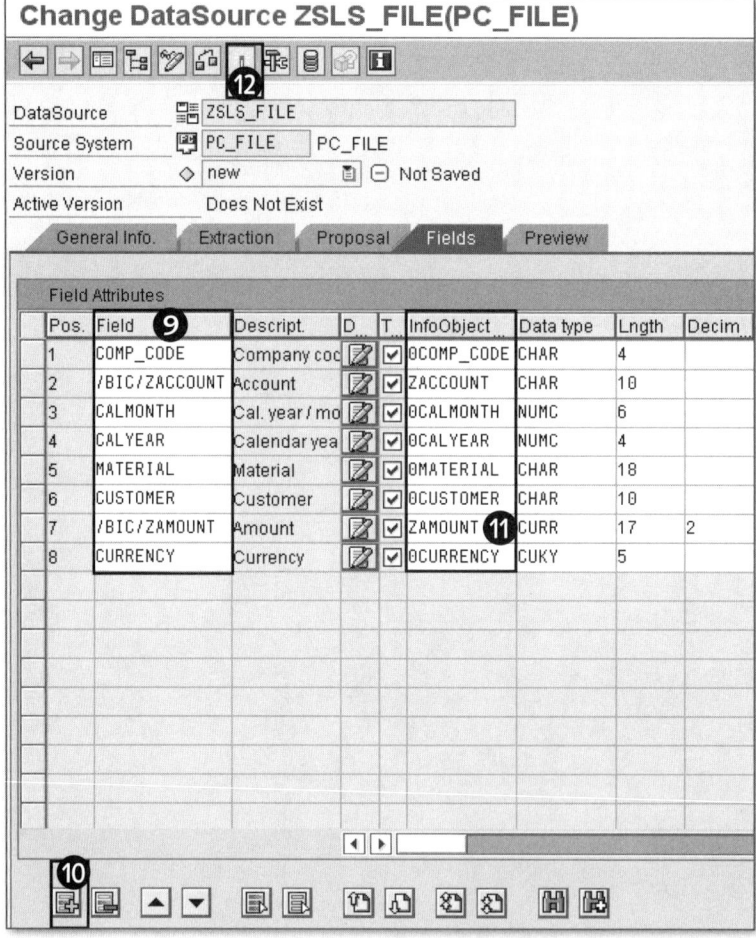

Figure 4.4 Create a Flat File DataSource for Sales Data—Part C

When the DataSource is successfully activated, an equivalent PSA table is automatically created by the system. The structure of the PSA table mirrors the structure of the file layout of the source data.

4.1.2 Creating Transformations

In SAP NetWeaver BW, the data coming from a source system is loaded into the DataSource or PSA in its original form as sent from the source system. The *transformation* process, however, lets you apply rules to modify the data coming from a DataSource before it is loaded into an InfoProvider.

At least one transformation process is required before data reaches the data target. For our case study, we will create a transformation process to transform the data from the PSA associated with the Sales DataSource to the Sales InfoCube.

Perform the following steps to create a transformation that loads data from the Sales DataSource created earlier into the Sales InfoCube, as illustrated in Figures 4.1, 4.2, 4.3, and 4.4:

1. Open the Data Warehousing Workbench using Transaction RSA1
2. Select MODELING • INFOPROVIDER.
3. Under the Sales Management InfoArea, right-click on the Sales Actual InfoCube and select the Create Transformation option from the context menu (Figure 4.5, ❶).
4. In the Create Transformation window, select the source of the transformation. Select the Object Type ("DataSource"), the DataSource ("ZSLS_FILE"), and the Source System ("PC_FILE") (Figure 4.5, ❷, ❸, and ❹).
5. Click on Enter (Figure 4.5, ❺).
6. The Transformation Create window appears (Figure 4.6). The system automatically proposes a mapping for the fields from the DataSource to the InfoObjects in the Sales Actual InfoCube. The proposal is based on the mapping of the InfoObjects in the Template InfoObjects column of the DataSource to the same InfoObject that exists as a characteristic or key figure in the Sales Actual InfoCube.

You may at times notice that some of the InfoObjects are not mapped. This is because data for these InfoObjects is not available in the DataSource; therefore, these values have to be directly set in the transformation. In these cases, select the appropriate InfoObject in the Rule Group: Standard Group table and double-click on it. There, you will have additional options to map the value for those InfoObjects.

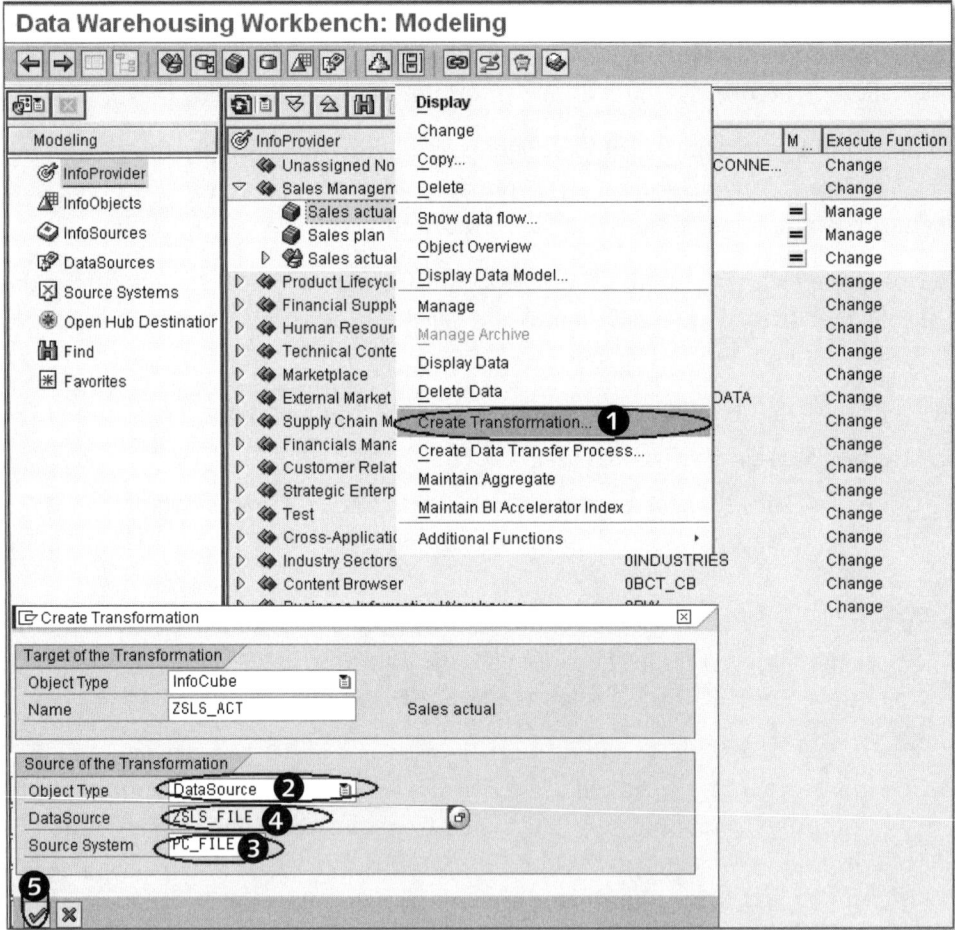

Figure 4.5 Create a Transformation—Part A

7. After all of the mappings have been assigned, click on the Activate button to save and activate the transformation object (Figure 4.6, ❻).

4.1 Loading Data into an InfoCube in SAP NetWeaver BW

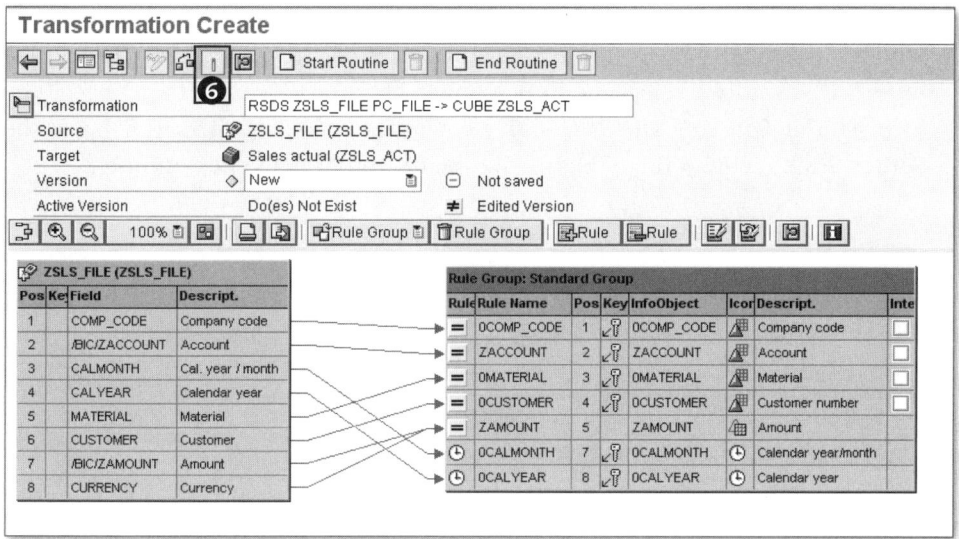

Figure 4.6 Create Transformation—Part B

4.1.3 Creating the Data Transfer Process (DTP)

The data transfer process (DTP) provides the ability to extract and load data from one persistent object to another.

> **Note**
>
> It is important to understand that the transformation process we created earlier only provides the rules for the extraction and loading of data. The DTP then uses the transformation to actually load the data from one persistent area to another.

For our case study, we want to define a DTP that extracts data from the Sales Actual File DataSource, uses the transformation process we created earlier, and loads the data into the Sales Actual InfoCube.

We will create a DTP by performing the following steps, as illustrated in Figures 4.7 and 4.8:

1. Open the Data Warehousing Workbench using Transaction RSA1.
2. Select MODELING • INFOPROVIDER.
3. Under the Sales Management InfoArea, right-click on the Sales Actual InfoCube and select Create Data Transfer Process from the context menu (Figure 4.7, ❶).

4 | Loading, Scheduling, and Managing Data

4. We are creating a DTP that loads data from the Sales Actual File DataSource, which we created earlier, to the Sales InfoCube. In the Creation of Data Transfer Process window, select the source object for the DTP. Enter the Object Type source ("DataSource"), the DataSource we created ealier ("ZSLS_FILE"), and the Source System ("PC_FILE") (Figure 4.7, ❷, ❸, and ❹) and click on Enter.

> **Note**
>
> A DTP can be created between a source and a target object only if a transformation process exists between the two objects.

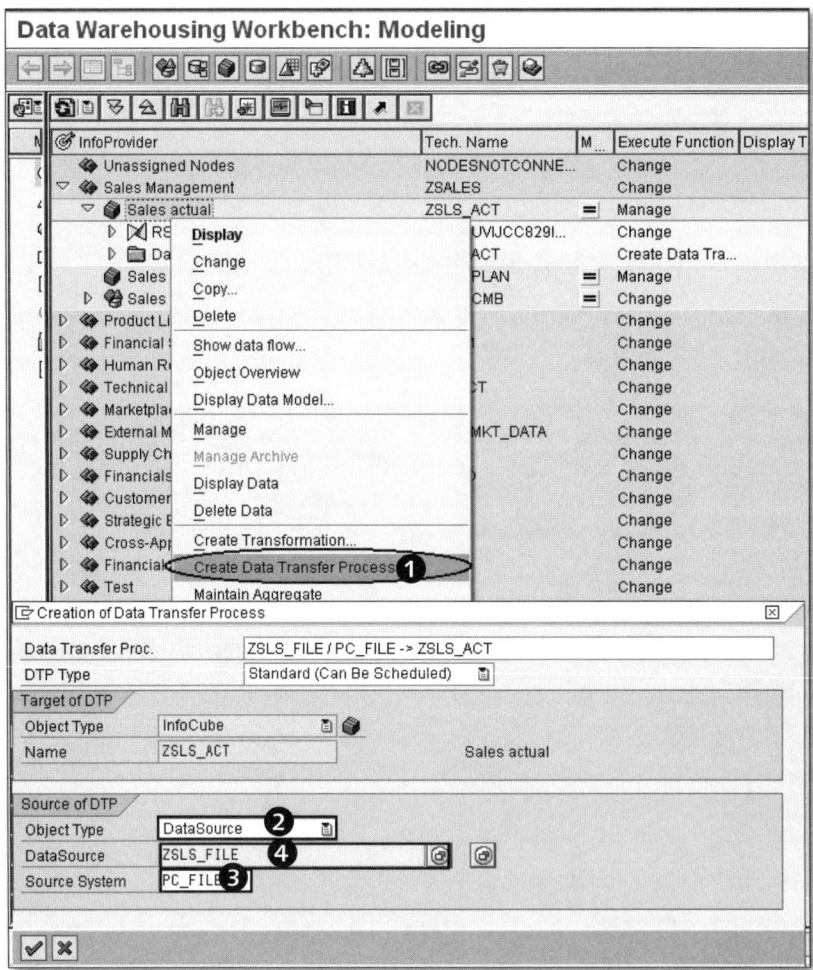

Figure 4.7 Create Data Transfer Process—Part A

136

5. In the Change Data Transfer Process window (Figure 4.8), select the extraction mode. If you select Full, all of the data from the source is loaded into the target. If you select Delta, only the changes made since the last time the data was extracted from this source is extracted into the target. Because we have sales and cost data for 2009, use the Full extraction mode.

6. Click on the Activate button to save and activate the DTP object (Figure 4.8, ❺).

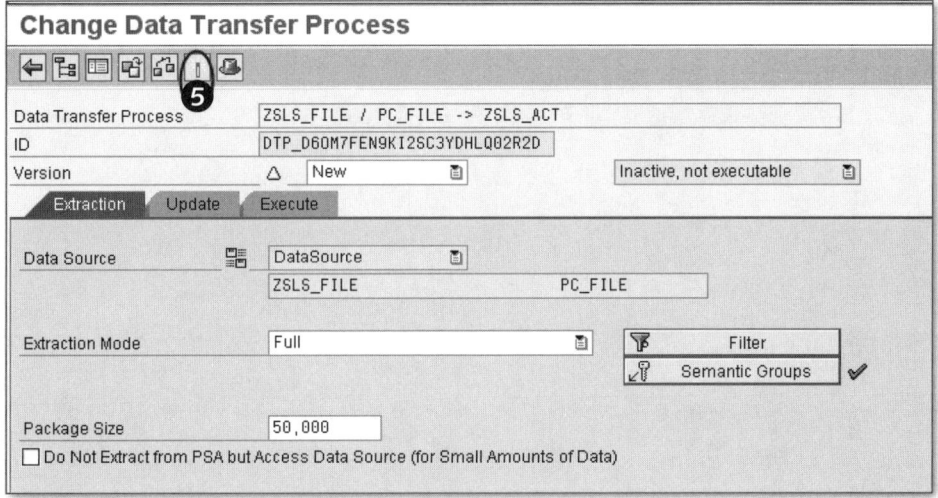

Figure 4.8 Create Data Transfer Process—Part B

4.1.4 Creating InfoPackages

In the previous steps, we configured objects such as the DataSource, transformation, and data transfer process that will be used to load sales actual data to the Sales InfoCube. However, the configuration of the objects by itself does not load the data; to do this, you must perform the following steps:

1. Schedule the loading of data from a DataSource to the PSA.
2. Schedule the load data from the PSA to a data target, which could be an InfoCube, DataStore, or InfoObject.

The InfoPackage is the object that is used to schedule the load of data from a DataSource to a persistent staging area (PSA). Create an InfoPackage for loading the sales data using the following steps, as illustrated in Figures 4.9, 4.10, and 4.11:

137

4 | Loading, Scheduling, and Managing Data

1. Open the Data Warehousing Workbench using Transaction RSA1.
2. Select MODELING • INFOPROVIDER.
3. Right-click on the Sales Actual File DataSource and select the option Create InfoPackage from the context menu (Figure 4.9, ❶).
4. In the Create InfoPackage window, enter the name of the InfoPackage ("Load sales data") and click on Enter (Figure 4.9, ❷ and ❸).

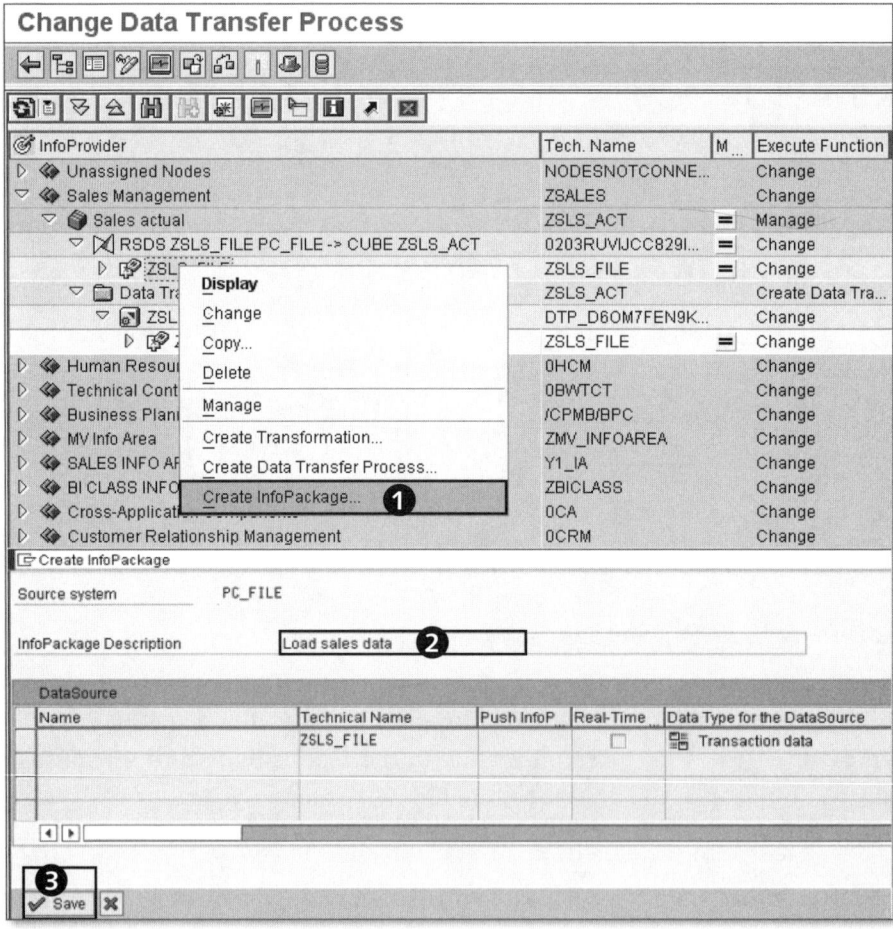

Figure 4.9 Create InfoPackage—Part 1

5. In the Scheduler (Maintain InfoPackage) window, select the Extraction tab (Figure 4.10, ❹).

6. Choose the Adapter, which determines whether the file you want to load exists on a local workstation or an SAP application server. Because this file exists on your PC, choose Load Text-Type File from Local Workstation from the dropdown list (Figure 4.10, ❺).

7. Enter the name of the file (*C:\Planning\US_SALESDATA.CSV*) that contains the sales and cost data for 2009 (Figure 4.10, ❻).

8. Specify the header rows to be ignored if you want the system to ignore header rows. (Refer back to Figure 4.1 for the layout of the file.) Because the first row of data contains the header, enter 1 in the Header Rows to be Ignored field (Figure 4.10, ❼).

9. Next to Data Format (Figure 4.10, ❽), select Separated with Separator (For Example, CSV) from the dropdown list, and, next to Data Separator, enter a comma (Figure 4.10, ❾).

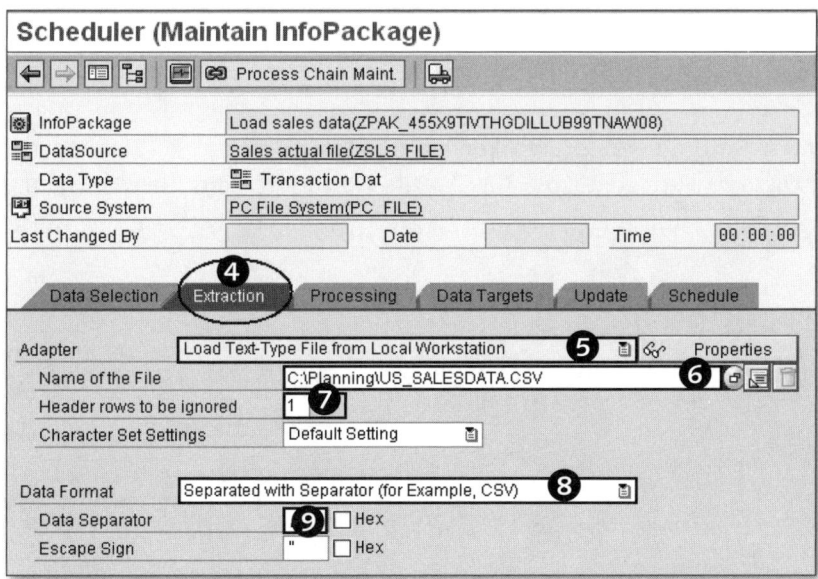

Figure 4.10 Create InfoPackage—Part 2

10. Select the Schedule tab (Figure 4.11, ❿). Ensure Start Data Load Immediately is selected (Figure 4.11, ⓫). Click on Start (Figure 4.11, ⓬). The data will now be extracted from the DataSource into the PSA. Click on the Monitor button to check the status of the extraction process (Figure 4.11, ⓭).

4 | Loading, Scheduling, and Managing Data

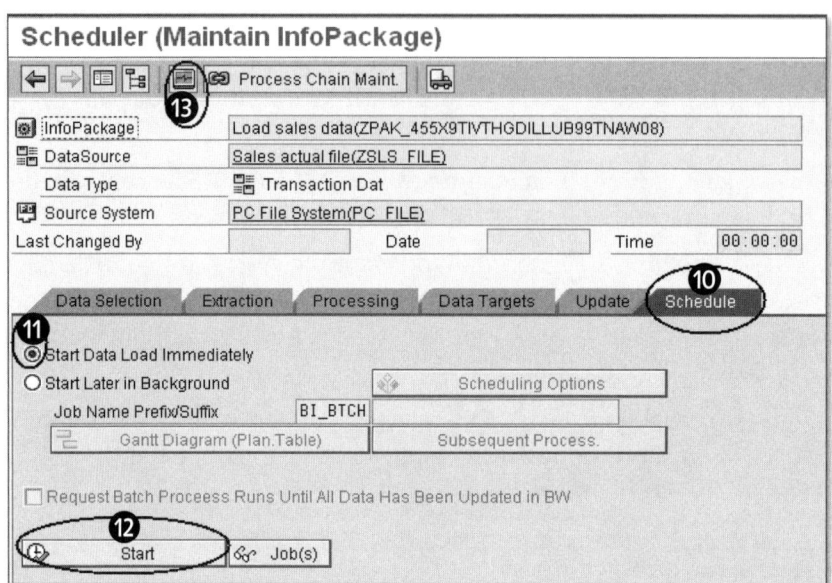

Figure 4.11 Execute InfoPackage

11. The Monitor – Administrator Workbench window in Figure 4.12 shows the status of the data extracted from the flat file DataSource into the PSA. If the data load is successful, the status of the load is displayed with a green traffic light.

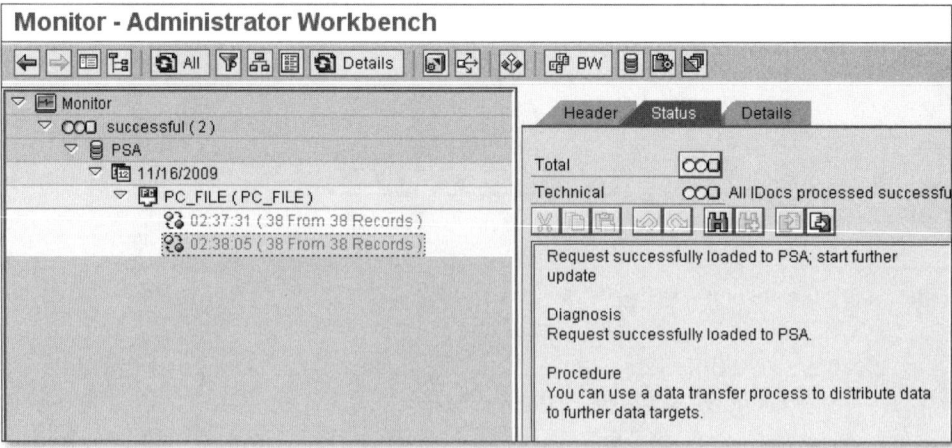

Figure 4.12 Monitor Status of InfoPackage

4.1.5 Load Data from the PSA to the Data Target

Now that we have loaded the data from the DataSource to the PSA, we are ready to schedule the load of data from the PSA to the Sales InfoCube using the data transfer process. The process applies the transformation when loading the data from the PSA to the data target.

1. Open the Data Warehousing Workbench using Transaction RSA1.
2. Select MODELING • INFOPROVIDER.
3. Locate the data transfer process created earlier under the Sales InfoCube, and double-click on it (Figure 4.13). The pane on the right displays the details of the DTP object.
4. Select the Execute tab and then click on the Execute button (Figure 4.13, ❶).
5. Click on the Monitor button to check the status of the load (Figure 4.13, ❷).

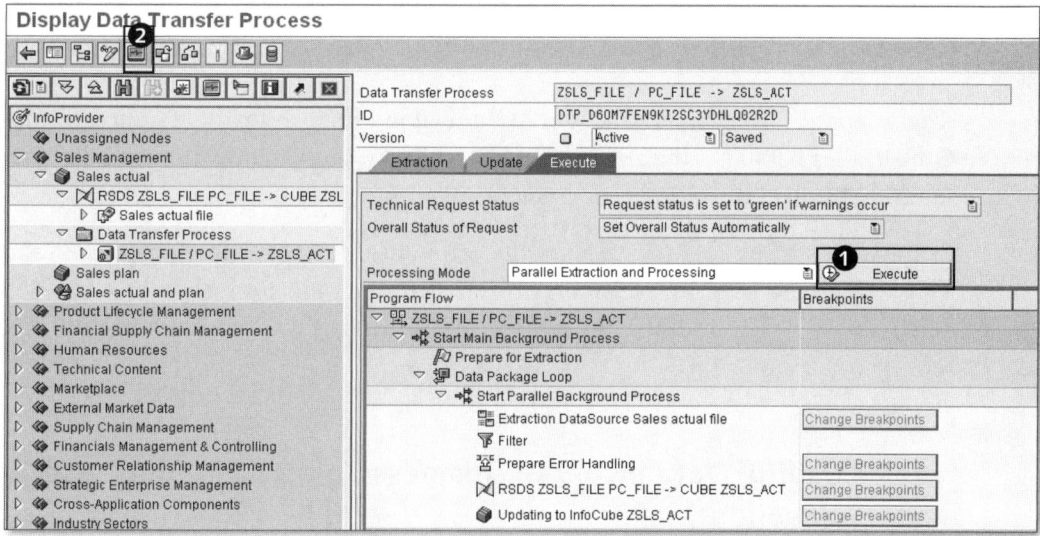

Figure 4.13 Execute Data Transfer Process

6. Return to the Data Warehousing Workbench by clicking on the back arrow button. Select the Manage option of the Sales InfoCube.
7. In the InfoProvider Administration window, select the Requests tab to see the requests that were loaded into the InfoCube.
8. Figure 4.14 shows the request loaded into the Sales InfoCube.

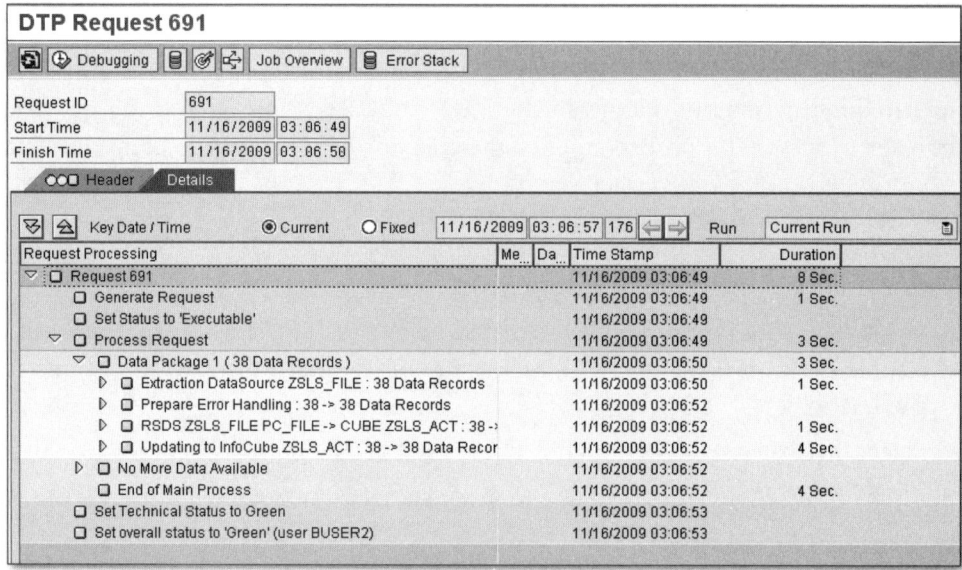

Figure 4.14 Monitor Data Transfer Execution Process

After reading this section, you should understand how to load data into an InfoCube using a flat file as the DataSource. Rich Bloom, Inc. can now use the sales data for 2009 in this InfoCube as the basis for planning in 2010.

In the next section, we will discuss the different options for loading master and transaction data into SAP BusinessObjects Planning and Consolidation. We will demonstrate different examples of how to load master and transaction data as it relates to our case study.

4.2 Loading Data into SAP BusinessObjects Planning and Consolidation

Two types of data exist in SAP BusinessObjects Planning and Consolidation: master data and transaction data. Master data is stored in a dimension, and transaction data is stored in an application. Although both master and transaction data can be manually entered into SAP BusinessObjects Planning and Consolidation, it may not be feasible to adopt this approach for large volumes of data. To automate the process of loading master and transaction data, SAP BusinessObjects Planning and Consolidation provides the following options:

- **Flat file**
  When this option is selected, master or transaction data can be loaded into a dimension or an application from a flat file. The flat file is the most flexible method to load data into a SAP BusinessObjects Planning and Consolidation application. In this case, the flat file is staged in the Application Folder area before it is loaded into the application.

- **InfoProvider in SAP NetWeaver BW**
  In the NetWeaver version of SAP BusinessObjects Planning and Consolidation, you can leverage the data in an InfoProvider in the SAP NetWeaver BW system. An InfoCube or DataStore object can be used as a DataSource to load data into an SAP BusinessObjects Planning and Consolidation application.

To begin, we will discuss the transformation and loading process in SAP BusinessObjects Planning and Consolidation. When loading data, extended features are available to transform and convert the data coming from a source file. The transformation definition serves to interpret the source of the data; it specifies the layout of the file, the different columns in the file, and how it should be loaded into the application. The conversion definitions are used when the source data should be interpreted differently before it is loaded into SAP BusinessObjects Planning and Consolidation.

4.2.1 Transformation and Conversion

The transformation file specifies the definitions used to interpret data coming from an external source before loading it into an SAP BusinessObjects Planning and Consolidation dimension or application. SAP BusinessObjects Planning and Consolidation provides the interface to create and maintain transformations in an Excel file. The transformation file includes three sections:

- Options
- Mapping
- Conversion

4 Loading, Scheduling, and Managing Data

Options

The Options section contains the options you want to use when interpreting the data from the external source. The options shown in Figure 4.1 can be specified in the Options section.

Option	Default Value	Description
AmountDecimal Point=<value>	Period	This option is used to specify the character to represent a decimal point. The default value to represent a decimal point is a "." (period).
		This is useful in countries where a value other than a period is used to denote a decimal point.
ConvertAmountDim=<dim_name>	Account	This option can be used to specify a dimension for amount calculations. The default value used for this option is the Account dimension.
		A formula should exist in the conversion file for the value specified here for the calculation to work.
CREDITPOSITIVE=YES|NO	YES	The default value for this option is "YES."
		If this option is set to "NO," all credit accounts (of type Owner's Equity and Income) will have negative sign.
FORMAT=DELIMITED/ FIXED/ VARIANT	There is no default value for this option	This is a required parameter.
		This specifies the format of the data in the input file.
DELIMITER	Comma	This option is applicable when the format option is set as "DELIMITED." This option is relevant when loading data directly from a file.
		Specify a value that matches the format of the input file.

Table 4.1 Options

Option	Default Value	Description
HEADER=YES/NO	YES	If the file includes a header row with column names, set the value of this option to "Yes."
		When a header is included, the column names in the header can be referred in the Mapping section of the transformation file to map the column names to the technical name of the target dimension of the application.
MAXREJECTCOUNT	Empty string	This option is used when validating the data from the external source and indicates the number of rejected records that can be tolerated before the validation process ends.
		An empty string represents 500 records.
		A value of "-1" indicates that processing should continue no matter how many rejected records are encountered.
		A positive value indicates the number of rejected records allowed before processing will end.
SUPPRESSCHARACTER	<TEXT>	This option will remove the value specified by <text> from the records.
		This is useful when certain pieces of text are not required when loading the data from an external source.
ROUNDAMOUNT = <INTEGER_VALUE>	Integer	This option rounds amount fields to the value specified in this option.
		The value for this option should be an integer number.
SKIP=<INTEGER_VALUE>	Integer	This option skips a given number of records from the top of the file as specified in this option.
		The value set should be an integer number.

Table 4.1 Options (Cont.)

Option	Default Value	Description
SKIPIF=<TEXT_VALUE1>|<TEXT_VALUE2>	Empty string	When text is specified for this option, a line will be skipped from the data file if it begins with the specified value. More than one text value can be specified when using this option, separated by the pipe delimiter.
SELECTION= <Dimension1_techname>,<Dimension1_value>;<Dimension2_techname>,<Dimension2_value>	Empty	This option is relevant only when extracting data from an InfoProvider in SAP NetWeaver BW. The dimension name is the name of the InfoObject used in the cube. The dimension value is the value for the InfoObject to be used when extracting the data. This option is useful when there is a need to selectively extract data from an InfoCube. Assuming a particular InfoCube includes two InfoObjects, Account and Material, the following selection will restrict the data into SAP BusinessObjects Planning and Consolidation for the "COGS" account and the "M1" material: SELECTION= 0Account, COGS; 0Material, M1.
FORMULA=		A Dimension can include a formula property to use in calculations. SAP BusinessObjects Planning and Consolidation provides functions that can be used in formulas. They are referred to as K2 functions. When functions are used in dimension formulas, the library file that includes these functions is specified here.

Table 4.1 Options (Cont.)

Option	Default Value	Description
CONVERT_INTERNAL=YES|NO		A conversion sheet can be used for each dimension to convert values coming from an external DataSource. The conversion sheet can have an internal value and an external value for a dimension member. The external value is the data coming from the external system. The internal value is how it would be stored in SAP BusinessObjects Planning and Consolidation. When this is set, the external value will be converted to the internal value when loading data. This option indicates whether the dimension member names should be compared with the internal names. This should be always set to "No."

Table 4.1 Options (Cont.)

The following is an example of the Options section in the transformation file.

```
*OPTIONS
FORMAT=DELIMITED
HEADER=YES
DELIMITER=','
AMOUNTDECIMALPOINT=
SKIP=0
SKIPIF=
VALIDATERECORDS=YES
MAXREJECTCOUNT=
ROUNDAMOUNT=
```

Mapping

The Mapping section specifies how external data is mapped to an SAP BusinessObjects Planning and Consolidation dimension or application. The mapping is defined by specifying a dimension to the left, and assigning it to the name of a column or the column number from an external file to the right. The name of the InfoObject is specified when data is extracted from an InfoProvider like an InfoCube.

The example that follows specifies the format to use when mapping a dimension to a column value from an external file. In this case, Entity is the name of the dimension in the application, and Company_Code is the column name for the data coming from the flat file. For this to work, the Options section should have the value for header parameter set to YES, and the first record in the file should have a column named "Company_Code."

```
Entity=Company_Code
```

The following is an example of a mapping when data is loaded from an InfoCube in SAP NetWeaver BW. In this case, Entity is the name of the dimension in the application, and 0COMP_CODE is the name of the InfoObject in the InfoCube.

```
Entity=0COMP_CODE
```

All dimensions in an SAP BusinessObjects Planning and Consolidation application should be mapped in the Mapping section of the transformation. It is possible that the flat file or data coming from an InfoProvider does not contain the values for all dimensions in an application. These dimensions should be assigned with the *NEWCOL(<text_value>) parameter in the Mapping section, where <text_value> is the value for the dimensions. This ensures a value is assigned to all of the dimensions during the load process.

Another example of a transformation that is often required when loading data from an external DataSource is to prefix the data coming from the source with a specific text string. For example, you may want to prefix all of the entity data coming from a flat file with the string "RB." This can be accomplished by specifying the following in the Mapping section:

```
Entity=*Str(RB) + Comp_Code
```

An example of a Mapping section is shown here:

```
*MAPPING
Account=Acct
DataSrc=New(FILELOAD)
Entity=*Str(RB) + Comp_Code
Category=Category
Time=Period
```

You have now seen a few examples of how to use the Mapping section. It supports more advanced features when assigning data. Table 4.2 describes the various mapping options.

Mapping Parameter	Description	Example
*COL(<NUMBER>)	This parameter can be set to assign the value of a dimension based on its position in the file. The <NUMBER> indicates the position of the column in the file.	Entity = *Col(4) This assigns the Entity dimension from the fourth column in the data file.
*COL(<NUMBER>, <POS1>: <POS2))	This parameter works the same way as the *COL(<NUMBER>) parameter and additionally provides a feature to select only a subset of the column value. <POS1> and <POS2> indicate the start and end positions within the column.	Entity = *Col(4,1,3). This assigns the Entity dimension from the fourth column in the data file. Only the value from the first three characters of this column will be used in the assignment.
*FCOL(A:B)	This parameter can be used to define multiple column values to a dimension.	Entity = *FCOL(2:5) In this example, the values from columns two to five in the data file will be assigned to the entity dimension.
*MVAL(A:B)	This parameter can be used when columns include consequence time periods in the file.	Time = *MVAL(5:9)
*NEWCOL(<TEXT_VALUE>)	In some cases, the data file may not contain the value for a dimension and it may be necessary to set a constant value for the dimension.	DataSrc=NEWCOL(FileLoad) The value for the DataSource dimension is set to the constant value "FileLoad" in this assignment.

Table 4.2 Mapping

Mapping Parameter	Description	Example
*str(<TEXT_VALUE>)	This parameter can be set when it is necessary to concatenate the data coming from a data file with other values. The text string can be used to prefix or suffix the column value.	Entity = *Str (BPC) + *Col(4) This assignment prefixes the string "BPC" to the data coming from the data file for the Entity dimension.
*pad	This parameter has similar functionality as the *str parameter, but it can be used to prefix the data coming from a file. *pad(SAP)	Entity = *pad(SAP)
*if(condition1(is true) action1;condition2 (is true) action2; action3)	If condition1 is true, action1 is performed. If condition1 is false, condition2 is executed. If condition2 is true, action2 is performed. If both condition1 and condition2 are not satisfied, action3 is performed.	Imagine that you have two columns, Source and Product, in the data file. You then want to apply the following rules when mapping the data: If you have the value "SAP" in the source field, you want to take the value of the product as it is coming from the file. If you have the value "LEGACY," you want to add two zeros to the product field. If neither "SAP" nor "LEGACY" is assigned to the Source field, you want to assign the value "Error" to the product field. This would look as follows: Product=*IF (source=*Str(SAP) then product;source=*Str(Legacy) then Str(00) + product;*str(ERR))

Table 4.2 Mapping (Cont.)

Conversion File

A *conversion file* associates the external values of data to equivalent internal values of dimension members in SAP BusinessObjects Planning and Consolidation. This is useful when data coming from a source does not match the data stored in SAP BusinessObjects Planning and Consolidation for a dimension. For example, the data coming from a file or an InfoProvider may not match how a dimension member value is stored in the SAP BusinessObjects Planning and Consolidation system, although they may mean the same. Using the conversion files, the external values can be mapped to the internal values.

When this conversion is required, you create a separate file or use a new spreadsheet for each dimension to define the conversions as necessary. The conversion sheet includes three columns: External, Internal, and Formula. The External column identifies how the data is coming from the external system. The Internal column defines how the data is stored in SAP BusinessObjects Planning and Consolidation. The Formula column can be added if any calculations are required. It is not mandatory to have a conversion file and is required only when there are conversions between external and internal values. For example, the following conversions can be defined for the Time dimension data:

- 200801 can be defined as the External column
- 2008.JAN can be defined as the corresponding Internal column

When data is loaded into an application that includes this conversion, any data that includes 200801 for the Time dimension from an external data source will be interpreted as 2008.JAN in SAP BusinessObjects Planning and Consolidation. You can also use the asterisk (*) and question mark (?) as wildcards in the External or Internal columns. An asterisk (*) refers to any string of characters, whereas a question mark (?) refers to a single character. You can skip a record containing an external value by setting the internal value as *SKIP. The Formula column can be used to represent any calculations. For example, you can have a formula to increase the revenue member of the Account dimension by 10%. This formula would read *value* × *1.10*. After the transformation and conversion files are created, the data can be loaded into the SAP BusinessObjects Planning and Consolidation dimension or application.

The actual process of loading data into SAP BusinessObjects Planning and Consolidation is performed using a data manager package. We will discuss this next.

4.2.2 Data Manager Packages

Data manager packages in SAP BusinessObjects Planning and Consolidation support a variety of tasks related to loading and maintaining data in a dimension or application. When a data manager package is executed, it in turn executes a corresponding process chain in SAP NetWeaver BW. A *process chain* automates the process of loading data in SAP NetWeaver BW. With the introduction of SAP BusinessObjects Planning and Consolidation for NetWeaver, new process types have been introduced in process chains to enable loading and managing the data for the SAP BusinessObjects Planning and Consolidation environment. Each data manager package is associated to a process chain in the SAP NetWeaver BW system. Process chains automate the process of loading and managing data in the SAP NetWeaver BW system.

There are four different types of data manager packages available to perform different tasks in SAP BusinessObjects Planning and Consolidation.

- **Data manager packages**
  The packages under this type are used for loading dimension and application data from flat files and InfoProviders in SAP NetWeaver BW.

- **Financial process packages**
  Financial process packages can be used for executing specific functions regarding planning and consolidation applications. They can be used for executing tasks related to allocation, currency translation, and consolidation functions.

- **System administration packages**
  These packages are related to management of the data. An example of a package under this type is archiving data.

- **Miscellaneous packages**
  Miscellaneous packages serve more of a utility value for SAP BusinessObjects Planning and Consolidation applications. The Import File and Send Mail data manager packages fall under this type and are useful for importing a file into SAP BusinessObjects Planning and Consolidation and then sending an e-mail to users. For this to work, e-mail services should be configured in SAP BusinessObjects Planning and Consolidation.

> **Note**
>
> Tables 4.3, 4.4, 4.5, and 4.6 list the common data manager packages that are used in SAP BusinessObjects Planning and Consolidation. If you do not see a data manager package you would like to use listed in one of these tables, you can easily create a new data manager package in SAP BusinessObjects Planning and Consolidation and associate it to a process chain that will perform a specific function.

The packages and process chains outlined in Tables 4.3, 4.4, 4.5, and 4.6 are delivered with the standard data manager packages.

Data Manager Package	Description	Process Chain
Import master data	This package is used for loading data into an SAP BusinessObjects Planning and Consolidation dimension.	/CPMB/IMPORT_MASTER
Import master data description	This package is used to load text data into a dimension.	/CPMB/IMPORT_DESCRIPT
Import transaction data	This package is used for loading transaction data using a flat file. The transaction file should be staged in the Application folder before it can be used in the data manager package. A transformation file is necessary to load transaction data in SAP BusinessObjects Planning and Consolidation for NetWeaver. The transformation file's reference in the transformation file should be available in the respective folder before the package is executed.	/CPMB/IMPORT
Import transaction data from InfoProvider	This package is used to load data from InfoProviders. The data can be extracted from different types of InfoProviders—InfoCube, DataStore objects, and MultiProviders.	/CPMB/LOAD_INFOPROVIDER

Table 4.3 Data Manager Packages

Data Manager Package	Description	Process Chain
Move transaction data	This package enables you to move data within the same application. A selection screen displays during the execution of the package. The following is the sequence of steps when this package is run: The data selected for the destination is removed from the corresponding InfoProvider. The data from the source is moved based on the selection. The data is deleted from the source for the selected data.	/CPMB/MOVE
Clear transaction data in InfoCube	This package enables you to clear or delete data in an SAP BusinessObjects Planning and Consolidation application. A selection screen displays during the execution of the package. On the selection screen, you must select a value for at least one dimension.	/CPMB/CLEAR
Copy transaction data	This package is used when you must copy transaction data within the same application. A selection screen displays during the execution of the package. This is very useful when you want to create a baseline of plan data for the next year. This can be done by copying the current year's actual data to next year's plan data. For example, the actual sales data for 2009 can be used as the baseline data for planning 2010 sales. This can be achieved using this package.	/CPMB/COPY
Append transaction data	When executing this package, the existing data is not affected. The data is appended to the existing application. This is available only when using a flat file as the data source.	/CPMB/APPEND

Table 4.3 Data Manager Packages (Cont.)

Financial Process Package	Description	Process Chain
Allocation	This package is used for executing the allocation logic.	/CPMB/ALLOCATION
FX restatement	This package runs the currency translation logic.	/CPMB/FX_RESTATMENT
IC elimination	This package is used to eliminate the intercompany transactions of the business. This is used primarily for the consolidation application and if there are transactions within the companies in the same group.	/CPMB/IC_ELIMINATION
IC booking	This package runs the IC booking logic	/CPMB/ICDATA
Opening balances	This package runs the opening balances logic to convert the ending period balances for a given period as the opening period balances for the subsequent period. This is relevant for balance sheet accounts when the closing balances for a period are carried forward as the opening balance of the subsequent period.	/CPMB/OPENING_BALANCES
Calculate ownership logic	This package runs the calculate ownership logic. This is applicable for consolidation applications.	/CPMB/OWNERSHIPCALC
Consolidation	This package is used for running the logic for performing financial consolidation when a business is composed of several independent entities.	/CPMB/LEGAL_CONSOLIDATION
Run CalcAccount	This package runs the CalcAccount logic	/CPMB/RUNCALCACCOUNT
Clear journal table	This package clears the journal table.	/CPMB/CLEAR_JOURNALS
Export journal table	This package export the journal table to an output file.	/CPMB/EXPORT_JOURNAL
Restore journal table	This package restores the journal table from a file.	/CPMB/RESTORE_JOURNALS

Table 4.4 Financial Processes Packages

System Administrative Package	Description	Process Chain
Validate logic file	This package validates a logic file for syntax.	/CPMB/ADMINTASK_VALIDATE
Validate transformation file	This package validates a transformation file.	/CPMB/VALIDATE_TRANSFORM
Validation	This package executes the validation rules as defined in the business rules for an application.	/CPMB/VALIDATIONS
Archive audit activity	When audit activity is enabled, a lot of data may be generated. This data has to be archived periodically. This package archives audit activity.	/CPMB/ARCHIVE_ACTIVITY
Archive audit data	This package archives application data.	/CPMB/ARCHIVE_DAT0041
Clear comments	This package clears comments from the comments table.	/CPMB/CLEARCOMMENTS
Light optimize	This package runs the light optimize process for an application. This process closes the open request, creates indexes, and updates database statistics. When the light optimize package is run from the Admin Console, it triggers a job to immediately execute this process chain.	/CPMB/LIGHT_OPTIMIZE
Full optimize	This works like the light optimize process. In addition, the data model of the InfoCube is also optimized.	/CPMB/FULL_OPTIMIZE

Table 4.5 System Administrative Packages

Miscellaneous Package	Description	Process Chain
Import and send mail	This package imports a file and e-mails the result to a list of users.	/CPMB/IMPORT_A_SEND_EMAIL
Import using FTP	This package imports a file into the current application.	/CPMB/IMPORT_USING_FTP

Table 4.6 Miscellaneous Packages

4.2.3 Process Chains

Process chains are used to automate the process of extracting, transforming, and loading data and provide different process types for managing data within the SAP NetWeaver BW and the SAP BusinessObjects Planning and Consolidation systems. To enable common tasks to be executed in SAP BusinessObjects Planning and Consolidation, SAP provides several standard process chains as out of the box functionality, ready to be used. The process chains provided by SAP have the prefix /CPMB and can also be enabled as Business Content. These process chains, created in SAP NetWeaver BW, are wrapped into a data management package in SAP BusinessObjects Planning and Consolidation.

The process chains are created and maintained using Transaction RSPC in the SAP NetWeaver BW system. Subsequently, data management packages are created in SAP BusinessObjects Planning and Consolidation and associated to the process chains created in SAP NetWeaver BW. Tables 4.3, 4.4, 4.5, and 4.6 list the process chains associated with data management packages.

As mentioned, process chains used for SAP BusinessObjects Planning and Consolidation applications are associated with the /CPMB namespace. You can also create custom process chains based on standard process chains, and adapt them to your requirements. Several process types are specifically provided for use in SAP BusinessObjects Planning and Consolidation applications.

Now that we have discussed transformation, conversion files, data management packages, and process chains, we will look into the process of loading data into a dimension using a flat file.

4.2.4 Loading Data from a Flat File into a Dimension

Rich Bloom, Inc. stores customer data, including the customer hierarchy, in a flat file. This data must be loaded from the flat file into the customer dimension. Before you load transaction data into an application, you need to load master data into a dimension. If a master data record (dimension member) is not available in a dimension when you load transaction data to an application, the transaction data load will fail.

We will now load the customer data for Rich Bloom, Inc. from a flat file into the RB_CUSTOMER dimension. Proceed as follows:

1. Log into the SAP BusinessObjects Planning and Consolidation Office Client, select the application set "ZRB_GM_PLAN," and select the application "ZRB_SALES_CMB."

2. The first step in the process is uploading the flat file to the Data Files folder of the application set. From the eData menu option, select the Data Upload option (Figure 4.15, ❶ and ❷). This opens the Data Manager – Upload dialog box.

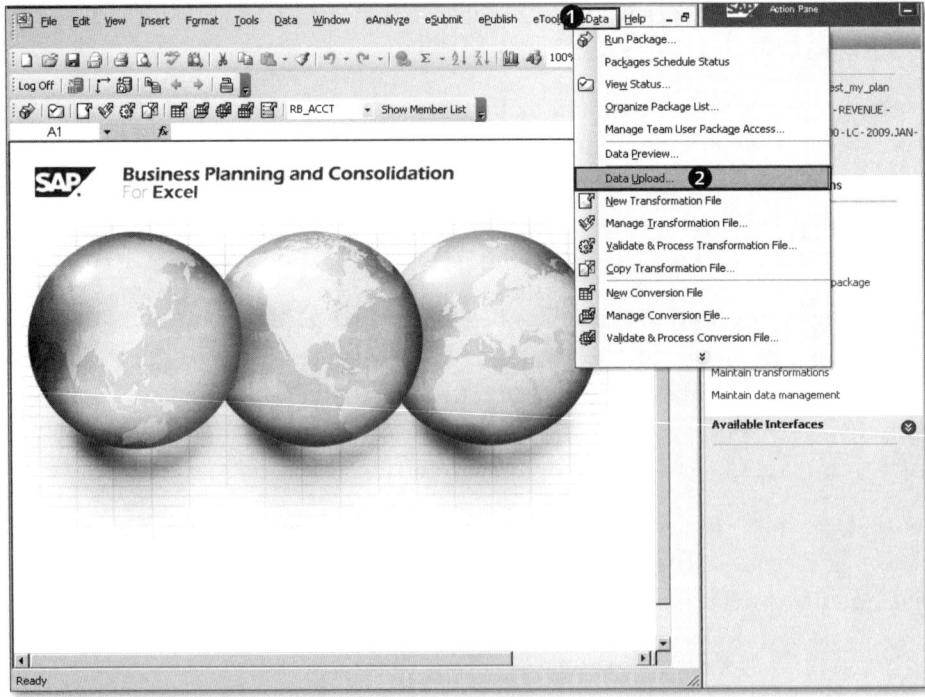

Figure 4.15 Loading Data from a Flat File into a Dimension—Part A

3. In the Data Manager – Upload dialog box, select the folder icon to locate the file (Figure 4.16, ❸ and ❹).

4. Select the folder under Destination File to store the file in SAP BusinessObjects Planning and Consolidation. This opens the Save dialog box. Select the destination file to store the file (Figure 4.16, ❺, ❻, and ❼). The destination file is in the Data Files folder under the application set of the SAP BusinessObjects Planning and Consolidation server.

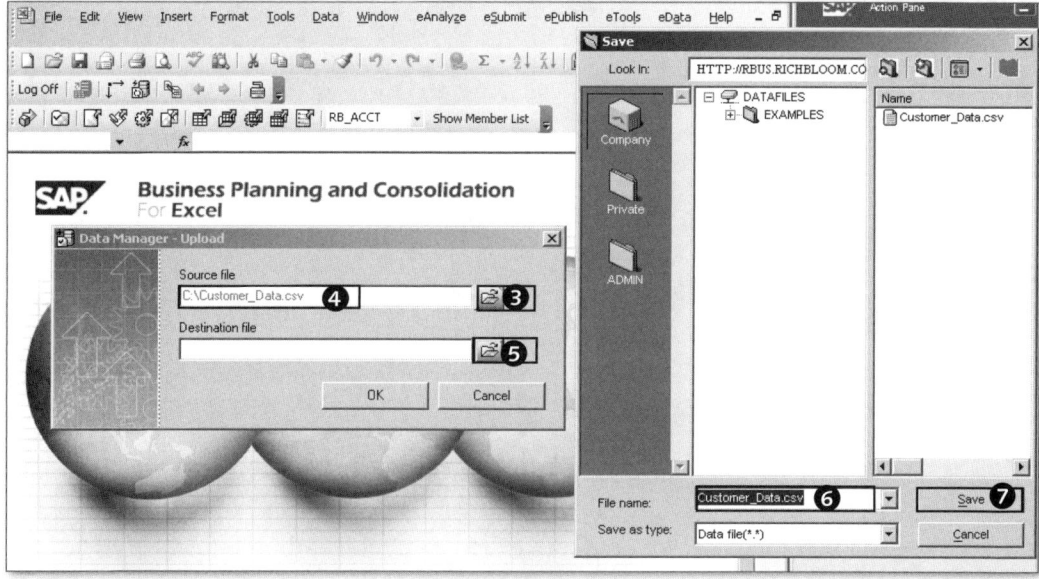

Figure 4.16 Loading Data from a Flat File into a Dimension — Part B

5. After the destination file is selected, click on OK (Figure 4.17, ❽).

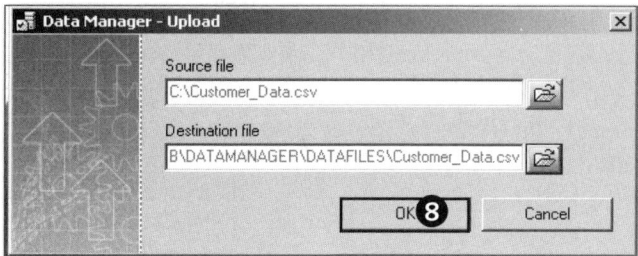

Figure 4.17 Loading Data from a Flat File into a Dimension — Part C

4 | Loading, Scheduling, and Managing Data

6. You are now ready to create a transformation file to define the structure of the file you will use to load data into the Customer dimension. From the eData menu option, select the New Transformation File option (Figure 4.18, ❾).

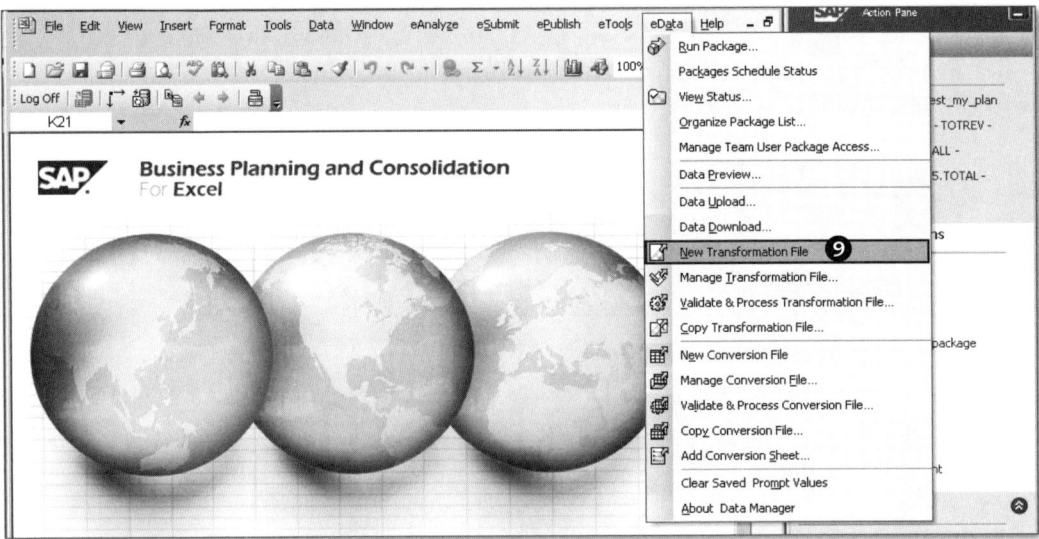

Figure 4.18 Loading Data from a Flat File into a Dimension—Part D

7. The flat file we are using is a comma-delimited file and contains the customer ID, description, and hierarchy for the customer data. The mapping is defined in the Mapping section. No data conversion is involved; therefore, we will not use the Conversion section. The transformation file is defined as shown in Figure 4.19, ❿. From the eData menu option, select the Validate & Process Transformation File option to validate and save the transformation file. This opens the Validate & Process Transformation dialog box.

8. In the Validate & Process Transformation dialog box, select the Data Type for which this transformation file should be used (Figure 4.20, ⓫), the technical name of the dimension into which the data should be loaded (Figure 4.20, ⓬), and the Data File that should be used as the source for this load (Figure 4.20, ⓭). Click on Save (Figure 4.20, ⓮).

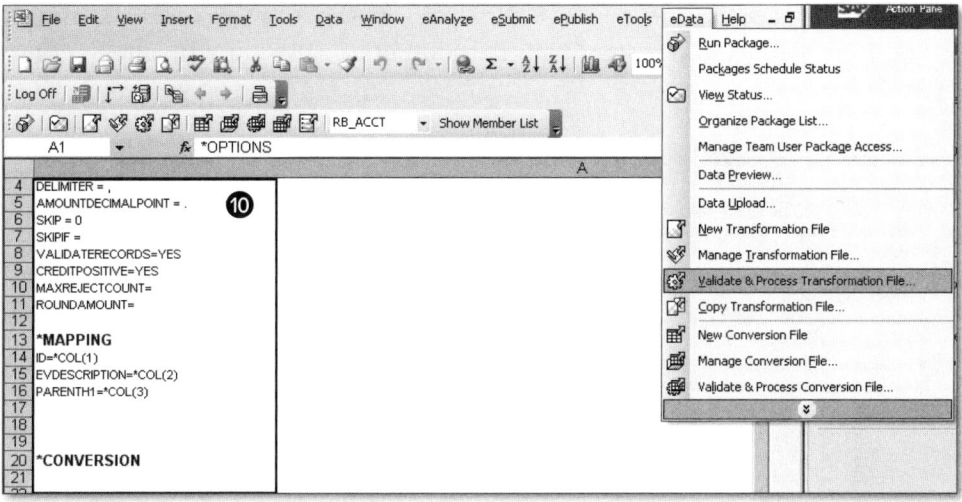

Figure 4.19 Loading Data from a Flat File into a Dimension — Part E

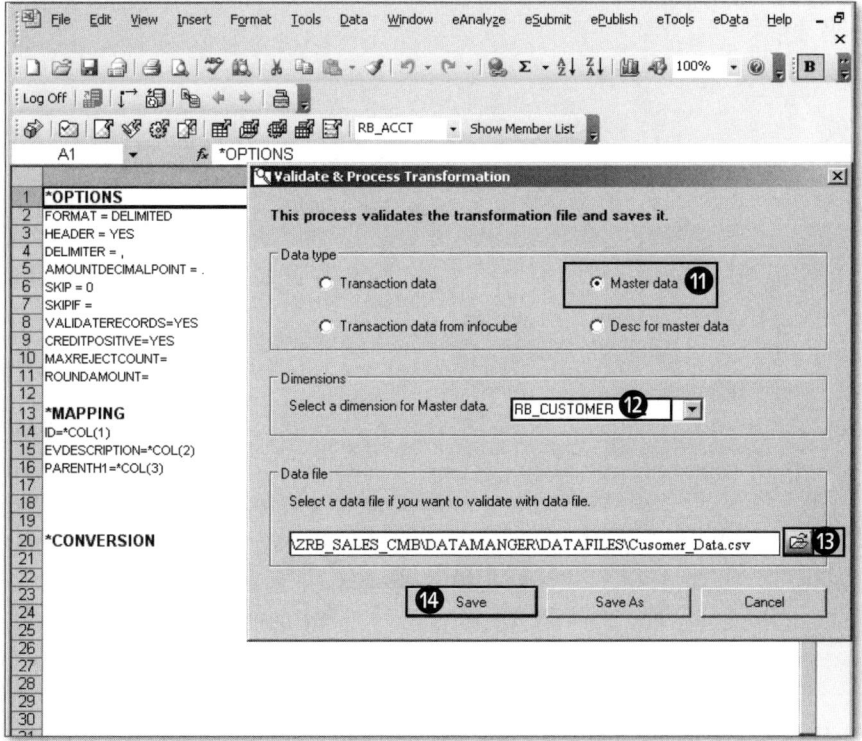

Figure 4.20 Loading Data from a Flat File into a Dimension — Part F

9. The system validates the transformation file with the structure of the dimension and the data file. The system will then output a log of the validation (Figure 4.21).

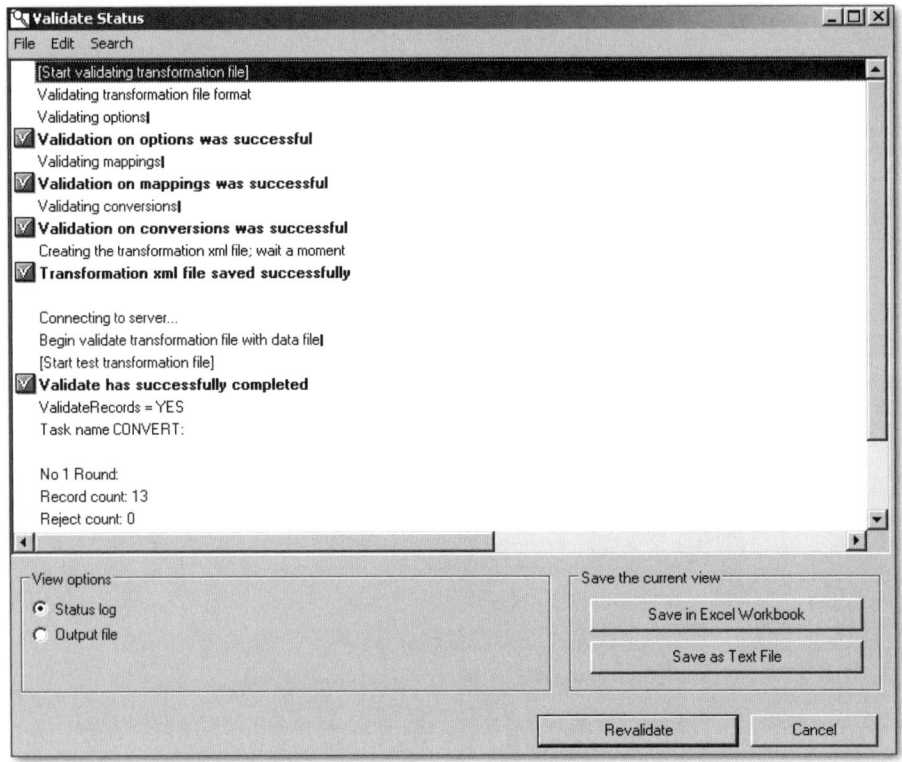

Figure 4.21 Loading Data from a Flat File into a Dimension—Part G

10. You are now ready to execute the data manager package to load the master data for customers. From the eData menu option, select the Run Package option to run a data manager package. In the dialog box that lists the data manager packages, select the Data Management group and execute the ImportMasterData data management package (Figure 4.22, ❺). Then, click on Run. This opens the Data Manager Run Package dialog box.

11. In the Data Manager Run Package dialog box, select the import file that should be loaded (Figure 4.23, ❻). You can also preview the data file you will load (Figure 4.23, ❼). Then, select the transformation file created in the earlier steps and enter the dimension name as "RB_CUSTOMER" for the Customer dimension (Figure 4.23, ❽ and ❾). Select the Run Now option, and click on

Finish (Figure 4.23, ⓴ and ㉑). Alternatively, if you want this to be loaded at a different time, you can select the Schedule option instead of running the package now.

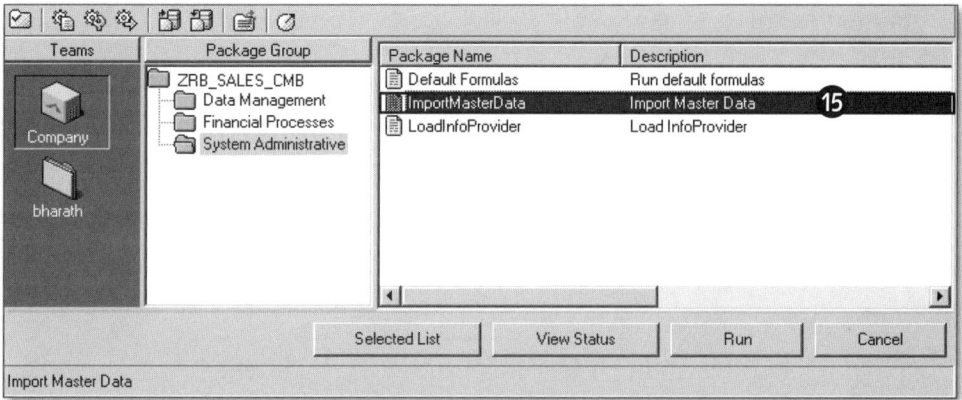

Figure 4.22 Loading Data from a Flat File into a Dimension—Part H

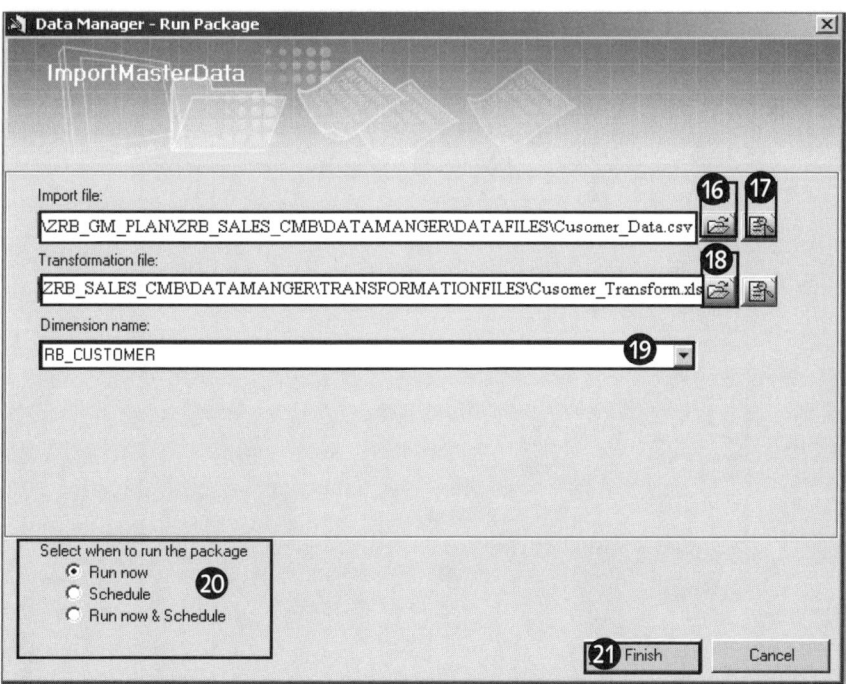

Figure 4.23 Loading Data from a Flat File into a Dimension—Part I

12. The job is scheduled as a background job, and the status of the job is refreshed every n seconds if the Refresh Status Every checkbox is checked (Figure 4.24). The status is displayed as InProgress, Completed, or Error. The log for the package can be displayed by selecting the package and clicking on the Detail button (Figure 4.24, ㉒).

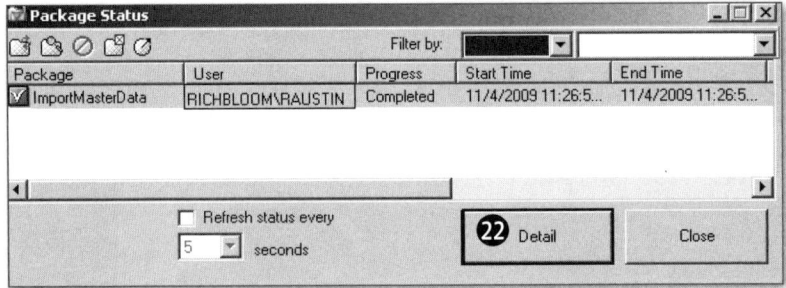

Figure 4.24 Loading Data from a Flat File into a Dimension—Part J

13. The detailed log of the package results is shown in Figure 4.25.

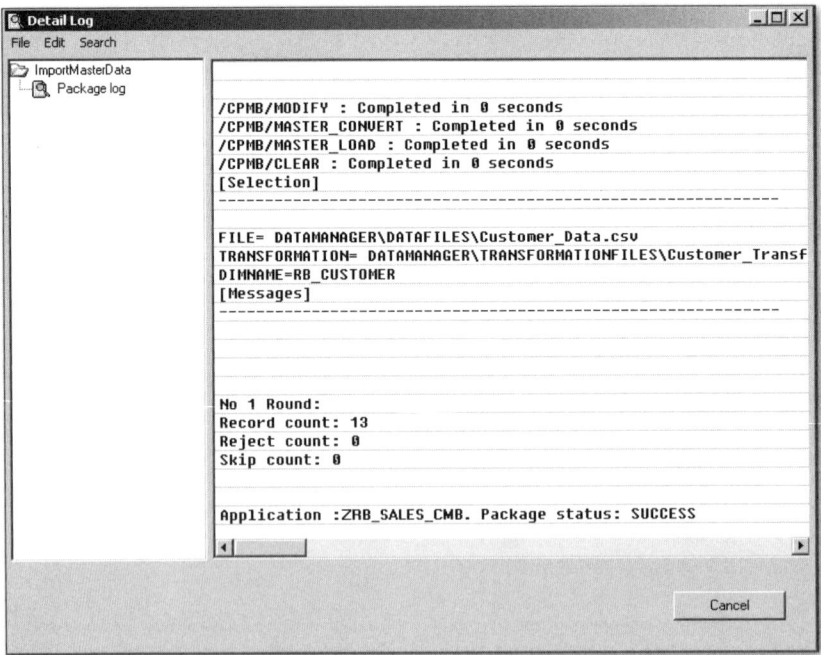

Figure 4.25 Loading Data from a Flat File into a Dimension—Part K

In this example, you have seen how to load master data from a flat file into a Customer dimension. In the next section, we will load the actual sales and cost data that is in the ZSLS_ACT InfoCube in SAP NetWeaver BW into the planning application in SAP BusinessObjects Planning and Consolidation.

4.2.5 Loading Data from an InfoCube into an SAP BusinessObjects Planning and Consolidation Application

Rich Bloom, Inc. stores its sales and cost data in the ZSLS_ACT InfoCube in SAP NetWeaver BW. This data needs to be loaded into the ZRB_SALES_CMB planning application in SAP BusinessObjects Planning and Consolidation. Follow these steps:

1. Log into the Office Client, select the ZRB_GM_PLAN application set, and select the ZRB_SALES_CMB application.

2. Create a transformation to define the structure of the data coming from the InfoCube and to map the InfoObjects in the InfoCube to the dimensions in the application. Pull the actual sales and cost data from the ZSLS_ACT InfoCube.

3. This InfoCube contains sales and cost data for various time periods. We want to extract the data only for the calendar year 2009. This requires us to specify an option in the transformation file to restrict the data to only that of 2009. The criteria to select the data only for this period can be specified in the Options section. The SELECT option is available for this purpose and can be used only when extracting data from an InfoCube.

4. In the Mapping section, map the dimension names in the application to the corresponding technical names of the InfoObjects in the InfoCube. The data in the Sales InfoCube does not include the data for the Category dimension. All of the dimensions in an SAP BusinessObjects Planning and Consolidation application must be mapped to an InfoObject or field from an external source when loading the data. When a value for a dimension is not supplied by the external data source, you can use the keyword *NEWCOL(<value>) to specify a value for the dimension. The <value> represents a member ID for the dimension. Map the Category dimension to the ACTUAL member ID value in the Mapping section. Similarly, set the Reporting Currency dimension to "LC" (local currency) for all of the data when loading data from the Sales InfoCube. Create a new transformation file with the definitions shown in Figure 4.26, ❶.

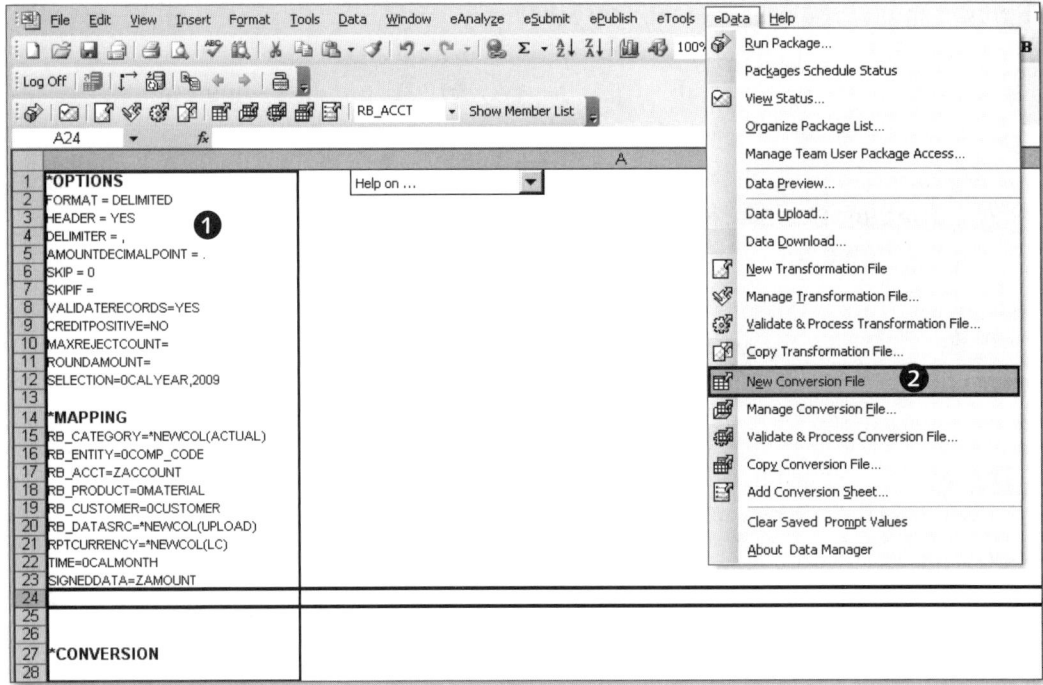

Figure 4.26 Loading Data from an InfoCube into an Application—Part A

5. The data for calendar month is in the YYYYMM format in SAP NetWeaver BW. This has to be converted into an equivalent SAP BusinessObjects Planning and Consolidation format for the Time dimension; therefore, you must define a mapping file for this conversion. From the eData menu option, select the New Conversion File option to create a new conversion file (Figure 4.26, ❷).

6. The conversion file contains three columns: External, Internal, and Formula. In the External column, specify the value coming from the external source. In the Internal column, specify the value as it is stored in SAP BusinessObjects Planning and Consolidation. The formula can be used for any calculations on amount values. Use the conversion file for the Time dimension, as shown in Figure 4.27, ❸. From the eData menu option, select Validate & Save the Conversion File to validate and save the conversion file (Figure 4.27, ❹).

7. The Save dialog box displays. Enter the file name as "RB_TIME" and click on Save (Figure 4.28, ❺ and ❻) for the conversion file. The conversion file is saved as an Excel file under the CONVERSIONFILES folder for the application set. The conversion file is validated with a message indicating that it was created successfully.

4.2 Loading Data into SAP BusinessObjects Planning and Consolidation

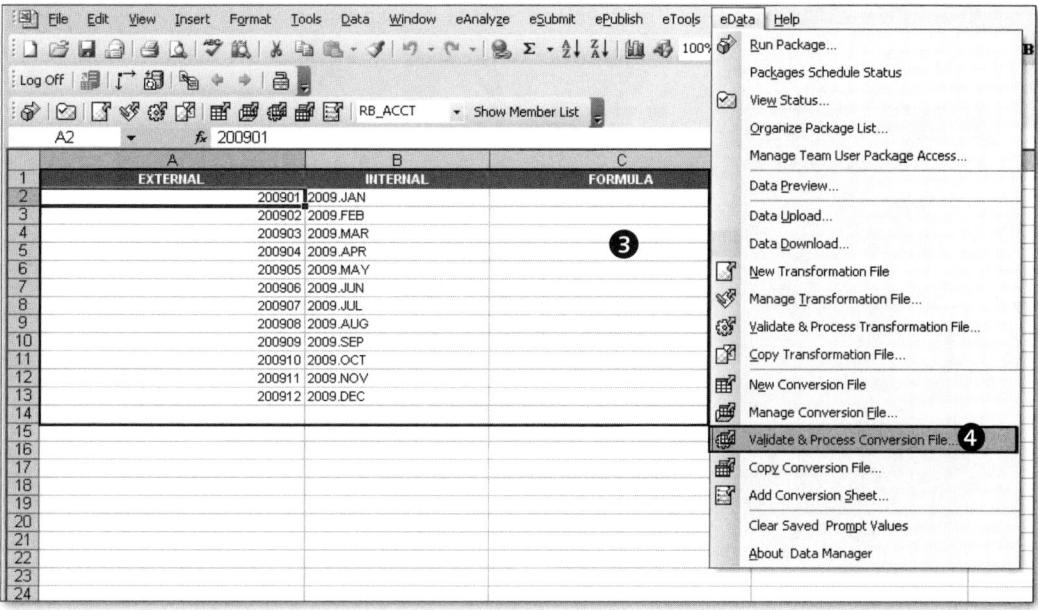

Figure 4.27 Loading Data from an InfoCube into an Application—Part B

Figure 4.28 Loading Data from an InfoCube into an Application—Part C

8. In the Conversion section, map the Time dimension to the conversion file created in the previous step, as shown in Figure 4.29, ❼.

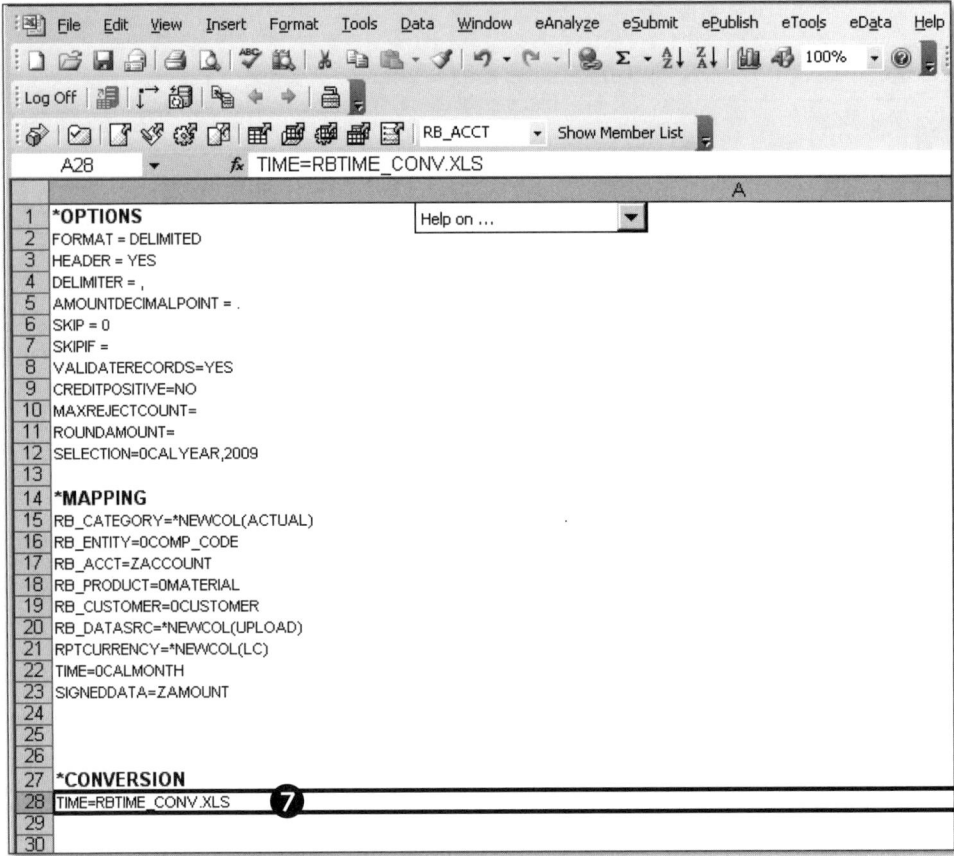

Figure 4.29 Loading Data from an InfoCube into an Application — Part D

9. Now, save the new transformation file you created in the previous step. You can optionally validate the transformation file for the options, mappings, and conversions specified in the transformation file during this process. You can see the log output of the validation in Figure 4.30.

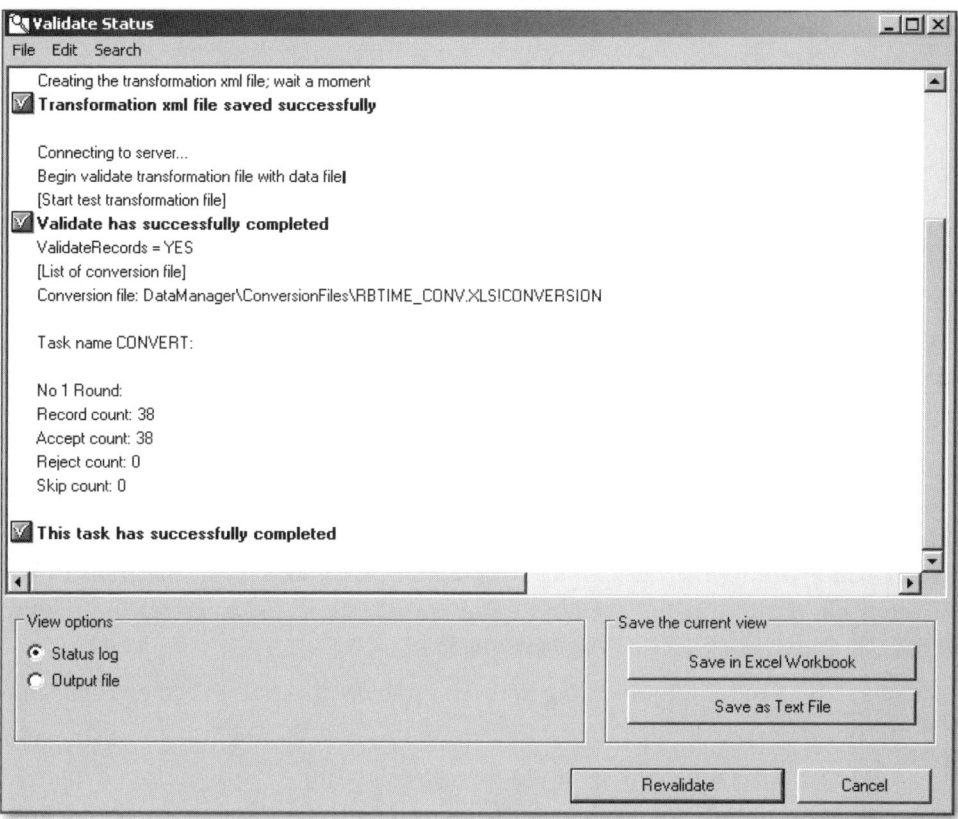

Figure 4.30 Loading Data from an InfoCube into an Application — Part E

10. You are now ready to execute the package to load the data from the ZSLS_ACT InfoCube into the SAP BusinessObjects Planning and Consolidation application. Select the LoadInfoProvider data manager package under the System Administrative group, and click on Run (Figure 4.31). This will open the Data Manager – Run Package dialog box.

4 | Loading, Scheduling, and Managing Data

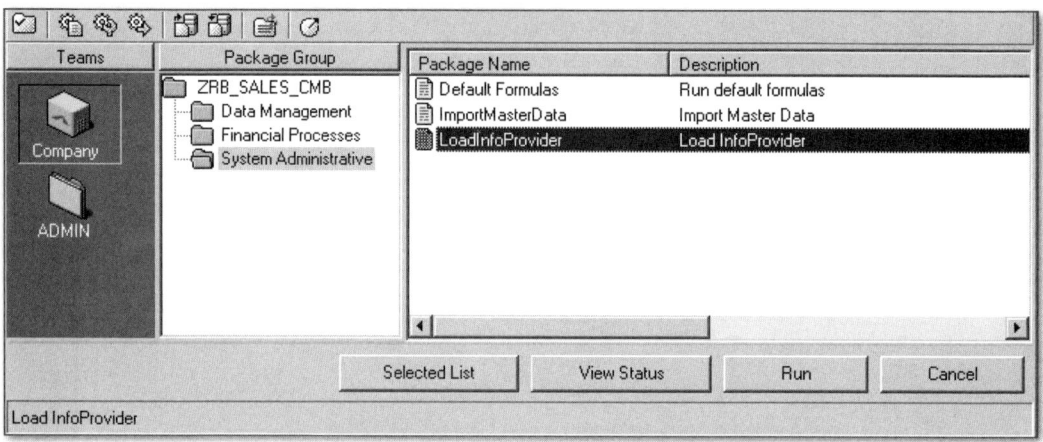

Figure 4.31 Loading Data from an InfoCube into an Application—Part F

11. In the Data Manager – Run Package dialog box, enter "ZSLS_ACT" as the InfoProvider from which to extract data (Figure 4.32, ❽). Select the transformation file created in the earlier step to use as the transformation file (Figure 4.32, ❾) when extracting data for this load.

12. Select the method of importing data from the database. Two options available for this:

    ▸ Merge: This option does not delete any data in the application. When an InfoCube sends data and the corresponding record exists in the application, the record coming from the InfoCube updates the existing data in the SAP BusinessObjects Planning and Consolidation application. If the record does not exist in the application, the record is added as a new record.

    ▸ Replace: When the Replace option is selected, the system deletes the records from the SAP BusinessObjects Planning and Consolidation application based on the values of the Category, Entity, and Time dimensions in the incoming records. All incoming data from the source for these values will be first deleted from the application and then replaced with the values coming from the source.

For our example, select Replace & Clear Data Values (Figure 4.32, ❿). The default logic can be executed when a data management package is run. We have not included any default logic for our application and choosing Yes or No should

170

not matter. However, as good practice, select Yes (Figure 4.32, ⓫). Click on Next to proceed to the next step (Figure 4.32, ⓬).

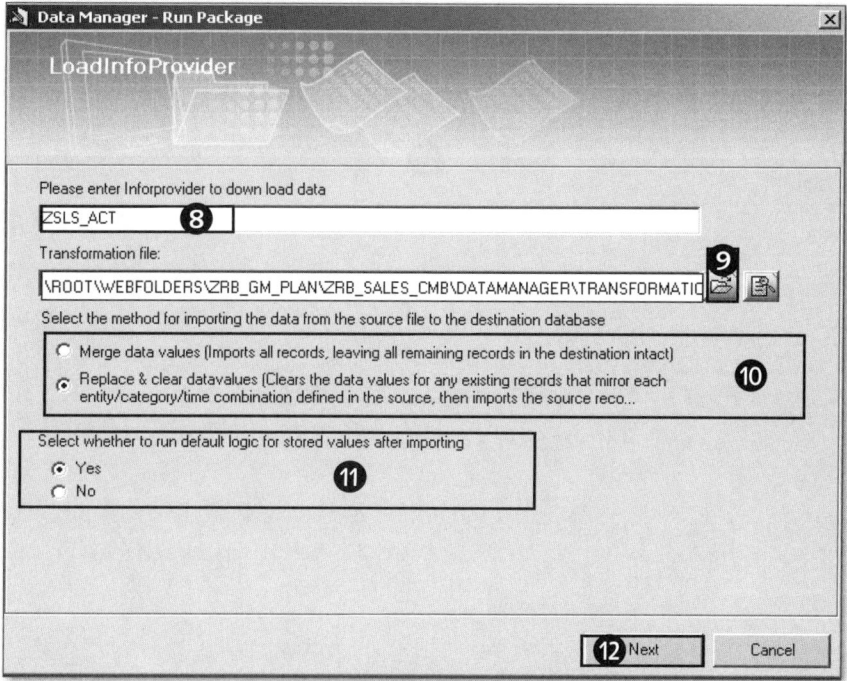

Figure 4.32 Loading Data from an InfoCube into an Application—Part G

> **Note**
> The name of the InfoCube you enter to use as the source data of the load is case-sensitive.

13. The work status lets you control updates to the data in an application. We will discuss work status in detail in Chapter 9. For this example, select Yes, Check for Work Status Settings Before Importing so that you do not allow any updates if the work status for the updated data region does not allow for updates (Figure 4.33, ⓭). Select the Run Now option to immediately execute the package and click on Finish (Figure 4.33, ⓮ and ⓯).

171

4 | Loading, Scheduling, and Managing Data

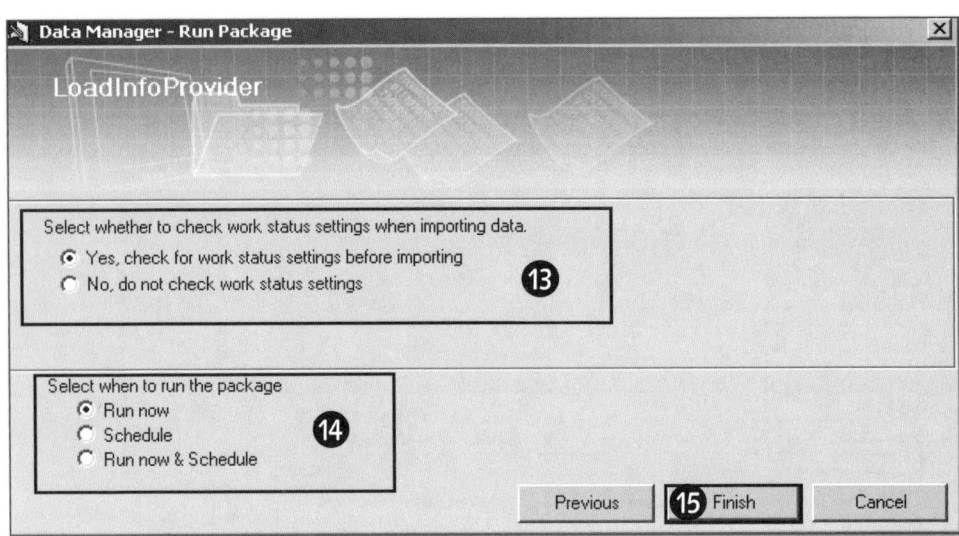

Figure 4.33 Loading Data from an InfoCube into an Application—Part H

14. The Package Status dialog box is displayed. After the package has run successfully, click on the Detail button to display the log for the package (see Figure 4.34).

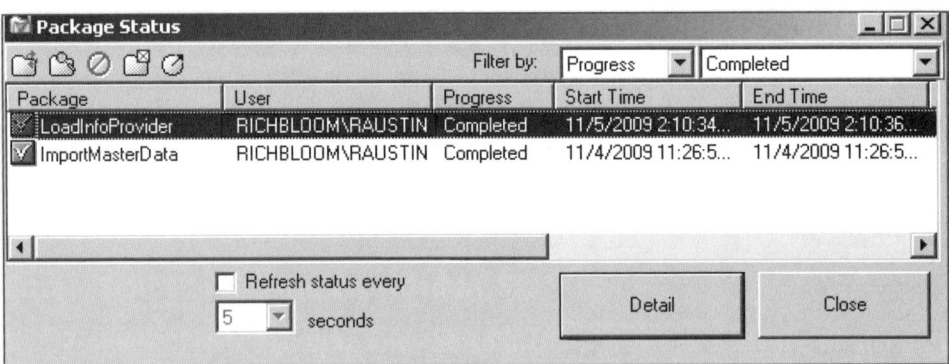

Figure 4.34 Loading Data from an InfoCube into an Application—Part I

15. The log displayed in Figure 4.35 displays the details of the package executed, along with the records processed.

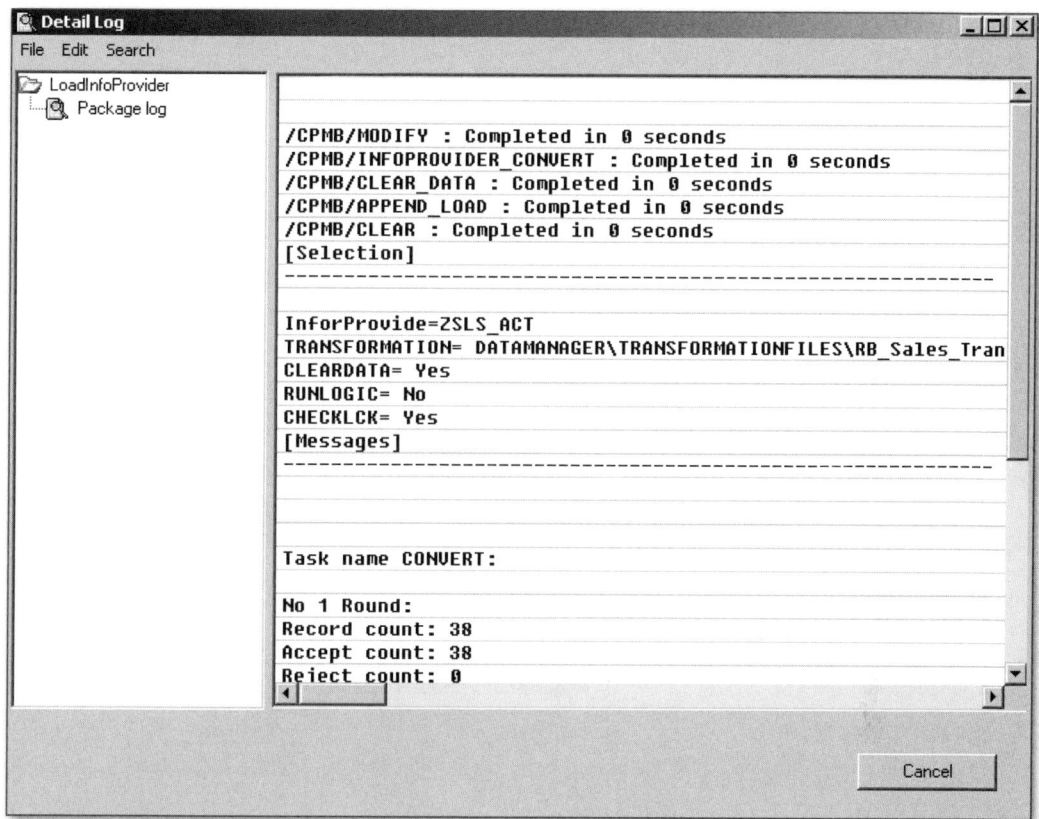

Figure 4.35 Loading Data from an InfoCube into an Application—Part J

In this example, you have seen how to load transaction data from an InfoProvider into an application in SAP BusinessObjects Planning and Consolidation. We loaded the actual sales data for 2009 from the Actual Sales InfoCube in SAP NetWeaver BW into the planning application in SAP BusinessObjects Planning and Consolidation. In the next section, we will create baseline plan data for 2010 by copying the sales and cost data for 2009 as the plan data for 2010.

4   Loading, Scheduling, and Managing Data

4.3   Copying Data Inside an SAP BusinessObjects Planning and Consolidation Application

To copy data inside an SAP BusinessObjects Planning and Consolidation application, follow these steps:

1. Log into the Office Client, select the ZRB_GM_PLAN application set, and select the ZRB_SALES_CMB application.

2. You are now ready to copy the actual sales and cost data for 2009 as the plan data for 2010. From the eData menu option, select the Run Package option. In the dialog box that lists the data manager packages, select the Data Management group, select the Copy data management package, and click on Run (Figure 4.36, ❶ and ❷). This opens the Data Manager Run Package dialog box.

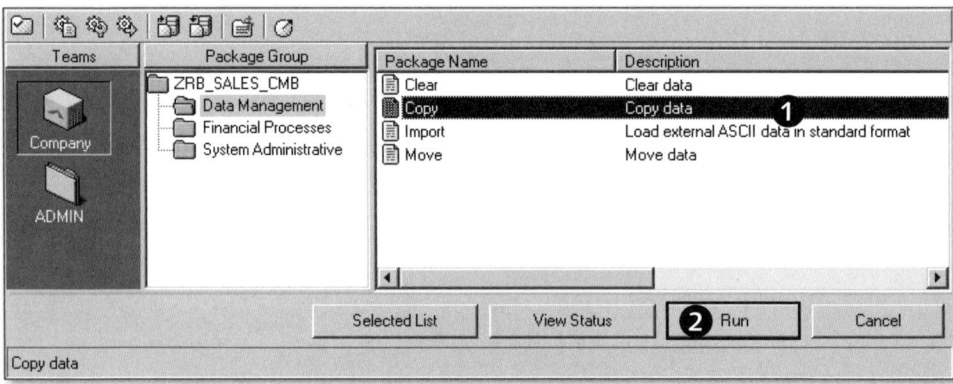

Figure 4.36   Copying Data inside an Application—Part A

3. Next, select the options to replace and clear data values, run the default logic, and check the work status before data is imported (Figure 4.37). Then, click on the Next button.

4. Our objective is to copy the data from the Actual Category for 2009 to the Plan Category for 2010. Under Source dimensions, click on the folder icon for RB_CATEGORY to select a member value for the Category dimension (Figure 4.38, ❸). This opens a dialog box to select values.

174

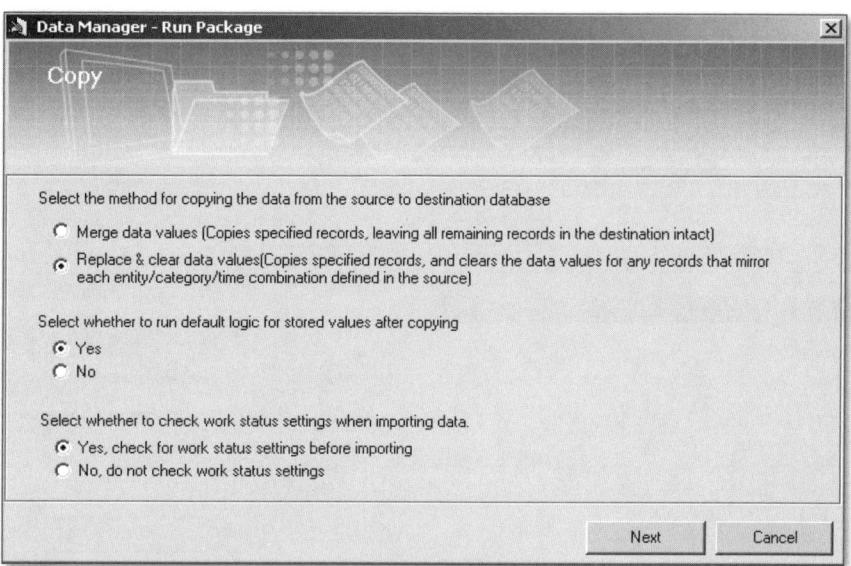

Figure 4.37 Copying Data inside an Application—Part B

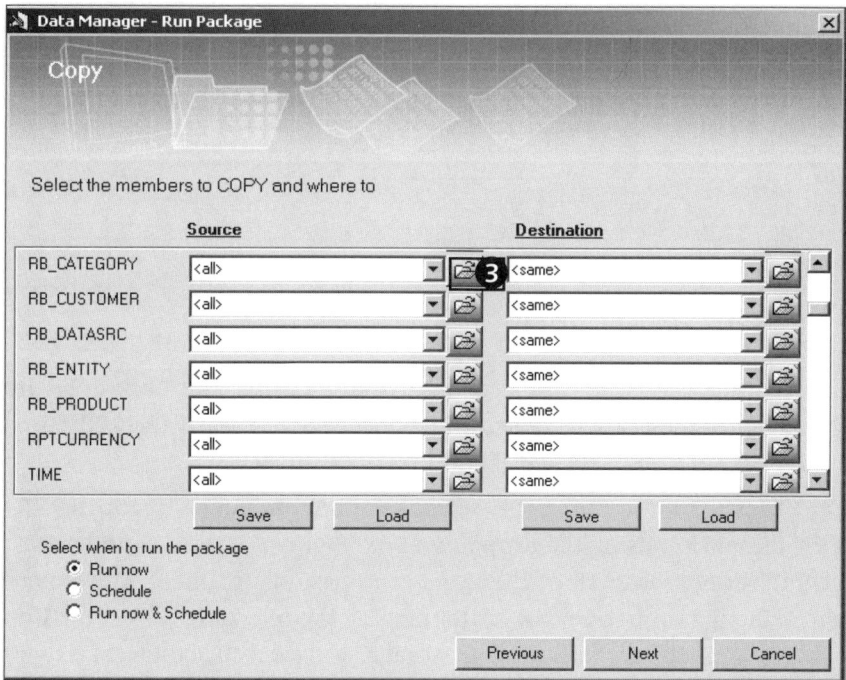

Figure 4.38 Copying Data Inside an Application—Part C

5. Select the ACTUAL member ID and click on Copy Selected (Figure 4.39, ❹ and ❺).

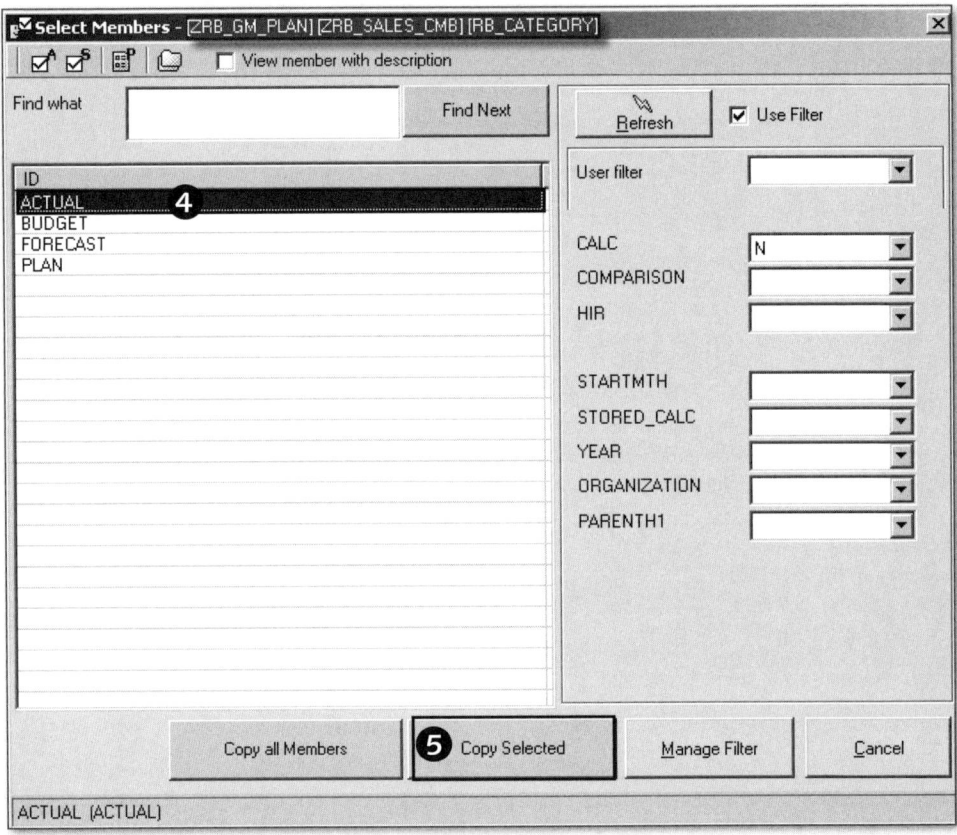

Figure 4.39 Copying Data inside an Application—Part D

6. Under Source dimensions, select the folder icon for TIME (refer back to Figure 4.38) to display a dialog box to select time periods. Select all of the 2009 time periods and click on Copy Selected (Figure 4.40, ❻ and ❼).

7. Now, under Destination dimensions, select the PLAN member ID for the RB_CATEGORY dimension using the dropdown box (Figure 4.41). Also under Destination dimensions, select all of the 2010 time periods for the TIME dimension, again using the dropdown box. After making the selections, select the Run Now option to immediately execute the package, and then click on Next (Figure 4.41, ❽ and ❾).

4.3 Copying Data Inside an SAP BusinessObjects Planning and Consolidation Application

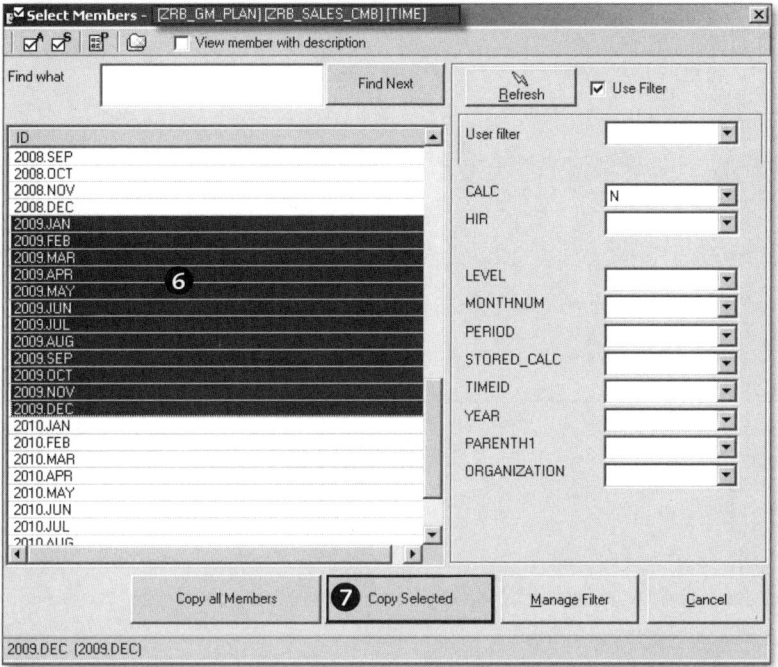

Figure 4.40 Copying Data inside an Application—Part D

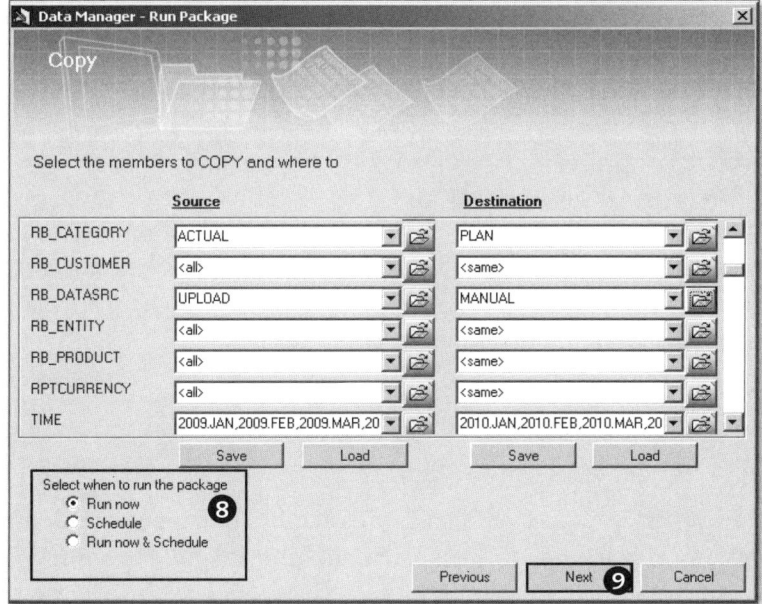

Figure 4.41 Copying Data inside an Application—Part E

In the next dialog box that displays (Figure 4.42), you are prompted to confirm your selections. Select Run Now to immediately execute the package; then click on Finish.

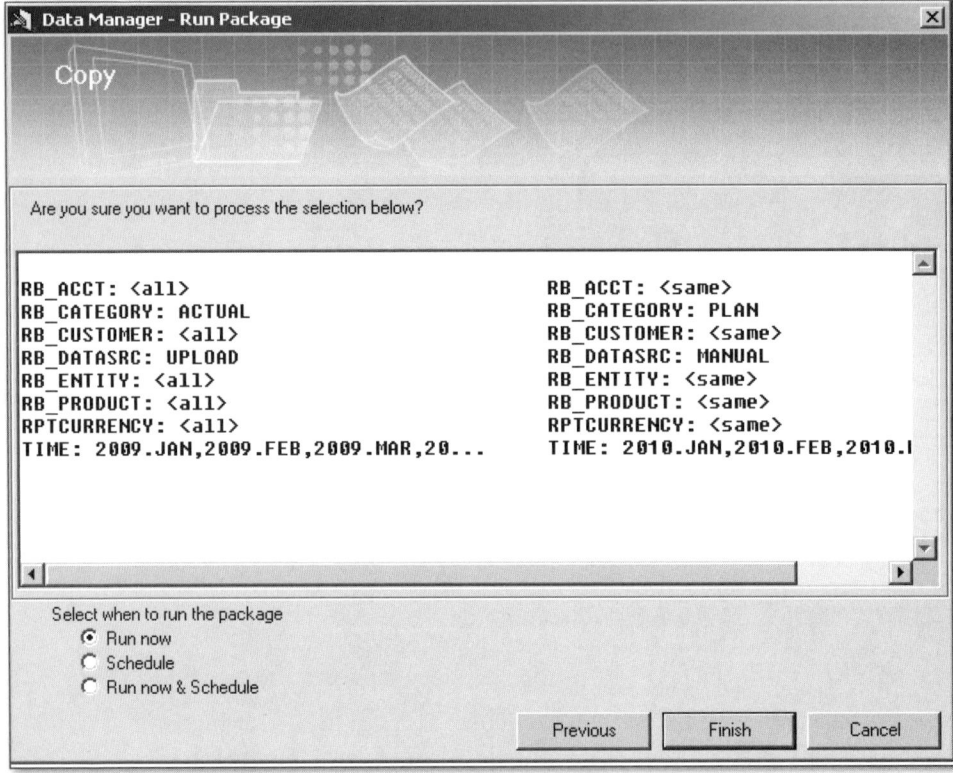

Figure 4.42 Copying Data inside an Application—Part G

You should now understand how to copy data within an application. At this point, we have created the baseline plan data for Rich Bloom, Inc. for 2010. This plan data can be revised as necessary to reflect market demand.

4.4 Summary

In this chapter, you learned how to load data from a flat file into an InfoCube in SAP NetWeaver BW. You also learned how to load data from a flat file to a dimension, and how to load from an InfoProvider in SAP NetWeaver BW to an application in SAP BusinessObjects Planning and Consolidation. In this process, you learned how transformation and conversion files are used when loading dimension and application data into SAP BusinessObjects Planning and Consolidation. To satisfy the requirements of our model company Rich Bloom, Inc., we performed the following actions to bring data into our planning application:

- Loaded the customer master data from a flat file into the Customer dimension.
- Loaded the actual sales and cost data for 2009 from an InfoCube into the planning application in SAP BusinessObjects Planning and Consolidation.
- Created baseline plan data for 2010 by copying the actual sales and cost data for 2009 to plan data for 2010.

In the next chapter, you will learn how to report the data available in SAP BusinessObjects Planning and Consolidation. You will also learn how to manually modify the data using input schedules.

5 Reporting, Planning, and Analysis in SAP BusinessObjects Planning and Consolidation

In this chapter, we will discuss how to report, plan, and analyze data using the SAP BusinessObjects Planning and Consolidation software, describing the various reporting and analysis options available in SAP BusinessObjects Planning and Consolidation. In the previous chapter, you learned how to load transaction data into an SAP BusinessObjects Planning and Consolidation application; in this chapter, we will describe the steps for setting up input schedules to enable users to manually create or modify data in an application.

Section 5.1 introduces you to the SAP BusinessObjects Planning and Consolidation for Excel and the SAP BusinessObjects Planning and Consolidation Web interface for creating reports in the application. We will begin by explaining the usage of the current view (CV) and Measure dimension in the context of reporting. We will then discuss the steps for developing reports with different types of standard templates (also called *dynamic templates*). Subsequently, we will explain how to build a custom report using Ev functions, which are standard functions used in reporting. In this context, we will discuss some of the options available to filter, expand, and format data. We will then present an overview of the web interface used for creating reports. We will conclude the section by providing tips for developing custom reports using structures and Visual Basic (VB) macros.

Section 5.2 discusses input schedules, and explains how to manually modify the data in an SAP BusinessObjects Planning and Consolidation application. When you set up an input schedule, you enable users to enter or modify data in an application; we will explore the different options available for this setup.

Section 5.3 summarizes what you have learned in this chapter and concludes that SAP BusinessObjects Planning and Consolidation provides an intuitive and robust interface for entering plan data, and reporting and analyzing data.

5.1 Reporting and Analysis in SAP BusinessObjects Planning and Consolidation

SAP BusinessObjects Planning and Consolidation provides an easy-to-use and powerful interface for creating reports and maintaining data. The reporting options for SAP BusinessObjects Planning and Consolidation can be classified under two broad categories:

- SAP BusinessObjects Planning and Consolidation for Excel
- SAP BusinessObjects Planning and Consolidation Web

An Excel interface is used to report data in SAP BusinessObjects Planning and Consolidation, which can also be integrated with Word and PowerPoint documents. SAP BusinessObjects Planning and Consolidation for Excel, however, is the primary tool used for planning, consolidation, and reporting.

The SAP BusinessObjects Planning and Consolidation Web interface can be used as a complementary tool to create and enable reports on the web.

The following are some of the key features of the reporting tool within SAP BusinessObjects Planning and Consolidation:

- **Offers Excel tools with SAP data storage**
  When you use the SAP BusinessObjects Planning and Consolidation for Excel tool, you can use the functions and features available in Excel and, at the same time, store the data in an SAP BusinessObjects Planning and Consolidation database. This enables users to use both Excel and a robust database for storing data, which will be necessary for high volume enterprise wide applications.

- **Provides dynamic templates**
  SAP BusinessObjects Planning and Consolidation offers standard templates, also called *dynamic templates*, which support different types of analysis commonly requested by businesses. Standard templates can be used to develop different types of reports, including monthly comparison reports, yearly comparison reports, trend reports, and variance reports. The ability to use these templates with very little development effort reduces TCO.

- **Allows you to customize standard templates**
  Standard templates can easily be customized to meet a particular business

requirement. This easy-to-customize feature makes standard templates more appealing.

- **Offers flexible ways to display data**
  The reporting interface is designed to provide maximum flexibility to display data. There is no code involved in creating a report. Using selection criteria, the report displays the data that is required for analysis. The system-supplied Measures dimension lets you view the data in different ways, either by period, quarter to date (QTD), or year to date (YTD).

- **Provides Ev functions**
  SAP BusinessObjects Planning and Consolidation for Excel provides *Ev functions*, a table of functions used for reporting. This aids in creating and delivering sophisticated reports for efficient data analysis.

- **Allows offline analysis**
  The data displayed in SAP BusinessObjects Planning and Consolidation reports can also be used for offline analysis. Specific features allow users to take the data from a report offline, modify it, and retract it back into SAP BusinessObjects Planning and Consolidation.

- **Enables data distribution**
  The data in an application can be distributed to other users who may or may not have access to SAP BusinessObjects Planning and Consolidation. This enables distributing data to users who may need access to it. These users can make changes to the data and send it back to SAP BusinessObjects Planning and Consolidation based on their level of access.

- **Facilitates data maintenance**
  In addition to reporting, SAP BusinessObjects Planning and Consolidation can be used for entering and modifying data. We will discuss this in detail when we talk about input schedules later in this chapter.

- **Provides features unique to planning and consolidation**
  SAP BusinessObjects Planning and Consolidation provides features that are used specifically in planning and consolidation applications. The ability to use spread, trend, and weight data makes it easy to allocate data and create projections for the future.

- **Offers standardized reports**
  The reporting functionality includes out-of-the-box system reports that can be displayed and executed on the web. They serve as a tool to analyze metadata

and to monitor changes to the objects in the SAP BusinessObjects Planning and Consolidation system.

5.1.1 SAP BusinessObjects Planning and Consolidation for Excel

The SAP BusinessObjects Planning and Consolidation for Excel interface is used to create reports and to enter and modify data in an application. This interface can be accessed from the Admin Console by selecting it from the Available Interfaces panel on the right side of the action pane.

You can also launch the reporting tool by directly launching the BPC OfficeClient application from the desktop. When you launch this tool, you are prompted to authenticate as a valid user in the system. This authentication is similar to when you log in to the Admin Console. After the system authenticates you as a valid user, you see the Excel interface in the action pane to the right. The action pane and menu options allow you to navigate the interface.

When you log in, the logon information and the application set you are logged into are displayed (Figure 5.1, ❶). The CV list displays the application and dimension member selections (Figure 5.1, ❷). The selections for the CV can be changed by clicking on the application or dimension members. To access a different application, click on the application; a new dialog box displays where you can select a different application in the application set. Similarly, when you want to make a different selection for a dimension, click on the current dimension member selection for that dimension; this displays a dialog box and enables a new value to be selected for that dimension.

In the lower half of the action pane, you can see a list of tasks from which you can select. The available tasks are as follows, and shown in Figure 5.1, ❸.

- **Reporting & Analysis**
  This task is used to create reports and analyze data in SAP BusinessObjects Planning and Consolidation.

- **Data Input**
  This task enables you to create input schedules for manually modifying data. We will look at this in detail in the next section about entering data into an application using input schedules.

- **Journals**

  Journals are used in consolidation applications when you want to make adjustments to data. We will talk about this in detail in Chapter 9.

- **Manage Data**

  This task is used to perform activities related to the maintenance of data. We looked at the features of using the Manage Data tasks when we discussed the process of loading data in the last chapter.

- **Open BPC System Reports**

  You can view system-supplied reports that serve as a tool to analyze metadata and monitor changes to objects by clicking on the Open BPC System Reports task. We will cover system reports in detail in Chapter 7.

In SAP BusinessObjects Planning and Consolidation for Excel, you can access the following interfaces from the Available Interfaces panel (Figure 5.1, ❹).

- BPC Web
- BPC for Word
- BPC for PowerPoint
- BPC Administration

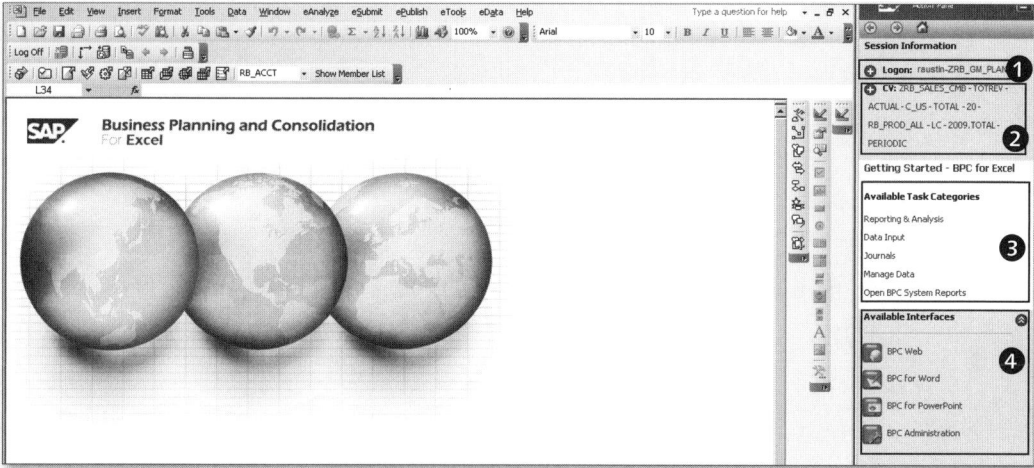

Figure 5.1 Reporting Interface for BPC—Part A

Clicking on the Reporting & Analysis task under Available Task Categories opens a set of tasks available for reporting data (Figure 5.2). Different types of reports can be built using the Reporting & Analysis Options interface. The following options are available under the Build New heading:

- **Open a Blank Workbook**
  This is used to create a new report.

- **Build a Report Using Drag & Drop**
  This task is designed to create a report using a graphical interface by dragging and dropping dimensions into the report.

- **Build a Report Using a Dynamic Template**
  This task is used to view a list of standard templates and to select a template that best fits your requirement for analysis (Figure 5.2, ❺).

Figure 5.2 Reporting Interface for BPC—Part B

The Reporting & Analysis Options interface also provides the following options under the Open Existing heading:

- **Open an Existing Report**
  This can be used to open an existing report stored on the SAP BusinessObjects Planning and Consolidation server.

- **Open an Existing Report from My Report Folder**
  This can be used to open an existing report created by you and saved on your desktop.

Before we dive into the steps of creating a report in SAP BusinessObjects Planning and Consolidation, we will explain the terms *current view* and *Measures* dimension, which are used in the context of reporting.

5.1.2 Current View

Current view (CV) allows users to select data that needs to be displayed in a report such as applications and dimension member values. If you want to make selections for a dimension, click on a dimension member in the CV. Figure 5.5 lists the options available when using the select member lookup dialog box to select dimension member values.

1. Click on the Customer dimension member in the CV section (Figure 5.3, ❶).
2. The member values for the dimensions are displayed in a new dialog box (Figure 5.3, ❷).
3. This screen provides an option to display the member data as a hierarchy or in table format (Figure 5.3, ❸).
4. The option shown in Figure 5.3, ❹, works like a toggle to select or deselect sibling members of the highlighted member.
5. The option shown in Figure 5.3, ❺, works like a toggle to select or deselect children of the highlighted member.
6. The option shown in Figure 5.3, ❻, is used to copy the selected members to a clipboard. The selection members can then be pasted in the worksheet.
7. The option shown in Figure 5.3, ❼, is used to locate a member. Clicking on this option opens a dialog box where you can enter a search criterion to locate a member in the dimension.

5 | Reporting, Planning, and Analysis in SAP BusinessObjects Planning and Consolidation

8. The option shown in Figure 5.3, ❽, is used for specifying additional filters for dimension member values displayed in this dialog box. Clicking on this option opens a filter window where you can specify the property values for which you want to see member data (Figure 5.3, ⓫). After the values are selected, click on the Refresh button (Figure 5.3, ⓬).

9. The option shown in Figure 5.3, ❾, is used for displaying the property member values of a member highlighted in the member list.

10. The option shown in Figure 5.3, ❿, is used to specify what happens when you double-click on a member. You can set the value to be transferred to the worksheet, or to use it as a toggle to expand or shrink the hierarchy when a member is double-clicked.

11. Click on OK to transfer the member value selected to the CV selection (Figure 5.3, ⓭).

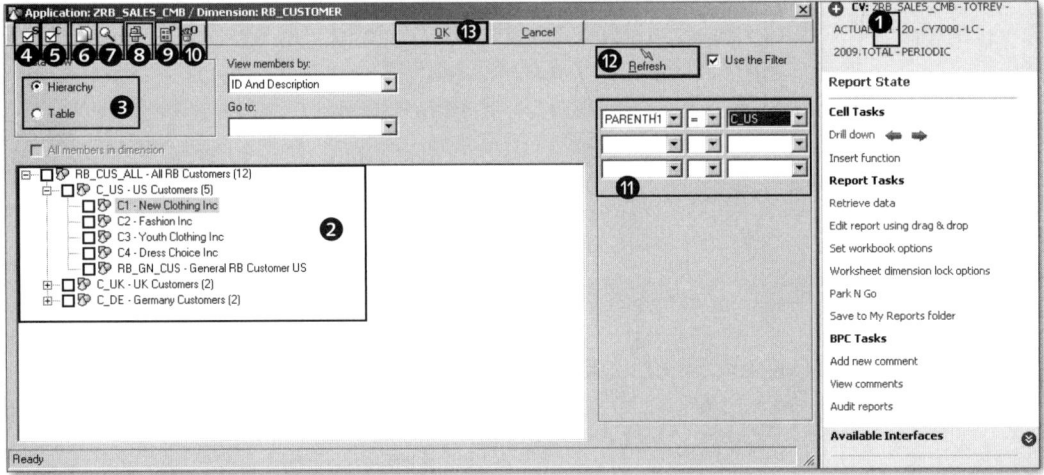

Figure 5.3 Current View Selections

5.1.3 Measures Dimension

It is important to discuss the importance of the Measures dimension in reports, because it impacts the way data is displayed in the report. The Measures dimension is used in conjunction with the Time dimension, and is available automatically in every SAP BusinessObjects Planning and Consolidation application.

The Measures dimension is used to report quantitative information for a particular period of time, using a formula that distinguishes between balance sheet accounts and profit and loss accounts and reports information accordingly. The information for balance sheet accounts is as of the end of the period; the information for profit and loss accounts is cumulative. There are three types of measures supplied with the Measures dimension that can be used in reports. They are as follows:

- **Periodic**
  This measure displays the data for the period for which the data is selected. For example, if you select the Feb 2010 period in your report, selecting the periodic measure displays the data for that period. For profit and loss accounts, the total value for the period is reported, and for balance sheet accounts, the ending balance for the period is reported.

- **Quarter to date (QTD)**
  This measure displays the quarter-to-date data up to the period selected. The system determines the quarter for the period displayed in the report, and cumulates the data from the beginning of that quarter to the period displayed in the report. For profit and loss accounts: If you select Feb 2010 and select the QTD measure, the data from the beginning of that quarter, Jan 2010, through Feb 2010 is reported. For balance sheet accounts: The ending balance for Feb 2010 is reported.

- **Year to date (YTD)**
  This measure displays the year-to-date data up to the period selected. For profit and loss accounts: If you select May 2010 and select the YTD measure, all of the data from the beginning of the year, Jan 2010, through May 2010 is reported. For balance sheet accounts: The ending balance for May 2010 is reported.

The data for an application can be stored either as periodic or YTD and the storage type is dictated by the web admin parameter associated with the application. The default storage type for an application is periodic.

The formula for the Measures dimension is maintained at the application level. You can view the formula in the SAP NetWeaver BW system using Transaction UJA_MAINTAIN_MEASURE_FORMULA. Enter the application set ID, application, and user ID. When entering the user ID, do not forget to enter the domain name along with the user ID (RICHBLOOM\RAUSTIN in our example).

Listing 5.1 shows the YTD measure for an application when data is stored periodically. The YTD measure formula, based on the type of account (profit and loss or balance sheet), either sums up the values from the beginning of the year or provides the balance as of the end of a period.

```
MEMBER [MEASURES].[YTD] AS 'IIF([%P_ACCT%].CURRENTMEMBER.PROPERTIES("2/
CPMB/ACCTYPE")="INC",SUM(PERIODSTODATE([%TIME%].[LEVEL00], [%TIME%].
CURRENTMEMBER),-[MEASURES].[/CPMB/SDATA]),IIF([%P_ACCT%].CURRENTMEMBER.
PROPERTIES("2/CPMB/ACCTYPE")="EXP",SUM(PERIODSTODATE([%TIME%].
[LEVEL00], [%TIME%].CURRENTMEMBER),[MEASURES].[/CPMB/SDATA]),IIF([%P_
ACCT%].CURRENTMEMBER.PROPERTIES("2/CPMB/ACCTYPE")="AST",([MEASURES].
[/CPMB/SDATA], CLOSINGPERIOD([%TIME%].[LEVEL02])),IIF([%P_ACCT%].
CURRENTMEMBER.PROPERTIES("2/CPMB/ACCTYPE")="LEQ",-([MEASURES].[/
CPMB/SDATA], CLOSINGPERIOD([%TIME%].[LEVEL02])),-[MEASURES].[/CPMB/
SDATA]))))';SOLVE_ORDER=3
```

Listing 5.1 YTD Measure Formula for Periodic Data

If you are familiar with MDX formulas, you can create your own formulas by using Transaction UJA_MAINTAIN_MEASURE_FORMULA.

You have now seen how to use the Measures dimension in SAP BusinessObjects Planning and Consolidation to report data for different periods. In the next section, we will discuss the steps to develop reports using dynamic templates.

5.1.4 Develop Reports Using Dynamic Templates

A *dynamic template* provides a quick entry point to create a report. Predefined templates are available for different types of analysis, and you can select a template that best supports your reporting need. The report can be further customized based on a particular business requirement.

Dynamic templates let you create a report quickly and reduce development effort. The templates serve a variety of standard analyses and can be used as the basis for developing a new report. A list of standard templates and their descriptions is shown in Table 5.1.

Template Name	Description
Trend	This report displays the current trend of data based on the Time dimension. You can have any dimension in the row. The Time dimension is used in the column to indicate current trends. You can display the data in the row as a hierarchy and the hierarchy levels can be customized.
Consolidating	This report displays the entity data in the rows and the Time dimension in the column.
Variance	This report displays the Category dimension in the column and any dimension in the rows. This report is used to calculate the variance between two different categories for a time period. The difference between the values (e.g., actual vs. budget) is displayed for the selected period.
Comparison with Prior Year	This report provides a comparison of the current and prior year's periodic and YTD values for different categories (e.g., plan vs. actual).
Comparison with 3 Year	This report provides for year over year comparisons.
Drill in Place	This report performs drill in place.
Sort On Values	This report sorts by data value.
Sort On Member	This report sorts by member descriptions.
Nested Rows	This report allows more than one dimension to be nested in the rows, and one dimension in the column.
Drill across dimensions	This report allows you to drill from one dimension to another in the rows.

Table 5.1 Standard Templates for Reporting

1. To create a report based on a standard template, click on Build a Report Using a Dynamic Template (Figure 5.2, ❺).

2. A new Report Wizard dialog box is displayed, showing the available templates (Figure 5.4). Clicking on a standard template displays a description of the template's purpose (Figure 5.4, ❻ and ❼).

3. For our example, select the Subtotals by Accounts (Trend) template, and click on Open (Figure 5.4, ❽).

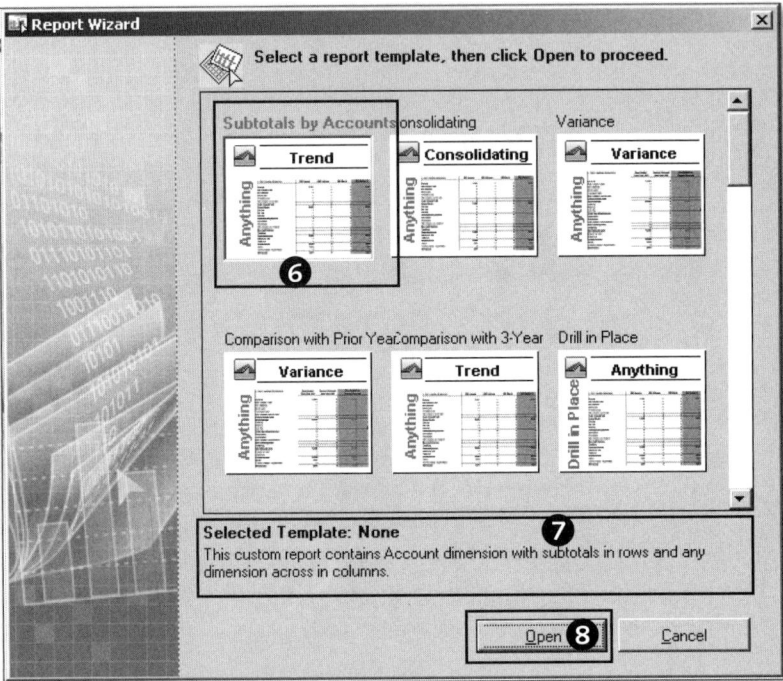

Figure 5.4 Reporting Templates in BPC—Part A

4. A report is now automatically built with the subtotals based on the Account dimension (Figure 5.5). The selection for the report is based on member values selected in the CV.

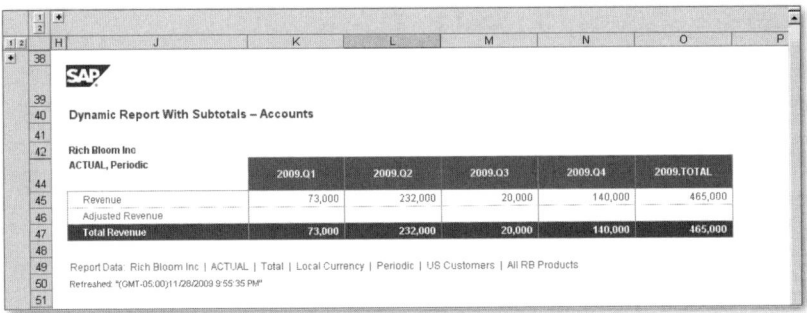

Figure 5.5 Reporting Templates in BPC—Part B

You have now seen how to use dynamic templates to build a report in SAP BusinessObjects Planning and Consolidation. Next, you will see how to build a report using Ev functions.

5.1.5 Developing Reports Using Ev Functions

A number of standard SAP BusinessObjects Planning and Consolidation functions are available for reporting and updating data in SAP BusinessObjects Planning and Consolidation. They can be used to perform tasks such as manage data, enter comments, and set work status for an application.

SAP provides a variety of functions, called Ev functions, to use for reporting and managing data. The EvDRE function is one of the main functions available for creating and configuring a new report in SAP BusinessObjects Planning and Consolidation. This function is entered in cell A1 of any blank workbook before configuring a report or input schedule. A list of Ev functions is shown in Table 5.2. The descriptions explain the purpose of each function and its usage in reports.

Function Name	Description	Example
EvSND	Used to send data to SAP BusinessObjects Planning and Consolidation using a cell as reference. This function can be used only in input schedules.	The following function can be inserted in a cell to enter and send a value. EvSND(R12,"Finance","SalesPlan", COGS,RB2, "Budget", "P1",2010. Jan") Any dimension in the application that is not specified in the send command is taken from the CV. The previous command sends the value in cell R12 of the worksheet. We are assuming the following application set and dimension members exist: Application set: Finance Application: Sales Plan Accounts: Cost of goods sold (COGS)

Table 5.2 List of Ev Functions

Function Name	Description	Example
		Entity: RB2 Category: Budget Product: P1 Time: Jan, 2010
EvAST	Returns the ID or the technical name of the current application set.	EvAST()
EvASD	Returns the description of the current application set.	EvASD()
EvAPP	Returns the ID of the current application.	EvAPP()
EvAPD	Returns the description of the current application.	EvAPD()
EvUSR	Returns the user name of the user currently connected to an application.	EvUSR()
EvSVR	Returns the server name of the server to which the user is connected.	EvSVR()
EvDIM	Returns the name of the dimension when a dimension type is specified. The following dimension types can be used: A (Account), E (Entity), C (Category), T (Time), R (Currency), U(x) (User Defined, where x is the number of the user-defined dimension)	EvDIM("E") This function outputs the name of the entity dimension for the current application.

Table 5.2 List of Ev Functions (Cont.)

5.1 Reporting and Analysis in SAP BusinessObjects Planning and Consolidation

Function Name	Description	Example
EvTIM	This function can be used to specify time offsets.	EvTIM("SalesPlan", 2010.Feb, 3) This function returns "2010.May" as the output. The first parameter, "SalesPlan," denotes the application. The second parameter denotes the time member on which the offset should be performed. The last parameter denotes the offset. A positive or negative value can be specified.
EvCVW	Returns the dimension member values set in the current view for an application.	EvCVW("Account") This function returns the value of the dimension member of the account dimension set in the CV.
EvGTS	Used to retrieve the data from an application based on dimension member selections that are passed to this function. If selection criteria are not specified for a dimension, the selections are taken from the CV.	EvGTS(AppName, ScaleValue, Member1, Member2,.. Membern)
EvPRO	Returns the property value of a specified dimension member.	EvPRO(AppName, Member, Property)
EvBET	Performs a better or worse comparison of two values, based on the account type property of the account member.	EvBET(AppName, AccountMember, Value1, Value2,...) This is a useful function when you are comparing actual data and budgets. For example, you can use this function to compare the Revenue account to see how well you have performed with respect to the budget.

Table 5.2 List of Ev Functions (Cont.)

Function Name	Description	Example
EvHOT	Used to link one report to another report. Clicking on a cell containing this function opens another report.	This is useful when it is necessary to jump from one report to another using the data in the original report as the context.
EvDRE	This is the main function used to configure new reports and input schedules. It is bi-directional and can be used to retrieve data and to enter or modify data. This function is optimized for large sets of data; we recomming using this function instead of EvSND or EvGET.	EvDRE(AppName, KeyRange, ExpandRange)
EvCOM	This function is also bi-directional and can be used to retrieve and send comments. The range to which the comment should be retrieved or from which it should be sent is specified, along with the dimension members with which the comment is associated.	EvCOM(CommentRange, AppName, Member1, Member2,...)
EvEXP	Performs row or column expansions.	EvEXP(AppName, Member, KeyRange, DataRange, ExpandDown(TRUE or FALSE))
EvMBR	Allows you to select a member from the Member Selector dialog box.	This is useful when you want to provide a custom button to let users select a dimension member from the list.
EvMNU	Allows you to create menu tasks that can be used as links to perform a number of SAP BusinessObjects Planning and Consolidation tasks. For example, a menu function can be created to open an input schedule when the link is clicked.	EvMNU(Macro Name, Display Name, Parameter)

Table 5.2 List of Ev Functions (Cont.)

1. To create a new report, select the Open a Blank Workbook task from the Build New list of tasks shown in Figure 5.2.
2. Enter "EvDRE()" in cell A1 in the new worksheet, and press Enter (Figure 5.6, ❶).
3. Click on Refresh Workbook to configure the settings for the new report (Figure 5.6, ❷).
4. This opens the BPC – EvDRE Builder dialog box. The available dimensions for the application are displayed (Figure 5.6, ❸). Drag the dimensions from this location to the columns and rows as required for your report.
5. In this example, we have pulled the RB_ACCT dimension to the rows, and the TIME dimension to the columns (Figure 5.6, ❹ and ❺).
6. Specify a dimension in the Spread Across Worksheets field if you want to create multiple EvDRE reports for each value selected for that dimension. For example, if want to create a profit and loss report for each entity in the organization as a separate worksheet, you can include the Entity dimension here.

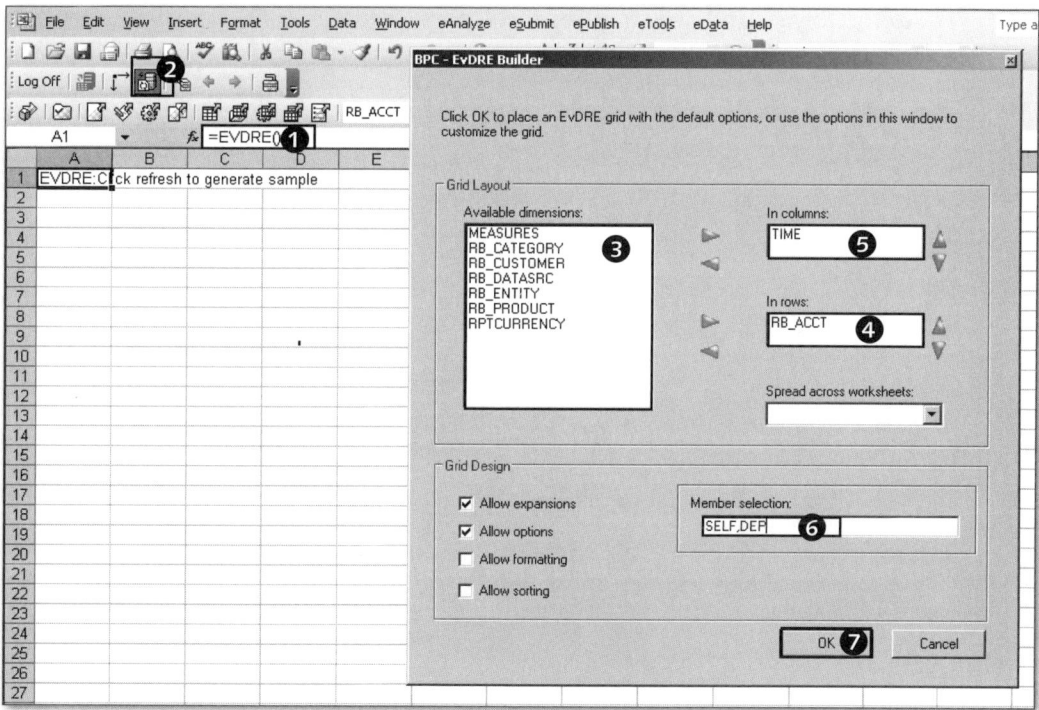

Figure 5.6 Creating an EvDRE Report—Part A

7. You can select the desired options in the Grid Design area to allow for expansions and for enabling formatting and sorting of data in the report. The Allow Expansions option is useful for allowing users to drill down to details.

8. The data is displayed based on the values selected in the CV. For the dimensions included in the rows and columns, specify how you want to select the dimension member values. In our example, we have specified the "SELF,DEP" member selection (Figure 5.6, ❻). This displays the member value selected in the CV, because we have included "SELF" in the selection. In addition, because we have specified "DEP," if the member value is a hierarchy node, then the dependent values are also displayed.

9. Click on the OK button when you have completed the selections (Figure 5.6, ❼).

10. This displays the report based on dimension member value selections in the CV (Figure 5.7). The data displays the actual sales for Rich Bloom, Inc. for 2009, and also lists the sales by quarters.

11. Click on the + sign that is available above column D to make further changes to the format and selections of the report (Figure 5.7, ❽). This will open the control panel of the report.

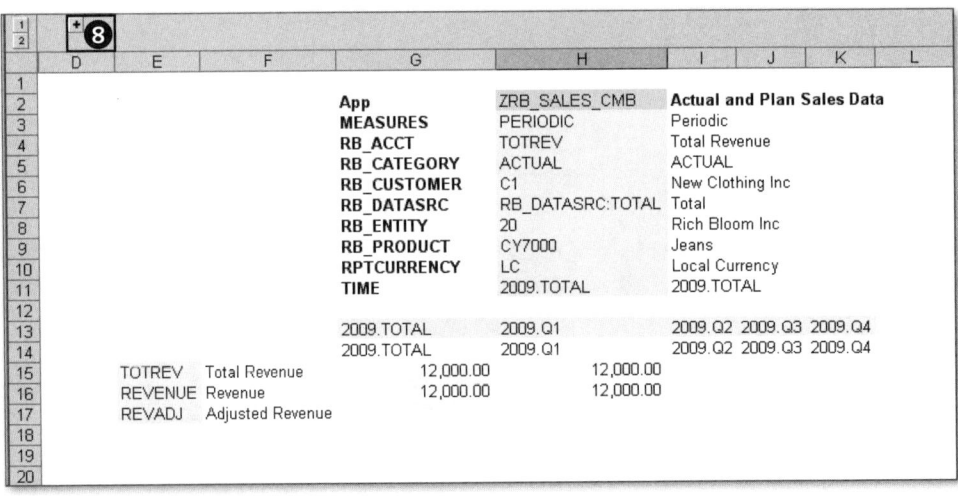

Figure 5.7 Creating an EvDRE Report—Part B

12. Let us assume that we want to see the sales totals by the individual months (January to December), not by quarters. The months are the base members for the Time dimension. Change the setting for the report to display only the base members for the Time dimension. Set the MemberSet parameter for the Time dimension to "BAS" (Figure 5.8, ❾).

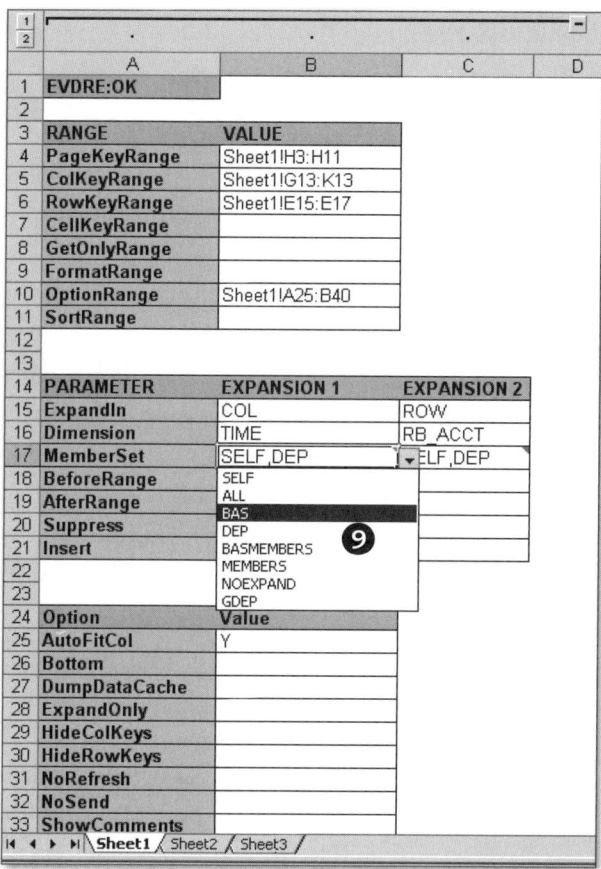

Figure 5.8 Creating an EvDRE Report—Part C

13. We will also display the Account Type property of the Account dimension member in the rows. To accomplish this, insert a new column using the Excel functionality between columns F and H (Figure 5.9, ❿). Under column G14, to the right of Account Description, enter a formula to retrieve the Account Type property of the accounts to be displayed in the rows (Figure 5.9, ⓫). To do this, select BPC Functions to see the list of functions, select the EvPRO function, and click on OK (Figure 5.9, ⓬, ⓭, and ⓮).

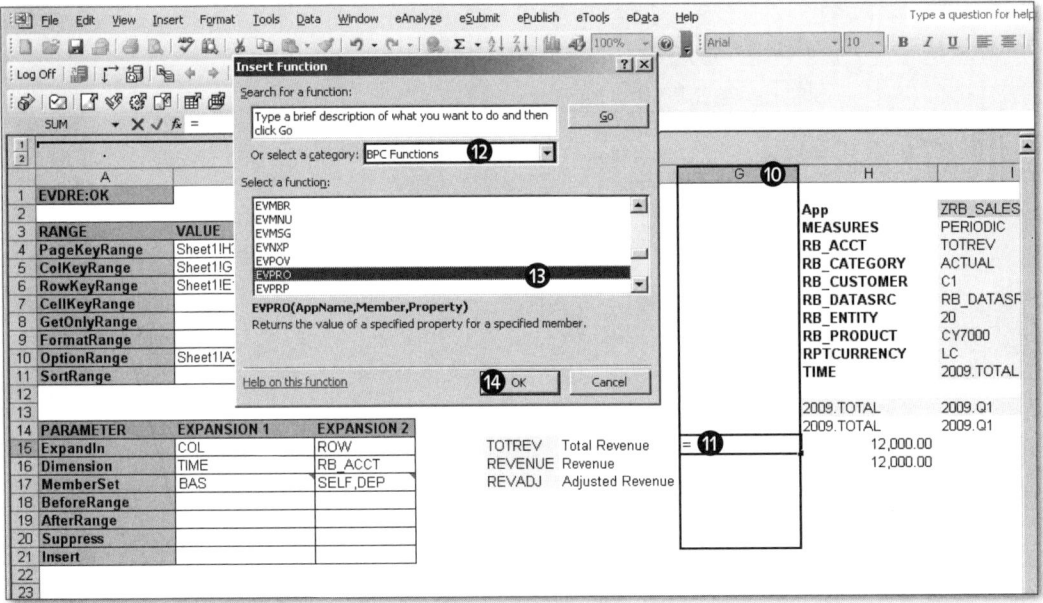

Figure 5.9 Creating an EvDRE Report—Part D

14. In the Function Arguments dialog box, enter "ZRB_SALES_CMB" as the name of the application, select the cell reference that corresponds to the first account member value displayed in the row for which you want to display the property, and specify "ACCTYPE" as the property name (Figure 5.10, ⓯). Click on the OK button to continue (Figure 5.10, ⓰). Then click on the Expand button (Figure 5.10, ⓱).

15. After clicking on the Expand button, the report shown in Figure 5.11 is displayed. It displays the total revenue for 2009.

Reporting and Analysis in SAP BusinessObjects Planning and Consolidation | 5.1

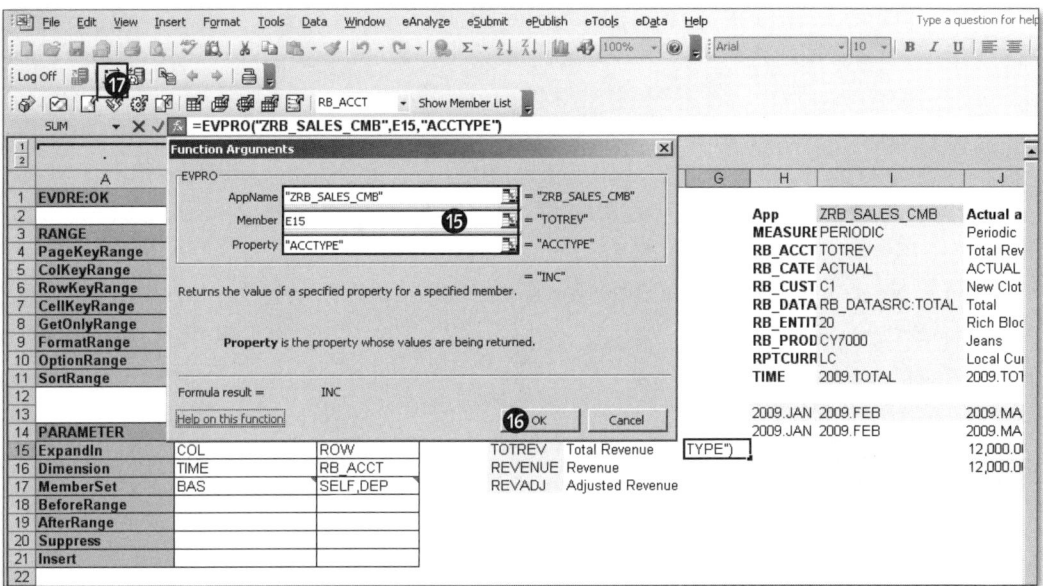

Figure 5.10 Creating an EvDRE Report—Part E

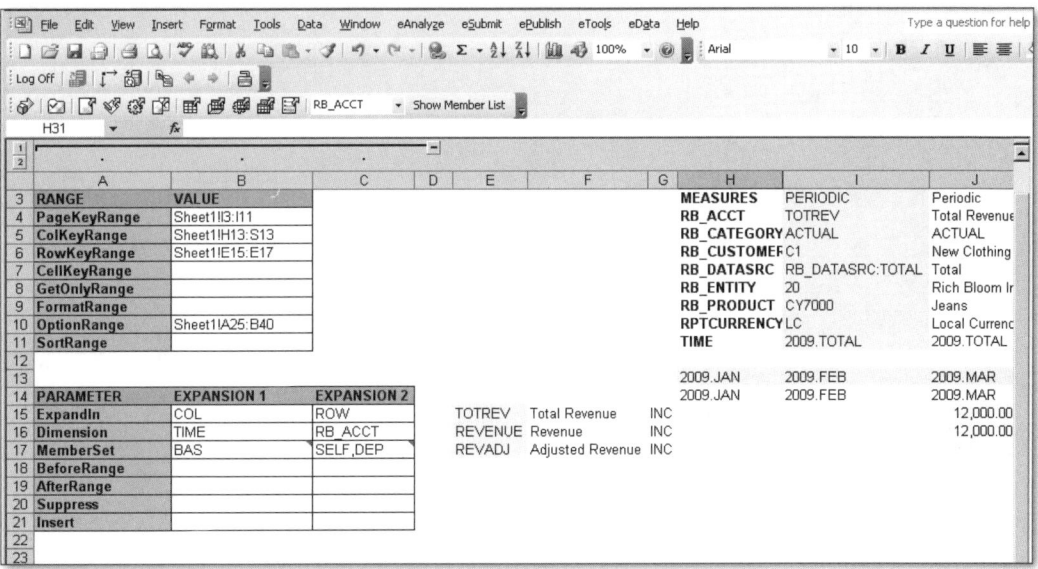

Figure 5.11 Creating an EvDRE Report—Part F

16. Next, we will display details of the Gross_Margin account on the report. First, modify the Account dimension member selection in the CV to point to the GROSS_MARGIN account (Figure 5.12, ⓲).

17. For the MemberSet parameters for the Account dimension that is displayed in the rows, select "BAS" and click on the Expand button to refresh the data (Figure 5.12, ⓳ and ⓴).This displays all of the base members for the Gross_Margin account on the report.

18. Next, we will build a filter for the Account dimension displayed in the rows by using the Build Filter feature in SAP BusinessObjects Planning and Consolidation. Right-click on the red icon that is displayed to the right of the MemberSet parameter for the account dimension (Figure 5.12, ㉑).

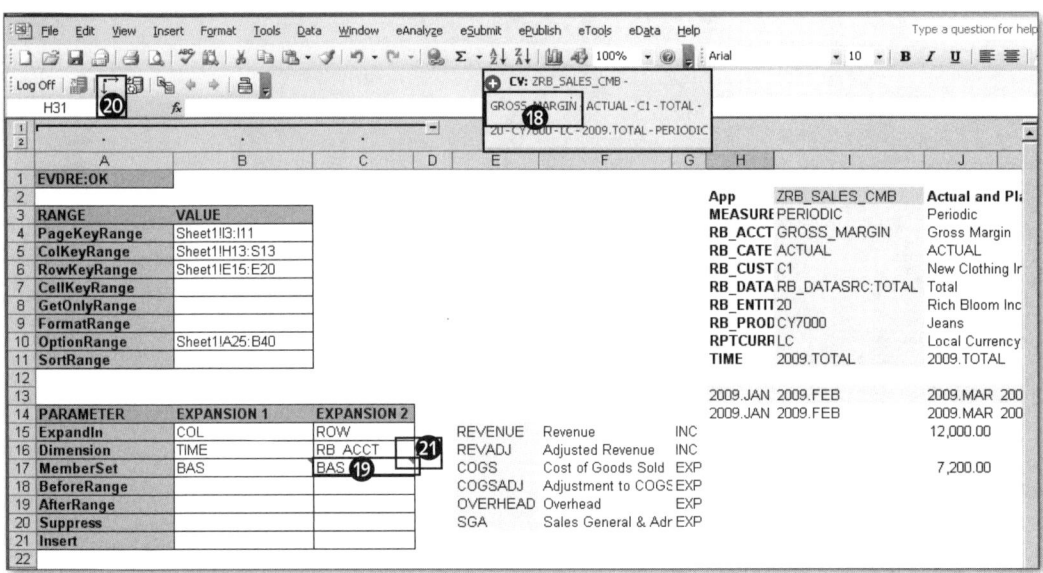

Figure 5.12 Creating an EvDRE Report—Part G

19. Now click on EVDRE: Builder Filter to make the selections for the Account dimension (Figure 5.13, ㉒).

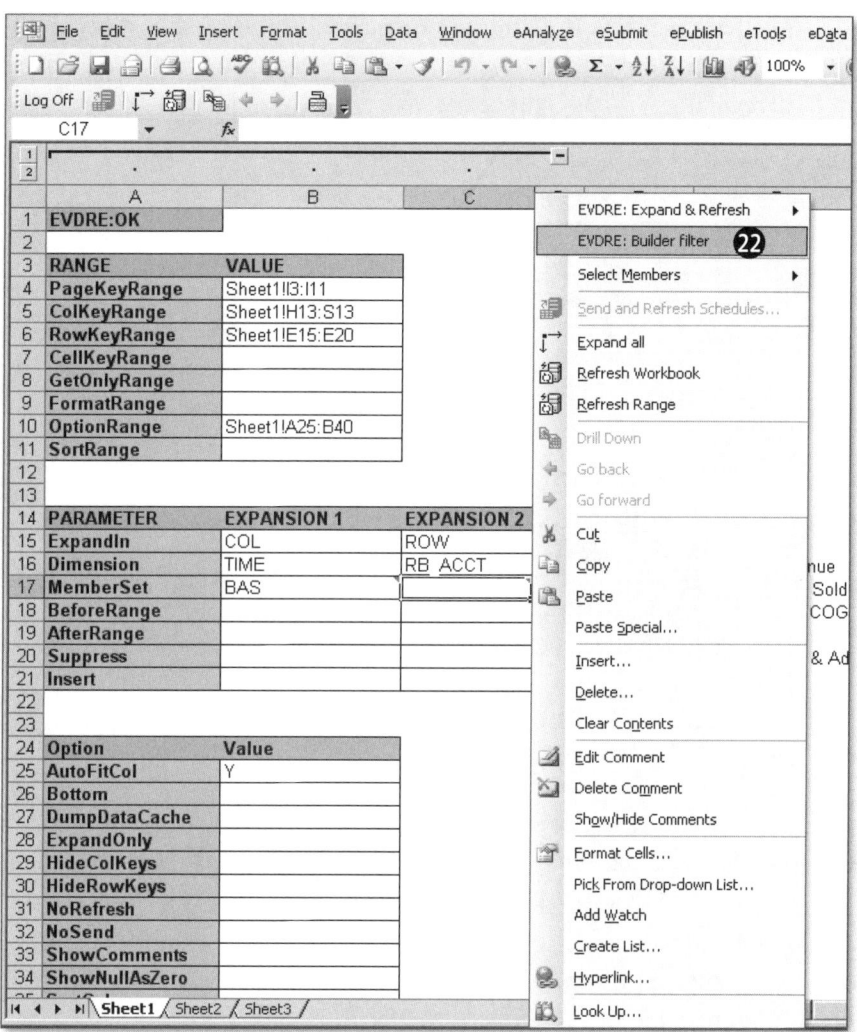

Figure 5.13 Creating an EvDRE Report—Part H

20. The Filter dialog box is displayed to define the selections for the data. Here, you can specify the property value used as a basis for selecting data. The interface also allows you to specify the selection criteria in multiple lines, using "AND" or "OR" expressions (Figure 5.14, ❷). After specifying the selections, click on Apply (Figure 5.14, ❷).

21. The selections you made in the filter are displayed in the MemberSet parameter for the Account dimension (Figure 5.14, ㉕). Now click on the Expand button to display the report (Figure 5.14, ㉖).

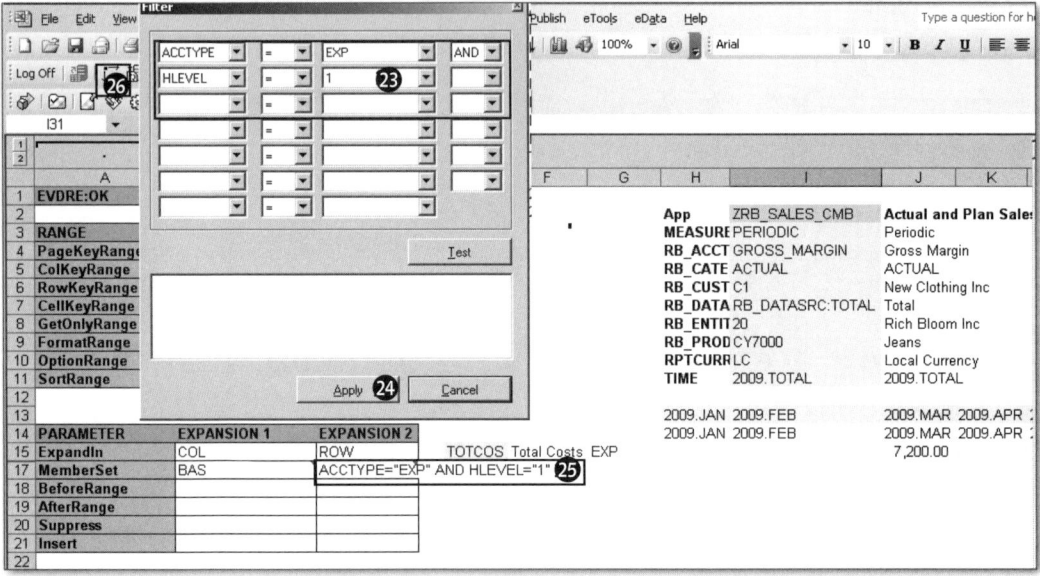

Figure 5.14 Creating an EvDRE Report—Part I

22. You are now ready to save the report. You can save it locally on your desktop by selecting the eAnalyze menu and then selecting the Save My Reports… option. By selecting this option, the report is available only to you.

23. We will save this report to the Company folder so that others in the organization can access this report. From the eTools menu option, select Save Dynamic Templates (Figure 5.15, ㉗). This opens the Save As dialog box.

24. Select the Company folder (Figure 5.15, ㉘). Specify the file name "Actual Sales Data for 2009" and click on Save (Figure 5.15, ㉙ and ㉚). This enables other users who have access to this folder to execute the report.

Reporting and Analysis in SAP BusinessObjects Planning and Consolidation | 5.1

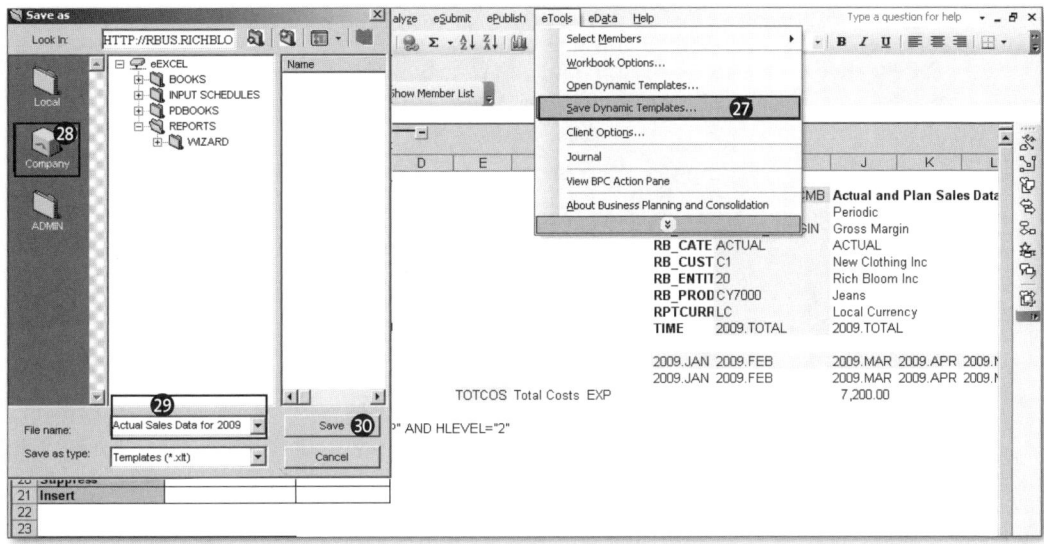

Figure 5.15 Creating an EvDRE Report—Part J

Now that we have discussed the creation of reports using EvDRE, we will review some of the options available to format the report. The formatting of reports is done in the control panel.

5.1.6 Control Panel

All EvDRE reports in SAP BusinessObjects Planning and Consolidation have a control panel where you can set expansion options, filter parameters, and formatting parameters. The following are the sections available in the control panel of a report:

- Range
- Parameter
- Options
- Format

Range

The Range section is used to specify the range of cells that will contain specific values. The parameters are described in Table 5.3.

205

Parameter	Description
PageKeyRange	Specifies the range of cells that contain the set of default dimension member values used to filter data for the page. If you specify ENTITY: US, UK, DE, all retrieved values contain the sum of values from entities US, UK, and DE.
ColKeyRange	Specifies the range of cells that contains the keys for columns in the report.
RowKeyRange	Specifies the range of cells that contains the keys for rows in the report.
CellKeyRange	Specifies the range of cells that will overwrite dimension member IDs used in ColKeyRange and RowKeyRange.
GetOnlyRange	Specifies a range of cells in an input schedule that should only retrieve (not send) values. The cells are designated as read-only.
FormatRange	Specifies the range of cells that contain the instructions to format data in the report.
OptionRange	Specifies the range of cells that contain options that can be set in a report such as Show Comments, Hide Column Keys, and so on.
SortRange	Specifies the range of cells that contain instructions to define sorting of data in rows of the report.

Table 5.3 Range Parameters

> **Note**
>
> Certain parameters such as *FormatRange*, *OptionRange*, and *SortRange* are available only when you select the respective option when creating the EvDRE report (refer back to Figure 5.6).

Parameter

The Parameter section is used to set parameters related to expansion and filters of a report or input schedule. We saw some examples of using these parameters when we developed the report using the EVDRE function earlier. Table 5.4 shows a list of parameters that can be set in this section.

Parameter	Description
ExpandIn	Specifies whether the expansion of a dimension needs to be done by row (ROW) or column (COL).
Dimension	Specifies the dimension for which you want to set the expansion and filter parameters.
MemberSet	Specifies the set of dimension member values to use to filter and display data for rows or columns in a report. You can either choose a specific value or use one or more of the following keywords: ▶ **SELF**: The current member. If you define the MemberSet as SELF, the expansion occurs on the current member. If you leave MemberSet blank, the system suppresses the expansion. ▶ **DEP**: All children of the current member. You can enter DEP (parent) to return the dependent members of a specified parent rather than using the parent from the page key range or current view. ▶ **BASMEMBERS**: All base members in the dimension. ▶ **BAS**: All base members below the current member. ▶ **NOEXPAND**: Do not expand. ▶ **ALL**: All dependents of current member.
BeforeRange	You use this parameter to dynamically insert rows and columns at the beginning of expansions.
AfterRange	You use this parameter to dynamically insert rows and columns of data at the end of expansions.
Suppress	Setting this parameter to Y, allows you to suppress rows and columns that contain zero or null values.
Insert	Setting this parameter to Y allows you to dynamically insert an explicit set of members before a current row or column of a report or input schedule.

Table 5.4 Parameters

Options

The Options section is used to set parameters related to a report or an input schedule. Table 5.5 shows a list of options that can be set.

Parameter	Description
AutoFitCol	Automatically adjusts the size of the columns containing the EvDRE ranges to fit the content after refreshing data.
Bottom	Shows only the specified number (n) of the lowest values in the entire data range.
DumDataCache	Writes the content of the data cache to the log file *EvDre_log.txt*.
ExpandOnly	Disables the refresh action and performs only an expansion, when requested. The system does not retrieve data from the database.
HideColKeys	Hides the column key ranges.
HideRowKeys	Hides the row key ranges.
NoRefresh	Prevents the system from refreshing data from the database.
NoSend	Prevents the system from sending data to the database.
ShowComments	Adds an Excel comment in any *DataRange* cell with a formula, if the value retrieved from the database differs from the one displayed by the formula.
ShowNullAsZero	Fills all empty cells in the data range with zeros.
SortCol	Sorts a given column.
SumParent	Inserts new rows with subtotals.
SuppressDataCol	Performs suppression on the defined columns directly in Excel.
SuppressDataRow	Performs suppression on the defined rows directly in Excel.
SuppressNoData	Prevents the suppression of zero values in the report.
Top	Shows only the specified number (n) of highest values in the entire data range.

Table 5.5 Options

Format

The Format section contains instructions for formatting data in a report or an input schedule. Table 5.6 shows a list of the columns in the Format section.

Parameter	Description
Criteria	Defines criteria for formatting data. The following are valid values: ▸ **CALC**: Applies to calculated values ▸ **INPUT**: Applies to non-calculated values ▸ **DEFAULT**: Applies regardless of criteria
Evaluate In	Defines the range for which the criteria must be evaluated. The following are valid values: ▸ **ROW**: Evaluate in rows ▸ **COLUMN**: Evaluate in columns ▸ **ROWCOL**: Evaluate in rows and columns ▸ **PAGE**: Evaluate in pages
Format	Lets you specify font attributes such as color, font size, font style, bordering, etc.
Use	Lets you specify which components of the formatting properties should be applied. The following are valid values: ▸ **ALL**: Apply all formatting properties ▸ **PATTERN**: Apply all pattern properties ▸ **NUMBER**: Apply all numbering properties ▸ **ALIGNMENT**: Apply all numbering properties ▸ **FONT**: Apply all font properties ▸ **FONTSTYLE**: Apply all font style properties ▸ **BORDER**: Apply all border properties ▸ **FRAME**: Apply all frame properties ▸ **STYLE**: Apply all style properties ▸ **CONTENT**: Apply all content properties ▸ **LOCK**: Apply LOCK property
Parameters	Lets you specify formatting instructions directly into text format.
Apply To	Lets you specify the sections of a report or input schedule to which a format should be applied. The following are valid values: ▸ **KEY**: Applies to row and column key ranges ▸ **HEADING**: Applies to text associated with keys ▸ **DATA**: Applies to data range ▸ **BLANK**: Applies to keys, heading, and data

Table 5.6 Format Parameters

Parameter	Description
NoRefresh	Prevents the system from refreshing data from the database
NoSend	Prevents the system from sending data to the database.
ShowComments	Lets you add an Excel comment in any DataRange cell with a formula, if the value retrieved from the database differs from the one displayed by the formula.

Table 5.6 Format Parameters (Cont.)

These parameter options allow you to develop customized reports to meet specific reporting requirements.

Recall that earlier, we discussed the CV and said that the values selected in it determine the selection of data in the report. At the same time, we also studied the ability to specify filter values in the control panel of the report; for example, by specifying dimension member values in the MemberSet. In the context of EvDRE reports, it is important to understand the order of precedence of the CV to determine how the values of filters are applied to a report or input schedule. In the next section, we will look at the order of precedence the system uses to apply filter values to reports.

Order of Precedence of the Current View

If filter definitions conflict with one another, the system uses the following order of precedence, from lowest to highest, to determine filter values. For example, the cell key, if it exists, takes precedence over the row key; the row key takes precedence over the column key; and the column key takes precedence over the page key. Refer to Table 5.7 for the order of precedence of the CV.

Rank	Description
1	The system CV, as defined by the CV bar.
2	The workbook CV, as defined in the workbook options.
3	The page CV, as defined in the PageKeyRange.
4	The column CV, as defined in the ColumnKeyRange.
5	The row CV, as defined in the RowKeyRange.
6	The cell CV, as defined in the CellKeyRange.

Table 5.7 Current View Order of Precedence

We have previously discussed the steps to create and format reports using the SAP BusinessObjects Planning and Consolidation for Excel interface. SAP BusinessObjects Planning and Consolidation also provides an interface to develop and display reports on the web. We will now discuss the steps involved in doing so.

5.1.7 Developing Reports Using SAP BusinessObjects Planning and Consolidation Web

From the SAP BusinessObjects Planning and Consolidation Web interface, you can develop reports using drag-and-drop. This provides you with an easy-to-use interface for developing reports, and users can start developing reports with little training. These types of reports are used less frequently when compared to Excel-based SAP BusinessObjects Planning and Consolidation reports but can be used by users who prefer to report on the web.

1. To build a report using drag-and-drop, click on BPC Web link in the list of available interfaces (refer back to Figures 5.1 and 5.2).
2. The web interface that displays is shown in Figure 5.16. Click on Live Reporting (Figure 5.16, ❶).This opens a new interface titled Live Reports List Options. Click on Build a Report Using Drag & Drop (Figure 5.16, ❶ and ❷).

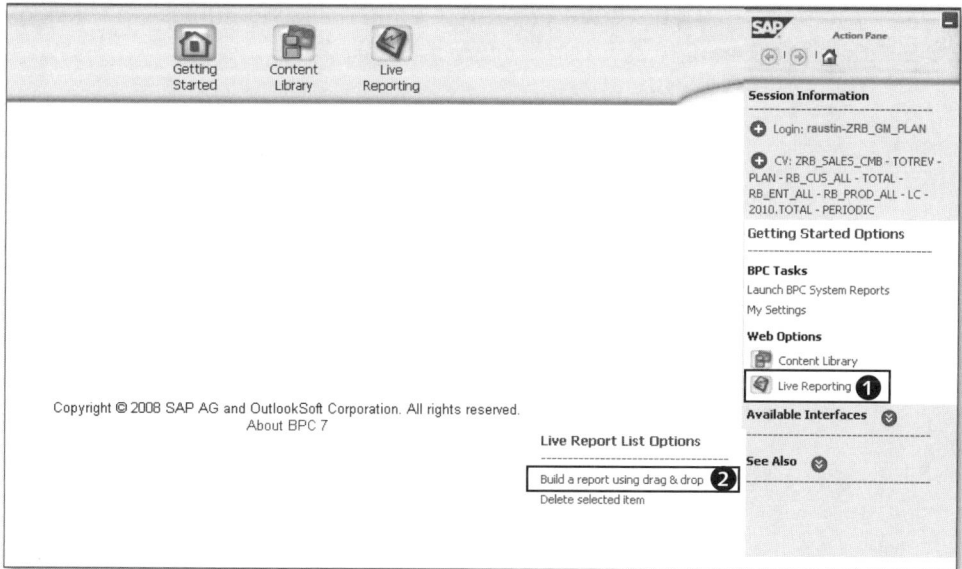

Figure 5.16 Creating a Report using Drag-and-Drop—Part A

3. Drag the RB_ACCT dimension to the rows, check the option Inherit Member Value from CV, and click on the green checkmark to continue (Figure 5.17, ❸, ❹, ❺, and ❻).

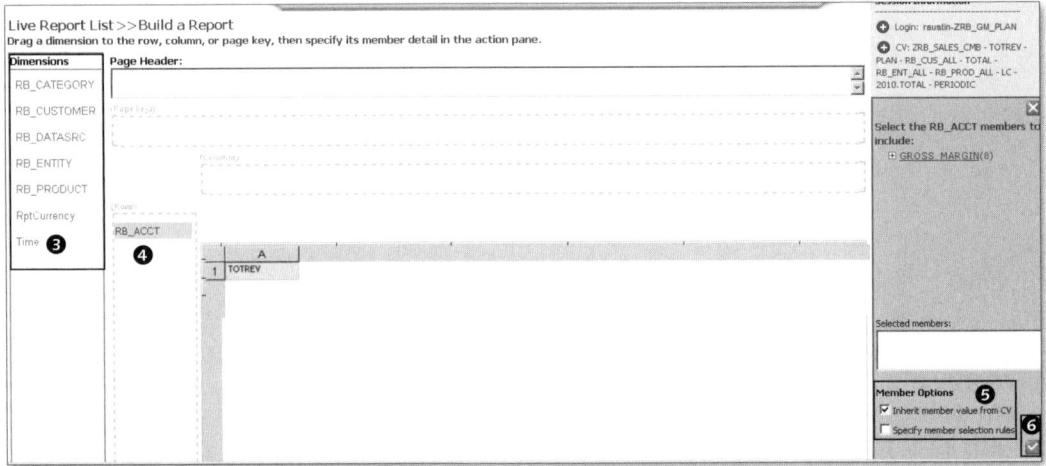

Figure 5.17 Creating a Report Using Drag-and-Drop—Part B

4. You have selected the RB_ACCT dimension for the rows. Now drag the Time dimension to the columns and select 2010.Total in the right pane as the filter for this report. Check the option Specify Member Selection Rules, and click on the green checkmark to continue (Figure 5.18, ❼, ❽, ❾, and ❿).

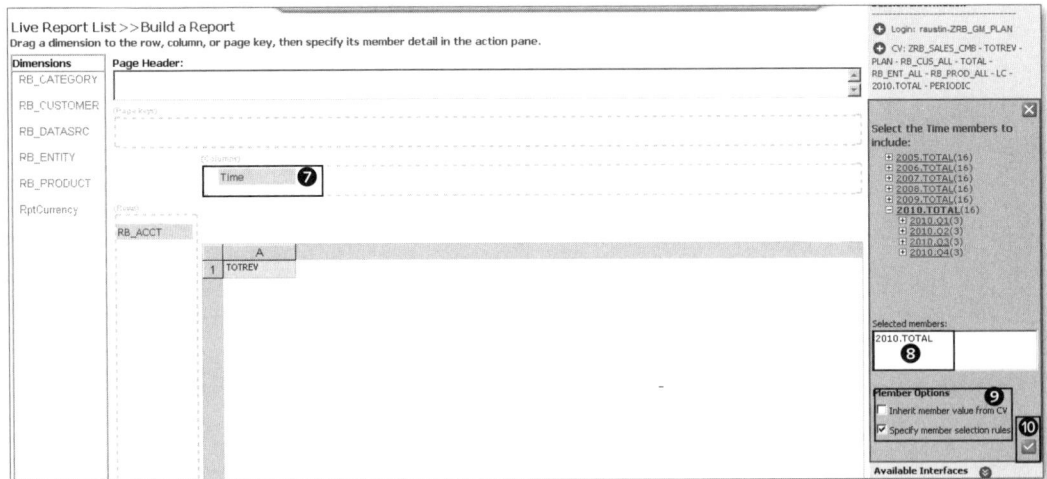

Figure 5.18 Creating a Report using Drag-and-Drop—Part C

Reporting and Analysis in SAP BusinessObjects Planning and Consolidation | 5.1

5. In the Member Selection Rule – Step 1 of 2 section, select Dependents Only of Selected, and click on the green checkmark to continue (Figure 5.19, ⓫ and ⓬).

6. In the Member Selection Rule – Step 2 of 2 section, select ID & Description and click on the green checkmark to continue (Figure 5.19, ⓭).

7. You are now prompted by the question "What would you like to do?" Click on Save Report (Figure 5.19, ⓮). You are prompted to enter the technical name and description of the report. Enter "RB_PLAN_2010" for the technical name and "Plan data for 2010" as the description (Figure 5.19, ⓯ and ⓰). Then, click on the green checkmark to continue.

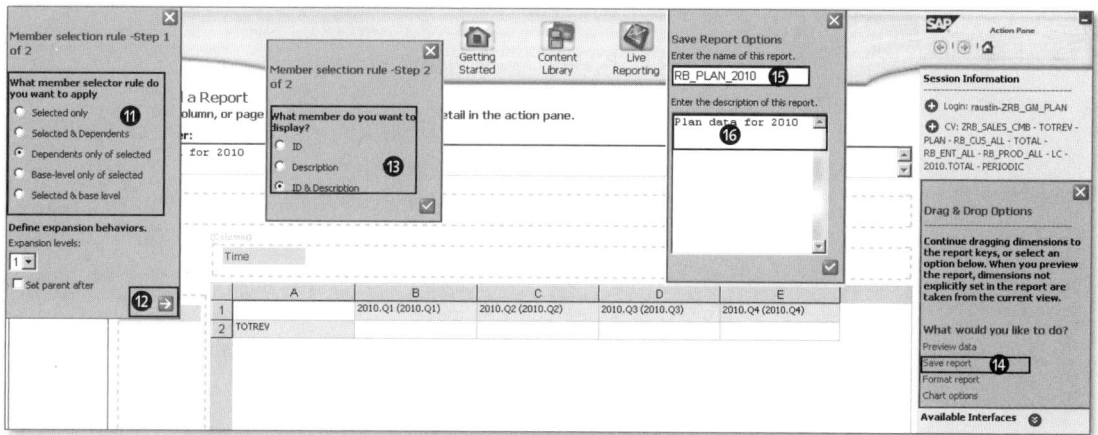

Figure 5.19 Creating a Report Using Drag-and-Drop—Part D

8. You can now access the report from the Live Report List. Click on the report to display it (Figure 5.20, ⓱ and ⓲). You can click on the plus icons to further drill down the report. For example, you can drill down on the totals displayed by quarter to see the data by month.

213

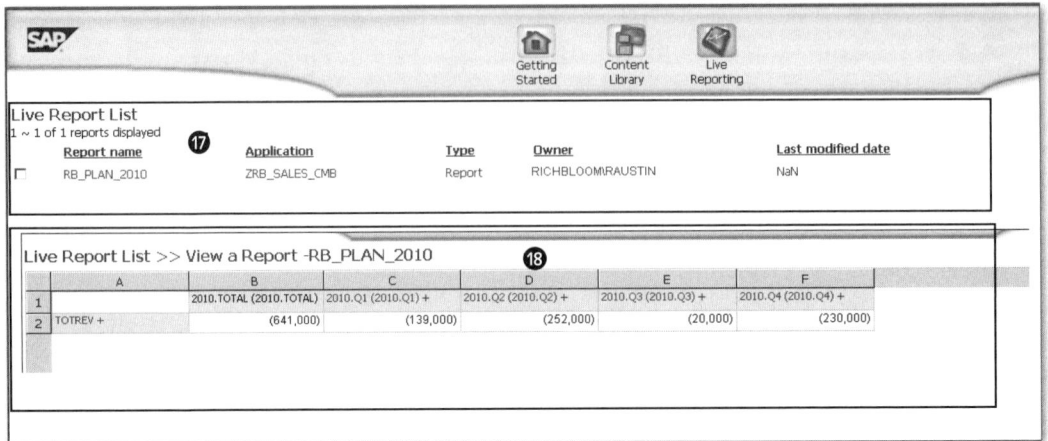

Figure 5.20 Creating a Report Using Drag-and-Drop—Part D

You have now seen how you can develop and deploy reports using the SAP BusinessObjects Planning and Consolidation Web interface. In the next section, we will provide you with tips to develop reports using structures and VB macros.

5.1.8 Developing Reports Using Structures and VB Macros

You may at times want to develop custom reports that group data displayed in each row using a specific criteria. For this, structures are used. In some reports, you may also want to use VB macros to calculate certain values.

Usage of Structures in Reports

We will now use the EvDRE function to create a report that displays the total revenue, total cost, and gross margin for all entities (grouped together) of our model company, Rich Bloom, Inc. There are many ways to develop a report to meet this requirement. We will develop this report using structures to demonstrate this function.

To create the report, identify the dimensions that will be used to create the grouping, and include these dimensions in the rows. Identify the dimension to be displayed in the column.

1. Start by creating an EvDRE report, and include the Account and Entity dimensions in the rows. You are including these dimensions in the rows because you want to create a row for a combination of values, based on accounts and entities in your structure. Include the Time dimension in the column. The CV is shown in Figure 5.21, ❶. All of the products have been selected because the report has to display the data for all of the products.

2. In the MemberSet parameter for the Account dimension, include the following accounts, each separated by a pipe sign. Each account will be displayed as a separate row in the report (Figure 5.21, ❷).

   "TOTREV|TOTCOS|GROSS_MARGIN"

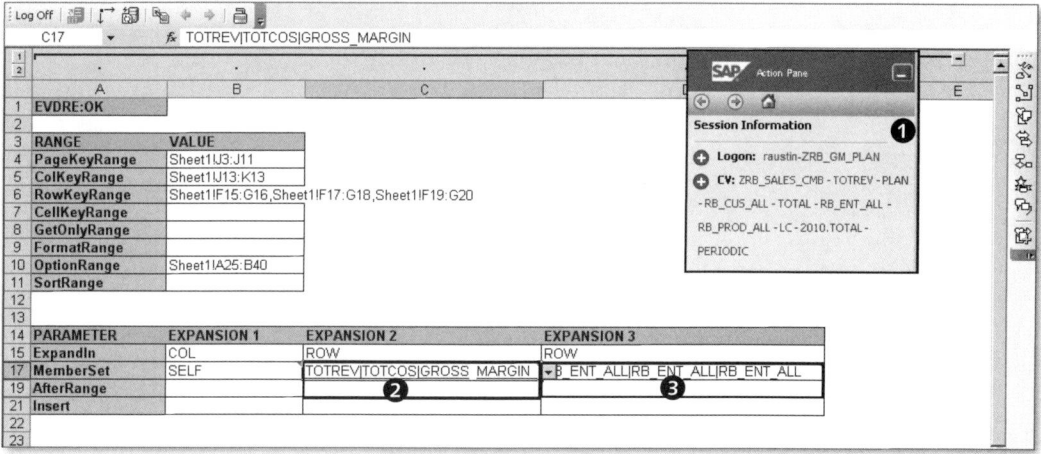

Figure 5.21 Creating a Structure in a Report — Part A

3. In the MemberSet for the Entity dimension, include the following entities, each separated by a pipe sign. Each entity will be displayed as a separate row in the report (Figure 5.21, ❸).

   "RB_ENT_ALL|RB_ENT_ALL|RB_ENT_ALL"

4. Enter the following value in the RowKeyRange, as shown in Figure 5.22, ❹ and ❺. Every combination should include at least two rows. Then, click on the Expand button to display the report.

   =EVRNG(F15:G16,F17:G18,F19:G20)

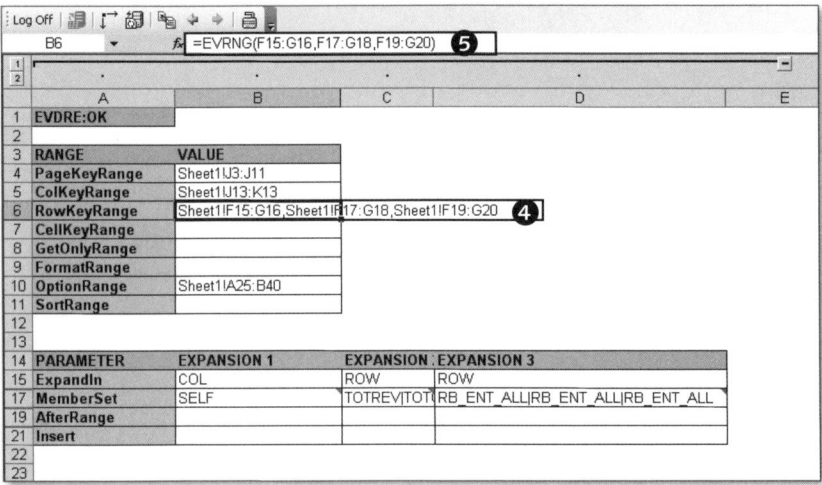

Figure 5.22 Creating a Structure in a Report—Part B

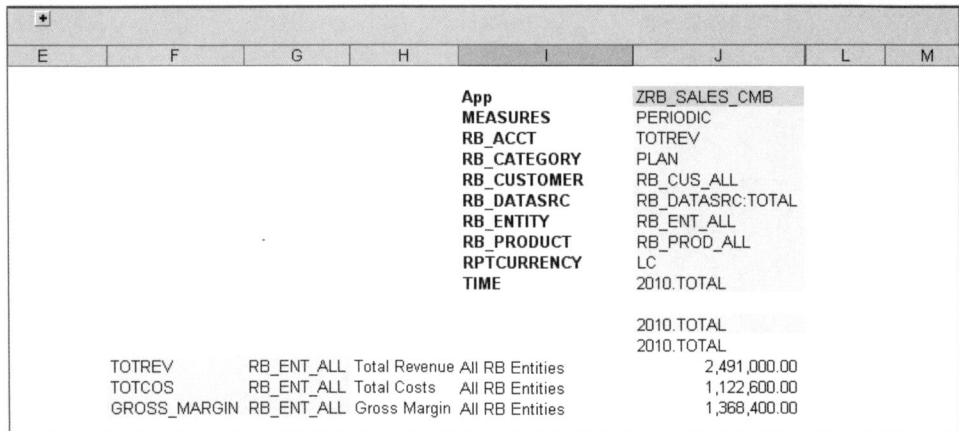

Figure 5.23 Creating a Structure in a Report—Part C

5. The report displays the data you requested (Figure 5.23). However, notice that the descriptions associated with the Account and Entity dimensions are displayed in the report. If you want to display only one description for each row, hide some of the columns that you do not want to display.

6. You can hide the row keys by setting the HideRowsKeys option to Y (Figure 5.24, ❻). This hides columns F and G. You can hide column H using the Hide option in Excel (Figure 5.24, ❼).

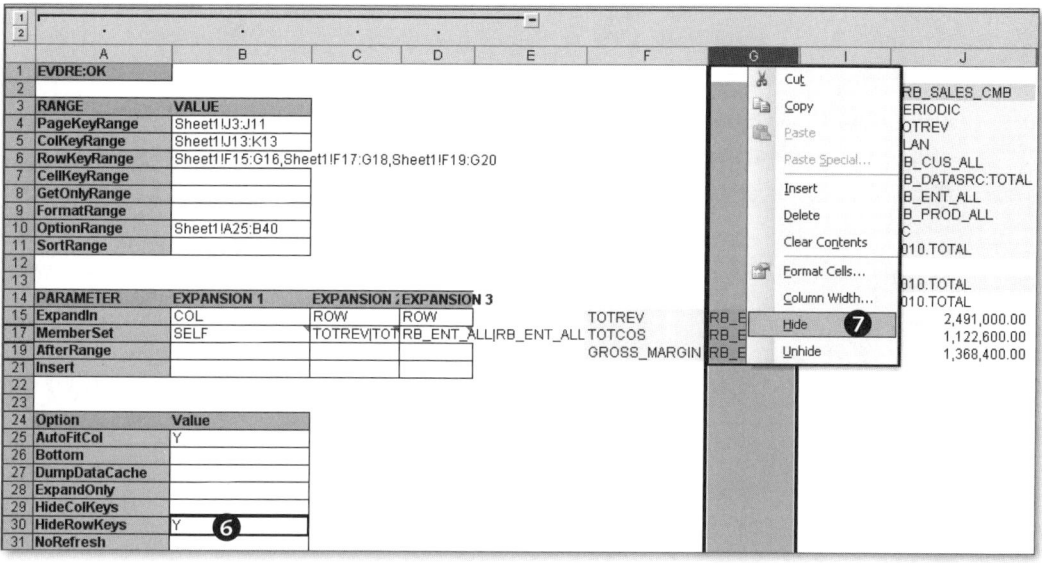

Figure 5.24 Creating a Structure in a Report—Part D

7. In the rows displayed in column I, enter the description for the row values to what you want to say (Figure 5.25, ❽). Save the report using ETOOLS • SAVE DYNAMIC TEMPLATE.

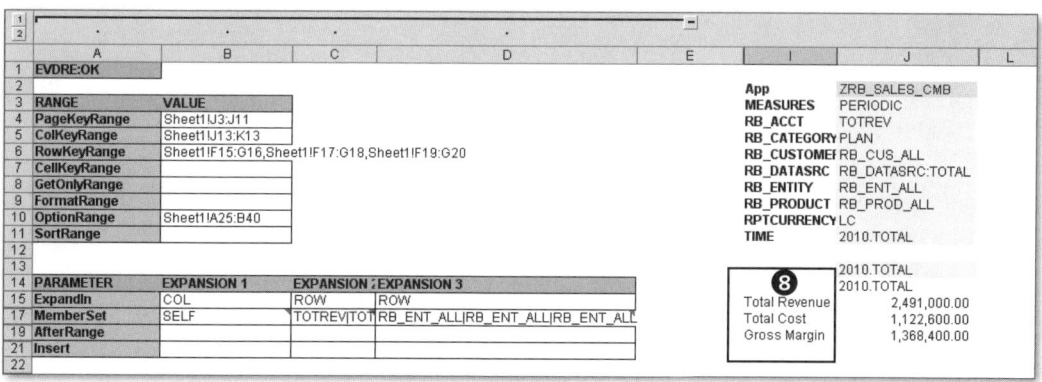

Figure 5.25 Creating a Structure in a Report —Part E

5 | Reporting, Planning, and Analysis in SAP BusinessObjects Planning and Consolidation

We have now created a report that groups data based on your requirements. Next, we will see how to use VB macros in reports.

Usage of Visual Basic Macros in Reports

We have an account called Gross Margin created as a member in the Account dimension. This account is set as a node of income and expense accounts. The gross margin is calculated by aggregating the values in the accounts. Now, instead of using the hierarchy for calculating the gross margin, we want to use a VB macro that subtracts total cost from total revenue to derive the gross margin.

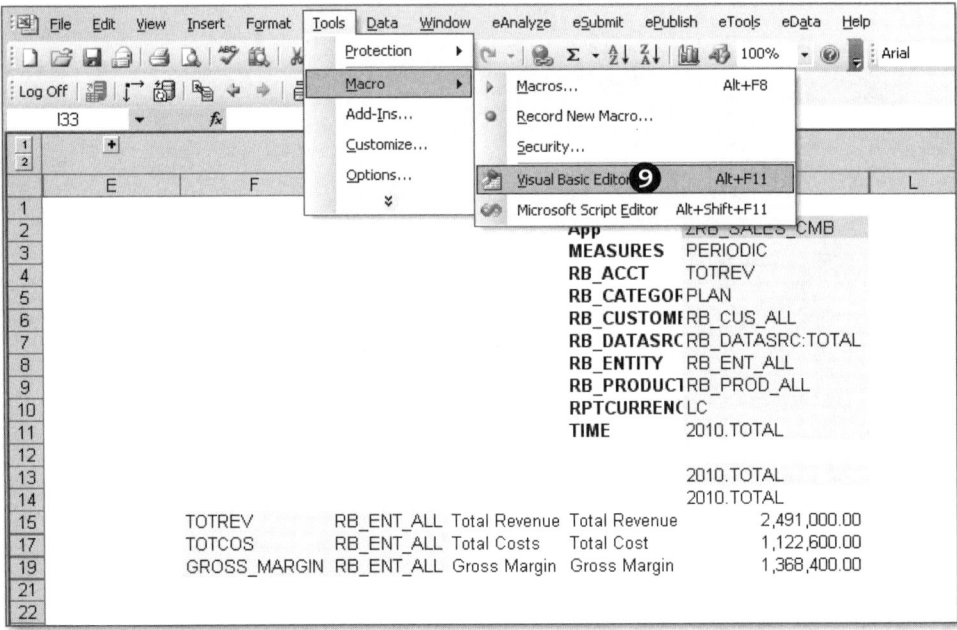

Figure 5.26 Usage of Visual Basic Macros in a Report—Part A

To perform this calculation, we must develop a macro using VB. Any time data is expanded in SAP BusinessObjects Planning and Consolidation; for this, the function AFTER_EXPAND is executed. We can include VB code in this function to perform certain specific tasks. In our example, we will use this function to derive the gross margin. The AFTER_EXPAND function should be in a separate module (Figure 5.27, ❿ and ⓫).

218

1. From the menu, click Tools and, under the Macro submenu, select Visual Basic Editor (Figure 5.26 ❾). Then, create a new module and include the code shown in Figure 5.27, ⓬.

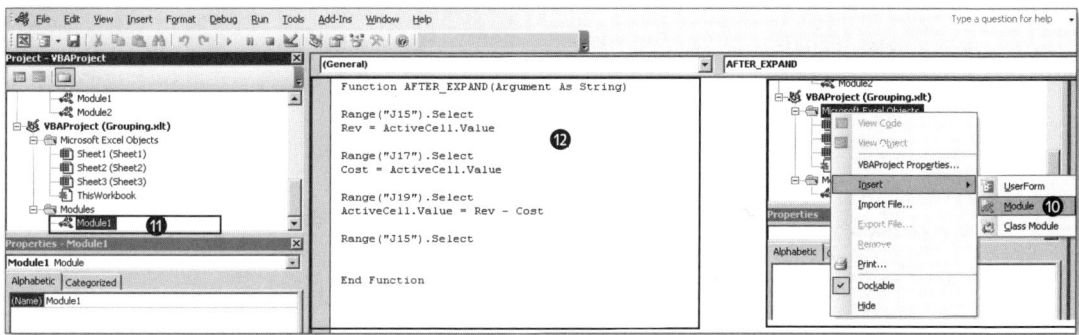

Figure 5.27 Usage of Visual Basic Macros in a BPC Report—Part B

2. This code reads the total revenues value in cell J15 and the total cost value in J17, and populates the gross margin in cell J19.

3. The last statement in the code is used to set the cursor in cell J15.

In this example, we coded our macro in the AFTER_EXPAND function. Depending on specific business requirements, you can execute a custom operation in any of the functions shown in Table 5.8.

Function
BEFORE_CHANGECVW
AFTER_CHANGECVW
BEFORE_REFRESH
AFTER_REFRESH
BEFORE_SEND
AFTER_SEND
BEFORE_EXPAND
AFTER_EXPAND

Table 5.8 Functions Where VB Macros Can be Coded

The name of the function tells you when the function will be executed; for example, the AFTER_CHANGECVW function is executed after changing CV values.

You should now understand how to create a report using VB macros. We coded the formula for the gross margin and populated a cell with this value.

Syntax for MemberSet

We will conclude this section by providing you with a few tips for developing syntax to specify member values for a dimension in the MemberSet. You should use the conventions and guidelines as shown in Figure 5.28 when developing the syntax.

Combination	Expression*	Example	Incorrect use case	Comment
Member ID + Member ID	[Member ID],[Member ID]	2006.Jan,2006.Feb ExtSales,ICSales	2006.Jan ,2006.Feb ExtSales , ICSales	Space is not allowed.
Member ID + Flag	[Member ID],[Flag]	Actual,DEP ICSales,BAS(2006.TOTAL) SalesKorea,LDEP(2,BalanceSheet) BAS(2006.Q1),2006.Q1	Actual DEP SalesKorea LDEP(2,BalanceSheet) BAS(2006.Q1) 2006.Q1	Space is not allowed.
			Actual or DEP SalesKorea or LDEP(2,BalanceSheet) BAS(2006.Q1) or 2006.Q1	'AND'/ 'OR' is not allowed.
Member ID + Filter	[Member ID],[Filter]	ExSales,ACCTYPE="INC"	ExSales ACCTYPE="INC"	Space is not allowed.
			ExSales or ACCTYPE="INC"	'AND'/ 'OR' is not allowed.
Flag + Flag	[Flag],[Flag]	SELF,DEP BAS,DEP(2006.Q1) LDEP(2),BAS	SELF DEP BAS DEP(2006.Q1) LDEP(2) ,BAS	Space is not allowed.
Flag + Filter	[Flag] and [Filter]	BAS(2006.Q1) and LEVEL="MONTH" Budget and Period="2006" LDEP(2,BalanceSheet) and Year="2007" SELF,,DEP and ACCTYPE="INC",ID=Account:SalesKorea MEMBERS and Group="ACTUAL"	Budget, Period="2008" MEMBERS Group="ACTUAL" LDEP(2,BalanceSheet) Year="2007"	Comma is not allowed.
			Budget or Period="2006" MEMBERS or Group="ACTUAL" LDEP(2,BalanceSheet) or Year="2007"	'OR' is not allowed.
Flag + ParentAfter	[Flag],[ParentAfter]	SELF,ParentAfter DEP(2006.Total),ParentAfter,SELF ParentAfter,MEMBERS and Acctype="INC" and Group="Profit & Loss"	SELF ParentAfter DEP(2006.Total) ParentAfter SELF	Space is not allowed.
			SELF or ParentAfter DEP(2006.Total) or ParentAfter or SELF	'AND'/ 'OR' is not allowed.
Filter + Filter	[Filter] and/or [Filter]	AccType="INC" or AccType="EXP" and calc="N" Year="2007" or Period="2006"	CALC="Y" and [YEAR="2006" or PERIOD="TOTAL"]	Bracket is not allowed.
			YEAR="2006",CALC="Y"	Comma is not allowed.

Figure 5.28 SAP AG Usage and Considerations of EvDRE for BPC 7.0M

After reading this section, you should now know how to create reports using standard templates. We discussed the usage of EV functions to develop custom reports, and you learned how to develop and execute reports on the web using drag-and-drop functionality. In the next section, we will explain how to use input schedules to enter and modify data in an application.

5.2 Planning in SAP BusinessObjects Planning and Consolidation Using Input Schedules

An input schedule is used for entering and modifying data in an application. For input schedule reports, data entered in the report can be validated and updated in the database.

The following are some of the uses and features of an input schedule:

- **Entry of data at the base member level**
  When using input schedules, the dimension member to be updated cannot be a hierarchy member. The rows in the input schedule should be base members. For example, if the Revenue account is a hierarchy member and is a parent of several base members, it cannot be directly used in the input schedule. The data needs to be entered only for the base members that make up the hierarchy member.

- **Concurrency lock**
  When data on an input schedule is sent for updating, the locks on the data are checked. These locks are also called *concurrency locks* and are designed to prevent two users from updating the same set of data at the same time. If two users enter data for the same selection and try to send the data to the database at the same time, only the user who obtained the lock first will be able to update the data. The user who sends the request for a lock later will get an error message stating that another user has already obtained the lock and that the update cannot happen at this time.

- **Work status**
  Work status can be configured to prevent changes from being made to data; for example, the plan data for 2010 can be set to the locked status so that no further changes can be made to the data. When a user attempts to modify data for a region that is locked, he receives a message indicating that the data cannot be modified due to work status locks. We will discuss work status in detail in Chapter 7.

▶ **Validation of data**

SAP BusinessObjects Planning and Consolidation for NetWeaver supports creating validations in the SAP NetWeaver BW system. For example, a validation can be set up to ensure transaction data entered for an entity located in the U.S. to accept USD as the currency. If data for an entity located in the U.S. is entered with EUR as the currency, the validation test fails and the data is rejected. Transaction UJ_VALIDATION is available for configuring validations in the SAP NetWeaver BW system. This is a new functionality that is available only in SAP BusinessObjects Planning and Consolidation for NetWeaver.

ABAP can be used to create custom logic to enforce validations when using this transaction. The validation mechanism can be used to configure validation rules that are checked before data is entered or updated. We will discuss how validations are used and set up in Chapter 6.

5.2.1 Standard Templates for Input Schedules

Similar to the standard templates used for reporting, standard templates are available for entering data. The standard templates for input schedules are also based on the EvDRE function. A list of standard templates used for input schedules is shown in Table 5.9.

Template Name	Description
Account Trend	The Account Trend input schedule is used for displaying and modifying the current trend of data based on the Time dimension. The account members are displayed in the rows, and time data is displayed in the columns.
Consolidating	The Consolidating input schedule contains Account Type members in the rows, and Entity members in the columns.
Entity Trend	The Entity Trend input schedule is set up similarly to the Account Trend template. The only difference is that the Entity Trend input schedule contains Entity members in the rows, and the Account Trend input schedule contains account members in the rows.
Nested Row	The Nested Row input schedule is set up so that no more than one dimension can be specified in the rows.
Comparative	The Comparative input schedule is defined to display account members in the rows and category members in the columns.

Table 5.9 Standard Templates for Input Schedules

5.2.2 Workbook Options

Before we go into creating an input schedule, it will be helpful to look at the various workbook options that are applicable for reports and input schedules. You can set the workbook options by selecting Workbook Options from the eTools menu. The available selections provide additional control and further customization features that may be required in a report or an input schedule. The settings for these options are available in Workbook Options, and are outlined in Table 5.10.

Workbook Option	Description
Type	The type indicates whether a workbook is a report or an input schedule.
	If the user needs to modify and update the data in an application, the report should be set as an input schedule report.
Refresh and Expansion	The following options are available to refresh data:
	▶ Refresh Workbook on Worksheet Update: This option refreshes the data when a change is made to an affected data cell.
	▶ Refresh After Data Send: When the workbook is an input schedule, a refresh is performed after sending the data.
	▶ Expansion on Workbook Open: When this option is selected, the expansion is automatically executed when the workbook is opened.
	▶ Expansion on Current View Change: When this option is selected, the expansion is executed automatically when there is a change to the expansion member in the current view.
	▶ Refresh by Sheet: When multiple worksheets are opened, selecting this option refreshes worksheets individually.
Allow Users to Change Options	If you check this option, non-administrators can also change the workbook options. If this option is not checked, only administrators can change workbook options.

Table 5.10 Workbook Options

Workbook Option	Description
Drilldown	This option specifies drilldown behavior. There are two options: ▶ Expand by Overwriting Rows: When this option is selected, the expanded members display the data below the expanded member, clearing the existing members. ▶ Expand by Inserting Rows: When this option is selected, the existing members are displayed below the expanded members. The existing members are not cleared.
Read Options for Comment	This option can be used to specify how a comment entered in SAP BusinessObjects Planning and Consolidation is displayed: ▶ Within Cell: Text is displayed inside the cell. ▶ As Excel Popup: Text is displayed in an Excel dialog box.
Set Maximum Expansion	This option is available to set the maximum columns and rows that can be displayed in the workbook. This option is used for performance reasons: ▶ The default number of columns is set to 100. ▶ The default number of rows is set to 1000. ▶ The maximum number of columns is 255. The maximum number of rows is 65,000. This setting determines the maximum rows and columns in the report.
Override Current View Settings	The workbook always uses the dimension members selected in the CV settings to display the report or input schedule. If you want to override the current view settings, you can specify a two-range dimension containing the dimension and member values. If you do so, the value of the dimension members specified here is used and overrides the current view settings. This applies only to EvDRE templates.

Table 5.10 Workbook Options (Cont.)

Workbook Option	Description
Save the Session CV with the Workbook	When you are running different reports in a session, the value in the CVs is used for all reports.
	When you want to use different member values for the same dimension in different reports, this option can be checked.
Set Worksheet Password	A specific SAP BusinessObjects Planning and Consolidation password may be set to secure the workbook. This password works differently from the Excel-based password. Do not use the Excel-based password in SAP BusinessObjects Planning and Consolidation, because expansions may not work properly.
Lock Status	The status below this heading indicates whether a workbook is open or locked.
	A workbook can be locked by selecting the Park N Go option from the eTools menu.

Table 5.10 Workbook Options (Cont.)

5.2.3 Developing an Input Schedule

We will now explain how to create an input schedule to manually enter and modify data.

1. The creation of an input schedule is similar to the creation of a report. First, create a report using the EvDRE function that has the Account dimension in the row, and the Time dimension in the column. Alternatively, we can also use the Data Input task that is available in the available task categories (refer back to Figure 5.1, ❸) to create the input schedule. The selections of dimension member values are shown in Figure 5.29, ❶.

2. After creating the report, select the eTools menu and then select Workbook Options. Select Input Schedule as the workbook type (Figure 5.30, ❷). This allows users to use the workbook to enter or modify data in an application.

3. The Refresh Options are used to automatically refresh the data when changes to CV selections are made (Figure 5.30, ❸). Click on the OK button (Figure 5.30, ❹) after you have set the options.

5 | Reporting, Planning, and Analysis in SAP BusinessObjects Planning and Consolidation

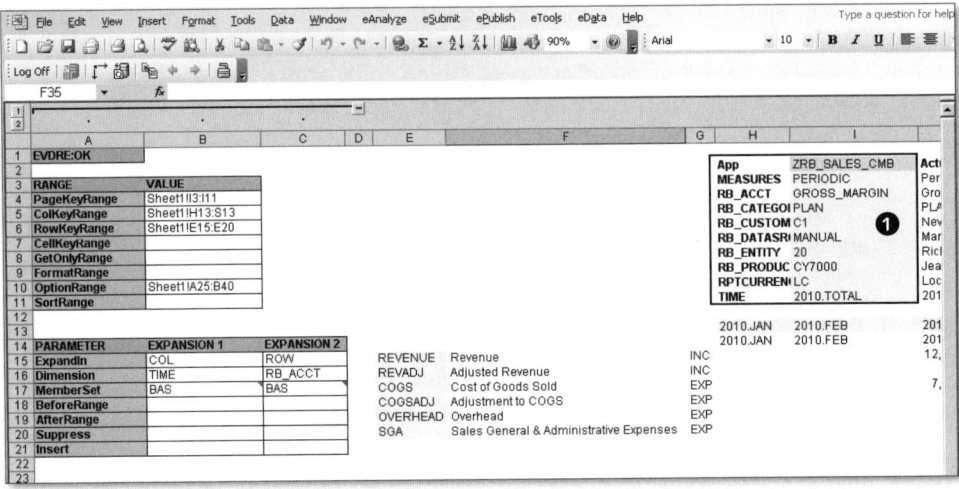

Figure 5.29 Creating an Input Schedule—Part A

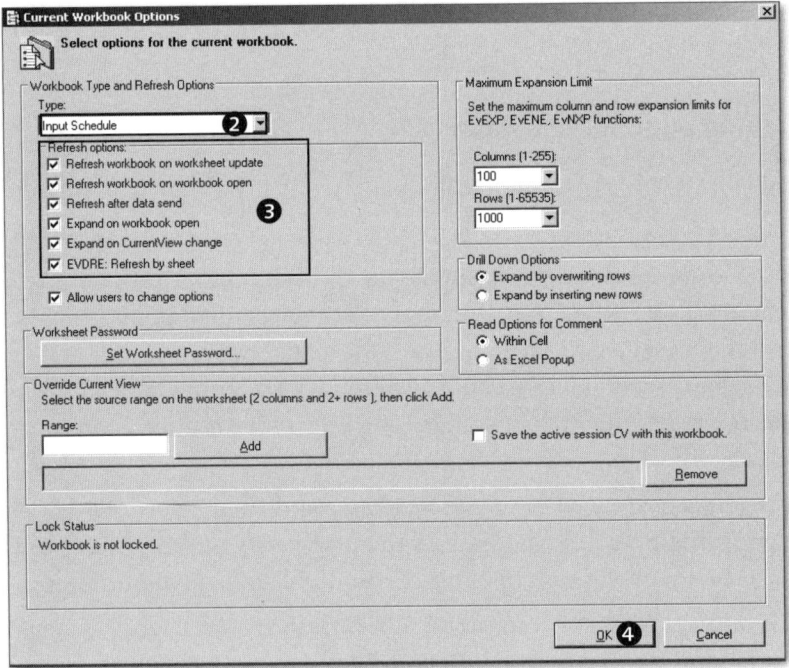

Figure 5.30 Creating an Input Schedule—Part B

4. After selecting the type of report to be an input schedule, click on Send and Refresh Schedule (Figure 5.31, ❺). This is required before the report can be used as an input schedule.

5. Enter "2,000" as the amount for February 2010 (Figure 5.31, ❻). Then, click on the Send and Refresh Schedule button again to send the data to the database. This opens the Send and Refresh Schedules dialog box. Choose Active Workbook and click on Refresh (Figure 5.31, ❼).

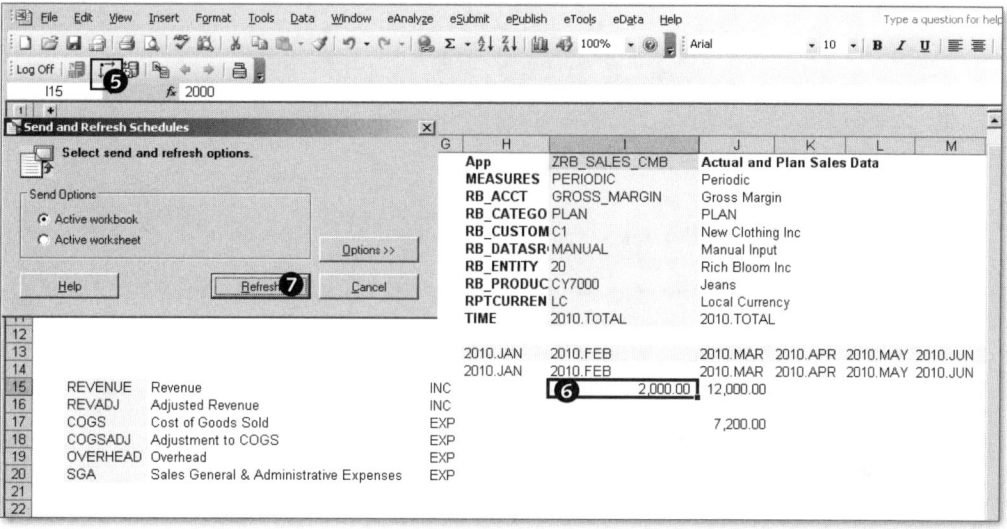

Figure 5.31 Creating an Input Schedule—Part C

6. The Business Planning and Consolidation dialog box is displayed, indicating the number of records that will be sent to the database and asking you to confirm the update to the database (Figure 5.32, ❽).

7. After you confirm the action to continue, a message log displays the details of the records updated in the database (Figure 5.32, ❾).

You should now understand how to create an input schedule. We will now discuss additional properties that can be set for an input schedule.

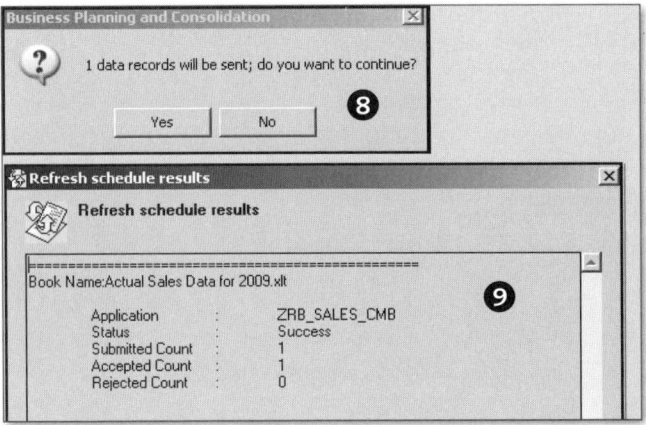

Figure 5.32 Creating an Input Schedule—Part D

5.2.4 Worksheet Dimension Lock Option

In the previous example, we used the selection of dimension member values in the CV for the input schedule. If you want to override the selection of dimension member values in the CV with other specific values for a report or input schedule, you can use the worksheet dimension lock options. The values specified here override the CV settings for the member, and any settings specified in the workbook options of a report or input schedule.

The worksheet dimension lock options are available under DATA INPUT • AVAILABLE TASK CATEGORIES • SCHEDULE TASKS (Figure 5.1, ❸).

5.2.5 Park N Go

Park N Go is a function that is available in SAP BusinessObjects Planning and Consolidation to lock either the CV or both the CV and the data in a report or input schedule. This function can also be used to take a workbook offline. This feature is useful when you want a user of a particular report or input schedule to use specific dimension member value selections when executing this report, and to prevent him from refreshing the data. Another application of this functionality is to take an input schedule offline, send it to a user who does not have access to SAP BusinessObjects Planning and Consolidation, have him enter data, and then bring the input schedule online for updating the data entered by the user.

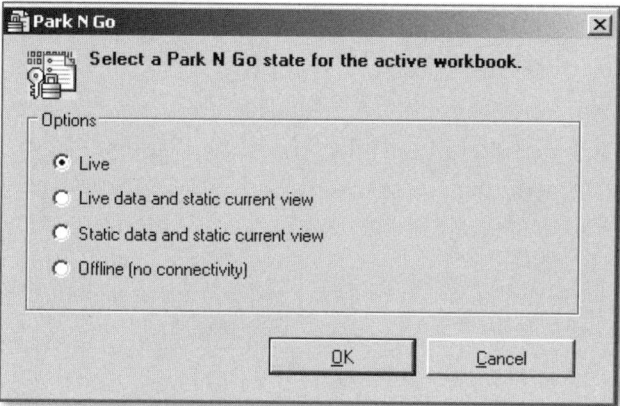

Figure 5.33 Park N Go

You can access Park N Go by selecting ETOOLS • PARK N GO and set one of the following options (Figure 5.33):

- **Live**
  This is the default setting for a report or input schedule.
- **Live Data and Static Current View**
  This option locks the CV in a report or input schedule. When a user changes the CV selections, the selections for the report or input schedule are not changed.
- **Static Data and Static Current View**
  This option not only locks the CV in a report or input schedule but also prevents the data in the report or input schedule from being refreshed.
- **Offline (No Connectivity)**
  Using this option, a workbook can be taken offline and distributed to users who do not have access to SAP BusinessObjects Planning and Consolidation. After these users have made changes to the data, the workbook can be brought online again by selecting the Live option.

5.3 Summary

In this chapter, we explained the steps for reporting, planning, and analyzing data in SAP BusinessObjects Planning and Consolidation. We discussed examples of how to use dynamic templates and create a custom report using the EV functions and explained how to create and deploy reports on the web. We then went on to create an input schedule, and explained how to use it for entering and modifying data in an application.

In Chapter 6, we will introduce you to different types of business logic that can be configured in SAP BusinessObjects Planning and Consolidation and see how it automates several tasks related to planning and consolidation. Here, you will learn how to configure business rules, develop K2 scripts, and set up validation.

6   Developing Business Logic in SAP BusinessObjects Planning and Consolidation

Every organization has rules and policies that guide its business processes and must be incorporated into IT applications; this is no different for planning and consolidation applications. In this chapter, we will discuss the different options available in SAP BusinessObjects Planning and Consolidation for defining logic and automating the process of deriving data and enforcing business rules.

In Section 6.1, you will learn how to use dimension formulas to perform calculations in SAP BusinessObjects Planning and Consolidation applications.

In Section 6.2, we will discuss the usage of K2 logic or script logic in SAP BusinessObjects Planning and Consolidation, and you will learn how it can be used to perform functions related to data management. (*Script logic* is a code-based logic that is used to meet complex business process requirements.)

In Section 6.3, we will discuss business rules and their usage in SAP BusinessObjects Planning and Consolidation. We will briefly look at how they are used to perform certain common tasks related to planning and consolidation. (We will also discuss business rules in Chapter 9, when we discuss the process of consolidating financial data for an organization.) In this section, we will explain how to perform currency translation, which is used in the context of planning and consolidation. Currency translation is a requirement for an organization that does business in more than one country and has transactions in different currencies.

In Section 6.4, we will discuss allocation. Allocation is commonly used by an organization to apportion expenses incurred by a common entity, such as a corporate entity, to other units based on certain drivers.

In Section 6.5, we will review the usage of BAdIs to define business rules in SAP BusinessObjects Planning and Consolidation. BAdIs are coded using the ABAP language, which provides additional flexibility when there is a need to write custom code. It also helps to leverage ABAP expertise in the organization when implementing SAP BusinessObjects Planning and Consolidation applications.

In Section 6.6, we will discuss validation of data in SAP BusinessObjects Planning and Consolidation, explaining how to use driver dimensions to define validation rules and enforce integrity of data.

We will start by discussing how dimension formulas are used to automatically calculate values in an SAP BusinessObjects Planning and Consolidation application.

6.1 Dimension Logic

In the last few chapters, we discussed how dimensions are used in SAP BusinessObjects Planning and Consolidation. We went through the process of defining a dimension and loading data into it, and talked about how it is integrated into an application and used in reporting. In Chapter 3, we explained that a dimension can have a property with a technical name of "Formula," which means that it contains formulas that aid in the automatic calculation of data. This process is referred to as *dimension logic*.

6.1.1 Dimension Formulas

To use dimension formulas, you must include a property with the technical name "Formula" to the dimension. This property contains a formula; for example, in the Account dimension, there could be a Gross Margin dimension member that has the formula property filled with a formula called "Total Revenues – Total Cost."

> **Note**
> Ensure that your formula property is set to be of sufficient length so that it can accommodate the formula defined for the member.

Certain rules apply to the formula property of a dimension. They are as follows:

- Formulas can be set only for base members and not hierarchy members of a dimension.
- When a formula is defined for a dimension member, you will not be able to directly enter any plan data for that member.
- In the formula, the name of the dimension should be used to refer to dimension members; however, the dimension name is not required for the Account dimension. For example, the formula property of dimension member Product 3 can be set as follows:

    [PRODUCT].[Product1] + [PRODUCT].[Product2]

    Note the usage of the technical name of the PRODUCT dimension in the formula.

- The dimension formula for the dimension member applies to all applications containing the dimension in the application set.
- SAP BusinessObjects Planning and Consolidation supports the use of addition, subtraction, multiplication, and division operators when defining formulas.
- Multi-dimension expressions can be used when defining formulas; these are especially useful for complex formulas. The list of MDX expressions that are available can be displayed by executing the BAPI_MDPROVIDER_GET_FUNCTIONS function module in the SAP NetWeaver BW system. The ApShell comes with a list of standard MDX formulas, available in the file *Mdxlib.lgf*. When maintaining dimension members to include MDX formulas, specify the name of this library file in the Options Sheet of the dimension member maintenance screen.
- The syntax of the formula is checked when dimension members are activated using the Process dimension option.
- When a formula is defined for a dimension member, the system calculates the result for the dimension member based on the formula at runtime. Including formulas for a dimension member can cause data retrieval to take more time depending on the amount of the data on which the formula has to work.

6.1.2 Solve Order

In the context of defining dimension formulas, it is important to understand the *solve order keyword*. In some reports, you may display more than one dimension member that is calculated based on a dimension formula, and the solve order function helps in resolving conflicts between two different formulas used in a report. In this situation, it sets the priority for which formula should be used.

For example, let us look at a scenario where you have the Account dimension with members Account 1, Account 2, and Account 3 in an application set. Account 3 is defined as a calculated member based on the following formula:

```
Account3 = [ACCOUNT].[Account1]/[ACCOUNT].[Account2]
```

Assume that the same application set includes another dimension, Product, with the members Product 1, Product 2, and Product 3. The Product dimension is defined as a calculated member based on the following formula:

```
Product 3 = [PRODUCT].[Product1] + [PRODUCT].[Product2]
```

Here, we have two calculated members, Account 3 for the Account dimension, and Product 3 for the Product dimension. For these dimension formulas, we can set the solve order function to set which formula should take precedence over the other. A formula that has the solve order defined as a lower value takes priority over others with a higher value; a formula that has the solve order defined as a value of 0 takes the highest priority. We will define the formulas to include the solve order function as follows:

```
Account3 = [ACCOUNT].[Account1]/[ACCOUNT].[Account2];Solve_Order=5
Product 3 = [PRODUCT].[Product1] + [PRODUCT].[ Product2];Solve_Order=50
```

Consider a report that contains the accounts in rows and products in columns. The format of such a report is shown in Table 6.1.

	Product1	Product2	Product3
Account1	120	130	250
Account2	5	5	10
Account3	24	26	50

Table 6.1 Demonstrate Solve Order

Now look at the value of the cell that intersects Account 3 and Product 3. The result is 24 + 26 = 50, not 250/10 = 25. This is because the Account formula takes precedence over the Product formula, because the value of solve order for the Account formula is less than that of the Product formula.

Now, let us create a Gross Margin dimension member in the Account dimension. We will calculate the gross margin by subtracting the total cost from total revenue. Recall from Chapter 3 that we set the gross margin as a hierarchy node of total revenue and total cost. To demonstrate the use of the Dimension formula, we will no longer have the gross margin as a hierarchy node. Instead, we will use gross margin as a base dimension member and define a dimension formula that calculates the gross margin.

We will now create a dimension formula for the Account dimension in our planning application.

1. Log-in to the BPC Admin Console, select the ZRB_GM_PLAN application set, and select the ZRB_SALES_CMB application.
2. From the Dimension Library, select the RB_ACCT dimension, and then click on the Dimension Members task in the right pane. You will see the list of dimension members for the Account dimension displayed.
3. The GROSS_MARGIN account was set as the parent for the TOTALREV and TOTALCOS members. Remove the parent relationship for the TOTREV and TOTCOS accounts, because we will be using a dimension formula to derive the value for the GROSS_MARGIN account.
4. Then, go to the cell that is the associated with the formula property for the GROSS_MARGIN account, and enter the formula as shown in Figure 6.1.
5. After entering the formula, process the changes for the Account dimension, then run a report that shows the gross margin account. The application now uses the formula to derive this value (Figure 6.2).

6 | Developing Business Logic in SAP BusinessObjects Planning and Consolidation

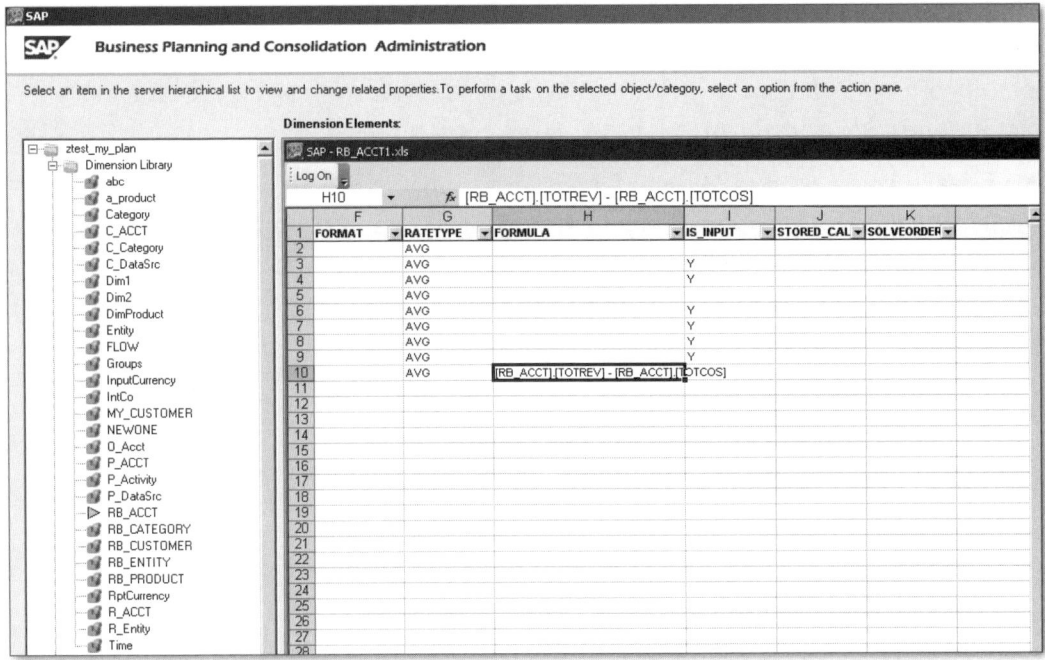

Figure 6.1 Creating a Formula for the Gross Margin Account

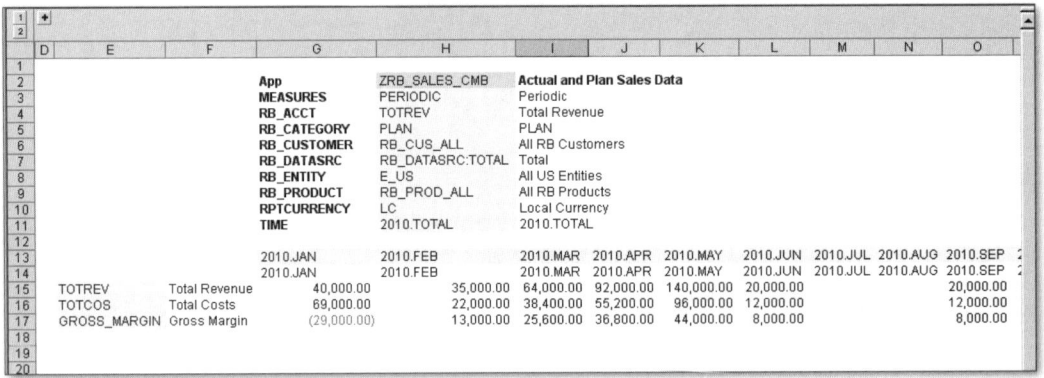

Figure 6.2 Reporting the Gross Margin Account using the Dimension Formula

In this section, we explained how to use dimension formulas to automatically calculate values. We also discussed the importance of using solve order when defining a formula, and how it can be used when multiple formulas are in conflict.

In the next section, we will explain the use of script logic in SAP BusinessObjects Planning and Consolidation and see how it can help us satisfy detailed business requirements that cannot otherwise be met using a standard SAP BusinessObjects Planning and Consolidation configuration.

6.2 Script Logic

At times, a business process may be so complex that a standard configuration is not enough to satisfy a requirement, or it may not be feasible to use dimension formulas. In these cases, script logic, or K2 logic, can be used to meet the requirement.

Consider a business scenario where you are planning sales for a future period. You copied last year's actual sales data as the basis of planning for the current year; however, due to changes in current demand, it is now necessary to adjust revenue based on the realities of the market, by, say, accepting a percentage value from the user to either increase or decrease revenue. This is a good candidate for script logic because it is not possible to meet this requirement using the standard SAP BusinessObjects Planning and Consolidation application or dimension logic. Script logic, on the other hand, can be used to increase or decrease revenues by a certain percentage for certain selections.

The script language provides full-fledged language support to write custom logic to meet a specific business requirement. The language constructs are similar to 4GL and can be easily included in an SAP BusinessObjects Planning and Consolidation application. They are powerful and efficient to use, especially when a lot of data needs to be processed.

A script file is used to create the code and is stored with the extension .LGF. We will now look at some of the common instructions used in script logic.

6.2.1 Script Logic Construct

In this subsection, we will discuss some of the commands used when developing script logic.

Pass Specific Dimension Members

It may be necessary to pass specific members to apply in the script logic. This can be achieved using the following coding instruction, which overrides any members selected for the dimension in the CV or prompt statements for that dimension. This will be helpful if you want to use only a specific member list in your script logic; more than one member can be specified when using this statement.

```
*XDIM_MEMBERSET {dimension name} = {member set}
```

The following instruction will use the member set ACTUAL, BUDGET for the Dimension category when processing the script file:

```
*XDIM_MEMBERSET Category = Actual, Budget
```

You can also use the *XDIM_MEMBERSET instruction with the "not equal to" operator, as follows:

```
*XDIM_MEMBERSET CURRENCY<>USD
```

If you want to read all of the members of a dimension, you can use the keyword <ALL>, as follows:

```
*XDIM_MEMBERSET INTCO = <ALL>
```

Adding Members to Existing Member Sets

A *member set* refers to a set of dimension member values that is selected for processing from an application in a script. You can add members to an existing member set using the following instruction:

```
*XDIM_ADDMEMBERSET {dimension} = {member set}
```

This will add the members specified in the instruction to the list of existing selections.

```
*XDIM_ADDMEMBERSET CURRENCY = LC
```

For example, if the user has selected the USD and EUR currency dimension members, the following instruction will also add the LC currency to the list of dimension members. This is helpful when you want to make sure a dimension member is always included in the list of members for that dimension.

Threshold for Maximum Number of Dimension Members Processed for a Dimension

In some cases, when the number of dimension members selected for processing is too high, the execution performance of the script logic may be impacted. In these cases, it may be necessary to break the queries into more than one to improve performance. The following instruction can be used to specify the threshold for the maximum number of dimension members before the query has to be split:

```
*XDIM_MAXMEMBERS {dimension} = {max number of members}
```

In the following instruction, if the number of entities to be processed exceeds the limit of 20 members, the query processor will break the query into multiple queries of no more than 20 entities each:

```
*XDIM_MAXMEMBERS Entity = 20
```

Storing and Retrieving Variable Values

You can build a dynamic set of members and store it in a variable using the following instruction, which enables the values of a particular dimension member ID or property value to be stored in a variable. The values stored in the variable can be used later in the logic.

```
*SELECT ({variable}, {what}, {from}, {where}
```

The following example shows how to store data in a variable using the *SELECT instruction:

```
*SELECT(%REPORTING_CURRENCIES%, ID, CURRENCY, [GROUP] = 'REP')
```

In this instruction, the user can retrieve the ID of all members in the CURRENCY dimension, where the GROUP property has the value REP. The <variable> is the %REPORTING_CURRENCIES%, the <what> is the ID that will be stored in the variable, the <from> represents the dimension to use, and the [GROUP] (<where>) represents the property to pull the data from the dimension specified in the <from>.

The values stored in the variable using the instruction can be used to set the member values for a dimension, as follows:

```
*XDIM_MEMBER_SET CURRENCY=%REPORTING_CURRENCIES%
```

In this case, %REPORTING_CURRENCIES% is the variable containing the values.

Members Passed to a Dimension

The %SET% keyword can be used to determine the members that are passed for a dimension. Additional members can be added using the following instruction:

```
*XDIM_MEMBERSET ENTITY = %SET%, SPECIAL_ENTITY
```

In this example, the "SPECIAL_ENTITY" entity is added to the entity dimension list.

Looping—WHEN/ENDWHEN Statement

The WHEN/ENDWHEN structure is used when it is necessary to update the current record and/or generate new records. The syntax of this structure is as follows:

```
*WHEN {criteria}
*IS {valid condition1}[,{valid condition2},…]
*REC[([FACTOR|EXPRESSION={Expression}[,{dim1}={member},{dim2}=…])] [*R
EC[([FACTOR|EXPRESSION={Expression}[,{dim1}={member},{dim2}=…])]] ….
[*ELSE] … …

*ENDWHEN
```

An example of usage is as follows:

```
*WHEN ACCOUNT.RATETYPE
*IS "AVG", "END"
*REC(FACTOR=-1, ENTITY=INTCO.ENTITY)
*ENDWHEN
```

In this example, the script logic reads all records that have the RATETYPE property equal to AVG or END and generates a new record that has a value equal to the current value, times the FACTOR. In addition, the value of the ENTITY dimension in the new record is set to the ENTITY property value associated with the INTCO dimension member of the current record. Values of all other dimensions are the same as that of the current record.

When there is no criterion to test, the following instruction can be used:

```
*WHEN *
*IS *
*REC(…)
*ENDWHEN
```

Looping — FOR/NEXT Statement

FOR/NEXT is a looping statement that allows you to apply logic to a specific set of records. The logic module supports any level of nesting of FOR...NEXT loops in the body of the logic files. The *FOR/NEXT structure can also be included inside a *WHEN/ENDWHEN structure to create new records.

The syntax for FOR/NEXT loop is as follows:

```
*FOR {variable1} = {set1} [ AND {variable2={set2}]
{text}
{text} …
*NEXT
```

The FOR/NEXT loop also supports up to two variables iterating on two independent sets of members. Here is an example:

```
*FOR %MYTIME% = %TIME_SET%
// logic content
*NEXT
```

COMMIT Statement

You can use the commit instruction anywhere in the code to commit or update the data to the database.

```
*COMMIT
```

Revaluing Using an MDX Statement

The following MDX statement can be used in an expression to revalue revenues to increase them by 10%.

```
[Account].[#Revenue] = [Account].[Revenue] * 1.10
```

The # sign is used to redefine the value posted to an account member. All calculated members should have ID preceded by the number sign (#).

LOOKUP / ENDLOOKUP Statement

The LOOKUP/ENDLOOKUP statement can be used in conjunction with a WHEN/ENDWHEN structure to retrieve ("lookup") values that may be needed either to calculate a new value or to define a criteria to be evaluated. The lookup can be performed in the current application or in a different application.

6 | Developing Business Logic in SAP BusinessObjects Planning and Consolidation

The lookup mechanism defines a relationship between the current record being processed and another record in a corresponding user-defined record set. For example, when performing currency translation, you may want to look up, in the RATE application, the value of the rate based on current entity, category, and period.

The syntax is:

```
*LOOKUP {App}
*DIM [{LookupID}:] {DimensionName}="Value" | {CallingDimensionName}
[.{Property}] [*DIM …]
*ENDLOOKUP
```

Where: {App} is the name of the application from which the values are searched; {DimensionName} is a dimension in the lookup application: {CallingDimension-Name} is a dimension in the current application; and {LookupID} is an optional identifier of the "looked-up" amount. This is only required when multiple values must be retrieved. Refer to the following example:

```
*LOOKUP RATE
*DIM R_ENTITY="GLOBAL"
*DIM SOURCECURR:INPUTCURRENCY=ENTITY.CURRENCY
*DIM DESTCURR1:INPUTCURRENCY="USD"
*DIM DESTCURR2:INPUTCURRENCY="EURO"
*DIM R_RATE=ACCOUNT.RATETYPE
*ENDLOOKUP
```

In this example, three different values are retrieved from the INPUTCURRENCY dimension (the rate of the currency of the current entity, the rate of the EURO currency, and the rate of the USD currency). Each of these values has been assigned a specific identifier (SOURCECURR, DESTCURR1, and DESTCURR2) that will be used somewhere in the WHEN/ENDWHEN structure.

Any dimension not specified in the lookup instruction is assumed to match with a corresponding dimension in the source application. In the example, the following instructions have been omitted, because they are redundant:

```
*DIM CATEGORY=CATEGORY
*DIM TIME=TIME.
```

You now know a few commands you can use when developing script logic. In the next section, we will explain how script logic can be executed.

6.2.2 Executing Script Logic

Script logic can be executed in two ways. It can be either included in the file DEFAULT.LGF and automatically executed when users enter or load data to an application, or it can be executed using a data manager package.

DEFAULT.LGF is a special type of script logic file that is executed when you load data or enter data using an input template. The SAP BusinessObjects Planning and Consolidation system runs the default logic indicated in the DEFAULT.LGF file of the application.

You can also execute a script logic file from the data manager. Using a data manager package, you can develop script logic to perform specific data management tasks and execute the script logic.

In the next section, we will explain how Rich Bloom, Inc. uses script logic to revalue plan data.

6.2.3 Creating Script Logic to Revalue Plan Data

Rich Bloom, Inc. wants to revalue the plan data for specific products, so we will now explain how this is done using script logic. In this example, we will create script logic that will allow a user to select specific products and specify a percentage by which to revalue the plan. The change in revenue will be posted to the REVADJ account.

We will first create a script logic file in SAP BusinessObjects Planning and Consolidation that contains the logic to perform revaluation. Then, we will create a process chain in SAP NetWeaver BW that can be used to execute script logic. Finally, we will configure a data management package in SAP BusinessObjects Planning and Consolidation that is associated with the script logic file and process chain and can be executed as needed.

1. Log into the BPC Admin Console and select the ZRB_GM_PLAN application set.
2. In the left pane, under ZRB_SALES_CMB, click on Script Logic (Figure 6.3, ❶); the action pane related to script logic is displayed on the right. Click on Create New Logic (Figure 6.3, ❷).
3. 3. In the New Logic dialog box, enter "REVALUE_PLAN" for Logic Name and click on OK (Figure 6.3, ❸ and ❹).

6 | Developing Business Logic in SAP BusinessObjects Planning and Consolidation

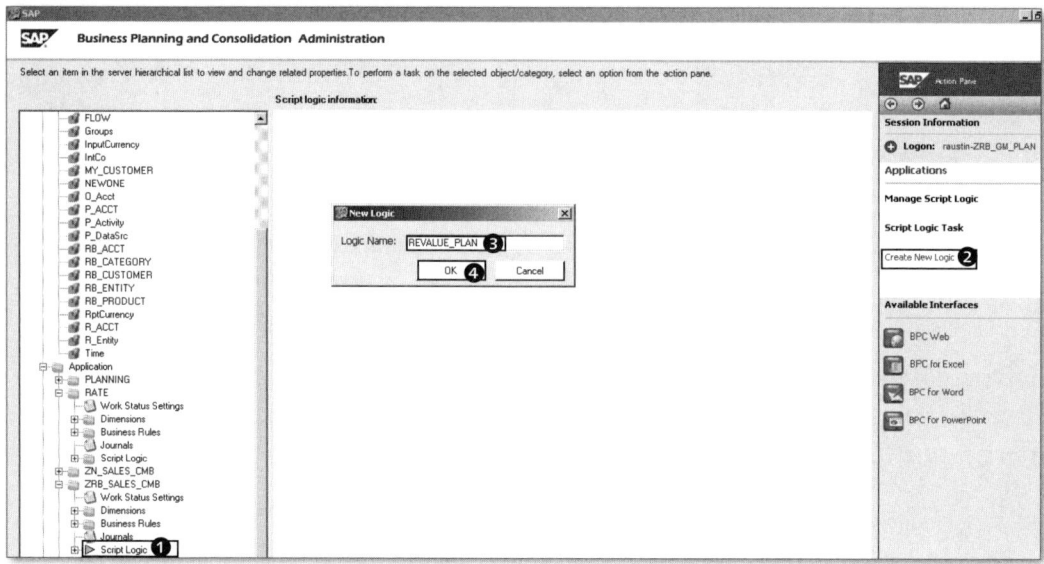

Figure 6.3 Creating Script Logic to Revalue Plan Data—Part A

4. Next, you can enter the script logic for revaluing the plan data. Enter the code as shown in Figure 6.4, ❺. The script is used to prompt the user to enter a percentage for revaluing revenue, and the increase or decrease in revenue is posted to the revenue adjustment account (REVADJ); it is calculated by multiplying the percentage increase/decrease (entered by the user) and the revenue amount. After entering the code, click on Validate and Save (Figure 6.4, ❻).

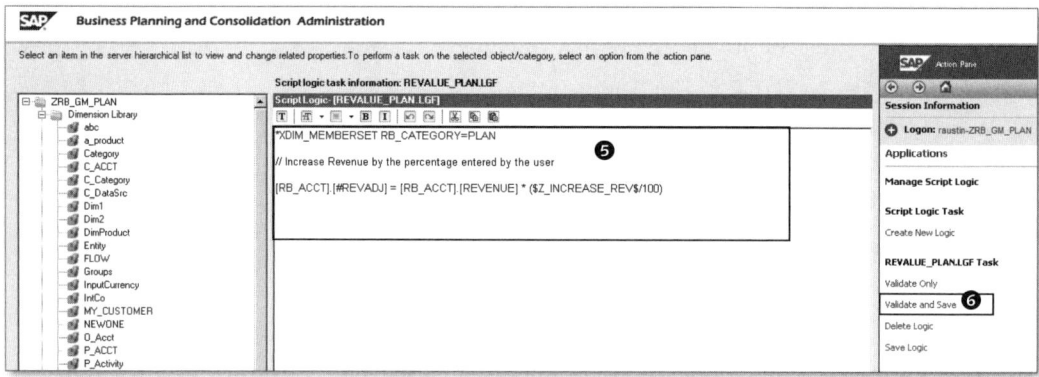

Figure 6.4 Creating Script Logic to Revalue Plan Data—Part B

244

5. Create a new process chain using Transaction RSPC in the SAP NetWeaver BW system, as shown in Figure 6.5. The process chain will include the Start process type and the following process types that are specific to SAP BusinessObjects Planning and Consolidation:

   ▶ Modify Dynamically
   ▶ Run Logic
   ▶ Clear BPC Tables

> **Note**
>
> The Clear BPC Tables process type is used in many SAP BusinessObjects Planning and Consolidation Process chains to clear temporary tables during processing.

6. Make sure you include the process types in the same order as shown in Figure 6.5. Every process type will be associated to a variant, and the variant for the Start process has to be unique for every process chain in the system. Create a new process variant for the start type.

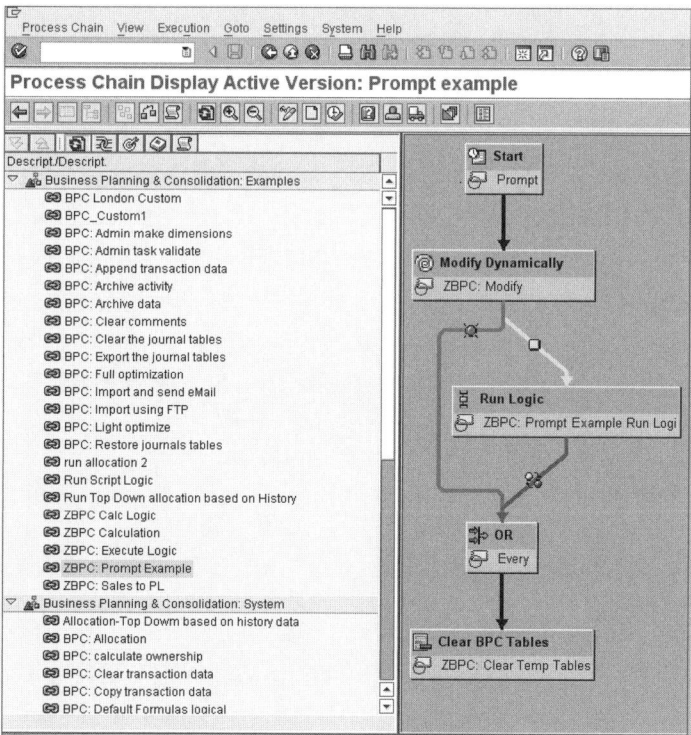

Figure 6.5 Creating Script Logic to Revalue Plan Data—Part C

6 | Developing Business Logic in SAP BusinessObjects Planning and Consolidation

7. Now, associate this process chain with a data package in SAP BusinessObjects Planning and Consolidation. To do this, go to SAP BusinessObjects Planning and Consolidation Excel, and log into the ZRB_SALES_CMB application. In the Excel interface, from the eData menu, select Organize Package List to create a new data package, and associate the process chain you created in the previous step to this package.

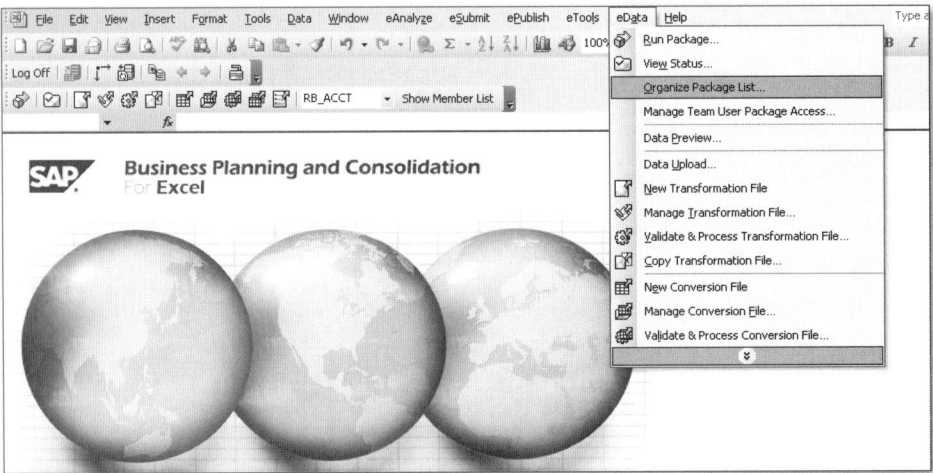

Figure 6.6 Creating Script Logic to Revalue Plan Data — Part D

8. This will open a new dialog box where you can maintain and create new packages. We will add this package under the System Administrative group. (This is just an example; you can place it into any group you want.) Click on the Add Package icon (Figure 6.7, ❼).

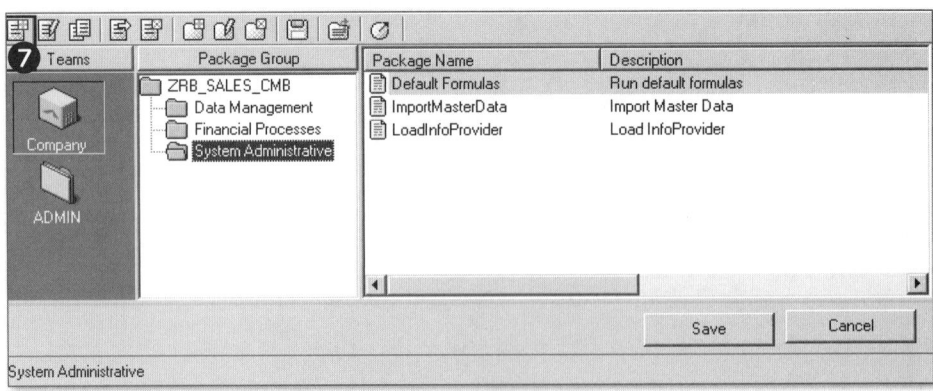

Figure 6.7 Creating Script Logic to Revalue Plan Data — Part E

246

9. Using the dropdown list, select the ZRB_PROMPT process chain you created in the earlier step in the SAP NetWeaver BW system (Figure 6.8, ❽). This process chain is run when this data package is executed. Enter "Increase Plan Revenue" as the package name (see Figure 6.8, ❾). Select the group where this package should belong using the dropdown box, and enter "Package to Increase Plan Revenue" for the description (Figure 6.8, ❿ and ⓫).

10. To give appropriate access to the package, specify whether users will be authorized to execute it. If you select User Package, users can execute the package. If you select Admin Package, only administrators can execute it (Figure 6.8, ⓬). After specifying the selection, click on the Add button (Figure 6.8, ⓭).

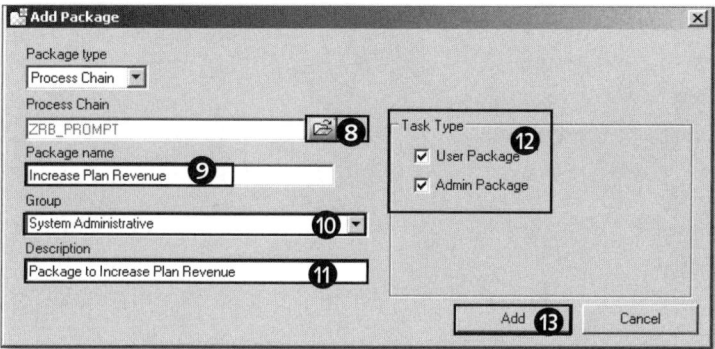

Figure 6.8 Creating Script Logic to Revalue Plan Data—Part F

11. 10. After you add the package, you will see the new package named "Increase Plan Revenue." Click on the Save button to save the package (see Figure 6.9, ⓮).

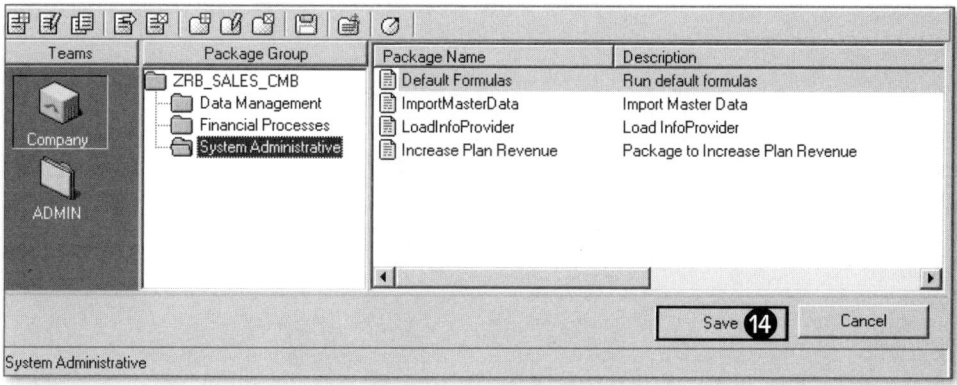

Figure 6.9 Creating Script Logic to Revalue Plan Data—Part G

6 | Developing Business Logic in SAP BusinessObjects Planning and Consolidation

12. Next, you need to associate the script logic file to the data management package. From the eData menu, select the Organize Package list to modify the data package you created. Select the Increase Plan Revenue package and right-click on the Modify option. The Modify Package dialog box displays; click on the icon (Figure 6.10, ⓯) to modify the package.

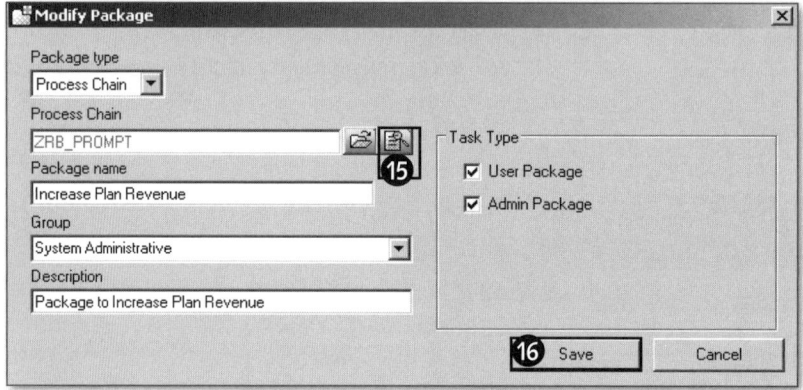

Figure 6.10 Creating Script Logic to Revalue Plan Data—Part H

13. The Data Manager Package View & Dynamic Script Editor dialog box displays. Click on Advanced to specify the package settings (Figure 6.11, ⓱).

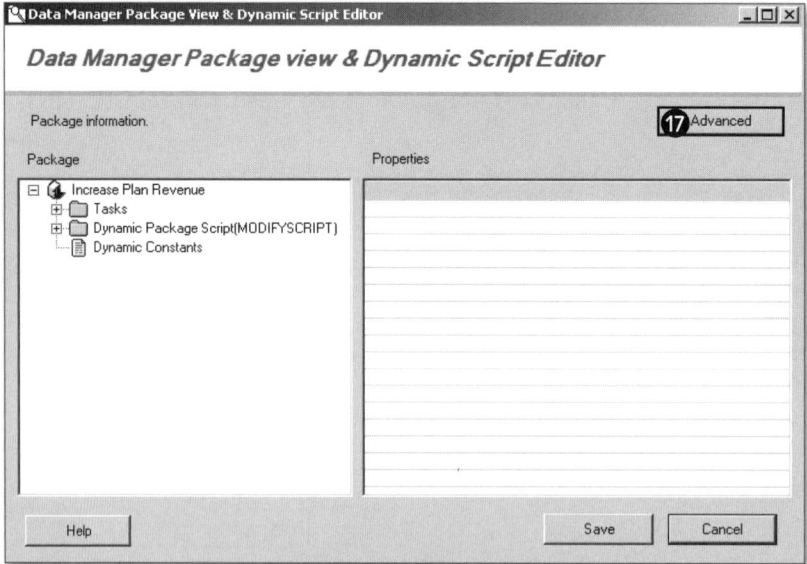

Figure 6.11 Creating Script Logic to Revalue Plan Data—Part I

248

14. Enter the code as shown in Figure 6.12, ⓲. The code is also provided here:

```
PROMPT(SELECTINPUT,,,,"%ENTITY_DIM%,%CATEGORY_DIM%,%CURRENCY_
DIM%,%TIME_DIM%,%DATASRC_DIM%,RB_CUSTOMER,RB_PRODUCT")
PROMPT(TEXT,%Z_INCREASE_REV%,"Input Revenue Increase in Percent",)
INFO(%EQU%,=)
INFO(%TAB%,;)
TASK(ZBPC_PROT_EXP_RUN_LOGIC,TAB,%TAB%)
TASK(ZBPC_PROT_EXP_RUN_LOGIC,EQU,%EQU%)
TASK(ZBPC_PROT_EXP_RUN_LOGIC,SUSER,%USER%)
TASK(ZBPC_PROT_EXP_RUN_LOGIC,SAPPSET,%APPSET%)
TASK(ZBPC_PROT_EXP_RUN_LOGIC,SAPP,%APP%)
TASK(ZBPC_PROT_EXP_RUN_LOGIC,SELECTION,%SELECTION%)
TASK(ZBPC_PROT_EXP_RUN_LOGIC,LOGICFILENAME,REVALUE_PLAN.LGF)
TASK(ZBPC_PROT_EXP_RUN_LOGIC,REPLACEPARAM,Z_INCREASE_REV%EQU%%Z_
INCREASE_REV%)
```

15. You can also copy the settings from a file. Note that in this seting, we are prompting the user to enter selection values for the Entity, Category, Currency, Time, Data Source, Customer, and Product Dimensions fields. We are also prompting the user to enter a percentage in the %Z_INCREASE_REV% field for revaluation. The name of the process variant we used in the process chain for the Run Logic task is ZBPC_PROT_EXP_RUN_LOGIC. In this code, we are also passing the values entered by the user to the process chain.

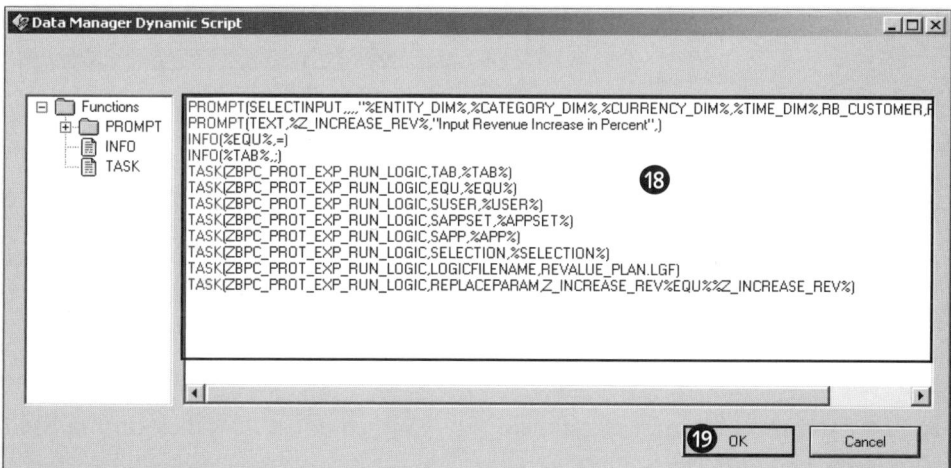

Figure 6.12 Creating Script Logic to Revalue Plan Data—Part J

16. Run a report to see the data before the revaluation is done (Figure 6.13).

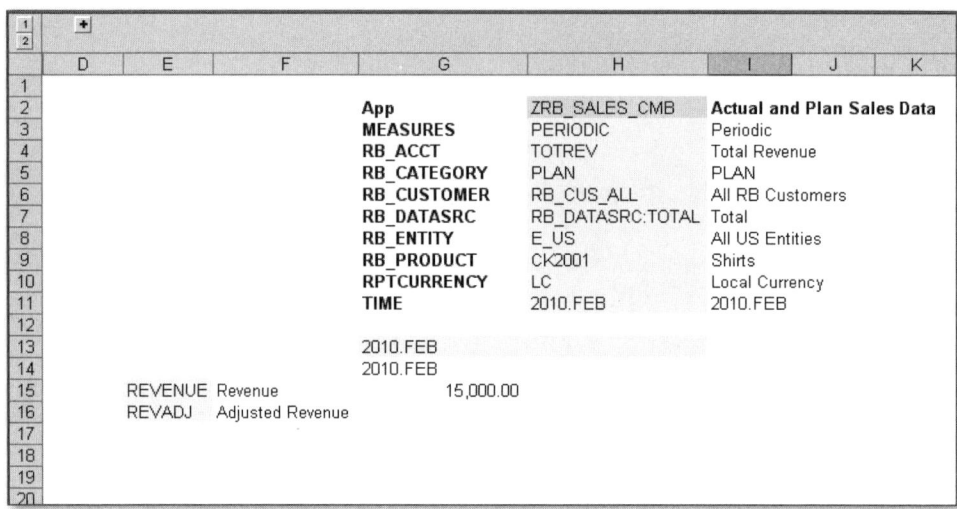

Figure 6.13 Creating Script Logic to Revalue Plan Data—Part K

17. You are now ready to execute the package to increase the plan revenue. From the eMenu menu option, select Run Packages. Select the Increase Plan Revenue package and click on Run (Figure 6.14).

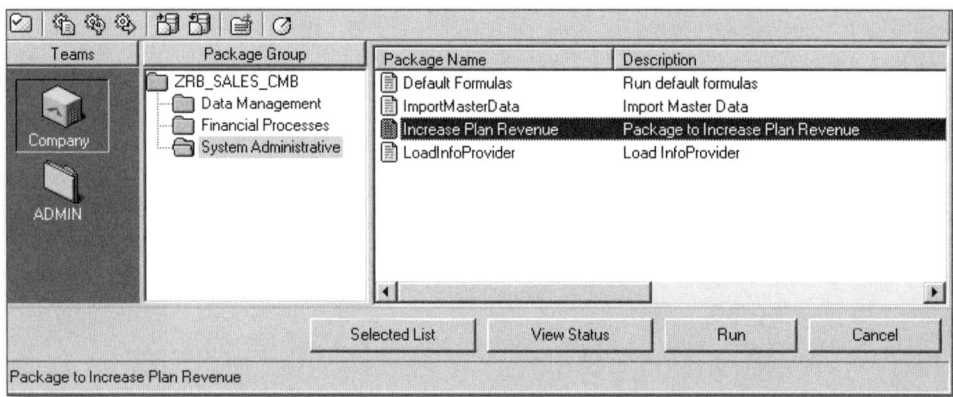

Figure 6.14 Creating Script Logic to Revalue Plan Data—Part L

18. Enter the revenue increase percent you want to effect and click on the Next button (Figure 6.15).

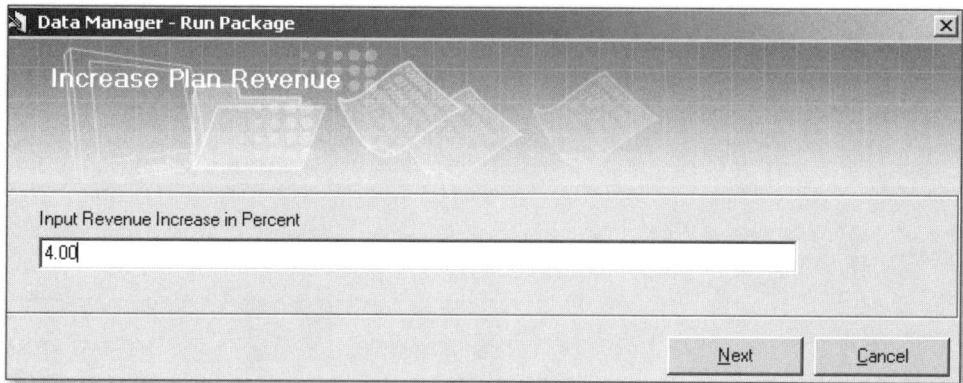

Figure 6.15 Creating Script Logic to Revalue Plan Data—Part M

19. You are prompted to enter the member value selections for the dimensions. Select Run Now and click on the Next button (Figure 6.16). Enter the selections for which you want to increase revenue, and click on Next to run the report. Note that we selected product CK2001 for revaluation.

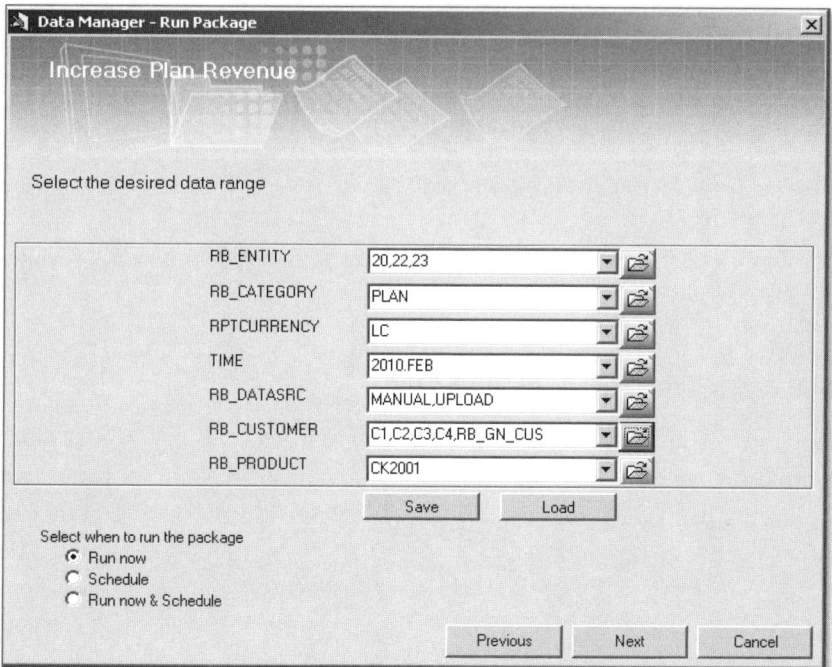

Figure 6.16 Creating Script Logic to Revalue Plan Data—Part O

20. Click on Run Now. You will see that product CK2001 has an amount posted to the revenue adjustment account, as shown in Figure 6.17. This amount represents revaluation to the revenue.

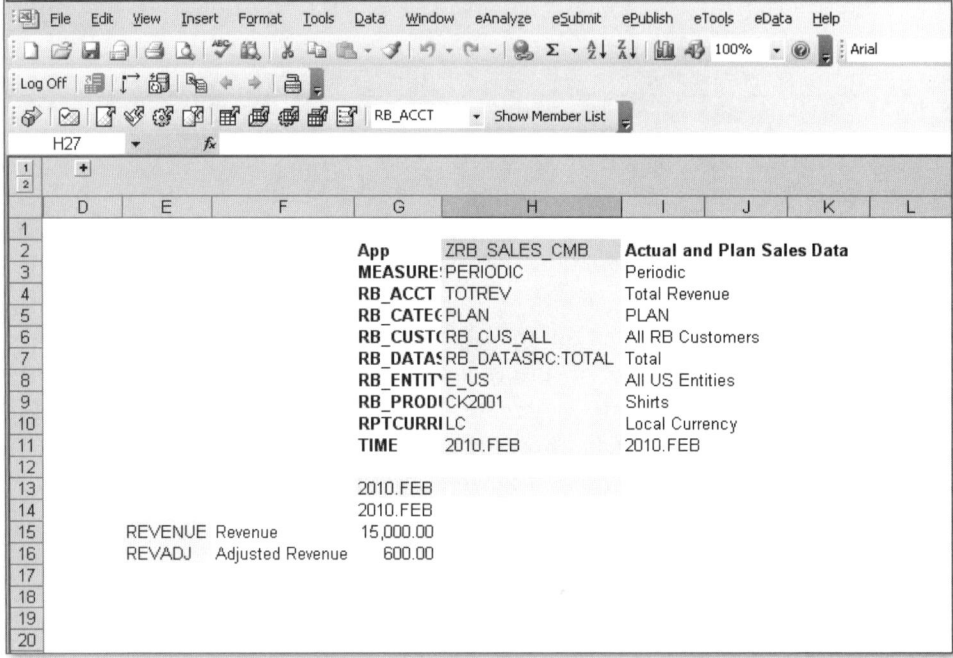

Figure 6.17 Creating Script Logic to Revalue Plan Data—Part P

You should now understand how to use script logic to revalue revenue for a certain period in an application.

6.2.4 Script Logic Files Provided by SAP

SAP BusinessObjects Planning and Consolidation provides a library of standard script logic functions, all of which have the file extension .LGF. Some of the script logic files are shown in Table 6.2. These files can be viewed in the SAP NetWeaver BW system by executing Transaction UJFS.

	Script File	Description
1.	Allocation.lgf	Used to run allocation logic.
2.	Calcaccount.lgf	Used to prepare cash flow; runs an account calculation business rule.
3.	Consolidation.lgf	Used to run a legal consolidation business rule.
4.	Copy_Opening.lgf	Used to run a balance carry forward business rule.
5.	FX_Trans.lgf	Used to run currency conversion.
6.	ICBooking.lgf	Used to run intercompany reconciliation and difference posting.
7.	ICData.lgf	Used to run intercompany reconciliation.
8.	ICElim.lgf	Used to run intercompany reconciliation.
9.	MDXlib.lgf	Library of MDX financial functions.
10.	System_Constants.lgf	Stores constant values for use within a script logic. The system constants file is located in the \\root\Data\Webfolders\<AppSet>\AdminApp\<App> folder.
11.	System_Library.lgf	Includes basic examples of a set of keywords.
12.	Validation.lgf	Used for running a validation rule.

Table 6.2 Script Logic Files provided by SAP

In the next section, we will discuss business rules and explain how they can be used in an application.

6.3 Business Rules

In the last section, you saw how you can code script logic to perform certain data management tasks. Instead of writing code, you can also configure *business rules* to perform certain tasks related to planning and consolidation. The code is already available in SAP function modules; you just need to call them in a script and pass the appropriate parameters to perform the desired function.

In this section, we will provide a brief introduction to the different business rules that can be configured in SAP BusinessObjects Planning and Consolidation. We will discuss setting up business rules to perform currency translation. (We also discuss business rules in detail in Chapter 9, when we discuss the process for consolidating data in SAP BusinessObjects Planning and Consolidation.)

To begin, we will discuss the different business rules that can be configured in SAP BusinessObjects Planning and Consolidation.

6.3.1 Account Transformation

Account transformation reads and aggregates the values posted to specific combinations of accounts, flow types, and data sources, and posts an aggregated amount under an alternate destination account, flow type, and data source combination.

6.3.2 Intercompany Booking

Accounting transactions between two different entities within an organization need to be eliminated when reporting consolidated financial results. The intercompany booking business rule allows business users to set rules to post intercompany transactions to an elimination entity; this rule automatically generates the postings needed to eliminate intercompany transactions when reporting financial results.

6.3.3 Carry-Forward

The carry-forward business rule is used to transfer the closing balances of a particular period into the opening balance of a subsequent period. This procedure is used to initialize the opening balance of a new reporting period with the closing balances from the last period.

6.3.4 Automatic Adjustments

The most important of the necessary adjustments for legal consolidation relate to the elimination of intercompany transactions between the various reporting units, and reclassifications and supporting of the applicable rules for the accounting of long-term investments. The automatic adjustment business rule supports the calculation and generation of these postings.

6.3.5 Currency Translation

An organization may have businesses in more than one country and conduct business transactions in many currencies. It is a statutory requirement to report financial results of the business in one currency; to do this, it is necessary to translate financial transactions in various currencies into one reporting currency, which is typically the currency of the corporate headquarters of the company. The currency translation business rule is used to translate all business transactions into one reporting currency.

The transaction data in SAP BusinessObjects Planning and Consolidation is stored in the currency in which the transaction is performed. This currency is referred to as the *transaction* currency, or the *local* currency. These transactions are then converted using the currency translation business rule to one reporting currency. This currency is referred to as the *group* currency or *reporting* currency.

We will now explain how to use the currency translation business rule to translate all financial transactions to one reporting currency.

SAP BusinessObjects Planning and Consolidation provides an application called the *rate* application. This is a supporting application used by financial and consolidation applications to store exchange rates that support currency conversion. It is important that the Category and Time dimensions in the rate application are identical to the respective dimensions in the application that uses the rate application for performing currency translation.

Note the following points that relate to the translation of currency:

- The application that requires currency translation must be created as a financial or consolidation application.
- An application can include only one dimension for indicating currency type. This is the dimension that states whether the transaction is in the local or group currency.
- The Entity dimension has a Currency property that denotes the local currency associated with an entity.
- The Currency dimension has a Reporting property. If a currency is marked as Reporting, currency translation can be used to convert transactions from the transaction currency to this reporting currency.

- The rate application contains the currency translation exchange rate to use for different periods and for different exchange rate types. The exchange rate type signifies the type of rate—for example, average rate or month-end rate—associated with the record in the rate application.
- The Rate Type property of the Account dimension is used for specifying the type of rate to be used for the translation.
- The TIMEID dimension must include the YEAR, PERIOD, TIMEID, and MONTH-NUM properties.
- The Data Source dimension must include the following properties:
  - DATASRC_TYPE, whose values include the following:

    I—Input

    M—Manual adjustment

    A—Automatic adjustment or elimination

    L—Data source level (use only for consolidation)
  - IS_CONVERTED, whose values include the following:

    N (or blank)—These members are ignored in the conversion

    Y—These members are converted from local currency (LC) into the desired currency

    G—These members are copied from the reporting currency of the group that is being translated into the currency member corresponding to the given group
- The Flow dimension is not mandatory for currency translation, but if it is included, the dimension must include the FLOW_TYPE property.
- The Inputcurrency dimension within the applicable rate application must include the MD property, whose values can be either M (for multiply rates) or D (for divide rates).

The currency translation program can be run in two modes: reporting currency mode and group currency mode. In reporting currency mode, transactions are translated from the local currencies to the reporting currencies. You should include the following script:

```
*RUN_PROGRAM CURR_CONVERSION
CATEGORY = %C_CATEGORY_SET%
```

```
CURRENCY = %RPTCURRENCY_SET%
TID_RA = %TIME_SET%
RATEENTITY = GLOBAL
......
*ENDRUN_PROGRAM
```

The group currency mode is used in an organization that is composed of a group of subsidiaries, and where the subsidiary data should be converted to one group currency.

```
*RUN_PROGRAM CURR_CONVERSION
CATEGORY = %C_CATEGORY_SET%
GROUP= %GROUPS_SET%
TID_RA = %TIME_SET%
RATEENTITY = GLOBAL
......
*ENDRUN_PROGRAM
```

In addition, you can maintain the currency conversion table to define the rules for currency translation. When the currency translation data manager package is run, the rules defined in this table are used during the currency translation process.

The details for setting up the business table for currency conversion are explained in Table 6.3.

Field Name	Description
Account Rate Type	Specify the account rate type to use in the currency translation. Examples of account rate type for an account are AVG, END, HIST.
	When the rate type of the source account is the same as defined in the rule, the criteria for using the business rule is met.
Source Flow	Specify the source flow as additional criteria to use in the translation. The value specified in this field can be one of the following:
	Base member
	Parent member
	A list of members is defined and filtered using a value of the DIMLIST property in the Flow dimension.

Table 6.3 Currency Translation Business Rule Table

Field Name	Description
Destination Account	Specify a base member as the destination account. If no value is specified for destination account, the value of the source account is used.
Destination Flow	Specify a base member for the destination flow. If no value is specified for destination flow, the value of the source flow is used.
Formula	Specify an arithmetic expression to define the currency translation. In the Formula field, the rates must be enclosed in square brackets, as follows: [END] - [AVG]
Force Closing	When the Force Closing flag is checked, an additional entry is generated where the destination flow is the closing balance. This is applicable for members in the Flow dimension where the property FLOW_TYPE is equal to the value CLOSING.
Apply to Periodic	When the application is a YTD application and must perform the currency translation based on periodic values, check the Apply to Periodic flag. When this flag is checked, the difference between the current period and prior period amount is calculated, and the formula is applied on the resulting amount. The result is added back to the prior period's value as written in the current period.
Entity FX Type	When a value is specified in Entity FX Type, the rule will be applied to all of the entity members that have a matching value in the FX_TYPE property of the Entity dimension.
Remark	A brief description of the business rule.

Table 6.3 Currency Translation Business Rule Table (Cont.)

We will now use an example to demonstrate how currency translation is set up and performed in SAP BusinessObjects Planning and Consolidation. One of the required dimensions for currency translation is DataSource. The planning application we use for our model company Rich Bloom, Inc. includes the DataSource dimension. The objective is to understand how to convert currency data from the British pound (GBP) to the U.S. dollar (USD).

Business Rules | **6.3**

We would normally load exchange rate data provided by a third-party vendor to the rate application. However, for our illustration, we will enter this information directly into the rate application.

1. Log into SAP BusinessObjects Planning and Consolidation for Excel, and access the rate application of your application set. Create an input schedule and enter the exchange rate for Jan 2010, as shown in Figure 6.18. The average rate for Jan 2010 is entered for the GBP and USD currencies. We want to translate the data from GBP into USD; therefore, a factor of 1 is entered for USD, and a factor of 1.50 is entered for GBP. Save the exchange rate data.

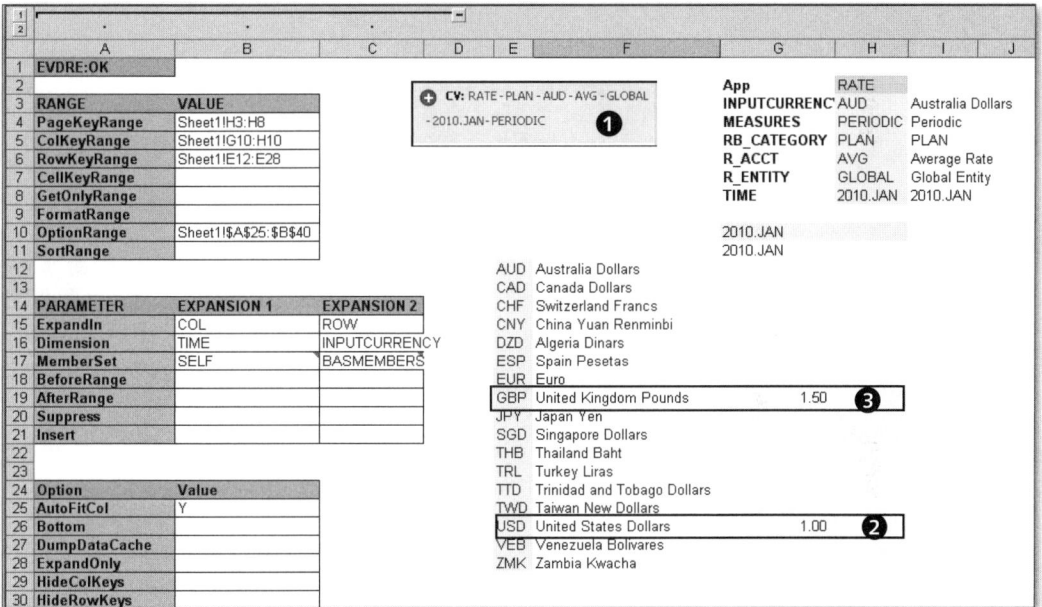

Figure 6.18 Performing Currency Translation—Part A

2. Log into BPC Admin Console, and select the application for which you want to perform currency translations. Enter the following code (Figure 6.19) in the FXTRANS.LGF file:

```
*RUN_PROGRAM CURR_CONVERSION
CATEGORY = %RB_CATEGORY_SET%
CURRENCY = %RPTCURRENCY_SET%
TID_RA = %TIME_SET%
RATEENTITY = GLOBAL
```

259

```
    OTHER = [ENTITY=%RB_ENTITY_SET%]
    //For more than one other scope parameter:
    OTHER = [ENTITY=%ENTITY_SET%;INTCO=%INTCO_SET%...]
  *ENDRUN_PROGRAM
```

Save and validate the logic file.

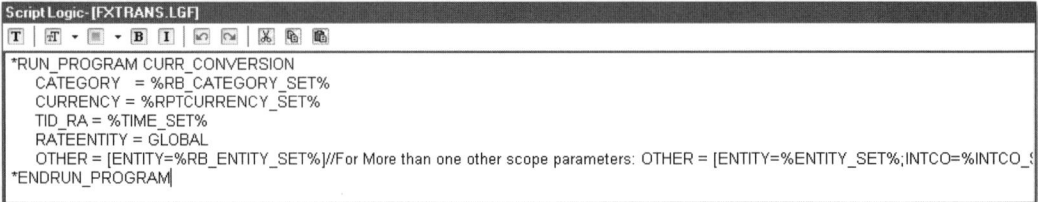

Figure 6.19 Performing Currency Translation—Part B

3. Execute a report to see the data before the currency translation is executed. The data associated with entity C2000 is shown in Figure 6.20, in local currency.

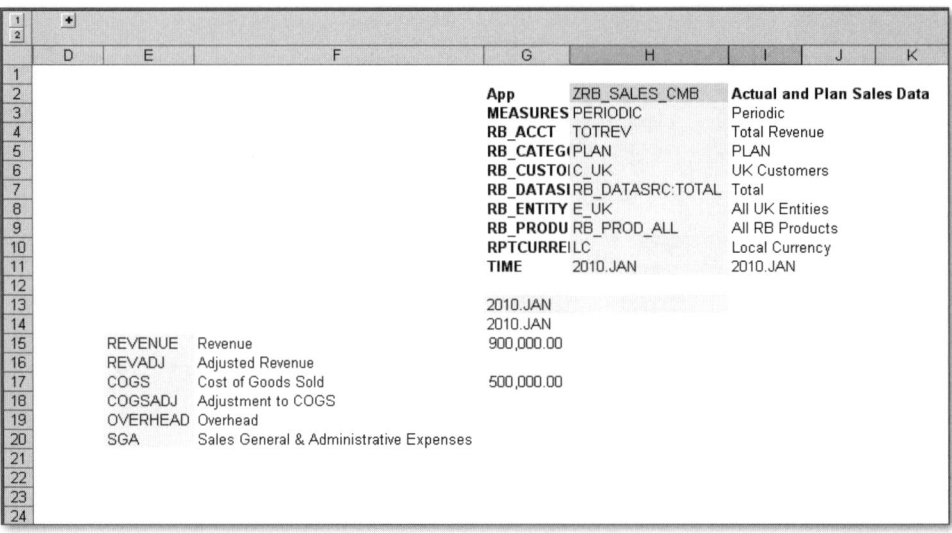

Figure 6.20 Performing Currency Translation—Part C

4. You are now ready to execute the FX Restatement currency translation data package (Figure 6.21).

Business Rules | **6.3**

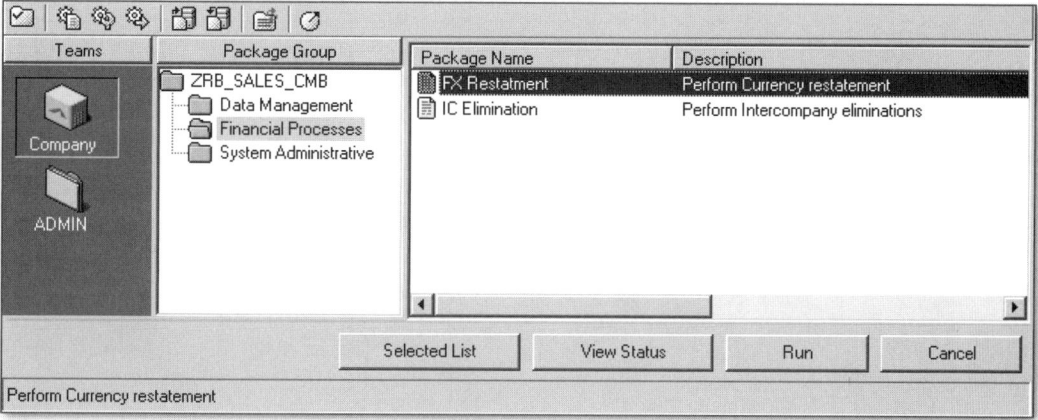

Figure 6.21 Performing Currency Translation—Part D

5. Execute the FX Restatement data package. The system will prompt you to enter parameter values (Figure 6.22). Our objective is to translate transactions in local currency to USD (US dollars). Select the report currency as USD.

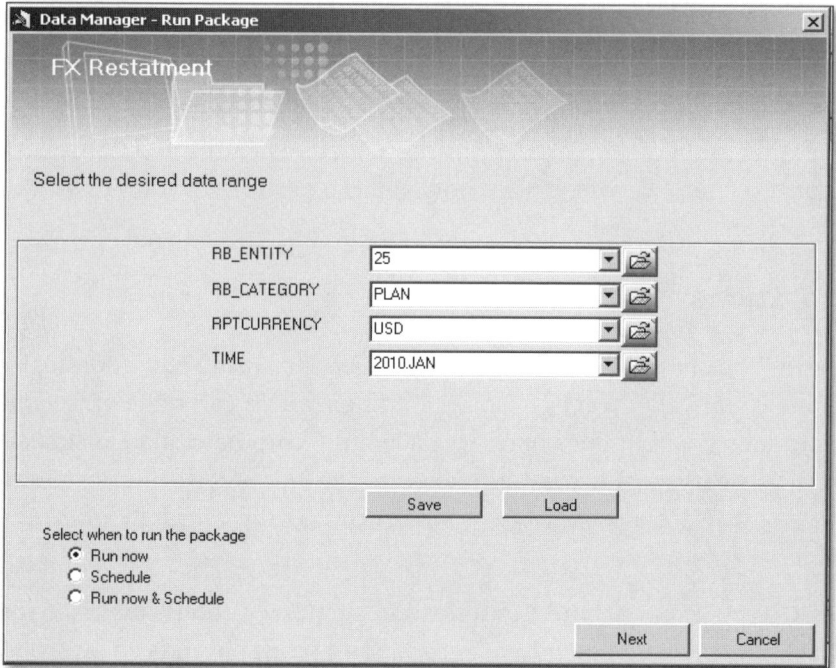

Figure 6.22 Performing Currency Translation—Part D

261

6. After you execute the data package, you will see that the data from the local currency has been translated to USD, based on the exchange rate specified in the rate application (Figure 6.23).

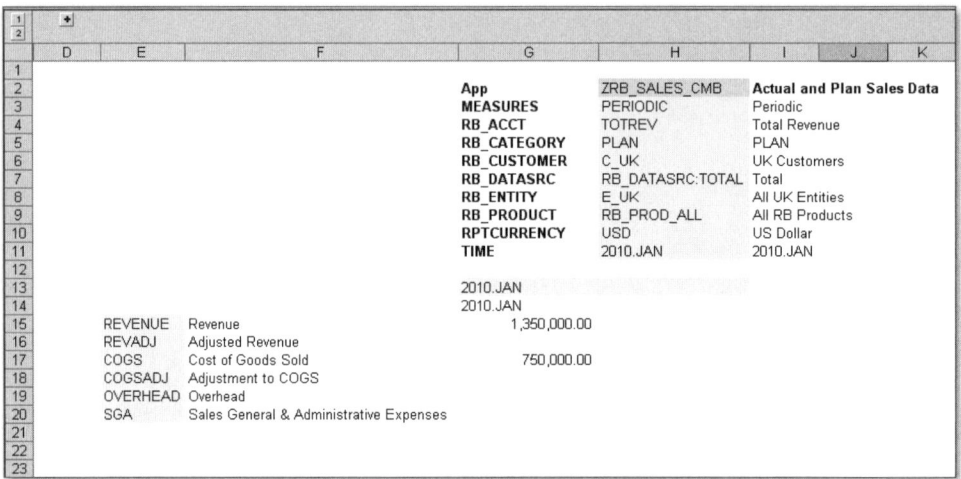

Figure 6.23 Performing Currency Translation—Part E

You now know how to translate financial transactions that are maintained in a local currency to a group currency. In this section, you have seen the different types of business rules that can be set up in SAP BusinessObjects Planning and Consolidation. In the next section, we will explain how you can perform allocations.

6.4 Allocations

There are several business reasons that drive the need for using allocation logic. Let us say, for example, that you have an organization with a corporate office and additional locations where it does business. When the corporate office incurs an expense, such as overheads, it has to be allocated to the other office locations based on criteria that depend on usage or work done by the corporate office for the other offices.

SAP BusinessObjects Planning and Consolidation supports a robust interface for allocating data. The allocation definition is coded as a script file and can be called from a data manager package. The script for allocating data is based on a table interface for the developer to specify how the allocation should be performed. This process provides the developer with an intuitive interface through which he can satisfy the business requirements for allocation.

An allocation is always made up of the following components:

- What needs to be allocated
- Where the results of the allocation must be written
- What driver should be used to perform the allocation
- How the allocation driver should be used; that is, what factor must be applied to the source amounts during the allocation process

You should have a clear understanding of these components before you begin coding the allocation logic. When you know what needs to be allocated, you can use the following syntax to code the allocation:

```
*RUNALLOCATION
*FACTOR={expression}
*NAME={allocation name}
*APP [WHAT={app name};] [ WHERE={ app name };] [USING ={ app name }]
*DIM {dim name} WHAT={set}; WHERE={set};[USING ={set};] [TOTAL={set}]
*DIM …
*ENDALLOCATION
```

Now let us discuss the following instructions in the code: *FACTOR and *DIM. The *FACTOR instruction can be used to define any arithmetic expression (written in the {expression} parameter), and may contain operands, parentheses, constants, and one or both of the keywords USING and TOTAL, representing respectively the amount coming from the USING region (i.e., the amount of the driver) and the amount coming from the TOTAL region (i.e., the sum of the drivers):

```
*FACTOR=USING/TOTAL
```

Another keyword supported by this parameter is COUNT, which represents the number of members into which one amount must be allocated. For example, when evenly allocating a yearly value into all months of a year, the administrator may use just the COUNT keyword.

```
*FACTOR=1/COUNT
```

6 | Developing Business Logic in SAP BusinessObjects Planning and Consolidation

With the *DIM keyword, you can define the set of members that each dimension should read for each specific region of the allocation (the WHAT, the WHERE, the USING, and the TOTAL regions).

Using the same logic, if you had to allocate rent expenses incurred by a corporate entity called "Admin" to other entities based on the respective percentage usage, you would have to code the following in your script logic. Note that the percentage is maintained in the application for each entity.

```
*RUNALLOCATION
*FACTOR=USING/100
*DIM ENTITY WHAT=ADMIN; WHERE<>ADMIN; USING<>ADMIN
*DIM ACCOUNT WHAT=RENTAL; WHERE=RENTAL; USING=PERCENTAGE
*ENDALLOCATION
```

To demonstrate this concept, we will now perform allocations so that Rich Bloom, Inc. can allocate the overhead expenses incurred at its corporate office (entity 22) to other entities in the U.S., based on the revenue generated by them for the period.

1. Looking at the plan data for Jan 2010, Rich Bloom, Inc.'s corporate office has planned overhead expenses for $20,000 (Figure 6.24). This has to be allocated to the other entities in the U.S., based on their total revenue for the same period.

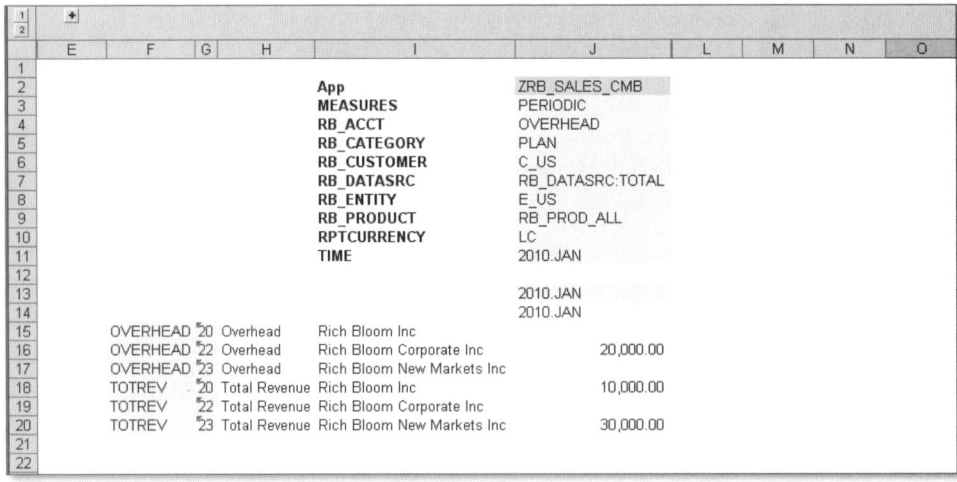

Figure 6.24 Performing Allocations — Part A

2. Enter the following code in the ALLOCATION.LGF script file for the application:

```
*RUNALLOCATION
*FACTOR=USING/TOTAL
*DIM RB_ACCT WHAT =OVERHEAD;WHERE=<<<;USING=REVENUE;TOTAL=<<<;
*DIM RB_ENTITY WHAT=22;WHERE=>>>;USING=>>>;TOTAL=BAS(E_US);
*DIM RB_CATEGORY WHAT=PLAN;WHERE=<<<;USING=<<<;TOTAL=<<<;
*DIM TIME WHAT=2010.JAN;WHERE=<<<;USING=<<<;TOTAL=<<<;
*ENDALLOCATION
```

Save and validate the script file (Figure 6.25). The logic allocates the overhead data for the period Jan 2010 from entity 22 to the other entities in the U.S., based on their sales revenue for that period.

Figure 6.25 Performing Allocations—Part B

3. You are now ready to execute the Allocation data manager package (Figure 6.26).

6 | Developing Business Logic in SAP BusinessObjects Planning and Consolidation

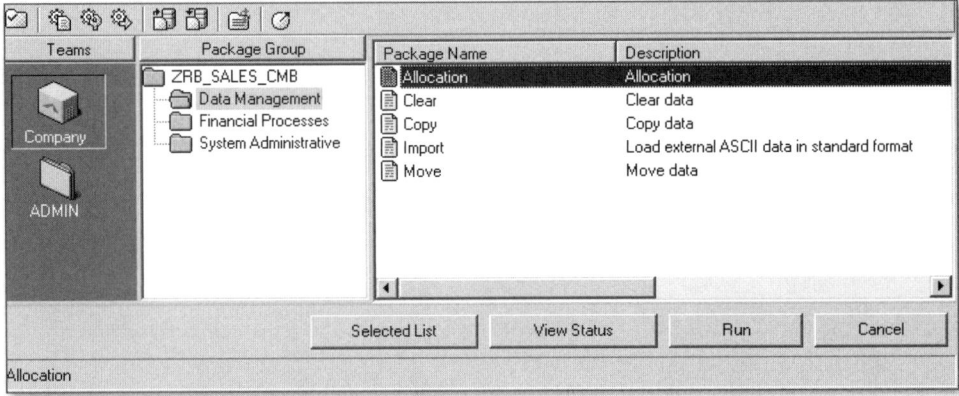

Figure 6.26 Performing Allocations—Part C

4. After the package has been executed, run the report to see how the allocation logic has worked (Figure 6.27). The overheads have been allocated from the corporate entity to the other entities, based on revenues.

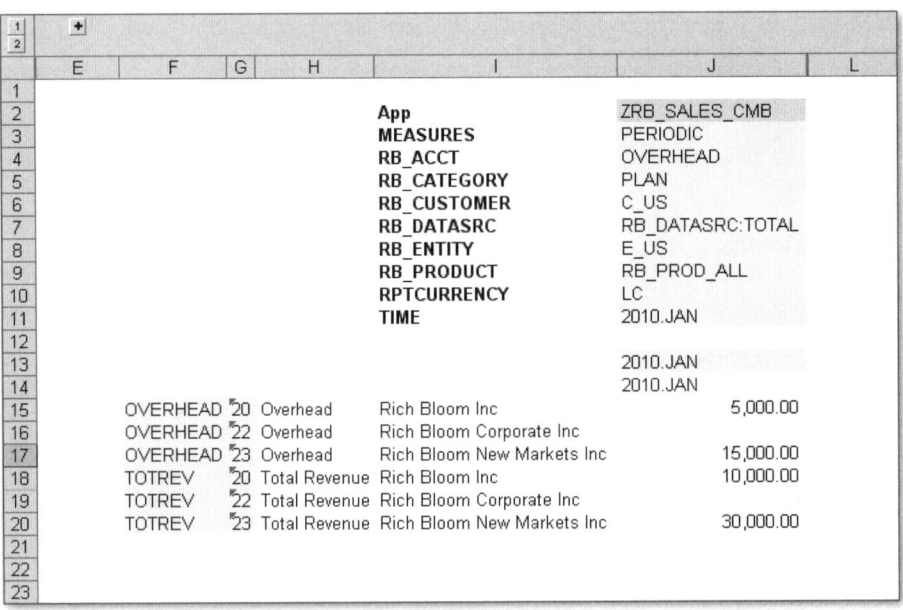

Figure 6.27 Performing Allocations—Part D

In this section, you have seen how allocation is performed in SAP BusinessObjects Planning and Consolidation. In the next section, we will discuss areas where you can write ABAP code to meet specific business requirements.

6.5 Using BAdIs to Code Logic

Some business processes require the use of additional logic to complement the existing SAP BusinessObjects Planning and Consolidation application framework. SAP Business Add-ins (BAdIs) can be used for this purpose, and can be created using ABAP in the SAP NetWeaver BW system. The rich language constructs in ABAP make it excellent for use in SAP BusinessObjects Planning and Consolidation applications. ABAP may also provide performance benefits when used in certain application scenarios.

You will need a basic understanding of object-oriented ABAP before you can develop BAdIs in SAP BusinessObjects Planning and Consolidation applications.

1. Use Transaction SE19 to create a BAdI, which should be based on enhancement UJ_CUSTOM_LOGIC and is provided for use in SAP BusinessObjects Planning and Consolidation applications. You are prompted to create a transport when you create a custom BAdI.
2. Specify the filter values for the BAdI implementation. These are the values that pass to the BAdI.
3. The UJ_CUSTOM_LOGIC~EXECUTE method is automatically created for the BAdI, because it is based on the UJ_CUSTOM_LOGIC enhancement. Enter the code for the BAdI here. The internal table CT_TABLE contains the data passed from the SAP BusinessObjects Planning and Consolidation application, which can be modified based on the business requirement.
4. Save and activate the objects created.
5. Create a script file in SAP BusinessObjects Planning and Consolidation to call the BAdI you have created. Refer to the following example:
   ```
   Syntax:
   *START_BADI <BADI_Name>
   <key1> = <value1>
   ```

```
<key2> = <value2>
..
*END_BADI
```

where <BADI_Name> is the name used in the BAdI. You can also pass the additional parameters <key1> and <key2>.

The execution of the BADI performs a default query and automatically writes back to the application. Set the QUERY parameter to OFF if you want to perform your own read inside the BAdI implementation; set WRITE to OFF to turn off the automatic write back of query results. You may code to write to another application from the BAdI.

6. Create a process chain that includes the run logic process to execute a data manager package. In the data manage package, adjust the prompts for the script to be executed.

7. You are now ready to execute the data manager package. This will execute the package and prompt for any parameters you specified in the BAdI.

You now know the steps for developing logic using BADIs in SAP BusinessObjects Planning and Consolidation. In the next section, we will discuss rules that can be configured to ensure data accuracy.

6.6 Validation

With the introduction of SAP BusinessObjects Planning and Consolidation for NetWeaver, a new and powerful feature has been introduced to enforce business rules and to prevent incorrect records from being entered or updated in the system. This ensures the accuracy of data in an SAP BusinessObjects Planning and Consolidation application.

The following rules apply to validation:

- Validation is performed in the SAP NetWeaver BW system using Transaction UJ_VALIDATION. You will need access to this transaction to access this interface.

- Only one dimension can be marked as the Driver dimension.

- Any dimension in an application can be specified as the Driver dimension for the purpose of validation. Different applications in a given application set can use any dimension as the Driver dimension.
- In the planning and consolidation application, the Account dimension is usually marked as the Driver dimension.
- Rules are defined so that only those records that meet the criteria can be saved to the application. Every time a record is updated for the application, including a Driver dimension, the rules are checked before the data is updated.
- When data is updated in SAP BusinessObjects Planning and Consolidation, and if the data does not comply with the rule defined, the record is rejected and an error message displayed.
- If the same dimension is used as the Driver dimension by more than one application in the application set, any rules created for that Driver dimension apply to all of the applications that share it.
- You can turn off the validation's functionality for an application using Transaction UJ_VALIDATION. When the validation is turned off, the rules for the application are not checked when data is updated. Validations can be set to apply to journals, manual updates, and data manager packages.
- Setting up validation rules does not require knowledge of ABAP; however, to set up advanced logic using code, the BAdI implementation is available. This provides additional ABAP functionality when a standard configuration for validation does not fully meet the requirement or when the process is complex enough to require the use of BADIs.
- Validation rules configured in the development system can be transported across the landscape.

We will now look at an example of setting up validation rules in the SAP NetWeaver BW system.

1. Log into the SAP NetWeaver BW system and execute Transaction UJ_VALIDATION. Identify the application set for which you want to set validation rules, and then click on Assign Driver Dimension (Figure 6.28, ❶ and ❷).

6 | Developing Business Logic in SAP BusinessObjects Planning and Consolidation

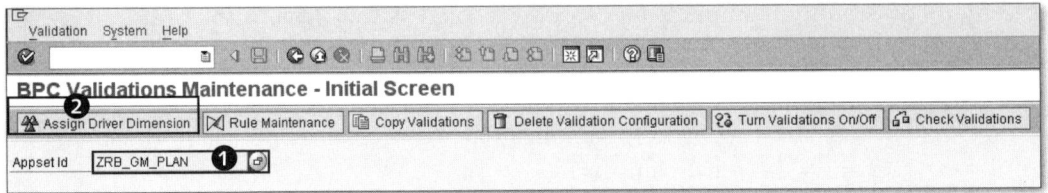

Figure 6.28 Creating a Validation Rule—Part A

2. All of the applications associated with the application set are displayed. Enter the dimension for the application for which you want to set the Driver dimension, and click on Save Driver Dimension Settings (Figure 6.29, ❸ and ❹). In our example, we are setting RB_ACCT as the Driver dimension for our planning application.

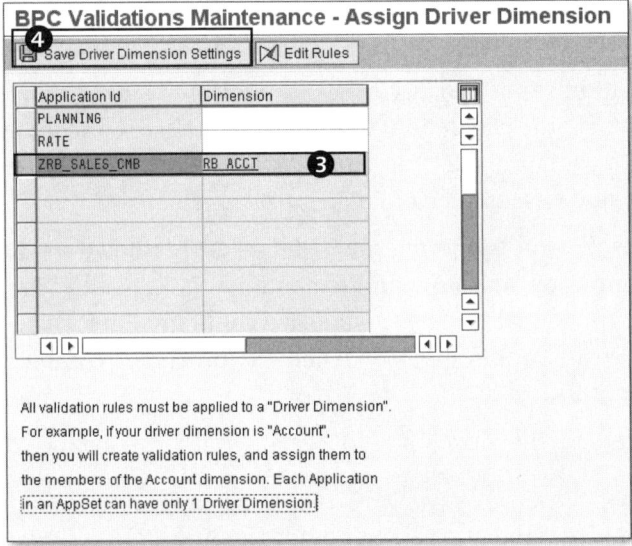

Figure 6.29 Creating a Validation Rule—Part B

3. After you have saved the Driver dimension settings, click on the back arrow. Here, you can create a new rule. Click on Create Rule to create a new validation definition (Figure 6.30, ❺).

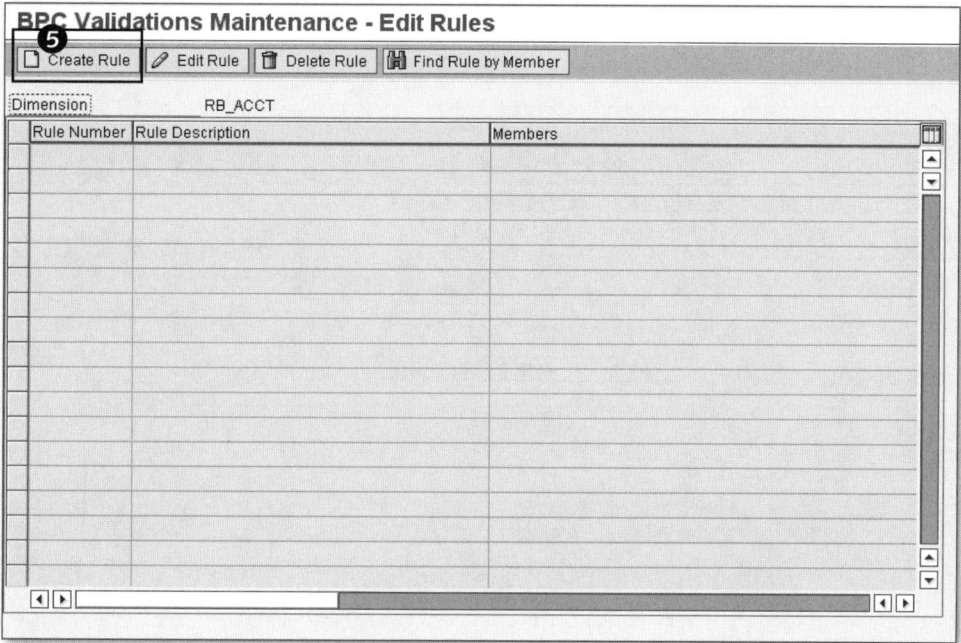

Figure 6.30 Creating a Validation Rule—Part C

4. Create a new account for corporate expenses and call it CORPORATE_EXP; this is the member for which you will be setting the validation. Select CORPORATE_EXP as the member of the Account dimension (Figure 6.31, ❻). Then, click on Add Dimension (Figure 6.31, ❼). Enter the following values in the first row for the columns:

```
Dimension   <RB_ENTITY>
Operator    <=>
Value       <22>
```

This defines the member value for the entity that can post values for this account. Entity 22 is the corporate office of Rich Bloom, Inc. under which corporate expenses are recorded (Figure 6.31, ❽). Other entities should not be able to charge corporate expense amounts.

5. Click on Save Rule, and click on the back arrow to go back to the previous screen (Figure 6.31, ❾).

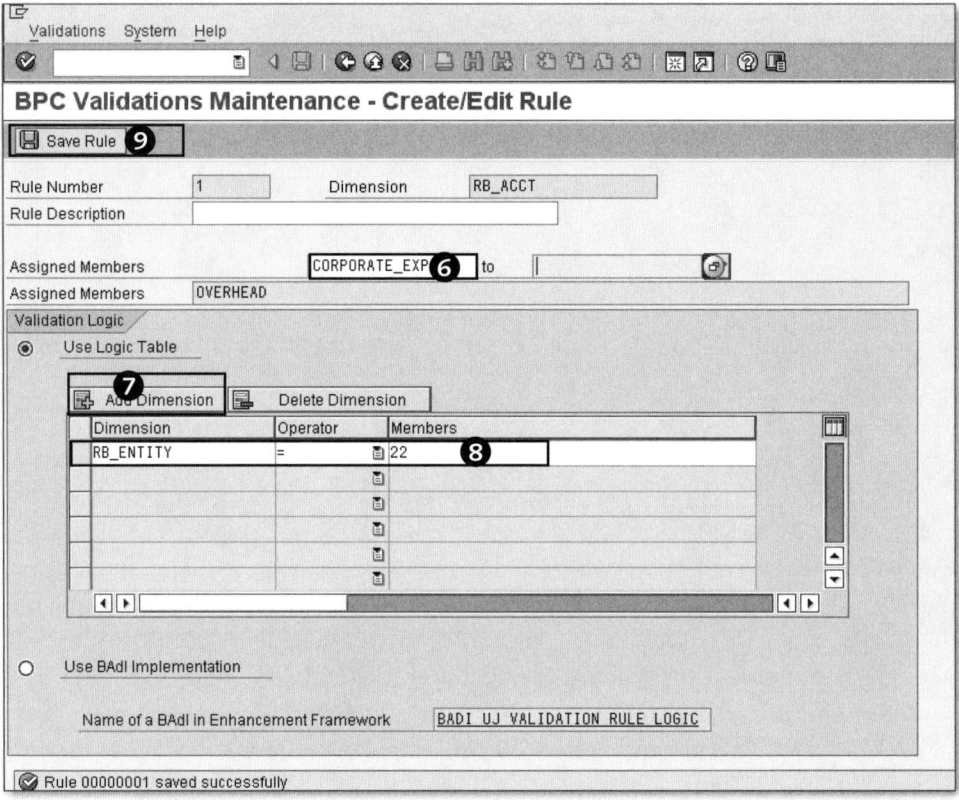

Figure 6.31 Creating a Validation Rule—Part D

6. You will now see the validation rule you created (Figure 6.32).
7. Click the green arrow to go back to the inital screen of Transaction UJ_VALIDATION, and click on the Turn Validation On/Off button to activate the validation rules (Figure 6.33, ❿).

Validation | **6.6**

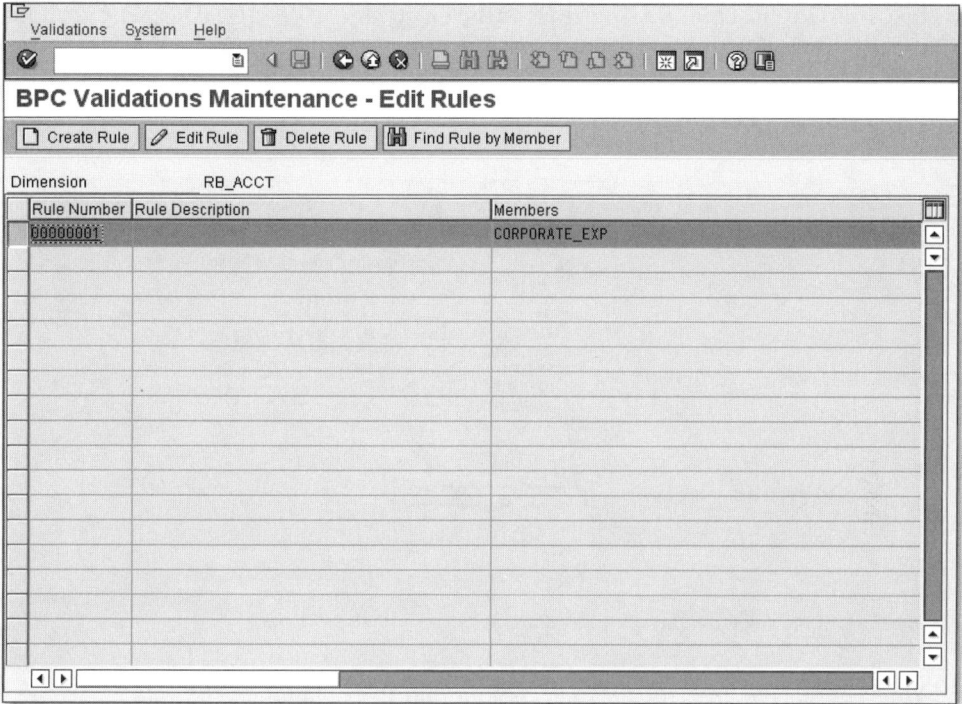

Figure 6.32 Creating a Validation Rule—Part E

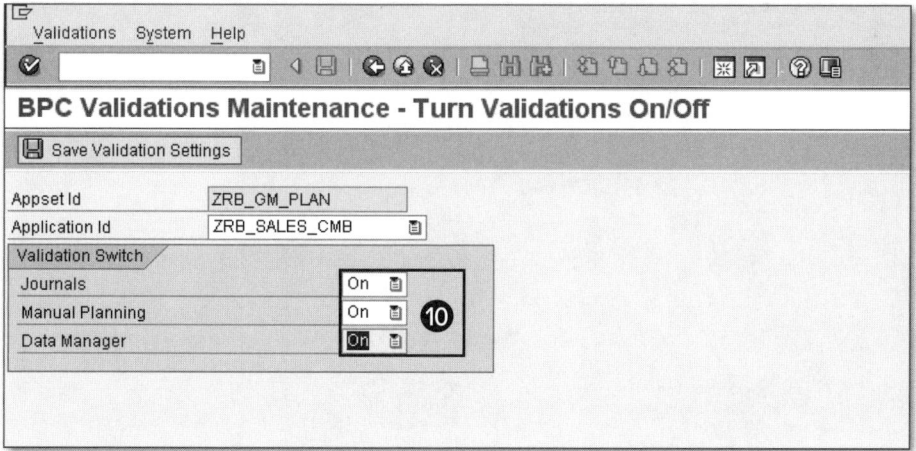

Figure 6.33 Creating a Validation Rule—Part F

8. Create an input schedule. Select 20 as the entity and OVERHEADS as the account member. Enter a value for CORPORATE_EXP, and send the data to the database (Figure 6.34). The system should disallow this transaction based on the validation rule created earlier.

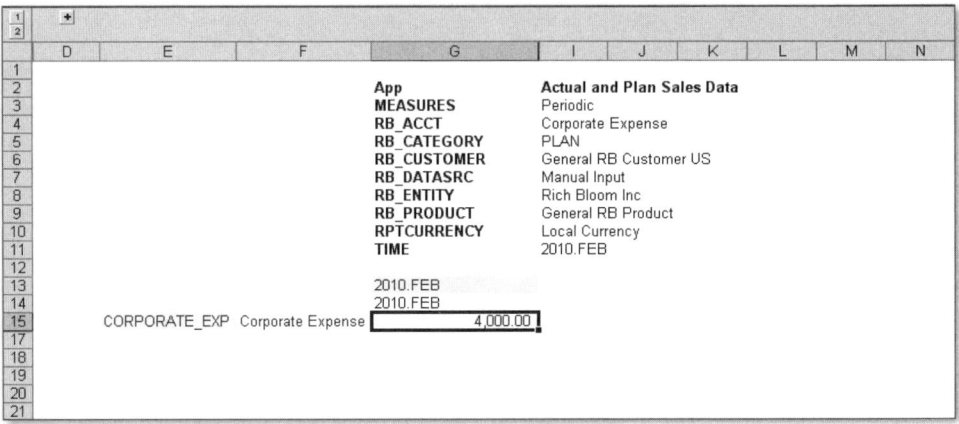

Figure 6.34 Creating a Validation Rule—Part G

9. You will receive an error message saying that the data failed the validation rule, because corporate expenses can only be posted to corporate entity 22.

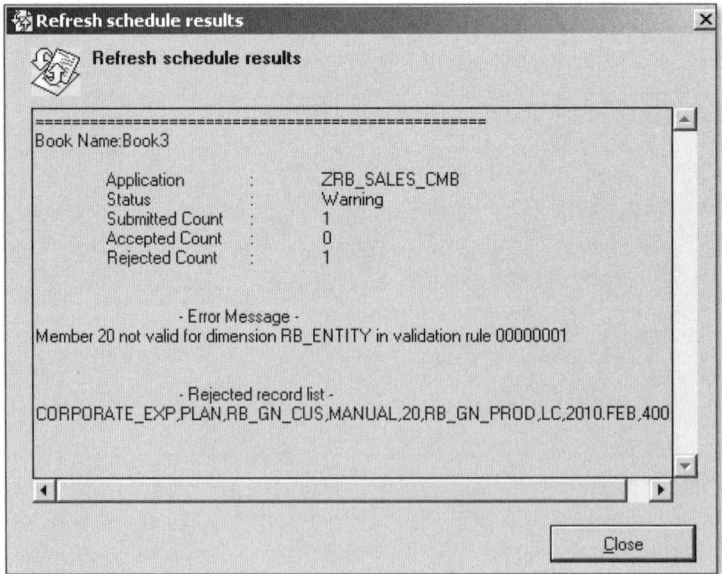

Figure 6.35 Creating a Validation Rule—Part H

You now know how to set up validation rules in the SAP NetWeaver BW system. This powerful functionality enforces data integrity in SAP BusinessObjects Planning and Consolidation applications.

6.7 Summary

In this chapter, you learned about the different options available to define logic in an SAP BusinessObjects Planning and Consolidation application. First, you saw how formulas can be defined as a property of a dimension member to automatically calculate values. Then, you learned about script logic, and saw how it provides a rich collection of statements to handle complex logic in applications.

We then discussed business rules to execute common planning and consolidation tasks, and explained how they can be used in place of developing detailed script logic. We showed examples of performing currency translation using the Rate application, and showed how to make allocations based on certain drivers.

You then saw how BAdIs can be used with SAP BusinessObjects Planning and Consolidation for NetWeaver. This is especially useful for coding complex application business requirements using ABAP.

Finally, we explained how to define validation rules in the SAP NetWeaver BW system to ensure data accuracy.

In the next chapter, we will review tools available in SAP BusinessObjects Planning and Consolidation to support collaboration. Specifically, we will review the *work status*, which is used to monitor the planning and consolidation process and protect data from further changes. We will also discuss options available to post comments, distribute and collect financial data, and develop a user interface using menus.

7 Process Management and Collaboration

This chapter introduces you to the collaboration tools and features available in SAP BusinessObjects Planning and Consolidation that facilitate the sharing and exchange of data. The objective of using these tools is to promote team dynamics and to enable users to make informed decisions on different business aspects.

Section 7.1 discusses how work status is configured to monitor and restrict changes to the data in an application. In particular, we will explain how work status can be used in a scenario where the current plan needs to be locked against further changes.

Section 7.2 explains how to add and view comments in SAP BusinessObjects Planning and Consolidation. Comments are used to provide context to information and to share perception and reasoning behind information in an application.

Section 7.3 explains how data or input schedules in SAP BusinessObjects Planning and Consolidation can be distributed to users as offline reports and how these reports can then be uploaded back into SAP BusinessObjects Planning and Consolidation after users make changes to the reports.

SAP BusinessObjects Planning and Consolidation can not only be used with Excel, but also with Power Point and Word. Section 7.4 shows you the steps involved in integrating SAP BusinessObjects Planning and Consolidation data with Word and Power Point documents.

Section 7.5 discusses the functions available in SAP BusinessObjects Planning and Consolidation for creating a menu-based application. Menus help users to view and execute periodic tasks in a planning or consolidation process.

We will begin by explaining the use of work status and how it is configured to restrict changes to the data in an application.

7 Process Management and Collaboration

7.1 Work Status

In SAP BusinessObjects Planning and Consolidation, work status serves the important function of protecting changes to data stored in an application. It enables a subset of data, also referred to as a region of data, to be assigned a work status and helps you monitor the status of the data throughout the planning cycle.

Work status can be set for any region of data, based on the dimensions selected for maintaining work status for an application. (If you are familiar with SAP planning tools such as SAP NetWeaver Business Planning and Simulation and SAP NetWeaver BW Integrated Planning, you may have heard the term "data slices" used alternately in those environments to describe the same thing.)

Work status helps you meet the objective of protecting and monitoring data as follows:

- Work status gives an organization more control over its data and defines the tasks that can be performed by each user. It differs from standard data access in SAP BusinessObjects Planning and Consolidation in that, after the work status is set as locked, even users who have write access to the data are restricted from performing data updates. For example, the data can be restricted from being updated by anyone in the organization after the plan data is approved by management.

- For each application set, you can define different work statuses such as unlocked, submitted, approved, and so on, depending on the process flow used by the organization. The work status defined for an application set is used by all of the applications in the set.

- You can also create a new work status, reorder the work status, edit the description of the work status, or delete a work status for an application set.

- Work status can be applied to the following activities:
    - Data manager (DM)
    - Journals (JRN)
    - Manual entry (MAN)
    - Comments (COMM)
    - Documents (DOCS)

- Work status applies to a set of data in an application, which is called a data region. For each application in the application set, you configure a set of dimensions to use for setting the work status. Only the dimensions selected in this configuration can be used to define the data region for setting the work status.
- To use work status, you have to select a minimum of three and a maximum of five dimensions in each application.
- When defining the dimensions for work status in an application, the system requires one dimension to be specified as the Owner dimension, which should include the Owner property. The members listed in this dimension should be updated with a user ID or team ID in the Owner property so that the IDs can be used for setting work status.
- A region of data can be selected for setting the work status. For example, if you want the plan data for all of 2010 to be locked from any changes in an application, this region of data can be set as locked.
- For a combination of work status and activity, you can define the following types of access:
    - All: When the work status for a data region is set to All, any user who has write access to the data region in the application can update data for the data region.
    - Locked: When the work status for a data region is set to Locked, no user can update data for the data region.
    - Owner: When the work status for a data region is set to Owner, only the user ID or team ID listed under the Owner property of the Owner dimension can update the data for the data region.
    - Manager: When the work status for a data region is set to Manager, only the user ID or team ID associated with the parent of the dimension member can update the data for the data region.
- You can set multiple owners as values in the Owner property of a dimension. Separate owner names with a semicolon. The owner name can be a user ID or team ID.
- SAP BusinessObjects Planning and Consolidation for NetWeaver supports the inclusion of the Account dimension for work status settings. The previous version of SAP BusinessObjects Planning and Consolidation did not support this.

- Work status also lets you monitor updates to unstructured data such as documents.
- Work status configuration is set by administrators at both the application set and application levels; therefore, administrators should be familiar with the business process and the different work status steps to perform this role. Administrators define the different work statuses and the types of users who can update data for a given work status. This serves the purpose of defining the users who can update data for a given work status.
- Changes to the work status definition will remove any existing work statuses set by users for all applications in the application set.
- Before you can use the dimension identified as the Owner dimension in setting a work status, you have to specify a hierarchy for it. The web administration parameter "APPROVALORG"—which is an application level parameter—identifies the hierarchy (H1, H2, H3, ... , Hn) to use in the work status. We will discuss setting this parameter in Chapter 8, when we discuss web administration parameters.
- When data is written back to a SAP BusinessObjects Planning and Consolidation application, the work status is checked for each individual record that is updated. If, for example, one of the records in the update failed the work status check, that record is rejected. The other records are updated successfully.
- In SAP BusinessObjects Planning and Consolidation for NetWeaver 7.5, functionality is available to generate and send email messages when there is a change to work status. (You will find more information on this new version of SAP BusinessObjects Planning and Consolidation for NetWeaver in Chapter 10.)

Let us take a look at a common scenario that requires the use of work status, using our sample company. In this scenario, the sales managers of Rich Bloom, Inc. enter the sales plan for the next year, which is then submitted to management for approval. After the plan has been approved, it should be protected from changes by anyone other than the owner of the entity, as follows:

1. Log into the ZRB_GM_PLAN application set and click on the Work Status option in the left pane (Figure 7.1, ❶).

2. In the center pane, you will see the different work statuses in the rows and the activities in the columns. The intersection identifies who can update the data for the combination of work status and activity (Figure 7.1, ❷). The work status defined here applies to all of the applications in the application set.

3. In the right pane, you can see the options to maintain work status for an application set (Figure 7.1, ❸). You can also create a new work status using the options listed here.

4. Select Owner for manual activity (MAN) to ensure that only the owner of an entity can modify the data when the work status is set to Approved (Figure 7.1, ❹).

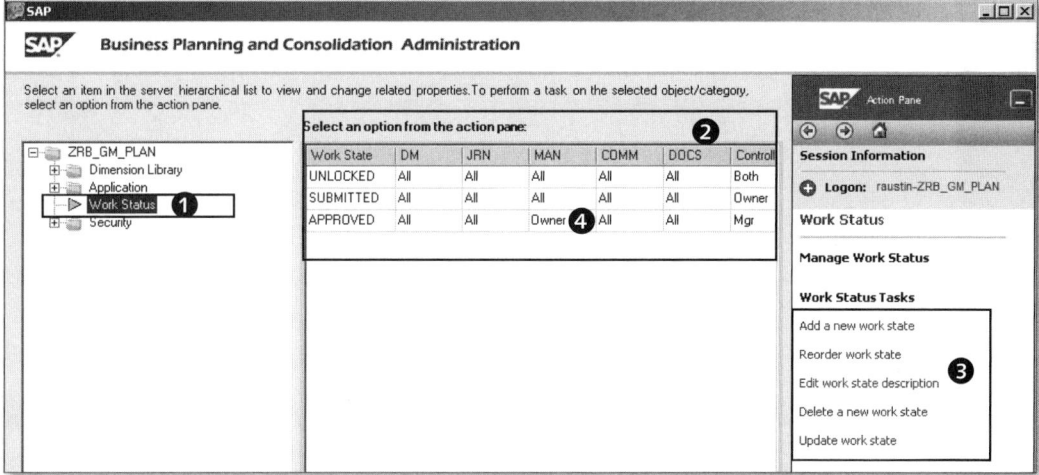

Figure 7.1 Configuring Work Status to Lock Data—Part A

5. Select the sales plan application, ZRB_SALES_CMB, and identify the Category, Entity, and Time dimensions as the dimensions to be used for setting work status for the application (Figure 7.2, ❺). As discussed earlier, you can select a maximum of five dimensions to set work status, and you are required to set one dimension as the Owner dimension, which should include an Owner property. We selected the Entity dimension as the Owner dimension in our example.

7 | Process Management and Collaboration

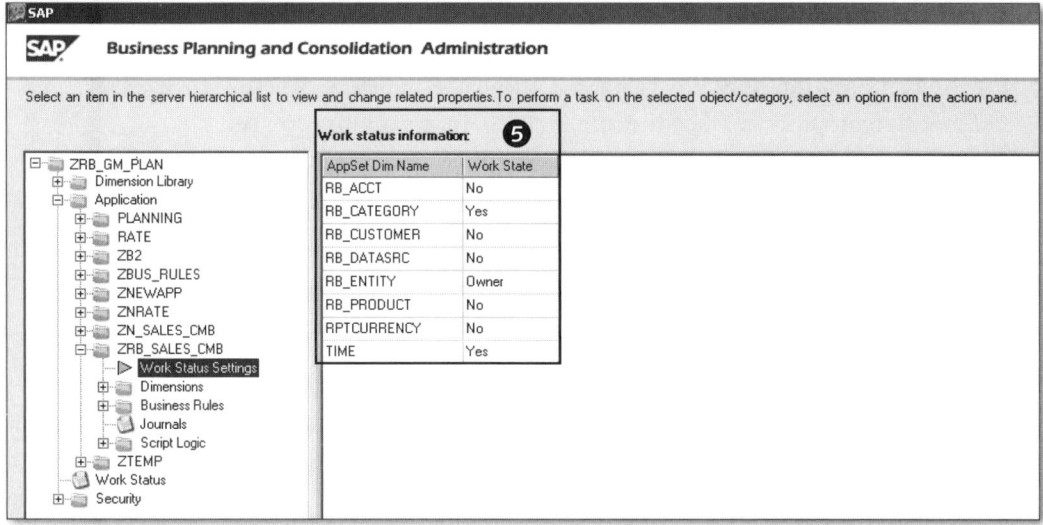

Figure 7.2 Configuring Work Status to Lock Data—Part B

6. Select the RB_ENTITY dimension under Dimensions in the left pane, and enter the owner value for the members in the dimension. The Owner property identifies who is the owner of the entity. In our example, SHILL (Shawn Hill) is identified as the owner (Figure 7.3, ❻). You can also enter a team in the Owner property, or multiple owners separated by semicolons.

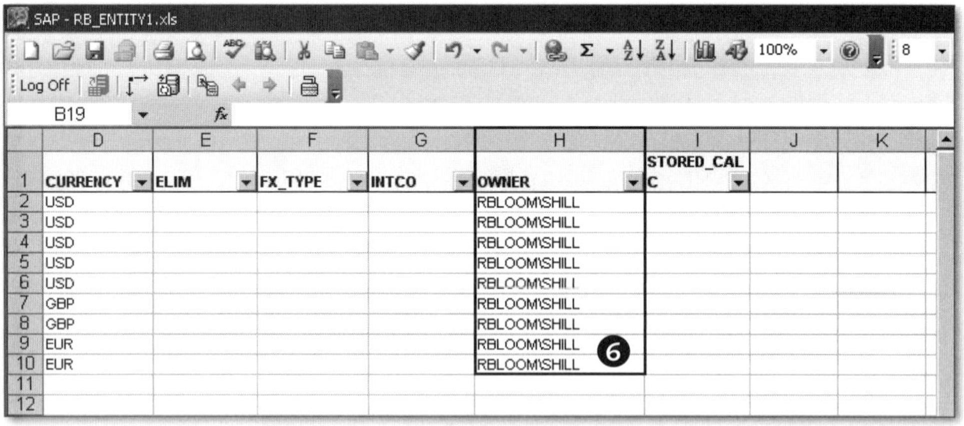

Figure 7.3 Configuring Work Status to Lock Data—Part C

282

7. Let us say that you have different entity members that fall under a higher level hierarchy node. The owner property value associated with the higher level entity node is the implied manager of the entities that fall under the node. The hierarchy used to maintain this relationship of owner and manager is known as the *approval organization hierarchy*. We can use the SAP BusinessObjects Planning and Consolidation Web interface to set the APPROVALORG parameter for the ZRB_SALES_CMB application (Figure 7.4, ❼).

Figure 7.4 Configuring Work Status to Lock Data—Part D

8. Select H1 as the APPROVALORG for this application (Figure 7.5, ❽). In this case, hierarchy H1 of the Entity dimension is used to determine the implied manager of entities.

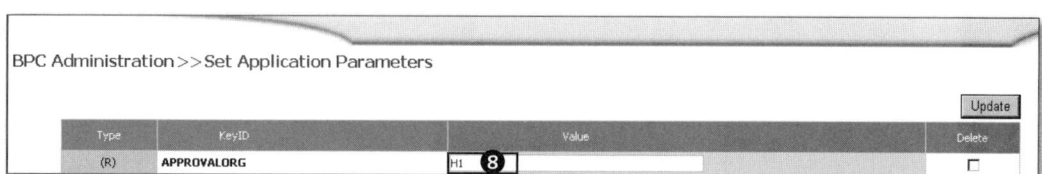

Figure 7.5 Configuring Work Status to Lock Data—Part E

9. From SAP BusinessObjects Planning and Consolidation for Excel, use the eSubmit menu and select the Modify Work Status option (Figure 7.6, ❾).

7 | Process Management and Collaboration

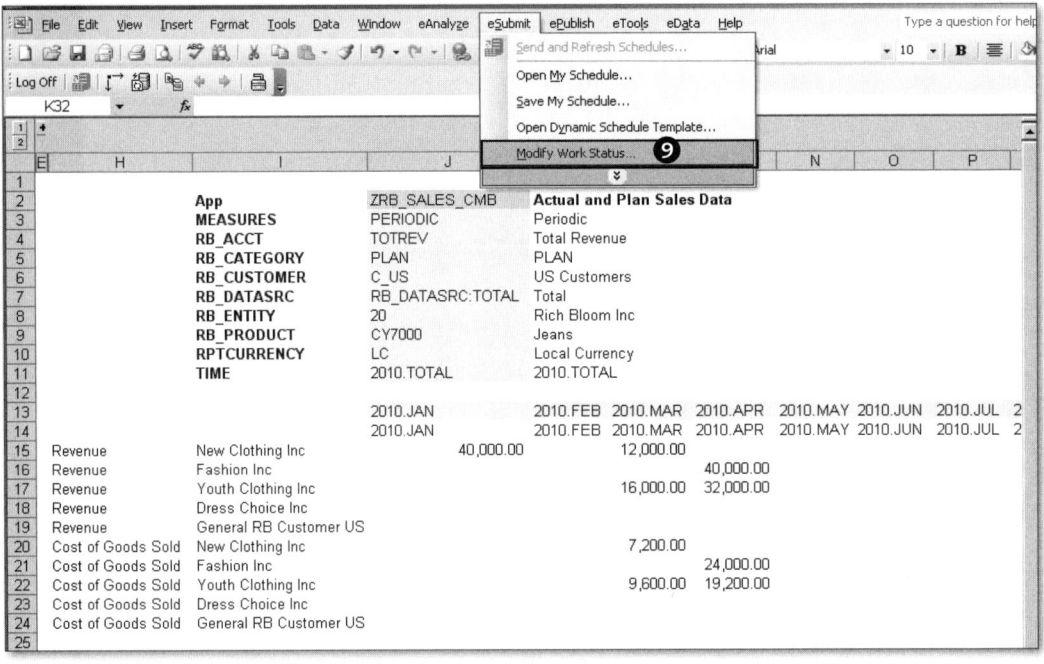

Figure 7.6 Configuring Work Status to Lock Data—Part F

10. You will now be directed to the web interface and required to authenticate your SAP BusinessObjects Planning and Consolidation credentials. Specify the member values to use for specifying the work status, and make the selections specified in ❿ of Figure 7.7, as follows:

    ▸ Category: Plan
    ▸ Entity: 20
    ▸ Time: 2010.Total

    Click on the green checkmark to continue.

11. Include all of the children for the selections by checking on Include Children in the Data Region (Figure 7.7, ⓫). This will apply the work status selection for all of the time periods in 2010. Select Approved as the work status and click on Enter.

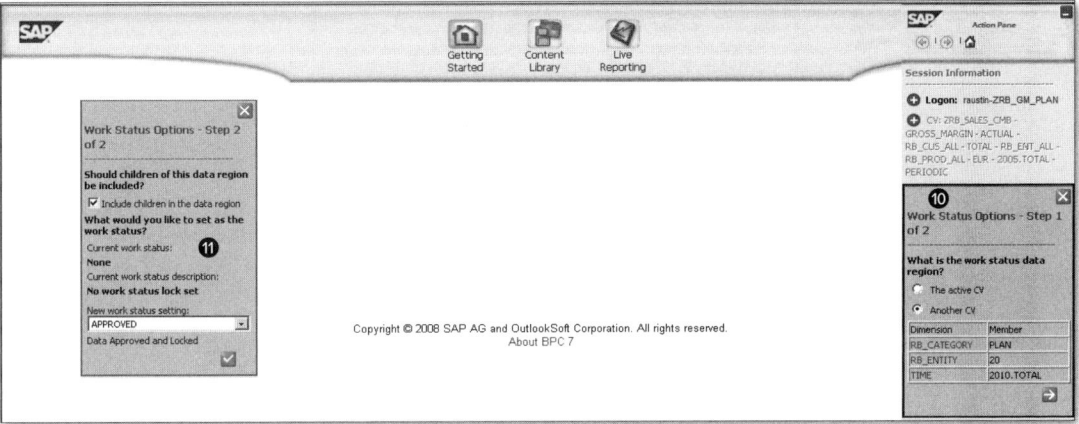

Figure 7.7 Configuring Work Status to Lock Data—Part G

12. Now, from SAP BusinessObjects Planning and Consolidation for Excel, create an input schedule and enter or modify plan data for entity 20 for the Jan 2010 period (Figure 7.8, ⓬). Then, send the data to the database.

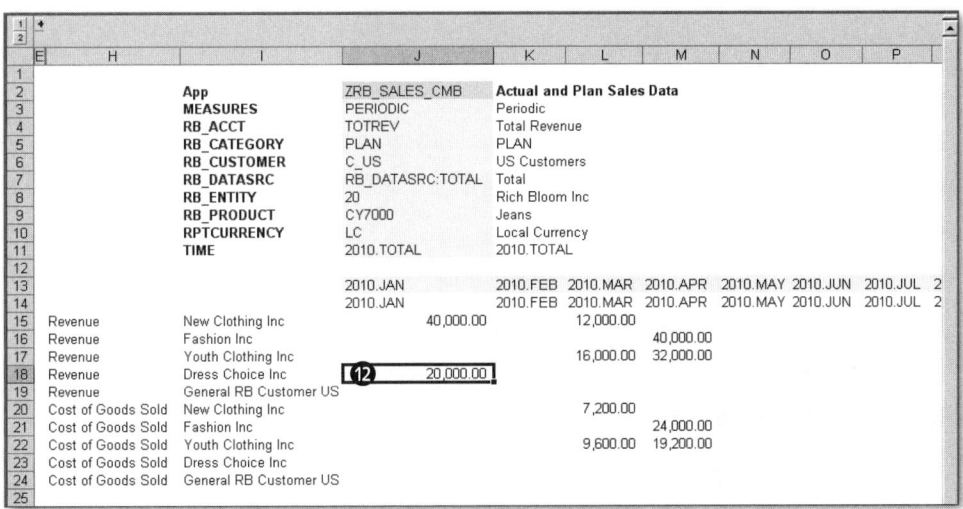

Figure 7.8 Configuring Work Status to Lock Data—Part H

13. You will notice that the update fails with an error message indicating that the work status check has failed. Because the work status is Approved, only the owner of the entity, Shawn Hill, can modify the data (Figure 7.9).

7 | Process Management and Collaboration

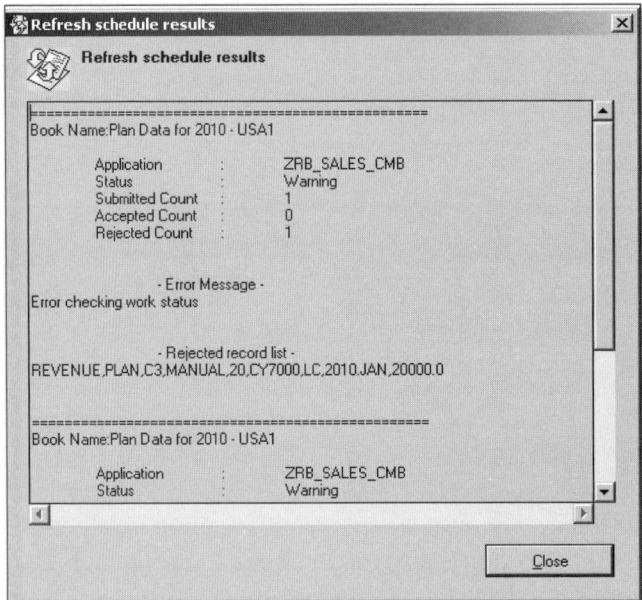

Figure 7.9 Configuring Work Status to Lock Data—Part I

In this section, we explained how to define work status types and select the dimensions to be used when assigning work status for an application. We also reviewed the steps for setting the work status for a data region, and explained how to use work status to lock data from being changed in an SAP BusinessObjects Planning and Consolidation Application.

In the next section, we will discuss how comments can be used in SAP BusinessObjects Planning and Consolidation.

7.2 Comments

Comments serve an important purpose in SAP BusinessObjects Planning and Consolidation; they enable users to enter free-form text about the data in an application. Information entered by users as comments can be viewed by others, and helps users in making better decisions. The following are important points about comments:

- The Comments interface can be accessed from the SAP BusinessObjects Planning and Consolidation for Excel, SAP BusinessObjects Planning and Consolidation Web, SAP BusinessObjects Planning and Consolidation for Word, and SAP BusinessObjects Planning and Consolidation for PowerPoint interfaces.
- You can set a comment for a specific current view selection from the SAP BusinessObjects Planning and Consolidation for Excel interface.
- A comment can be up to 265 characters. This is the Excel limit for a comment.
- You can create a comment for unstructured documents such as a Word or PowerPoint documents that are available in the content library of SAP BusinessObjects Planning and Consolidation.
- Users should have authorization to add, view, or delete comments. Authorization for these two tasks is necessary to add and manage comments: AddComment and ManageComment.
- When you create a comment, a keyword and priority can be assigned to the comment. You can then search for comments using either partial or full criteria based on these two parameters.
- You can run a report to get a detailed list of comments by history.
- The EvCOM function is used in SAP BusinessObjects Planning and Consolidation for Excel to send a comment to a database for a specific set of member values. The EvCGT and EvCGP functions are used to retrieve comments based on a specific set of member values.
- The value of the Comment application-level parameter determines whether comments can be maintained for an application. The parameter should be set to ON before comments can be posted for an application. We will discuss this setting in detail in Section 8.3, Web Administration Parameters.

7.2.1 Add Comments

There are two options to add comments from the SAP BusinessObjects Planning and Consolidation for Excel interface. You can add a comment either manually, or by using the EvCOM function for a particular selection of dimension member values. Follow these steps:

1. To add a comment manually, open a report or input schedule using the SAP BusinessObjects Planning and Consolidation for Excel interface. Click on the

Add New Comment task under BPC Tasks in the action pane on the right (Figure 7.10).

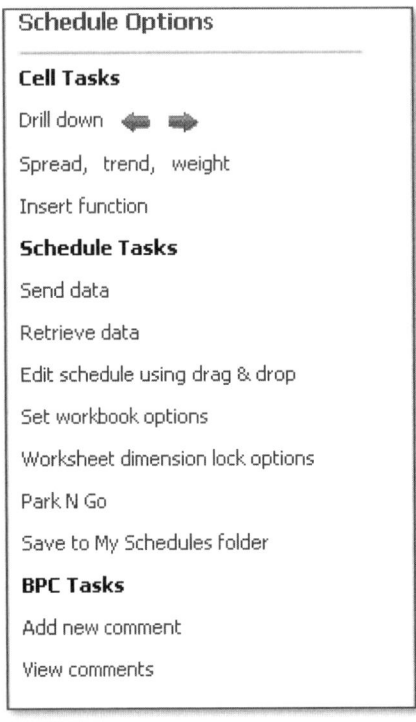

Figure 7.10 Steps to Add Comments—Part A

2. The system displays a dialog box, Enter a New Comment – Step 1 of 2, with the following options to create a comment (Figure 7.11):

   ▶ The Active Report or Schedule Cell: This option can be selected if a report or input schedule is open. Otherwise, this option is grayed out.

   ▶ The Active Current View: When this option is selected, the comment is associated with the values defined in the current view.

   ▶ Custom Current View: This option can be selected if you want to create a comment based on a custom CV. If this option is selected, the system prompts you to optionally select the dimension values to which the comment should apply. If a dimension is unchecked, that dimension is ignored for the comment.

For our example, select Custom Current View. Check only the Category, Entity, and Time dimensions for the comment. Select the following member values for entering the comment:

- RB_CATEGORY: PLAN
- RB_ENTITY: 20
- RB_TIME: 2010.TOTAL

Then click on the green arrow button.

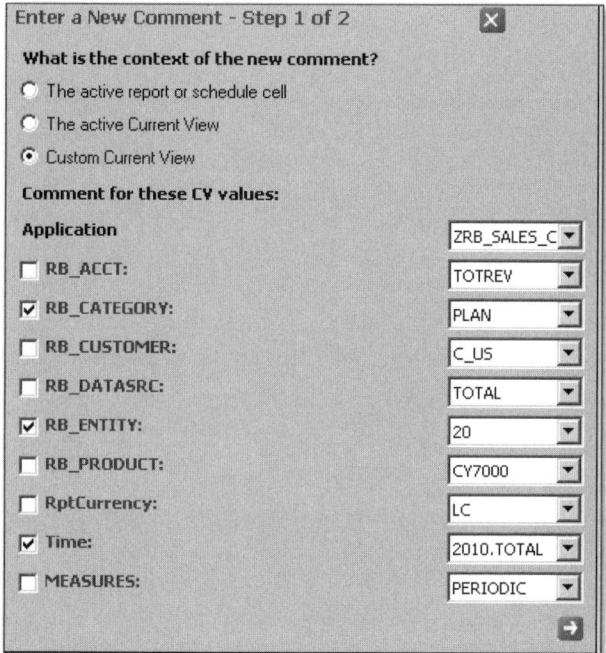

Figure 7.11 Steps to Add Comments—Part B

3. In the next screen, select the priority of the comment (Figure 7.12). The values High, Medium, Low, and No Priority can be selected.

4. You can optionally associate a keyword with the comment (Figure 7.12), which you can use later to retrieve the comment. You can enter a keyword of up to 30 characters.

5. Enter the comment (Figure 7.12).
6. Click on the green checkmark. This is the last step in the process of adding comments; the comment is then stored in the database.

Figure 7.12 Steps to Add Comments—Part C

We have now added a comment for a combination of dimension member values. Next, we will explain how to view comments.

7.2.2 Viewing Comments

Follow these steps to view comments:

1. Open a report or input schedule using the SAP BusinessObjects Planning and Consolidation for Excel interface and click on the View Comments task under BPC Tasks in the action pane on the right (Figure 7.10).

2. A dialog box, View Comments – Step 1 of 3, is displayed (Figure 7.13). You can view a comment based on one of the following selections:

    ▸ The Active Report or Schedule Cell: This option is available only if a report or input schedule is already open. Otherwise, this option is grayed out.

    ▸ The Active Current View: The system returns a comment associated with the selections in the active CV.

▶ Custom Current View: This option can be selected if you want to view a comment based on dimension values that is different from what is shown in the CV. If this option is selected, the system prompts you to select the dimension values to retrieve the comments. If no values are selected for a dimension, that dimension is ignored in the retrieval process.

> **Note**
> Only the dimensions that were checked when creating the comment should be selected when retrieving the comment.

After making your selections, click on the green arrow to move to the next step.

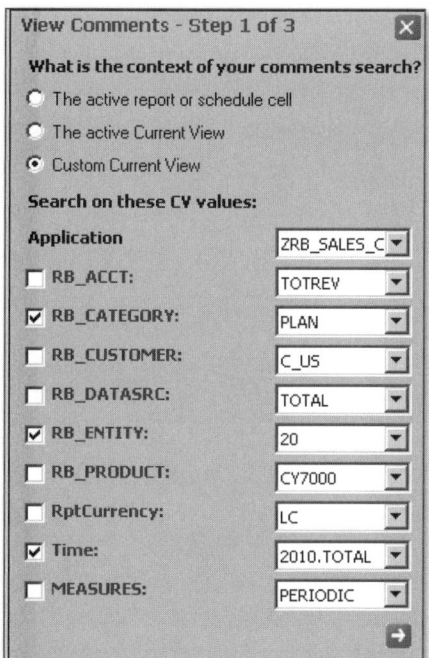

Figure 7.13 Steps to View a Comment—Part A

3. A new dialog box is displayed (Figure 7.14), and the system asks: "Do You Want to Include Comment History?" If you want to view the history of the comments associated with this selection, select the Show Comment History checkbox.

4. Select the priority level of the comments you want to view.

5. Select the keyword criteria to use when searching for comments. You do not need to enter the complete keyword, and you can use a partial keyword in the search for comments. After making your selections, click on the green arrow to proceed to the next step.

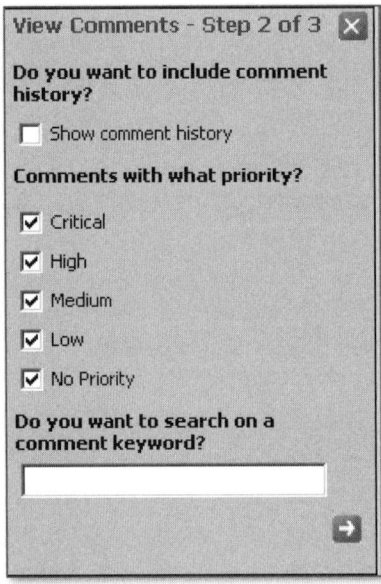

Figure 7.14 Steps to View a Comment—Part B

6. You will now be prompted to select an option based on the origin of the comment (Figure 7.15):

    ▶ Comments From Anyone: This selection returns all comments that were entered by all users. For our example, use this option.

    ▶ Comments From Myself: This selection returns only the comments you entered (based on your user ID).

    ▶ Comments From Another: This selection returns comments added by a specific user. When you select this option, you will have to select the particular users whose comments you want to view.

7. You can also specify a date criteria if you want to search comments by a date range. Now, click on the green checkmark.

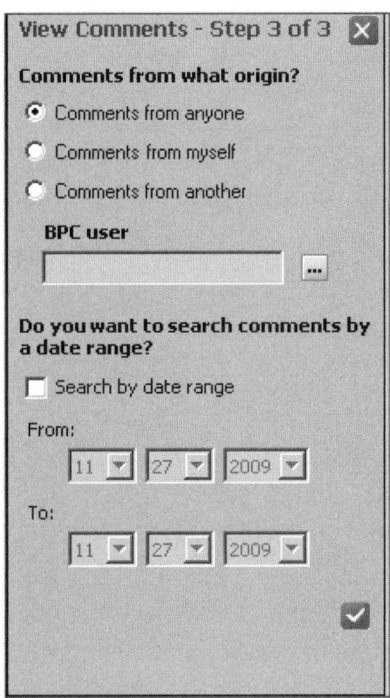

Figure 7.15 Steps to View a Comment—Part C

8. The comments page opens on the web (Figure 7.16). Before the page is displayed, you must authenticate your credentials by entering your user ID and password. The comments page is composed of two tables:
   - Data Region with Comments: This table displays the dimension members that were selected in the criteria for displaying comments. This table can include more than one row based on the selection criteria and will display only the selections for which comments exist.
   - Comments for the Selected Data Region: This table displays all of the comments associated with a given data region as displayed in the Data Region with Comments table. Click on a row in the Data Region with Comments table to display the associated comments in this table. The following information is displayed for each comment displayed in this table:
     — Comment: Displays the comment entered by the user for this selection.
     — Priority: Denotes the priority of the comment.
     — Keyword: Displays any keyword associated with the comment.

7 | Process Management and Collaboration

— Originator: Displays the user who originally created the comment.

— Date: Denotes the date when the comment was originally created.

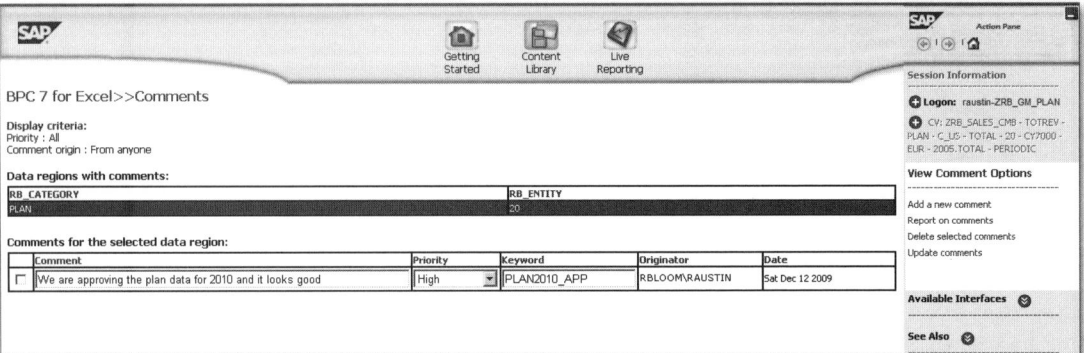

Figure 7.16 Steps to View a Comment—Part D

9. On the right side of the action pane (Figure 7.16), you will find options to add a new comment, report on comments, delete selected comments, or update comments. To delete a comment, select a comment displayed in the comments for the selected data region, and click on Delete Selected Comments. Here, you can also update the description of a comment, its priority, or its keywords, and then click on Update Comments to effect the updates.

You now know how to maintain and view comments. In the next section, we will explain how to report on comments.

7.2.3 Report on Comments

Comments can also be viewed by selecting the Launch BPC System Reports option from the SAP BusinessObjects Planning and Consolidation Web interface for your application (Figure 7.17, ❶). The menu option to run system reports is located under BPC Tasks.

Click on Launch BPC System Reports and you will see Comments Report under the Application Reports tasks in your left pane (Figure 7.17, ❷).

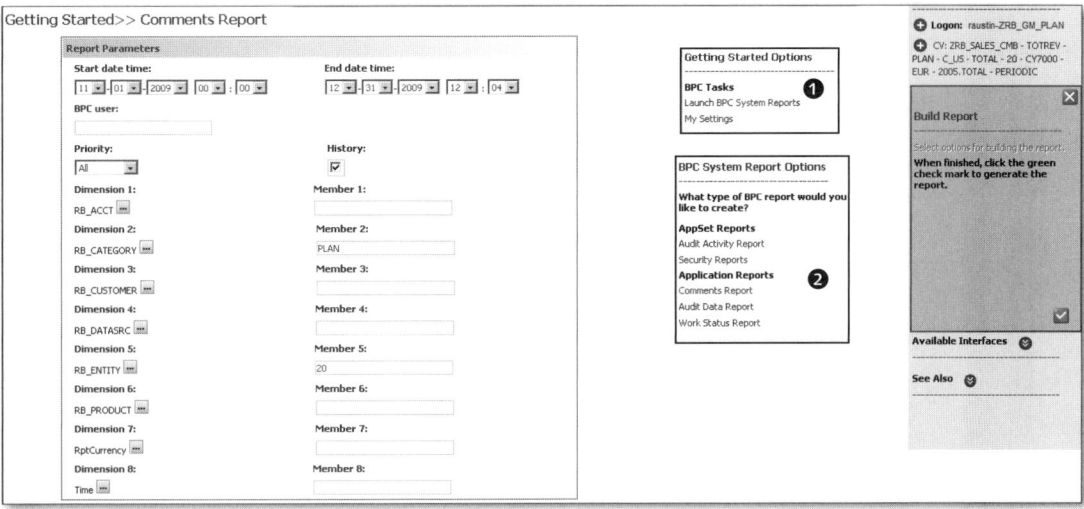

Figure 7.17 Reporting a Comment—Part A

You can generate a report of comments based on the following selections:

- Start Date: Specify the start date when the comment was created.
- Start Time: Specify the start time when the comment was created.
- End Date: When you specify the start date, you can specify the end date for comments to be included in the report.
- End Time: When you specify the start time, you can specify the end time for comments to be included in the report.
- SAP BusinessObjects Planning and Consolidation User: If you want the report to include comments for only a particular user, you can specify the ID of the user.
- History: Check this option if you want the report to include not only the latest comment but also a history of all of the comments for a selection.
- Priority: Indicate the priority of comments to be included in the report.
- Dimension Values: Specify the dimension member values if you want to see comments based on specific values. A blank for a dimension member indicates that you want all values for that dimension to be reported.
- Set Portrait: This setting indicates how you want to display the report. The available options are Portrait and Landscape.

After you make your selections, click on the green checkmark in the action pane to display the comment report (Figure 7.18).

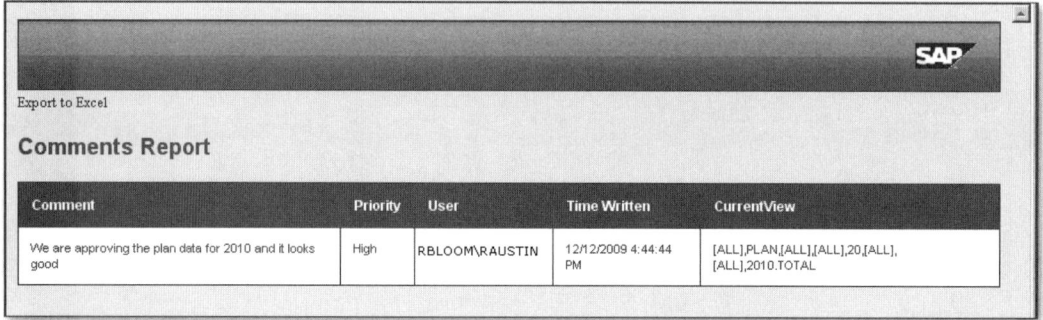

Figure 7.18 Reporting a Comment—Part B

You now know how to create comment reports. Next, we will review some of the Ev functions that are available to maintain and view comments.

7.2.4 Ev Functions for Comments

You can use the following standard Ev functions in SAP BusinessObjects Planning and Consolidation for Excel to create, update, or display comments:

- **EvCOM**
  You can use the EvCOM function to send a comment to the database. The values specified in this function should reference the application name and dimension values with which this comment must be associated. If a member value is not specified, the value for the dimension is automatically taken from the CV of a report or schedule.

- **EvCGT**
  You can use the EvCGT function to retrieve a comment from the database for an application and member values. Similar to the EvCOM function, if a dimension member value is not specified, the value for the dimension is automatically taken from the CV of that report or schedule.

You should now know how to add and view comments, including how to use SAP BusinessObjects Planning and Consolidation reports from the SAP BusinessObjects Planning and Consolidation Web interface. In the next section, we will explain how distribution and collection is used to distribute reports and input schedules. We will also explain how to use the Distribution and Collection interface to update data from an offline input schedule into SAP BusinessObjects Planning and Consolidation.

7.3 Distribution and Collection

The Distribution and Collection interface in SAP BusinessObjects Planning and Consolidation allows a user to share the data in SAP BusinessObjects Planning and Consolidation with other users who may or may not have access to the system. It also enables the data to be entered in offline mode and be reloaded back into SAP BusinessObjects Planning and Consolidation.

The distribution and collection menu options can be accessed from the SAP BusinessObjects Planning and Consolidation for Excel interface via the ePublish menu. You must have the necessary authorization to use this functionality.

The process of sending a report or input schedule in offline mode is referred to as *distribution* in SAP BusinessObjects Planning and Consolidation. The data included in this report can be used by others who may need access to this information for analysis and decision making. Sometimes users who travel may not be able to connect to SAP BusinessObjects Planning and Consolidation to access information in an application; distribution facilitates the process of getting data to the necessary users via email, and also aids in collaboration.

A user can update the data in an input schedule in offline mode and push the changes back to the SAP BusinessObjects Planning and Consolidation system. The process of updating the data from an offline input schedule back to SAP BusinessObjects Planning and Consolidation is referred to as *collection*.

The report or input schedule generated using the distribution list is a snapshot of the data at a specific point in time. When a user sends a report or an input schedule using a distributor, the data can be placed in a folder or sent as an email to users. If the report or input schedule is sent via email, the SAP BusinessObjects Planning and Consolidation system should be configured to send email to users.

The process of defining reports or input schedules for distribution is managed using distribution lists. You can specify more than one report or input schedule when defining the distribution list; if you are sending data as an email message, you can list the users who should receive the report and what data should be sent. A distribution list with the definition of the reports or input schedules can be saved in XLS or XLT format.

After a distribution list is created, the list can be executed to generate the reports and input schedules defined in the distribution list, and the distribution list can be executed immediately or scheduled in the background. This job is executed on the machine of the user who schedules the job.

When data is generated using the distribution option, the access available for the user who schedules the distribution governs the content of the report or input schedules. Ensure that the user executing the distribution list has sufficient member access to the data requested in the distribution list. If the user does not have access to the data, the distribution list fails to execute and returns a message saying that the user does not have sufficient authorization to run the reports. A report or input schedule generated using distribution can be viewed directly in Excel; there is no need to use any of the interfaces.

When a file is created or sent as an email after the generation of reports or input schedules using the distribution process, anyone who has access to that file or email can view the generated data, because the information is offline at that time. This has to be taken into consideration when data is distributed using this process, especially if the generated data is sensitive and should be kept confidential.

There are three primary interfaces that can be used to distribute and collect data:

- **Distribution lists**
  This interface is used to create and maintain distribution lists. The list identifies the reports, schedules, and selections for generating the data.

▶ **Offline Distribution Wizard**
This interface is used to schedule execution of the distribution list. The job can be scheduled to run immediately, or it can be scheduled as a future job to be run later.

▶ **Collection**
This interface is used only for input schedules that were distributed earlier. Using this interface, data entered or modified into an offline input schedule can be updated in the planning application.

7.3.1 Creating a Distribution List

We will now explain how to create a distribution list for the input schedule displayed in Figure 7.19. Recall that we created this input schedule in Chapter 5.

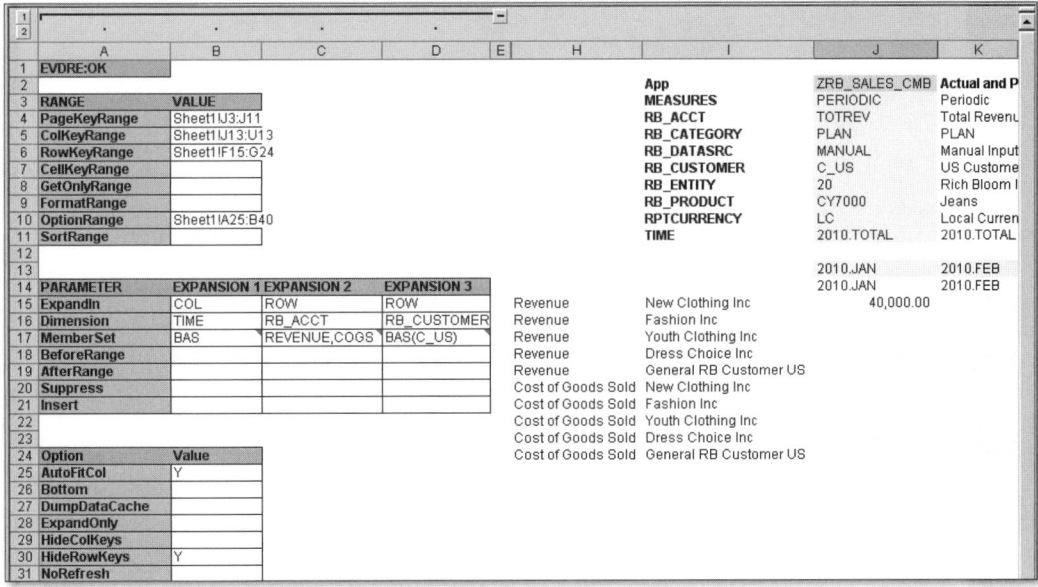

Figure 7.19 Creating a Distribution List—Part A

To access the distribution list, log into the SAP BusinessObjects Planning and Consolidation for Excel interface. You need access to the Manage Distributor List task under Collaboration to maintain distribution lists.

1. Go to the EPUBLISH menu. Select MANAGE DISTRIBUTION LIST and select NEW. You are prompted to select a template to create the new distribution list. (Figure 7.20).

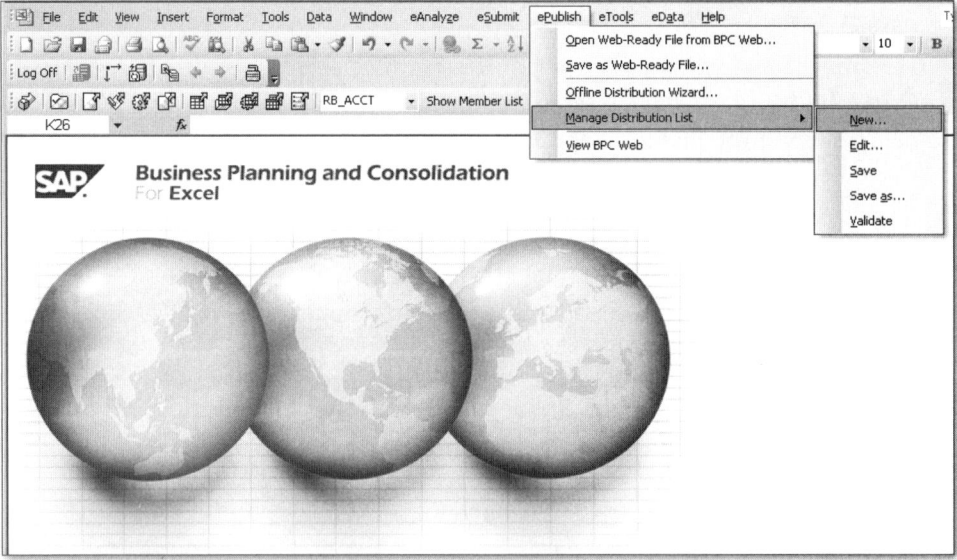

Figure 7.20 Creating a Distribution List—Part B

2. This opens up the distribution template (Figure 7.21), which contains a placeholder to enter the name of a book. This applies to the entire distribution list. A distribution list can include multiple sections, and each section denotes a report or an input schedule. Enter the following parameters for the distribution template:

   ▶ BOOK: Every distribution list has a name assigned to it. Specify the name of the book here.

   ▶ SECTION: A distribution template can contain one or more sections, and a section is defined for each report or input schedule. Enter the name of the section here.

   ▶ REPNAME: In this parameter, specify the report or input schedule you want to use in a section of the distribution list.

- FIXKEY: This field is used to specify fixed filters for the report; specify the static selections. You can have more than one FIXKEY field for the different dimensions in your application; for example, you may have a need to always run a report for the PLAN category. In this case, the FIXKEY is used to specify the fixed values you want to use to run the report.
- VARKEY: The VARKEY field specifies the dimensions values to use to burst the report. You can specify more than one dimension in this field. If you want a user to receive the report, specify the user here. The user receives the report for the selections corresponding to that user, which allows you to only send users the data they really need. (This is applicable only if you are distributing your report as an email message.) If multiple values are selected for a dimension specified in the VARKEY field, multiple reports are created when executing the report. In the example shown in Figure 7.21, a report will be generated for each entity that is under the E_US hierarchy.
- SECTIONEND: This denotes the end of the section.

The email configuration in SAP BusinessObjects Planning and Consolidation should be set if you want to email reports or input schedules using the distributor. Also, email addresses should be maintained and current for the user in SAP BusinessObjects Planning and Consolidation.

> **Note**
>
> If you do not specify a dimension available in your application in the FIXKEY or VARKEY fields, the values for the dimension are taken from the CV of the user who is scheduling the report.

3. Validate the distribution list you just created. When the distribution list is validated, the system checks to see whether all mandatory fields are entered, and also checks the syntax of the distribution list.
4. Save the distribution list. A user who wants to create a distribution list and save it to the company folder needs access to the Update to Company Folder task that falls under File Access.

7 | Process Management and Collaboration

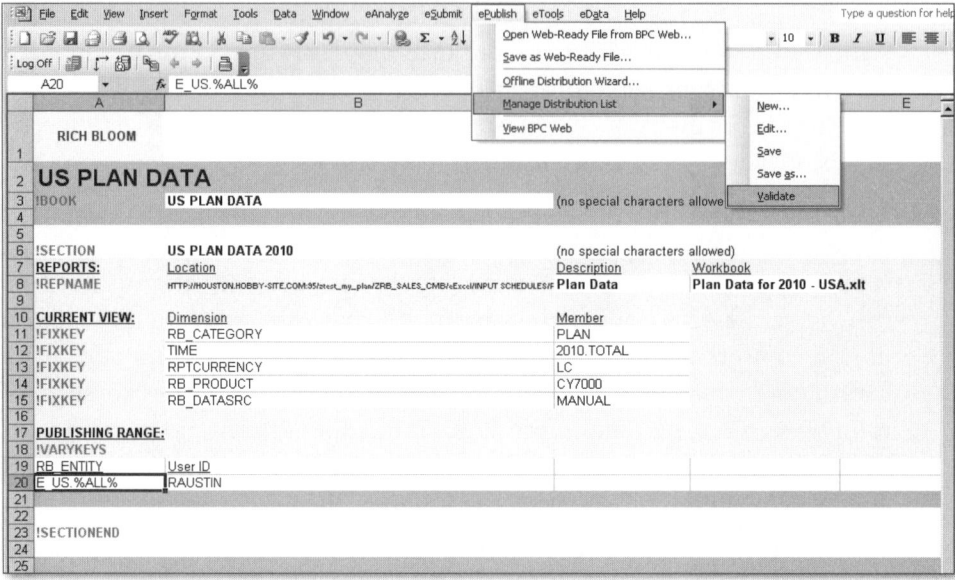

Figure 7.21 Creating a Distribution List—Part C

Now that we have created a distribution list, we can execute and distribute it as an offline report or input schedule.

7.3.2 Offline Distribution Wizard

Before using the Offline Distribution Wizard, ensure that you have the necessary access. You will need access to the PublishOffline task that falls under Collaboration.

1. Go to the EPUBLISH menu and select OFFLINE DISTRIBUTION WIZARD (Figure 7.22). You are prompted to either select the distribution or the collection process. Under Distribution, there are two options for running the template:

    ► Lockdown and Send Mail: When this option is selected, the system prompts you to select a distribution list and then requires you to specify the sender, subject, and body details of the email message. Additional options are available if you want to receive confirmation that the message was received, or if you want to send the report as a ZIP file.

▶ Lockdown and Save to Folder: When this option is selected, the system prompts the user to select a distribution list and specify a folder location where the reports or schedules selected in the distribution list should be saved.

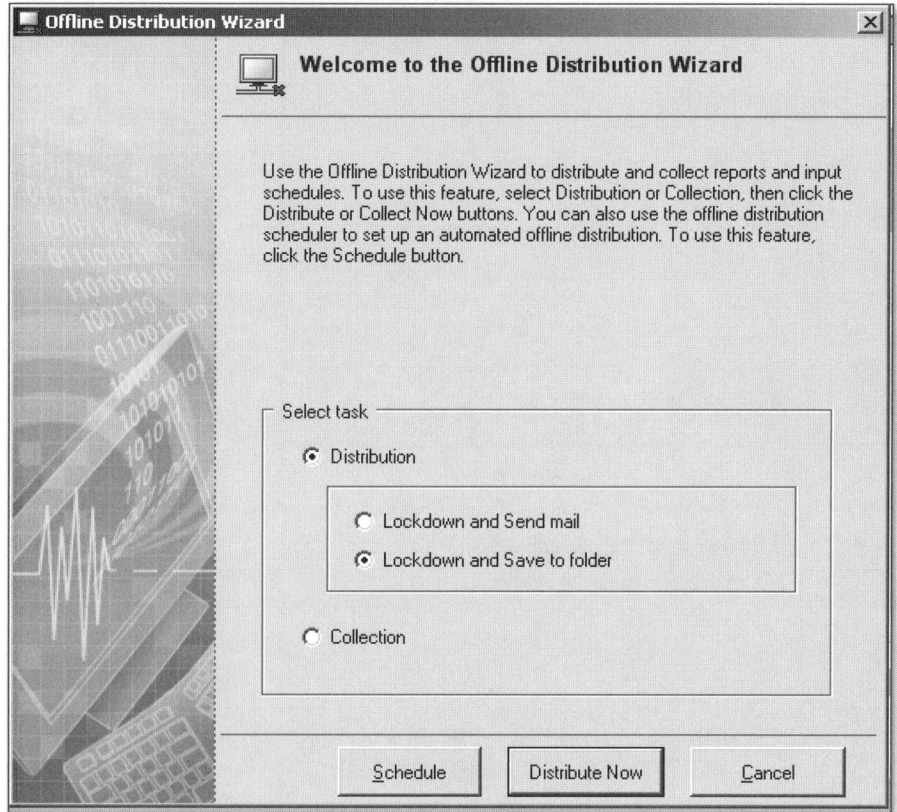

Figure 7.22 Offline Distribution Wizard—Part A

2. Select the distribution list you want to execute, and specify the folder in which you want to the files to be created (Figure 7.23). Click on the Next button.
3. You are then prompted to select the sections in the distribution list you want to distribute (Figure 7.24). After making your selections, click on the NEXT button.

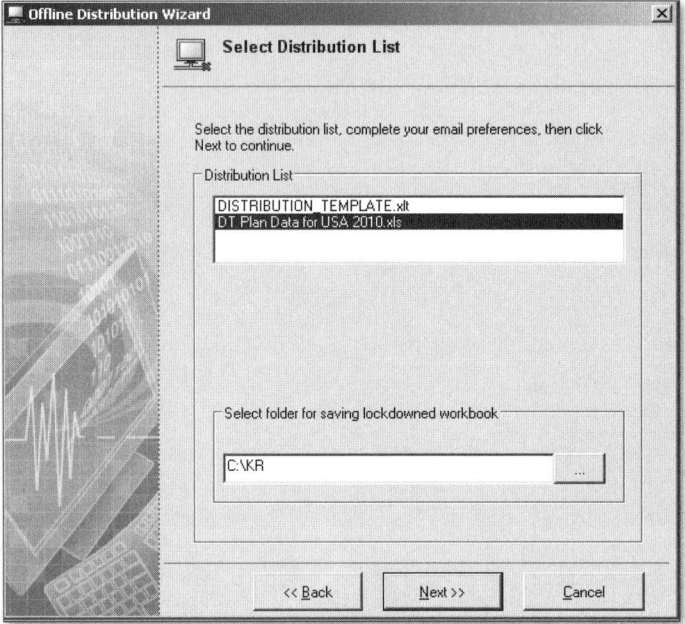

Figure 7.23 Offline Distribution Wizard—Part B

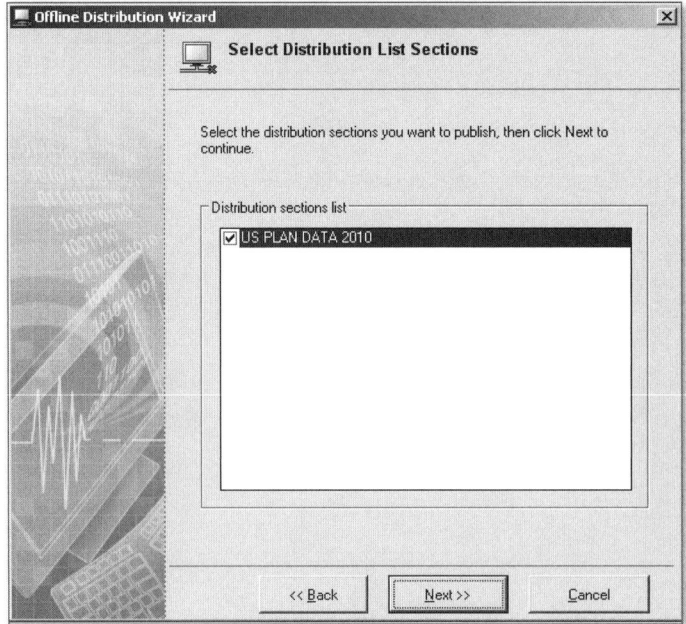

Figure 7.24 Offline Distribution Wizard—Part C

4. The next dialog box confirms the reports that will be created and the selections that will be used in creating the reports (Figure 7.25). Click on the Process button to continue.

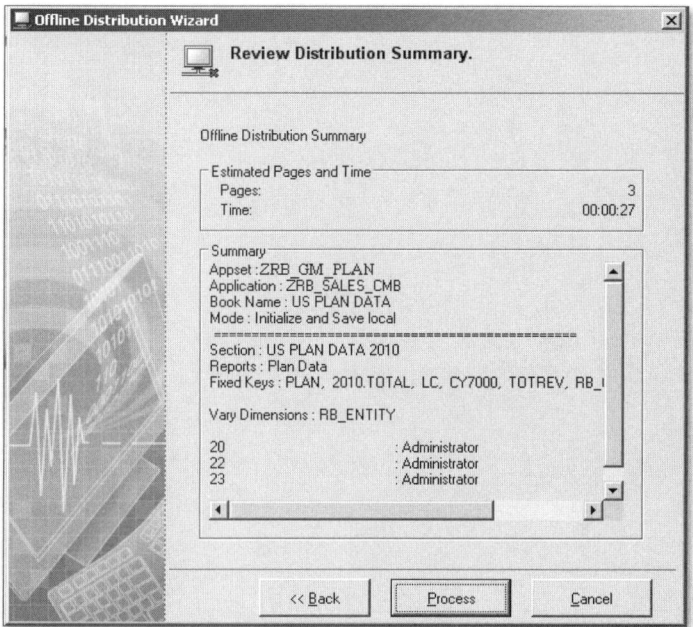

Figure 7.25 Offline Distribution Wizard—Part D

5. The distribution list is now executed on the client machine. In this case, the client is the user who is scheduling this process for execution. The reports and input schedules specified in the distribution lists are opened, the CV is changed based on the selections defined there, and the data is refreshed and saved in the folder specified when executing the list. A message confirms that the reports were distributed successfully. Click on FINISH to complete the distribution process (Figure 7.26).

The files are generated in the folder specified in the distribution list (Figure 7.27). The naming convention of the reports or input schedules generated by the distributor is as follows:

- The report recipient or user ID name as specified in the VARKEY field in the distribution list.
- The VARKEY value specified in the distribution list section.
- The name of the report specified in the distribution section.

7 | Process Management and Collaboration

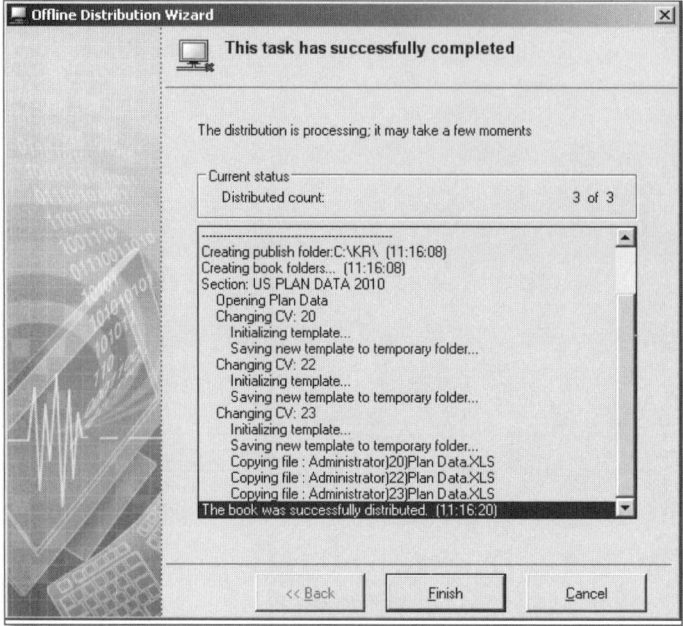

Figure 7.26 Offline Distribution Wizard—Part E

> **Note**
> More than one file or email may be generated based on the selections in the VARKEY field of the distribution list.

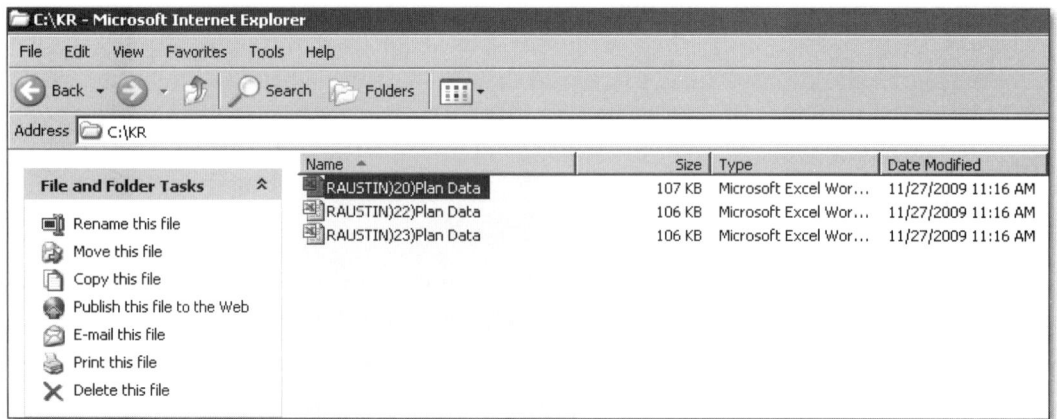

Figure 7.27 Offline Distribution Wizard—Part F

306

> **Note**
> Do not keep a distribution list open when you want to use the Offline Distribution Wizard to execute it.

7.3.3 Collection

Collection applies only to input schedules that were distributed using the Offline Distribution Wizard. Input schedules that are distributed as an offline report can be updated offline, and then the updates can be pushed back to SAP BusinessObjects Planning and Consolidation.

You need sufficient authorization to collect data; specifically, you need access to the SubmitData task that falls under Analysis and Collection. The distribution list we ran included an input schedule; we will now change one of the records in the input schedule and push the data back to SAP BusinessObjects Planning and Consolidation using the Collect interface (Figure 7.28).

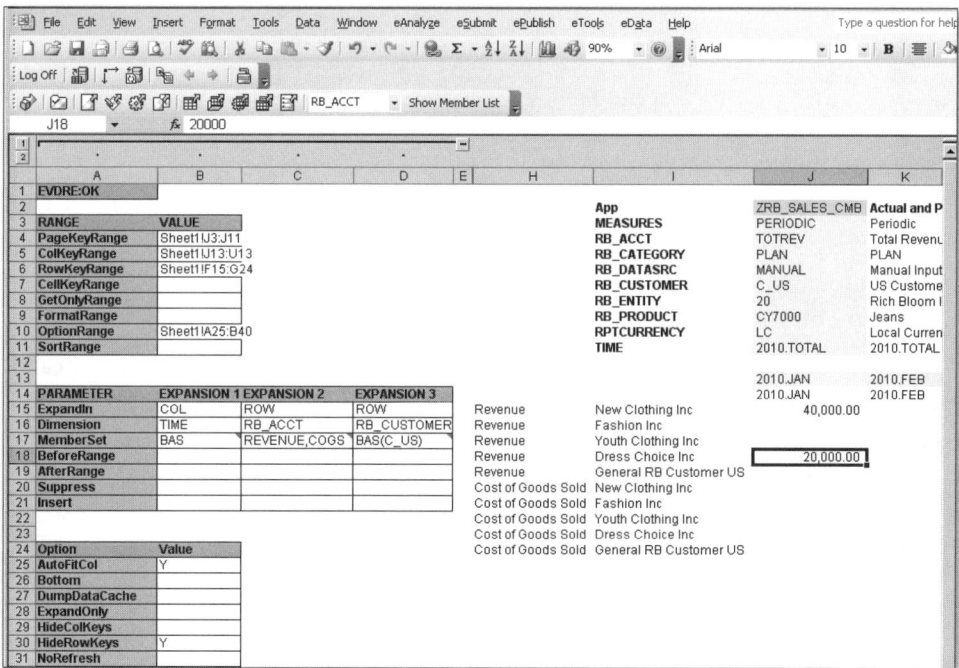

Figure 7.28 Steps in Collecting Data—Part A

1. Go to the EPUBLISH menu and select OFFLINE DISTRIBUTION WIZARD. You are prompted to select the distribution or collection task; select COLLECTION and click on the COLLECT NOW button to collect the data (Figure 7.29).

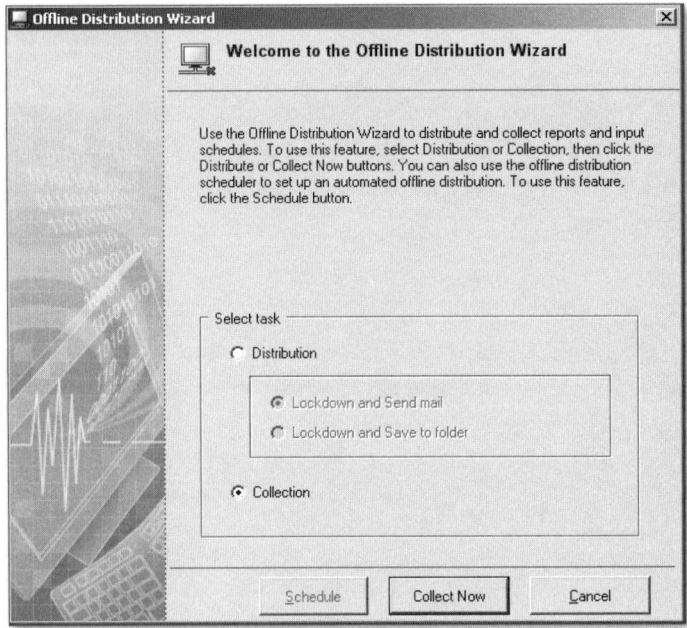

Figure 7.29 Steps in Collecting Data—Part B

2. The next dialog box displays two options for collecting data (Figure 7.30):
   ▶ Outlook Mail Box: When this option is selected, data is collected from an email message attachment.
   ▶ Local Folder: When this option is selected, data is collected from a file located on your local computer. When you specify a folder, you can specify the folder and files from which you want to collect the data. More than one file can be selected in this step.
3. Select the files to collect and click on the Next button.
4. After the files are selected, a dialog box indicates that the data in the files will be processed (Figure 7.31). Click on the Process button.

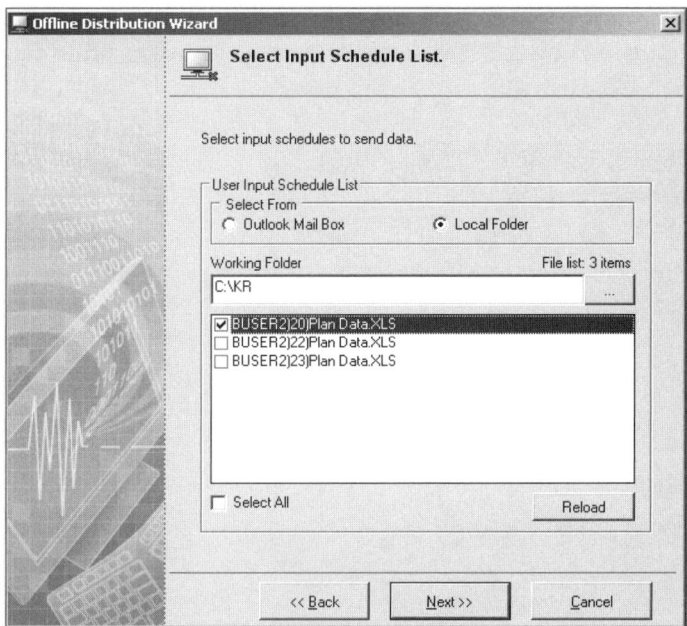

Figure 7.30 Steps in Collecting Data—Part C

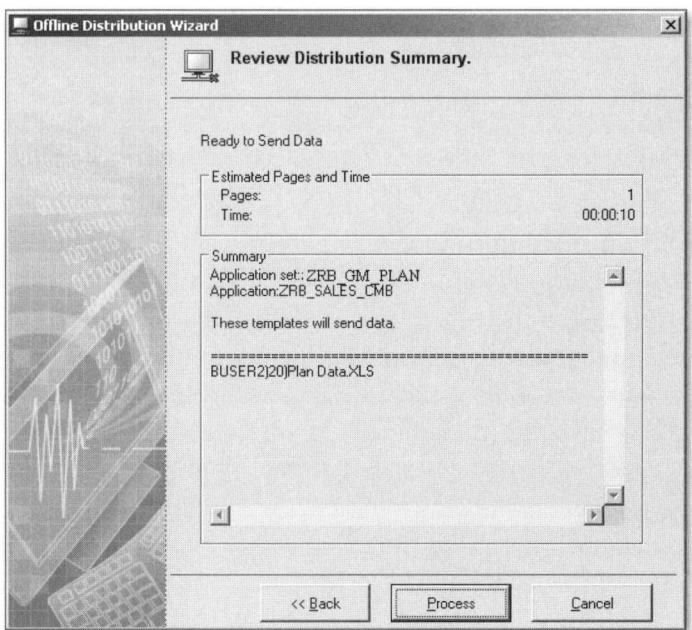

Figure 7.31 Steps in Collecting Data—Part D

5. During the update process, all of the validations defined for the application are checked before the data is processed. The number of records processed is displayed in the dialog box (Figure 7.32).

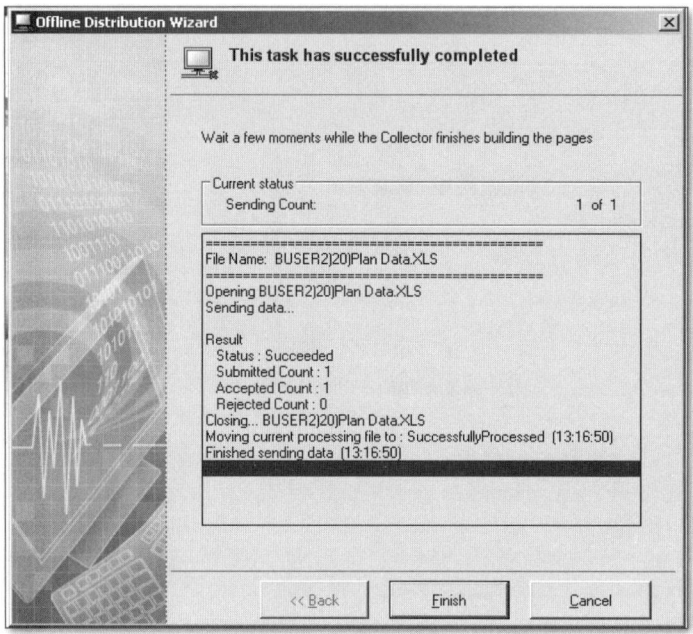

Figure 7.32 Steps in Collecting Data — Part E

6. All of the processed files are moved to the SUCCESSFULLYPROCESSED folder, as shown in Figure 7.33.

You have now seen how the distribution and collection functionality works in SAP BusinessObjects Planning and Consolidation. It is a powerful feature for generating and distributing reports and can be tailored to run multiple reports for different selections from a single distribution template. The ability to distribute input schedules in offline mode, and the ability to update those schedules offline and push them back into SAP BusinessObjects Planning and Consolidation, is another key feature of the interface. Although data is entered offline, all of the validations for the application are enforced when the data is pushed back to SAP BusinessObjects Planning and Consolidation.

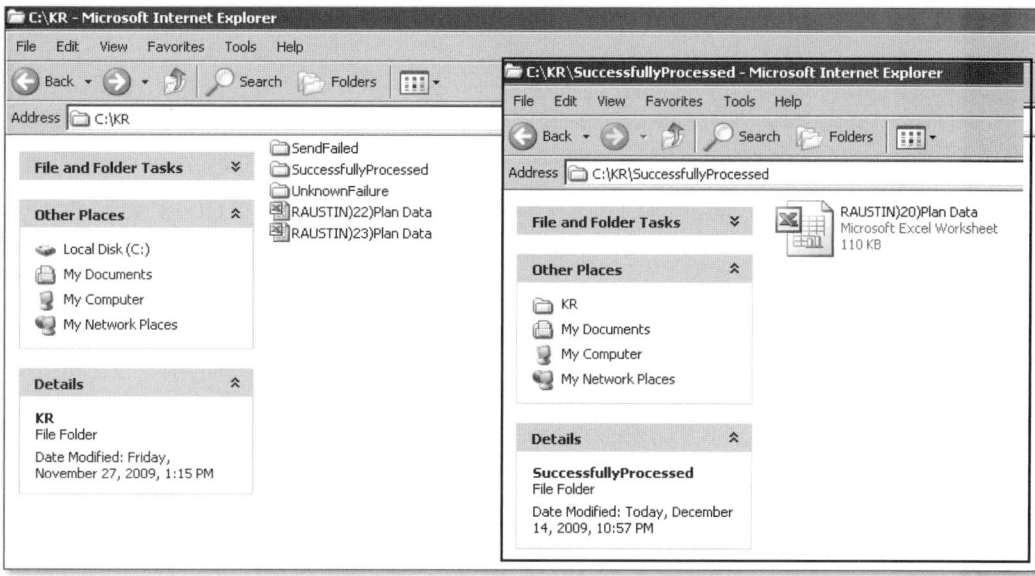

Figure 7.33 Steps in Collecting Data—Part F

In the next section, we will explain how Word and PowerPoint interfaces are used to integrate SAP BusinessObjects Planning and Consolidation data into those types of documents.

7.4 Integrating SAP BusinessObjects Planning and Consolidation Data into Word and PowerPoint

SAP BusinessObjects Planning and Consolidation allows you to not only integrate data into Word and PowerPoint, but also to embed objects such as input schedules into these documents. You can also add and view comments from this interface. The following tasks are available when using the Word and PowerPoint interfaces:

- **Insert BPC Data**
  The Insert BPC Data task in the action pane is used for inserting SAP BusinessObjects Planning and Consolidation data into a Word or PowerPoint document. After you add the Insert BPC Data object into a document, the placeholder represents the dimension members specified in the current view. You can view the selection by placing the cursor on the object.

- **Insert BPC for Excel Object**
  When this task is selected, a dialog box prompts you to select a report or input schedule. When an input schedule is inserted into a document, the changes can be updated in SAP BusinessObjects Planning and Consolidation.

- **Comments**
  The Add New Comment and View Comment tasks in the action pane can be used to add and view comments.

- **Retrieve All Data**
  When you have inserted a link for the data in the CV using the Insert BPC Data task, you can retrieve the value for this selection using the Retrieve All Data task.

- **Expand All**
  When you insert an SAP BusinessObjects Planning and Consolidation for Excel object in a document, you can click on the Expand All task in the action pane to use the expansion functions in SAP BusinessObjects Planning and Consolidation.

- **Send All Data**
  When an input schedule created in SAP BusinessObjects Planning and Consolidation for Excel is inserted into a document, the change made to the input schedule can be updated to the database.

When an object is inserted into a document, you can only retrieve the data from SAP BusinessObjects Planning and Consolidation; you cannot use it to update the data. We will now use a simple example to show you how you can use the SAP BusinessObjects Planning and Consolidation for Word interface to insert SAP BusinessObjects Planning and Consolidation data into a document. The SAP BusinessObjects Planning and Consolidation for Word and SAP BusinessObjects Planning and Consolidation for PowerPoint interfaces can be accessed from the SAP BusinessObjects Planning and Consolidation Admin, SAP BusinessObjects Planning and Consolidation Excel, and SAP BusinessObjects Planning and Consolidation Web interfaces.

1. Access the SAP BusinessObjects Planning and Consolidation for Word interface. A list of menu options under BPC TASKS and DOCUMENT TASKS is displayed (Figure 7.34).

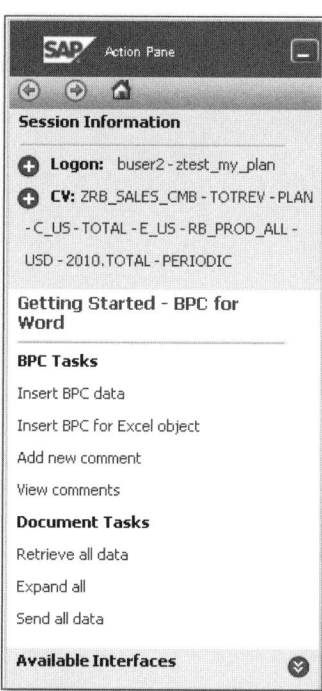

Figure 7.34 Integrating SAP BusinessObjects Planning and Consolidation Data into Word—Part A

2. Open a new Word document as shown in Figure 7.35. Then, click on INSERT BPC DATA, and insert this object into your Word document. The member selections in your CV are used to retrieve the data. Place the cursor on the object to view the selections SAP BusinessObjects Planning and Consolidation will use to retrieve the data.

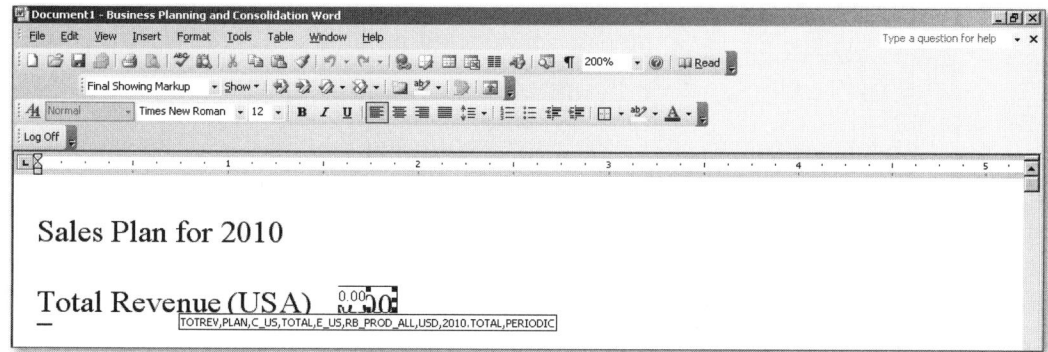

Figure 7.35 Integrating SAP BusinessObjects Planning and Consolidation Data into Word—Part B

3. You can right-click on the object inserted in the previous step to display the properties of the object (Figure 7.36).

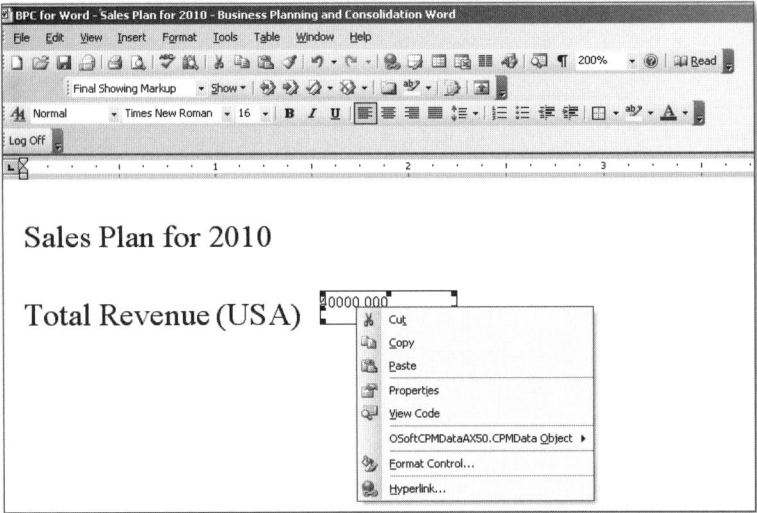

Figure 7.36 Integrating SAP BusinessObjects Planning and Consolidation Data into Word—Part C

When you click on the Retrieve All Data task under Document Tasks in the action pane, the data from SAP BusinessObjects Planning and Consolidation is retrieved and displayed for the objects inserted in the Word document, as shown in Figure 7.37.

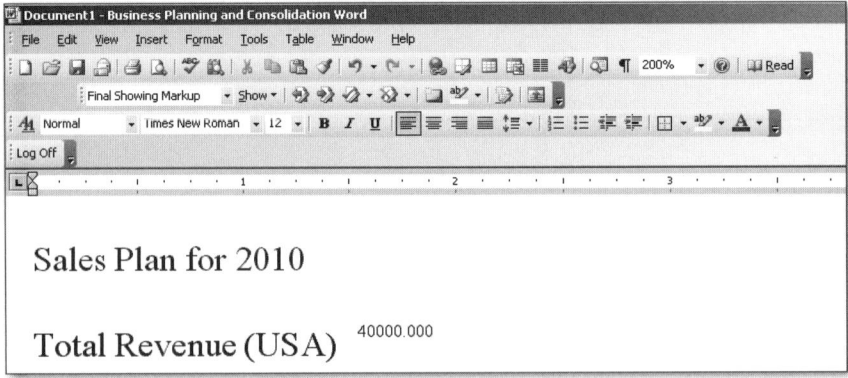

Figure 7.37 Integrating SAP BusinessObjects Planning and Consolidation Data into Word—Part C

In this section, we explained how to interface SAP BusinessObjects Planning and Consolidation data into Word and PowerPoint documents. In the next section, we will explain how you can use menus to view and execute tasks in planning or consolidation processes that need to be performed on a periodic basis.

7.5 Menus

SAP BusinessObjects Planning and Consolidation provides a standard set of EvMNU functions that can be used in SAP BusinessObjects Planning and Consolidation for Excel to launch common tasks such opening a report or executing a data package.

Two options are available when using the EvMNU functions: you can create them as standard Excel functions or include them inside a VB macro. The following is the syntax for using the EvMNU function as an Excel formula:

- **EvMNU**
  MacroName, DisplayName, Parameter.
- **MacroName**
  This is the menu command for executing a common task such as setting the member value in the CV for a dimension or updating data from an input schedule to the database.
- **Display Name**
  This is the text the user clicks on to launch the menu task. It is an optional parameter.
- **Parameter**
  Some macro commands require additional parameters. For example, to execute a report, the name of the report to be run is required as a parameter in the command.

Table 7.1 lists the menu commands used in SAP BusinessObjects Planning and Consolidation.

Menu Command	Description
MNU_eANALYZE_REFRESH	Recalculates reports.
MNU_eANALYZE_OPENMY	Opens the MyReports report folder.

Table 7.1 List of EvMNU Functions

Menu Command	Description
MNU_eANALYZE_OPENSTANDARD	Opens the report library in the eExcel/Reports directory.
MNU_eANALYZE_SAVEMY	Saves the report to the MyReports folder.
MNU_eANALYZE_REPORTWIZARD	Launches the dynamic template report dialog box.
MNU_eSUBMIT_REFSCHEDULE_SHEET_NOACTION	Sends data without clearing or refreshing.
MNU_eSUBMIT_REFSCHEDULE_SHEET_REFRESH	Sends data and refreshes the worksheet.
MNU_eSUBMIT_REFSCHEDULE_SHEET_CLEARANDREFRESH	Sends data and clears and refreshes the worksheet.
MNU_eSUBMIT_REFSCHEDULE_BOOK_NOACTION	Sends data without clearing or refreshing the worksheet.
MNU_eSUBMIT_REFSCHEDULE_BOOK_NOACTION_SHOWRESULT	Sends data without clearing or refreshing the worksheet, and shows the result in a window on successful send.
MNU_eSUBMIT_REFSCHEDULE_BOOK_REFRESH	Sends the workbook and refreshes the data.
MNU_eSUBMIT_REFSCHEDULE_BOOK_CLEARANDREFRESH	Sends the workbook, clears the data, and refreshes the workbook.
MNU_eSUBMIT_REFRESH	Refreshes the schedule without sending data.
MNU_eSUBMIT_OPENSTANDARD	Opens the schedule library. No parameter is allowed for NetWeaver; the default settings open the eExcel directory.
MNU_eSUBMIT_OPENMY	Opens the MySchedules folder.
MNU_eSUBMIT_SAVEMY	Saves the input schedule to the MySchedules folder.
MNU_eSUBMIT_SCHEDULE	Opens the dynamic schedule template dialog box.
MNU_eSUBMIT_MODIFY	Opens the work status action pane in SAP BusinessObjects Planning and Consolidation Web.

Table 7.1 List of EvMNU Functions (Cont.)

Menu Command	Description
MNU_ePUBLISH_OPENPUBLICATION	Opens the SAP BusinessObjects Planning and Consolidation Web directory. Parameter = directory path.
MNU_ePUBLISH_PUBLISHSHEET	Publishes a worksheet to SAP BusinessObjects Planning and Consolidation Web.
MNU_ePUBLISH_OFFLINE_WIZARD	Opens the Distribution Wizard.
MNU_ePUBLISH_OFFLINE_NEW	Creates a new offline report.
MNU_ePUBLISH_OFFLINE_EDIT	Edits offline options.
MNU_ePUBLISH_OFFLINE_SAVE	Saves the offline report.
MNU_ePUBLISH_OFFLINE_SAVEAS	Opens the Save As dialog box.
MNU_ePUBLISH_OFFLINE_VALIDATE	Validates an offline report.
MNU_ePUBLISH_VIEWeDASH	Opens SAP BusinessObjects Planning and Consolidation Web.
MNU_eTOOLS_CHANGEAPP	Opens the Change Application Set dialog box.
MNU_eTOOLS_MEMBERSELECTOR_x	Opens the member lookup for the specified dimension type. The dimension types are: A: Account C: Category E: Entity T: Time F: Measures I: Intercompany Dimension types D, S, and U are not supported.
MNU_eTOOLS_FUNCTIONWIZARD	Opens the Function Wizard.
MNU_eTOOLS_EXPAND	Expands all dynamic expansions.
MNU_eTOOLS_REFRESH	Refreshes reports and input schedules from the server.
MNU_ETOOLS_PARKNGO	Opens the Park N Go dialog box.
MNU_eTOOLS_JOURNAL	Opens the journal form. (Only available if journals are set up on the server.)

Table 7.1 List of EvMNU Functions (Cont.)

Menu Command	Description
MNU_eJOURNAL_QUERY	Opens the Journal Manager (only available if journals are set up on the server).
MNU_eJOURNAL_REPORT	Opens the Journal Report Wizard (only available if journals are set up on the server).
MNU_eTOOLS_OPENSTANDARD	Opens the template library.
MNU_eTOOLS_SAVESTANDARD	Saves to the template library.
MNU_eTOOLS_DRILLDOWN	Performs drilldown on the current cell.
MNU_eTOOLS_DRILLDOWN_BACK	Reverses the last drilldown.
MNU_eTOOLS_DRILLDOWN_FORWARD	Performs a drilldown that was undone by the DRILLDOWN_BACK task.
MNU_eTOOLS_DATAMANAGER	Opens the Data Manager and adds the eData menu.
MNU_eTOOLS_OPTION	Opens the Client Options dialog box.
MNU_eTOOLS_WBOPTION	Opens the Workbook Options dialog box.
MNU_eTOOLS_ABOUT	Opens the About BPC dialog box.
MNU_eData_RUNPACKAGE	Opens the Data Manager Run Package dialog box. Allows users who have access to run database packages.
MNU_eDATA_SELECTPACKAGE	Opens a specific data manager package. The syntax for this command is MNU_eDATA_SELECTPACKAGE(<package name>, <package file path>, <teamname>, <package group>) EvMNU(A1,A2).
	For only this menu command, the parameters are part of the MacroName; therefore, you must leave the Parameter section blank. For example, if you have MNU_eData_SelectPackage("import","examples/import.dts","HQ") in cell A1, and FX Restatement in cell A2, your EvMNU function would be:
MNU_eDATA_VIEWSTATUS	Opens the Data Manager View Status dialog box.

Table 7.1 List of EvMNU Functions (Cont.)

Menu Command	Description
MNU_eDATA_ORGANIZEPACKAGE	Opens the Data Manager Organize Package dialog box.
MNU_eDATA_MANAGESITEPACKAGE	Opens the Data Manager Manage Team User Package Access dialog box.
MNU_eDATA_DATAPREVIEW	Opens the Data Manager Data Preview dialog box.
MNU_eDATA_DATAUPLOAD	Opens the Data Manager Data Upload dialog box. Allows users who have access to upload data files to the server and perform data transformations.
MNU_eData_DataDownLoad	Opens the Data Manager Data Download dialog box. Allows users who have access to download data files from the server.
MNU_eDATA_NEWTRANSFORMATION	Creates a new data manager transformation sheet.
MNU_eDATA_OPENTRANSFORMATION	Opens the Data Manager Open Transformation dialog box.
MNU_eDATA_SAVESTRANSFORMATION	Opens the Data Manager Save As Transformation Sheet dialog box.
MNU_eDATA_NEWCONVERSIONFILE	Creates a new data manager conversion file.
MNU_eDATA_OPENCONVERSIONFILE	Opens the Data Manager Open Conversion File dialog box.
MNU_eDATA_SAVECONVERSIONFILE	Saves the active conversion file.
MNU_eDATA_SAVEASCONVERSIONFILE	Opens the Data Manager Save as Conversion File dialog box.
MNU_eDATA_CLEARPROMPTVALUE	Clears saved data manager prompt values.
MNU_eDATA_TESTTRANSFORMATIONWDATA	Opens the Data Manager Test Transformation with Data dialog box.
MNU_ETOOLS_TASKPANE	Shows the ActionPane.
MNU_ESUBMIT_MANAGE_DYNAMICHIERARCHIES	Opens the Dynamic Hierarchies dialog box.

Table 7.1 List of EvMNU Functions (Cont.)

Menu Command	Description
MNU_ESUBMIT_REFSCHEDULE_SHEET_NODIALOG_SHOWRESULT	Sends the active sheet without any dialog box. Shows the Result dialog box.
MNU_ESUBMIT_SENDDATA	Sends data only (not refresh data).
MNU_ESUBMIT_COMMENT	Sends comments only, not refresh comments.
MNU_ESUBMIT_SENDDATA_AFTER_COMMENT	Sends data first.
MNU_ESUBMIT_COMMENT_AFTER_SENDDAT	Sends comment first.

Table 7.1 List of EvMNU Functions (Cont.)

The following macro sets the CV for the Time dimension to 2007.Jan. Select a specific cell, and enter the command as a formula, as shown in Figure 7.38 (❶ and ❷).

`EvMNU("SETCV", "SET TIME", "Time=2007.Jan").`

When a user clicks on the cell, the Time dimension in the CV is set to 2007.Jan.

The following macro launches a report. Select a specific cell and enter the command as shown in Figure 7.38 (❸ and ❹).

`EvMNU("OPENFILE", "View Plan Report", "Reports/Plan_2010.xls").`

When a user clicks on the cell, the Plan_2010.xls report in the Reports folder is executed.

1. You can optionally assign a macro to invoke a command. From the Excel menu, select VIEW • TOOLBARS • FORMS to display the tool bar to add form objects. Click on the button object and add it into the Excel worksheet (Figure 7.39, ❺).

2. Right-click on the object and select the Edit Text option to edit the text displayed for the object.

3. To assign a menu command to the button, right-click on the object and select the Assign Macro option (Figure 7.39, ❻). This opens the Assign Macro, where you specify the name of a macro (Figure 7.39, ❼). For example, the MNU_ETOOLS_MEMBERSELECTOR_C macro command opens the member selection dialog box for the Category dimension and enables the user to select a value. When a user clicks on the button, the command is executed.

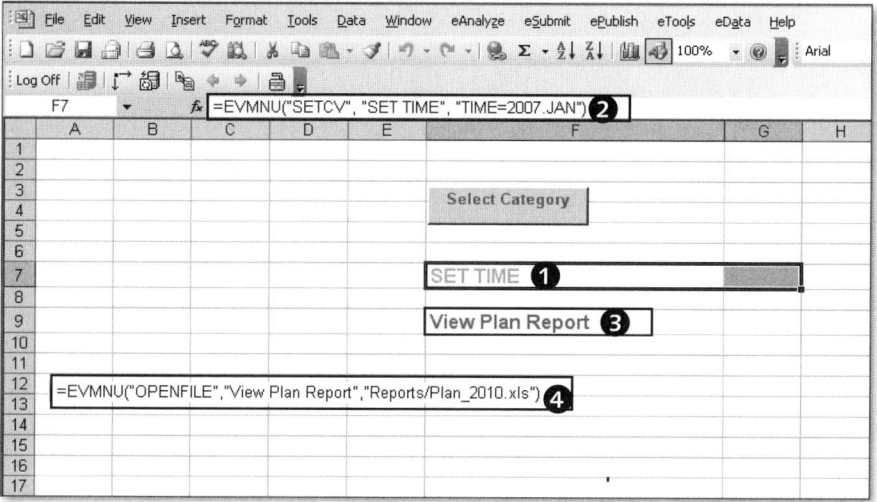

Figure 7.38 SAP BusinessObjects Planning and Consolidation Menu Command

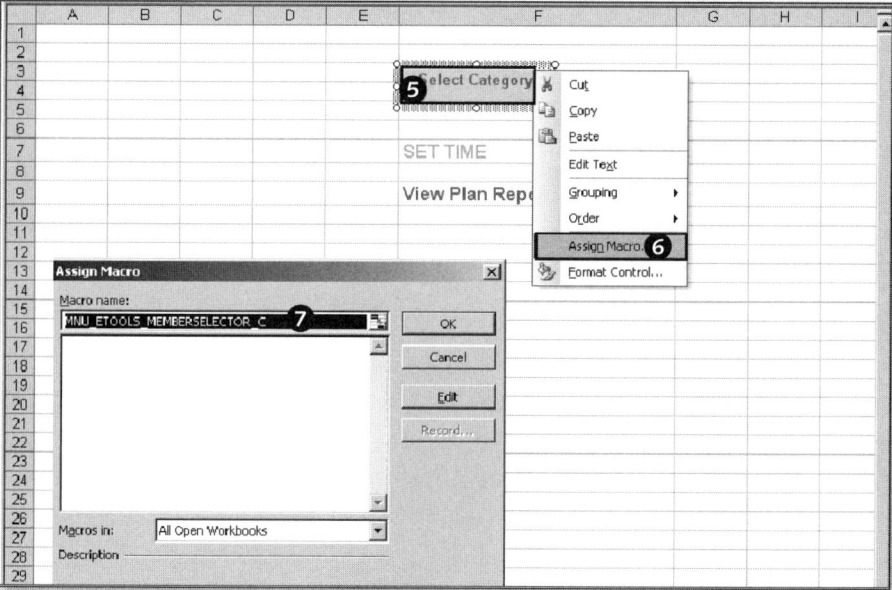

Figure 7.39 SAP BusinessObjects Planning and Consolidation Assign Macro Command

Commands can also be invoked using a VB macro. When you include them inside a VB macro, you can include multiple EvMNU commands as a macro and make them available to users.

To create a VB macro, select VIEW • TOOLBARS • CONTROLTOOLBOX from the Excel menu; this displays the toolbar for adding objects. Click on the button object and insert it into the Excel worksheet. The following VB macro opens the Data Manager Run Package dialog box:

```
Private Sub CallDM_Click()
Application.Run ("MNU_eData_RUNPACKAGE")
End Sub
```

You now know how to develop menus that help users execute periodic planning and consolidation tasks.

7.6 Summary

In this chapter, you learned about key collaborative features available to monitor, lock, share, distribute, and collect data in SAP BusinessObjects Planning and Consolidation. You learned how work status is used to lock data from changes and to enable workflow in applications. Next, you learned how comments can be entered and viewed in SAP BusinessObjects Planning and Consolidation. We then discussed the distribution and collection features for distributing data, which allow users to update data and send it back into the planning application using the collection interface. We also discussed the SAP BusinessObjects Planning and Consolidation interfaces for Word and PowerPoint. Finally, we discussed how to create a menu-based application for users to view and execute planning and consolidation tasks.

In the next chapter, we will discuss essential tools to help with the smooth functioning of your SAP BusinessObjects Planning and Consolidation system. We will explain the process of transporting objects from the development system to the quality assurance and production systems, and also discuss key topics such as locking, administration parameters, statistics, audits, and document management.

8   Essential Tools for Building Applications

This chapter discusses the essential tools in maintaining an SAP BusinessObjects Planning and Consolidation application. SAP offers a robust tool to manage changes to objects made in the development environment and provides an easy-to-use interface for moving them across the system landscape. The SAP BusinessObjects Planning and Consolidation system is delivered with tools that are used to manage locking, enable statistics, activate audit, store unstructured data, and manage security.

In Section 8.1, we will explain how to transport SAP BusinessObjects Planning and Consolidation objects from the development to the quality assurance and production systems. The parameters and settings used to manage the transport process are explained in detail and will help you gain a sound understanding of how to manage transports in your organization. In addition, you will be able to identify the difference between transporting SAP BusinessObjects Planning and Consolidation objects and standard SAP NetWeaver BW objects.

In Section 8.2, we will explain the locking concept used in SAP BusinessObjects Planning and Consolidation for NetWeaver and technical details about how the planning application handles locks and maintains the integrity of data. We will also look into the configuration tables that are available to customize the locking parameters for an application.

In Section 8.3, we will discuss the parameters that can be set for an application set, and the applications that belong to an application set. You will see how these parameters influence the functionality of an application.

In Section 8.4, we will introduce you to how statistics can be enabled for an application and the benefits it provides in managing the performance of your application.

In Section 8.5, we will introduce you to how auditing can be enabled for an application and the benefits it provides in monitoring the changes made in your application.

In Section 8.6, we will discuss how the content management tool in SAP BusinessObjects Planning and Consolidation is used to store, manage, and enforce the security of unstructured data.

In Section 8.7, we will discuss security, which is an important component in any application. SAP BusinessObjects Planning and Consolidation offers two types of security: one to manage the tasks a user can perform and one to determine the data-level access a user has in an application. In this section, you will learn how to set up security for your applications in SAP BusinessObjects Planning and Consolidation.

We will start by looking at the interface used for transporting objects in SAP BusinessObjects Planning and Consolidation and how it differs from the standard process of transporting objects in the SAP NetWeaver BW system.

8.1 Transporting SAP BusinessObjects Planning and Consolidation Objects

SAP supports a landscape that includes development, quality assurance, and production systems to develop, test, and implement an application. The process of development begins, appropriately, in the development system. When development is complete, unit testing is performed, and the development objects are transported to the quality assurance system where they are tested extensively to confirm that the functionality works as expected. This is normally the system where integration/user acceptance tests are performed. When the testing is completed successfully in the quality assurance system, the changes are moved to the production system. This process should be followed assiduously to avoid any issues of unintended changes going into production, leading to serious consequences. SAP BusinessObjects Planning and Consolidation for NetWeaver supports the process of moving objects from one system to another via the transport mechanism.

In SAP BusinessObjects Planning and Consolidation version 5.1, the transport mechanism was not available, because the product was not integrated with the SAP system. The process used in this version was to move or do a backup of objects in the development system and then restore them in the target system. With the integration of SAP BusinessObjects Planning and Consolidation with NetWeaver, transport functionality is available to transport objects across the system landscape. The transport process in SAP BusinessObjects Planning and Consolidation for NetWeaver leverages the existing framework in SAP systems to transport objects. Using this tool, objects that need to be moved across the landscape can be identified and sent in a streamlined and controlled fashion, reducing any problems in this process.

SAP Best Practices does not recommend doing any development type activity in the production system because objects should be fully tested before they are moved; however, there are cases where the customer needs to modify objects directly in the production system. In these scenarios, you can modify the configuration to make changes directly in production. This is especially true in reporting, where there may be a need to create ad-hoc reports directly in the production system.

The transport mechanism involves the following steps:

1. Create or modify objects in the development system.
2. Perform unit testing in the development system.
3. Create a transport request in the development system for the objects created or modified.
4. Transport the request to the quality assurance system.
5. Perform integration/user acceptance test in the quality assurance system.
6. Move the objects to the production system.

The existing framework in SAP NetWeaver BW is used for transports, and the mechanism now supports the ability to manage SAP BusinessObjects Planning and Consolidation objects. The process used for transport, however, is different from what is used for transporting SAP NetWeaver BW objects; in the SAP NetWeaver BW system, Transaction UJBPCTR is used to create and manage transport requests for SAP BusinessObjects Planning and Consolidation objects.

Only application sets can be transported in SAP BusinessObjects Planning and Consolidation, but any application set, including the ApSHELL, can be transported. When an application set is transported, all of the subobjects under the application set are also transported. The application set must be offline before a transport request is created in the source system, and the application set in the target system should be offline before the transport is imported.

When a transport request is created for an application set, the system creates entries in two shadow tables, UJT_TRANS_HDR and UJT_TRANS_OBJ, and inserts the objects for the application set. The UJT_TRANS_HDR table contains an entry for the application set that is selected, and the UJT_TRANS_OBJ table includes the metadata for the application set objects. When the transport request is sent from a source system, the entries in the transport from these two tables are compared with the objects in the target system and synchronized.

Follow these steps to transport objects:

1. Execute Transaction UJBPCTR to create a transport and click on the green checkmark (Figure 8.1, ❶ and ❷). You are prompted to create the transport request in the following screen.

2. In the Request Type section, select one of the three options for creating the transport request (Figure 8.1, ❸).

    ▸ Insert/Modify Request: This option lets you create a new transport request for an application set.

    ▸ Deletion Request: This option lets you delete an application set in the target system you previously transported.

    ▸ Only Update Shadow Tables: If you previously created a transport for an application set and have not yet released it, you can use this option to update the shadow tables for any changes made to the application set since that point.

3. In the Parameters section, select the application set you want to transport (Figure 8.1, ❹).

4. After a transport request is created, it has to be released. The Release Request Directly option under the Additional Parameters section can be checked if you want to create a transport and immediately release it after making your selections.

5. After making the selections, click on Execute (Figure 8.1, ❺).

6. The next screen prompts you to enter a description for the transport request. Enter a short description and click on the Save icon (Figure 8.2, ❻ and ❼).

8.1 Transporting SAP BusinessObjects Planning and Consolidation Objects

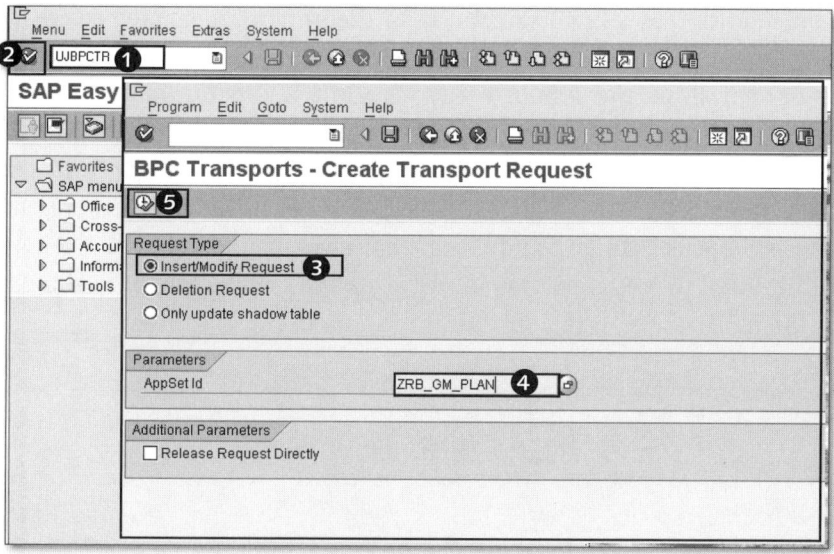

Figure 8.1 Transporting an Application Set—Part A

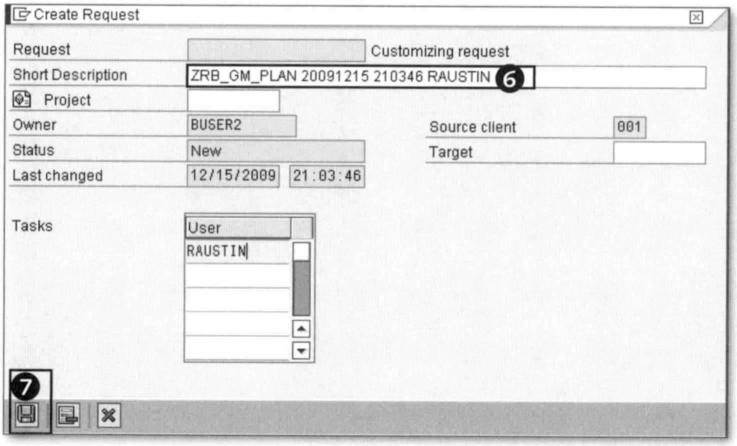

Figure 8.2 Transporting an Application Set—Part B

There is a difference in the way SAP NetWeaver BW objects are transported as compared to how SAP BusinessObjects Planning and Consolidation objects are transported. For transporting SAP NetWeaver BW objects, you select the transport option in the administrator's workbench and select the options to transport the objects. Also, when a user creates a transport request for an SAP NetWeaver BW object, and another user modifies the same object before that transport is released, the transport is written as an additional task in the same request created by the original user. However, in the case of SAP BusinessObjects Planning and Consolidation, the system allows the second user to create a new request. The shadow tables UJT_TRANS_HDR and UJT_TRANS_OBJ include the updated entries for the application set, and, as a result, either of the transports can be released and sent to the target system. SAP NetWeaver BW objects are not included when creating an SAP BusinessObjects Planning and Consolidation transport request. They are automatically created in the target system, based on the comparison of the objects included in the transport with the objects in the target system.

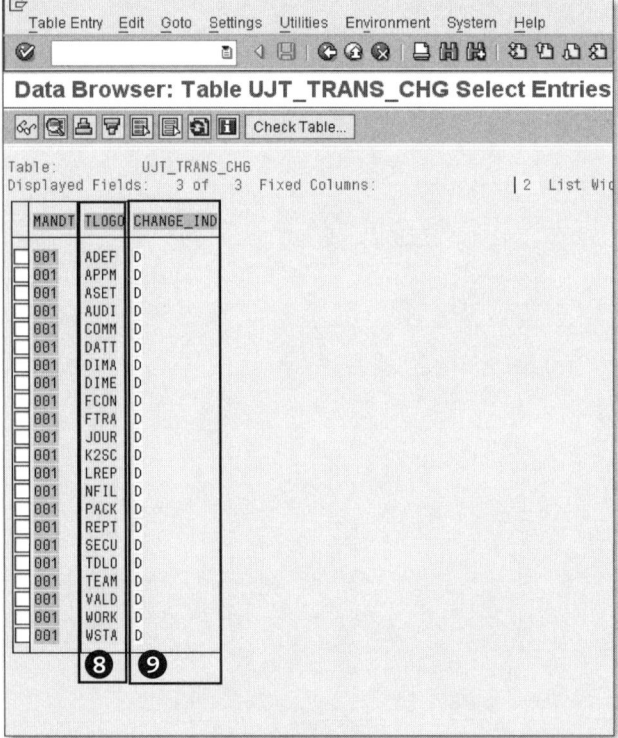

Figure 8.3 Object Changeability in SAP BusinessObjects Planning and Consolidation—Part A

Table UJT_TRANS_CHG represents the object changeability table in SAP BusinessObjects Planning and Consolidation and contains the entries for all subobjects in an application set (Figure 8.3, ❽). (Subobjects include applications, scripts, reports, journals, comments, security objects, etc.) The table includes a field called

CHANGE_IND to indicate whether the object can be changed in the system (Figure 8.3, ❾). If this indicator is set to P for an object, it cannot be transported and is not included in a transport request. All objects that have the CHANGE_IND field set to D are transported when a transport request is created. The data in this table can be modified using Transaction SM30 to customize the transport process.

You can view the description of the objects in this table by double-clicking on a record (Figure 8.4). Position the cursor on the TLOGO field and click on the drop-down button to display the values for this field (Figure 8.4, ❿). This displays all of the text value descriptions for the objects (Figure 8.4, ⓫).

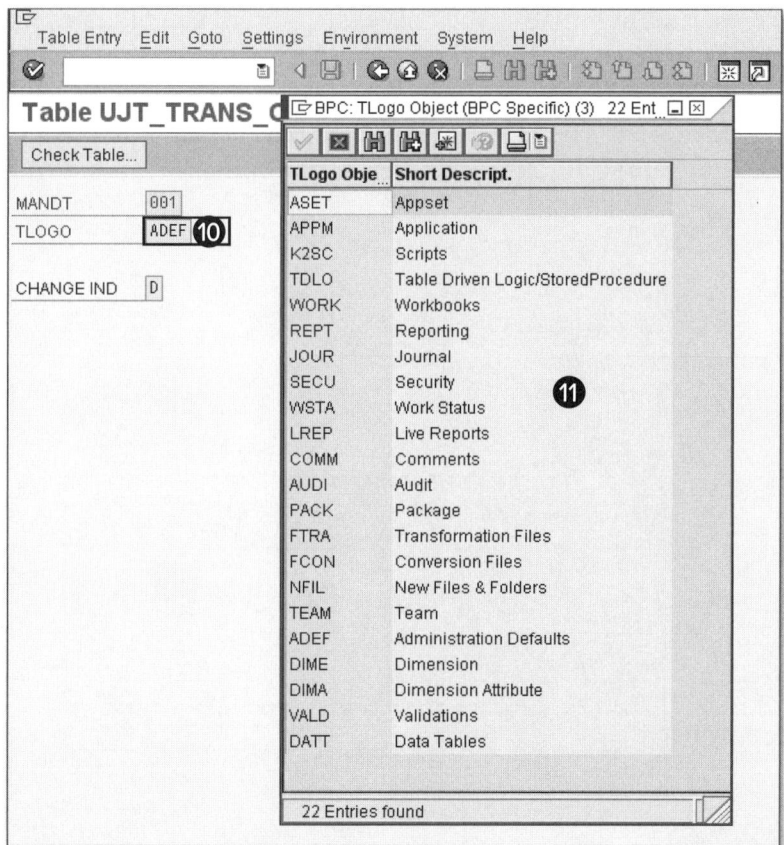

Figure 8.4 Object Changeability in SAP BusinessObjects Planning and Consolidation—Part B

8 | Essential Tools for Building Applications

When an application is created in SAP BusinessObjects Planning and Consolidation, the system creates directories and files in the background. The directories created during this process are used to store script files, journal templates, reports, input templates, etc. for an application. The directories and files created under an application set can be viewed using Transaction UJFS; this is the file service utility used in SAP BusinessObjects Planning and Consolidation.

During the transport process, these files may need to be transported as well. The settings in Table UJT_TRANS_FIL determine the directories and files that are transportable (Figure 8.5). The TLOGO field in the table defines the type of object to be transported, and the PATTERN_ID field determines what is transported. When you double-click on a row in this table, you can see the pattern that indicates the files that are to be transported (Figure 8.5, ⓬). Files/directories under subobject NFIL (new files and folders) are only transported to the target system when there is a new application being created in the target system. Data manager files cannot be transported. Similar to the UJT_TRANS_CHG table, the entries in the table can be modified using Transaction SM30.

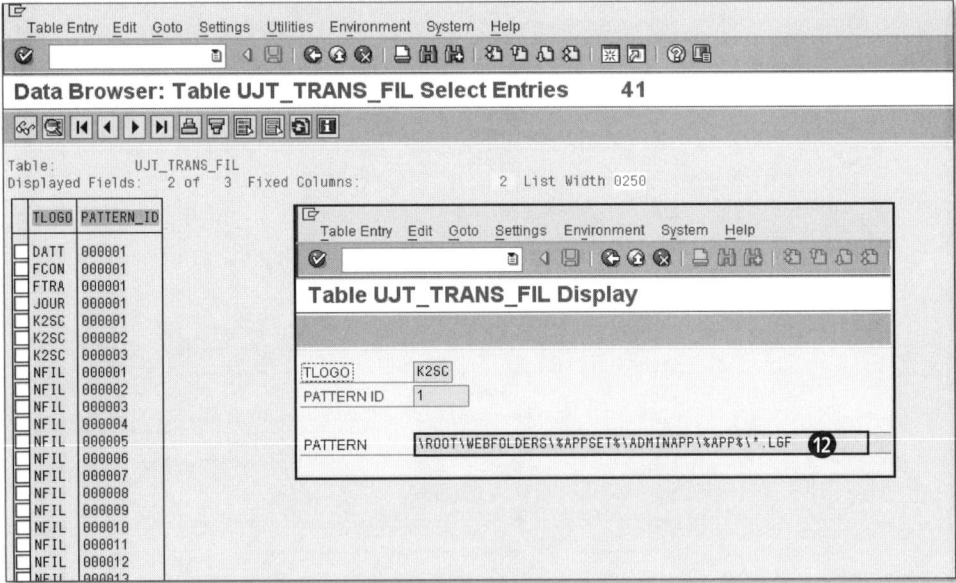

Figure 8.5 Directories and Files Transport Options

SAP BusinessObjects Planning and Consolidation objects should not be transported using the standard process for transporting SAP NetWeaver BW objects, because this will create errors in transport and issues when activating objects in the target system.

The standard configuration and authorization must be in place before transport requests can be released in the SAP NetWeaver BW system. After a transport request is created or released in the development system, you can view it using Transactions SE09 or SE10.

The transport administrators on the Basis team should perform the job of importing the request into the target system. After the transport is imported, you can view and display the logs, which provide detailed information on how the transport was processed in the target system, and errors, if any.

> **Note**
>
> The value of the CHANGE_IND in Table UJT_TRANS_CHG determines which objects can be changed in the system. If this indicator is set to D, the object can be changed. This option is available so that customers can adjust the object changeability of objects in the production system.

You should now understand how to use the transport process to move objects from the development to the quality assurance and production systems. Next, we will review the locking process used in SAP BusinessObjects Planning and Consolidation when data is updated for an application.

8.2 Concurrency Locking

Locking is an important concept to understand and consider during application development. The purpose behind locking is to prevent two users from updating the same data at the same time. The application should prevent this from happening to avoid data inconsistency.

We will first discuss the approaches to locking.

8 | Essential Tools for Building Applications

8.2.1 Approaches to Locking

The approach to locking can be considered from two viewpoints. Locking can be granular; that is, locking can be set at the record level on the data that is updated. This approach has the advantage of locking only the records that are updated. However, this is likely to take more time, because every record that needs to be updated is locked during the process. This option also consumes more memory, because you will be acquiring locks for every record that is updated.

The second approach is to lock based on a range of data. With this approach, locking is based on the range of data the user is updating. This makes it faster for the system to acquire locks but has the disadvantage of making it easy for you to lock more records than necessary. Although the end objective is to prevent two users from updating the same region of data, it is necessary to achieve a balance when using these options.

SAP BusinessObjects Planning and Consolidation for NetWeaver uses the concept of *concurrency locking*, which is based on a mixture of these options. We will now discuss the locking features in SAP BusinessObjects Planning and Consolidation for NetWeaver.

8.2.2 Locking Features in SAP BusinessObjects Planning and Consolidation for NetWeaver

In SAP BusinessObjects Planning and Consolidation, data is uploaded to the database when data is loaded using the data manager package and when data is updated via manual update using the interfaces for Excel, Word, and PowerPoint. (Data is updated even when journals are posted, which we will discuss in more detail in Chapter 9.) During the update process, data integrity must be maintained so that two users do not update the same region of data at the same time. It is also important to ensure that one user does not overwrite data entered by another user.

SAP BusinessObjects Planning and Consolidation for NetWeaver uses the concept of *concurrency locking* to lock data during updates. Concurrency locking comes into play only when a user sends data to update the database; no locks are obtained in SAP BusinessObjects Planning and Consolidation prior to the update when the user enters data.

Note

Locking in SAP BusinessObjects Planning and Consolidation is mandatory. There are no settings available to bypass locking.

The concepts behind locking differ between SAP BusinessObjects Planning and Consolidation and the other tools for planning used in SAP NetWeaver BW, namely SAP NetWeaver Business Planning and Simulation, and SAP NetWeaver BW Integrated Planning. In these tools, data is locked when a user opens the planning template to enter plan data for a particular selection. In SAP BusinessObjects Planning and Consolidation, data is locked only when the plan data is saved. However, the same framework for locking is used by all three tools.

8.2.3 The Locking Process in SAP BusinessObjects Planning and Consolidation for NetWeaver

SAP BusinessObjects Planning and Consolidation for NetWeaver obtains locks only when a user initiates the process to update data. This update is also referred to as the *write back* process. The request for update sent by the user is split into packets, and the default size of a packet is 40,000 records. This setting is governed by the PACKAGE_SIZE parameter in Table UJR_PARAM (Figure 8.6), and can be changed by modifying the default settings using Transaction UJR0 for an application in the application set.

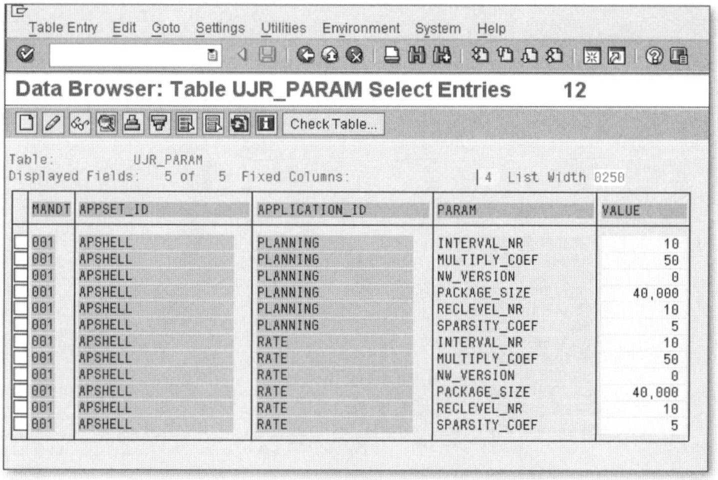

MANDT	APPSET_ID	APPLICATION_ID	PARAM	VALUE
001	APSHELL	PLANNING	INTERVAL_NR	10
001	APSHELL	PLANNING	MULTIPLY_COEF	50
001	APSHELL	PLANNING	NW_VERSION	0
001	APSHELL	PLANNING	PACKAGE_SIZE	40,000
001	APSHELL	PLANNING	RECLEVEL_NR	10
001	APSHELL	PLANNING	SPARSITY_COEF	5
001	APSHELL	RATE	INTERVAL_NR	10
001	APSHELL	RATE	MULTIPLY_COEF	50
001	APSHELL	RATE	NW_VERSION	0
001	APSHELL	RATE	PACKAGE_SIZE	40,000
001	APSHELL	RATE	RECLEVEL_NR	10
001	APSHELL	RATE	SPARSITY_COEF	5

Figure 8.6 Parameter Table for Concurrency Locking

The packet of data for update is analyzed, and the region of data that should be locked is determined and set. The SAP BusinessObjects Planning and Consolidation system determines whether it needs to perform record-level locking or to lock a range of data.

Record Level Check

When the number of records to be updated is less than 10, record-level locking is used. The value of 10 is set in the parameter RECLEVEL_NBR in the UJR_PARAM table and can be configured to a different value for an application in the application set, based on the requirements of that application. To modify this parameter, execute Transaction UJR0 and click on the green checkmark (Figure 8.7). When the RECLEVEL_NBR parameter is set to a high number, updates may take longer to complete and result in higher memory usage due to the time it takes to obtain locks.

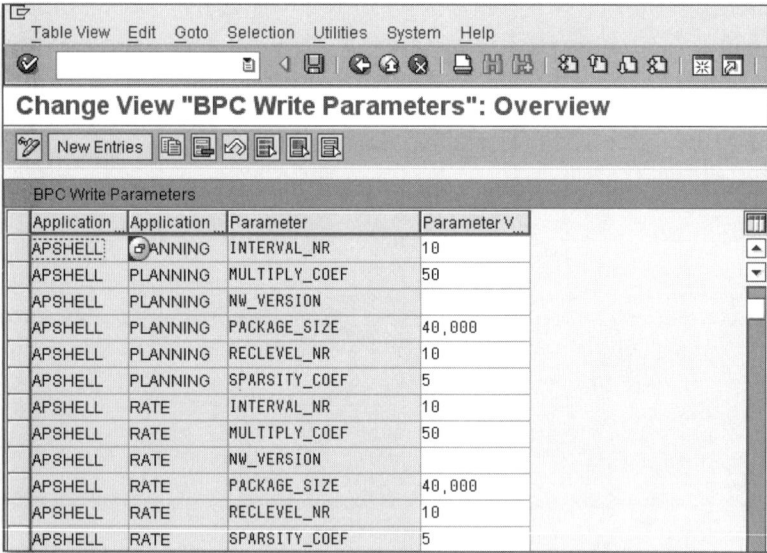

Figure 8.7 Customizing Concurrency Locking Parameters

Sparsity Check

When the number of records is equal to or higher than the value in the parameter RECLEVEL_NBR, a sparsity check is performed. The sparsity check is carried out as follows.

First, the system determines the number of unique members in each dimension in the record set and then multiplies the number of unique member counts of each dimension to arrive at a value. For example, assume that there are four dimensions, and the numbers of unique dimension members in the dimensions are as follows:

- Account: 15
- Time: 3
- Category: 2
- Entity: 1

When you multiply these numbers, the value is 90. We will call this value X. Next, the system multiplies the total number of records to be updated by the sparsity coefficient parameter SPARISITY_ COEF in Table UJR_PARAM. We will call this value Y. The default value for the SPARISITY_ COEF parameter is 5. The value of this parameter can be changed using Transaction UJR0.

If $X > Y$, the record set is considered to be sparse. If the number of records to be updated in this example is 14, the value of Y would be 14 × 5 = 70. Because $X > Y$, the record set would then be considered to be sparse.

If records are sparse, the number of unique dimension member values for each dimension is determined and sorted in ascending order. The unique member records of each dimension are multiplied until the value of the MULTIPLY_COEF parameter in Table UJR_PARAM is reached.

For example, let us say there are four dimensions and the numbers of unique dimension values in the dimensions sorted in ascending order are as follows:

- Entity: 1
- Category: 2
- Time: 3
- Account: 15

Let us also say that, for this application, the value of MULTIPLY_COEF is 50. Now, multiply the unique dimension member counts in the Entity and Category dimensions; the value is 1 × 2 = 2, which is less than 50. Next, multiply the value obtained in the previous step by the unique Time dimension's member count, which results in a value of 2 × 3 = 6. This value is still less than 50. Continue multiplying the value obtained in the previous step by the unique Account dimension's member count, and you obtain a value of 6 × 15 = 90. At this point, the value exceeds the MULTIPLY_COEF value of 50. In this case, individual values in the Entity, Category, and Time dimensions are locked. The range of values in the Account dimension is also locked.

If records are not sparse, all of the members of dimensions that have 10 or fewer distinct values are locked. The value of 10 is dependent on the INTERVAL_NR parameter in Table UJ_PARAMETER, and can be modified using Transaction UJR0. For those that have 10 or more distinct values, the system creates a lock between the low and high values for the member values in that dimension.

If the system is able to obtain locks, the locks are obtained and the data is updated. After the data is updated, the locks are released. If there is more than one package to update, the system processes the next package to obtain the locks using the same process for that package, and updates it.

If the system is not able to obtain locks for a package, the update for that package and the subsequent package fails with an error indicating the system was not able to obtain locks for the update. However, the package(s) for which the system was able to obtain locks, and for which data was processed successfully, cannot be rolled back. For example, let us say that there were three packages to update for a request sent by a user. Assume that the system was able to successfully acquire locks on the first package and update the data in the application, but was not able to acquire locks on the second package. As a result, the second package and the subsequent updates fail, even though the first package was updated in the cube and contains the changes made by the user.

The failed packages can be run again, because only delta values are posted by SAP BusinessObjects Planning and Consolidation during this update. An overview of the concurrency process is shown in Figure 8.8.

> **Note**
>
> For journals, the delta mechanism is not used when posting values. The package size for journals is set to 99,999,999 to ensure the concept of packages is not used when updating data using journals.

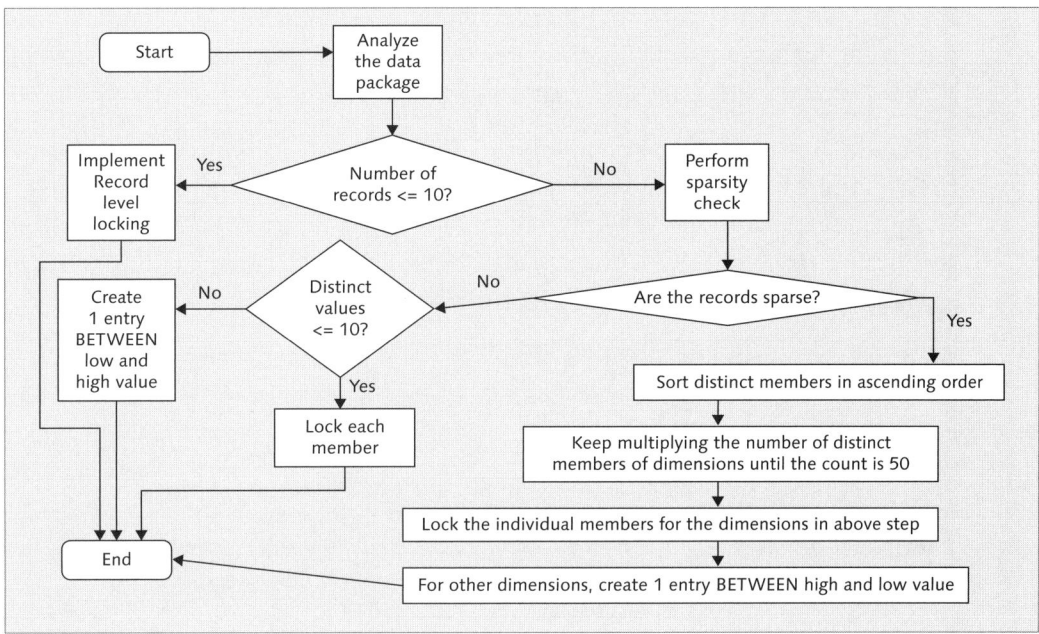

Figure 8.8 Concurrency Locking Process

In the next section, we will discuss the use of web administration parameters and see how they influence application behavior.

8.3 Web Administration Parameters

Web administration parameters influence the behavior of applications. Two types of web administration parameters can be configured in SAP BusinessObjects Planning and Consolidation:

- **Application set parameters**
  The parameters defined under this type apply to all applications in an application set.

- **Application parameters**
  The parameters defined under this type apply to each application in the application set.

Some parameters are required; others are optional. If a parameter is required, you can accept the default values. Make sure you have the appropriate security defined to make changes to the web parameters.

In the SAP BusinessObjects Planning and Consolidation Web interface, select the BPC Administration task under Available Interfaces. In the following screen, select SetAppSet Parameters or Set Application Parameters under Web Admin Tasks to access the parameter screen. You can modify the CV to select the application set or application for which you want to set the parameters.

Table 8.1 lists the parameters that can be defined for an application set, and Table 8.2 lists the parameters that can be defined for an application. Required parameters are indicated explicitly.

Parameter Name	Description
ALLOWEXTENSIONS	Defines the file extensions of files the system allows users to upload to the application, including data manager files, content library files, web-ready files, and library files. When set to ALL, SAP BusinessObjects Planning and Consolidation allows all extensions. The default value is ALL. (Required.)
ALLOW_FILE_SIZE	The maximum file size SAP BusinessObjects Planning and Consolidation allows users to upload. The default value is 100 MB. (Required.)
AVAILABLEFLAG	Controls whether the system is offline or not. "Yes" means the system is online and available for sending data to the database. You can take the system offline by changing the value to "No." (Required.)
AVAILABLEMSG	The message that displays to users who try to access an application that is offline. (Required.)
AVAILABLEURL	The name of the web page to display to users who try to access an application that is offline (AVAILABLEFLAG = No). (Required.)
DEFAULT_EXTENSIONS	The file extensions the system allows users to upload by default: XLS, XLT, DOC, DOT, PPT, POT, XML, MHT, MHTML, HTM, HTML, XLSX, XLSM, XLSB, ZIP, PDF, PPTX, PPTM, POTX, POTM, DOCX, DOCM, DOTX, DOTM, CDM, TDM, PNG, GIF, JPG, CSS, MRC. Also see ALLOWEXTENSIONS.

Table 8.1 Parameters for Application Set

Parameter Name	Description
LANDINGPAGEITEM	This parameter is used to customize the initial page that is displayed when you access the SAP BusinessObjects Planning and Consolidation Web interface. To customize the Getting Started page on SAP BusinessObjects Planning and Consolidation Web, contact your system administrator.
LOGLEVEL	Used by an application set to control the level of the ABAP log, which you view via Transaction SLG1. LOGLEVEL has the following possible values: 0 — None: Log is off. 1 — Error: Log only error, abort, and exit messages. 2 — Warning: Log warning, error, abort, and exit messages. 3 — Info: Log info, status, error, abort, and exit messages. 4 — Trace: Log info, status, error, abort, exit, and trace (highly detailed) messages.
MAXLRCOLUMNS	The maximum number of columns to display in a live report in SAP BusinessObjects Planning and Consolidation Web. The value includes header and data columns.
MAXLRROWS	The maximum number of rows to display in a live report in SAP BusinessObjects Planning and Consolidation Web. The value includes header and data rows. For example, if you specify a value of 5, one heading row and four data rows are displayed.
SMTPAUTH	The authentication method of the SMTP server. 0 = Anonymous 1 = Basic 2 = NTLM This setting does not change the method on the SMTP server but must match the type of authentication enabled on it. Failure to set this appropriately can result in errors from the email server. (Required.)
SMTPPORT	Port number for your SMTP email server. The default is port 25, the default SMTP server port number. (Required.)

Table 8.1 Parameters for Application Set (Cont.)

Parameter Name	Description
SMTPSERVER	The name or TCP/IP address of the SMTP email server the system uses to send email. (Required.)
SMTPUSER	The user name from which email in the system originates. (Required.)
TEMPLATEVERSION	Current version number of the dynamic templates in the application set. Whenever you add to or change the input schedule or report dynamic templates, you should increment this version number so that users automatically receive the new templates when they log into this application set. (Required.) You can also reset the template version from the Admin Console.

Table 8.1 Parameters for Application Set (Cont.)

Parameters	Description
APPROVALORG	If you want to use the work status feature, you must use this field to identify the hierarchy level (H1, H2, H3, ..., Hn) for which you want to track the work status of deliverables. You can define only one hierarchy for each application within an application set. For alternate organizations, "No Status" displays when viewing those members in the work status screen. If this field is blank, work status tracking is disabled.
BPC_STATISTICS	When set to ON, various SAP BusinessObjects Planning and Consolidation modules write detailed runtime statistics to Tables UJ0_STAT_HDR and UJ0_STAT_DTL. You can use this information to monitor system performance. Valid values are ON and OFF. (Required.)
Calculation	This parameter is used for the account transformation of business rules. This value can be changed in the Change Application Type menu in Modify Application.
IntcoBookings	This parameter is used for the intercompany booking of business rules. This value can be changed in the Change Application Type menu in Modify Application.

Table 8.2 Parameters for Application

Parameters	Description
Opening Balance	This parameter is used for opening business rules. This value can be changed in the Change Application Type menu in Modify Application.
JRN_REOPEN_PROPERTY	A custom journal module assumes that the property named UB must be present in the Account dimension to further filter the journals to reopen. The default is Group. If Group is specified, there is no need to modify the Account dimension.
ORG_OWNERSHIPCUBE	The default value is OWNERSHIP. (Required.)
ORG_INTCO	The default value is I_NONE, which should also be a member ID in the INTCO dimension in the ownership application if using dynamic hierarchies. (Required.)
ORG_ACCOUNTOWN	The default value is PGROUP. (Required.)
ORG_ACCOUNTLIST	The default value is METHOD,POWN,PCON. (Required.)
ORG_PARENTPROPERTY	This parameter is used with dynamic hierarchy statutory applications when defining fixed hierarchies. The value must match the value in the ParentProperty property value of entities in the statutory application's supporting ownership application. (Required.)
OWNERSHIP_APP	The name of the ownership application. If this parameter does not exist, by default, the consolidation procedure searches for an application named OWNERSHIP. (Required.)
YTDINPUT	This parameter controls whether data is input in YTD format. Valid options are 1, which means YTD format; or 0, which means periodic format.

Table 8.2 Parameters for Application (Cont.)

In the next section, we will discuss the steps involved in collecting statistics in SAP BusinessObjects Planning and Consolidation, and the benefits this offers.

8.4 Statistics

The statistics tool in SAP BusinessObjects Planning and Consolidation is designed to measure the performance of SAP Business Planning and Consolidation applications and to gather information about how the system is used. It is similar to the tool used in SAP NetWeaver BW for collecting statistics to analyze the time taken to load and report data on SAP NetWeaver BW objects.

The statistics data collected allows you to measure load times and retrieve data. Using these statistics, you can identify bottlenecks and take timely action before they become bigger issues. This is a valuable tool that can help with maintaining a smoothly running SAP BusinessObjects Planning and Consolidation system.

The statistics tool can record the time taken to execute the following modules for an application:

- **Shared query engine**
  Using the statistics tool, you can display the time taken to retrieve data from an InfoCube for a given report.
- **Write back**
  You can measure the time taken to update data in an InfoCube.
- **K2 or script logic**
  This will help you measure the time taken to execute script logic.

The default value for the BPC_STATISTICS parameter is Off, but it must be set to On (at the application level) before SAP BusinessObjects Planning and Consolidation can collect statistics for an application (Figure 8.9).

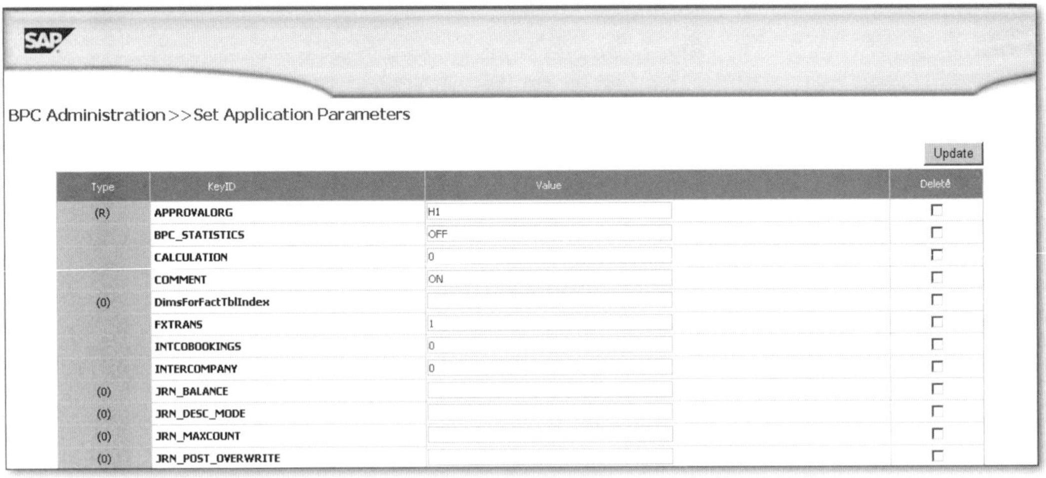

Figure 8.9 Web Parameter to Turn On Statistics

The statistics recorded are stored as header and detail records in SAP NetWeaver BW. The header data represents user actions, and the detail data represents the events associated with the actions. For example, the header data may represent the user action of sending data for update in SAP BusinessObjects Planning and Consolidation; the detail data then represents the individual events associated with this action—such as checking whether the user is authorized to make changes, and checking the work status to confirm that the data is not locked. All of these represent the detail events associated with the action initiated by the user.

The different actions for which you can collect statistics are listed in Table UJ0_ACTION. You can collect statistics on the following types of actions:

- Read data through SQE
- Run K2 script logic
- Write back data

Different types of events are associated with an action. The list of events that is used in SAP BusinessObjects Planning and Consolidation is displayed in Table UJ0_EVENTS.

Some of the common events during the course of writing back data are as follows:

- Check security
- Check validation
- Check work status
- Obtain concurrency locks

After the web parameter for collecting statistics for an application is set to On for an application, statistics data is collected in Tables UJ0_STAT_HDR and UJ0_STAT_DTL.

You can view statistics on an application using Transaction UJSTAT (Figure 8.10 and 8.11) and select the data based on the GUID, user, start date, start time, action, application set, and application:

- **Statistics Session**
  This is a system-generated value used as the key for the action or the event under which it is stored.

- **User ID**
  This represents the user who initiated the action or event.
- **Statistics Start Date**
  This is the start date of the action or event.
- **Statistics Start Time**
  This is the start time of the action or event.
- **Action ID**
  This describes the action performed.
- **AppSet**
  This denotes the application set to which this record pertains.
- **Application**
  This denotes the application driving the event or action.

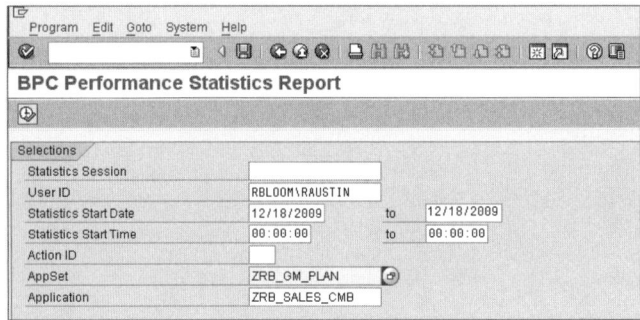

Figure 8.10 Displaying Statistics—Part A

Hierarchy	AppSet ID	Appl. ID	Seq	Start Date	Start Time	Runtime	T Runtime	C Runtime	Nr of Recs
Shared Query Engine Read	ZRB_GM_PLAN	ZRB_SALES_CMB	0	12/18/2009	00:45:15	0.531000	0.531000	0.531000	0
Unwrap XML	ZRB_GM_PLAN	ZRB_SALES_CMB	1	12/18/2009	00:45:14	0.000000	0.000000	0.000000	0
Run Axis Query	ZRB_GM_PLAN	ZRB_SALES_CMB	2	12/18/2009	00:45:14	0.000000	0.531000	0.531000	5
Check Validation for Axis Query	ZRB_GM_PLAN	ZRB_SALES_CMB	3	12/18/2009	00:45:14	0.062000	0.062000	0.062000	0
Check Member Security (Axis)	ZRB_GM_PLAN	ZRB_SALES_CMB	4	12/18/2009	00:45:15	0.000000	0.000000	0.062000	0
Get Dimension and Member Information	ZRB_GM_PLAN	ZRB_SALES_CMB	5	12/18/2009	00:45:15	0.094000	0.094000	0.156000	0
Build Sub Queries for Multiple Hierarchies	ZRB_GM_PLAN	ZRB_SALES_CMB	6	12/18/2009	00:45:15	0.000000	0.000000	0.156000	0
Miscellaneous Processing Time	ZRB_GM_PLAN	ZRB_SALES_CMB	7	12/18/2009	00:45:15	0.000000	0.000000	0.156000	0
Run Sub Query for Measures	ZRB_GM_PLAN	ZRB_SALES_CMB	8	12/18/2009	00:45:15	0.000000	0.375000	0.531000	5
Miscellaneous Processing Time	ZRB_GM_PLAN	ZRB_SALES_CMB	9	12/18/2009	00:45:15	0.000000	0.000000	0.156000	0
Process Slicer	ZRB_GM_PLAN	ZRB_SALES_CMB	10	12/18/2009	00:45:15	0.000000	0.000000	0.156000	0
Run Sub Query for Multiple Hierarchies	ZRB_GM_PLAN	ZRB_SALES_CMB	11	12/18/2009	00:45:15	0.000000	0.375000	0.531000	5
Process Axis	ZRB_GM_PLAN	ZRB_SALES_CMB	12	12/18/2009	00:45:15	0.000000	0.000000	0.156000	0
Process Formula	ZRB_GM_PLAN	ZRB_SALES_CMB	13	12/18/2009	00:45:15	0.000000	0.000000	0.156000	0
Axis Query Kernel	ZRB_GM_PLAN	ZRB_SALES_CMB	14	12/18/2009	00:45:15	0.000000	0.375000	0.531000	5
Wrap xml after QUERY	ZRB_GM_PLAN	ZRB_SALES_CMB	30	12/18/2009	00:45:15	0.000000	0.000000	0.531000	0

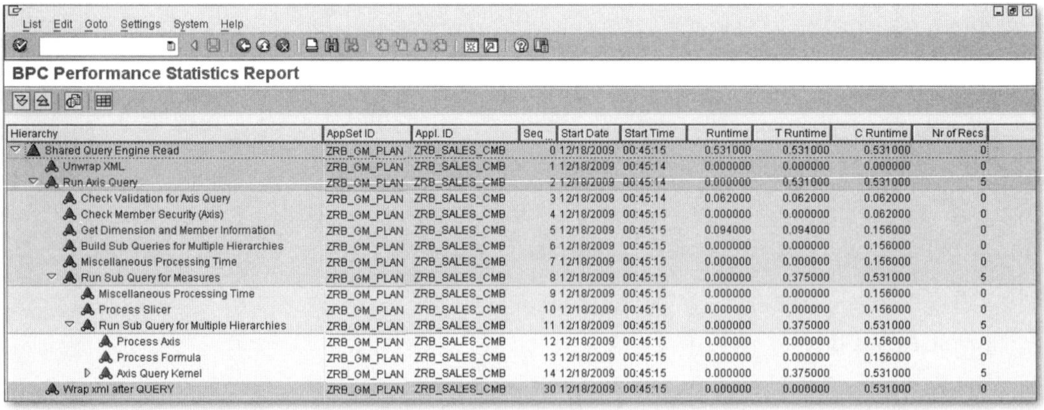

Figure 8.11 Displaying Statistics—Part B

You can delete all statistics for an application set or application using the program UJ0_STATISTICS_DELETE (Figure 8.12). It is not possible to selectively delete statistics records from an application set or application.

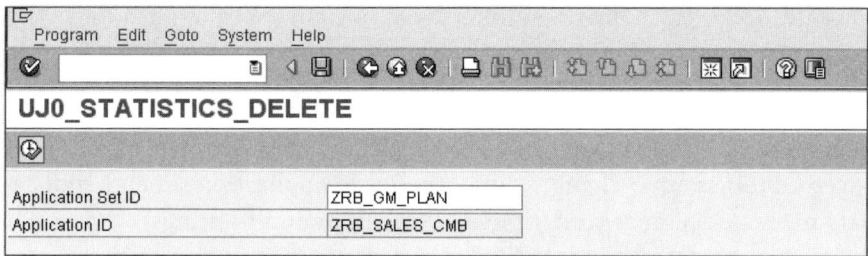

Figure 8.12 Deleting Statistics Data

In this section, we discussed how to collect and view statistics for an application. In the next section, we will explain how to turn on the audit functionality and view audit information.

8.5 Audit

The audit functionality in SAP BusinessObjects Planning and Consolidation provides the framework for monitoring changes to application configuration and data. SAP BusinessObjects Planning and Consolidation for NetWeaver supports these two categories for auditing and provides the functionality to safeguard the SAP BusinessObjects Planning and Consolidation system. There are two types of audits:

- **Activity audit**
  This audit type is used to record changes to metadata. The audit captures any changes to application sets, applications, and dimensions. It is defined at the application set level.
- **Data audit**
  This audit type captures changes to transaction data and is applicable for an application.

The configuration for activating audits is enabled in the web interface. To activate an activity or data audit, select the BPC Administration task under Available Interfaces. In the following screen, you will see two tasks under Web Admin Tasks: Manage Activity Audit, and Manage Data Audit.

The following actions can be performed for recording an activity audit:

- Add, modify, delete, or copy operations for application sets, applications, and dimensions.
- Make security changes (any changes to users, teams, tasks, or member profiles).
- Make web administration changes (any changes to application set and application parameters, document content management, or audit settings).
- View user activity (work status locks).

Activity audit data is stored in Tables UJU_AUDACTHDR and UJU_AUDACDET. Data audit data is stored in Tables UJU_AUDDATAHDR, /1CPMB/KIABGAD, and /1CPMB/KIGTQAD. Failed audit logs can be displayed using Transaction SLG1.

Audit data can be archived. Two standard process chains are provided to do this, one for archiving activity audit data and another for archiving data audit data. The two process chains available for this purpose are /CPMB/ARCHIVE_ACTIVITY and /CPMB/ARCHIVE_DATA. Reporting is not possible on audit data that has been archived.

Standard reports are available in SAP BusinessObjects Planning and Consolidation, and you can use filter criteria when reporting audit data. To access reports, select Launch BPC System Reports under BPC Tasks in the web interface.

You now know how to enable and view audit data. In the next section, we will explain how to use the content library to create and maintain unstructured documents.

8.6 Content Library

The content library interface is accessed via the SAP BusinessObjects Planning and Consolidation Web interface and is used for creating and sharing unstructured data such as documents and HTML. Documents are loaded via this interface, and the list of file types you can store in the content library are specified in the web administration parameters for the application set. You should have the appropriate access to upload and view documents; specifically, you need access to the CreateWebPage and ManageContentLib tasks to create a web page and to post documents.

8.6.1 Accessing the Content Library

The content library is used for storing documents and is accessed from the web interface by clicking on the Content Library icon. Existing documents in the document library are listed with the following information:

- **Title**
  This indicates the title of the document.
- **Type, subtype, and application context**
  These items can be used to provide more meaning to the document.
- **Team access**
  This identifies who is authorized to view documents and can be specified based on user ID or teams.
- **Date**
  This indicates the date on which the document was updated.

8.6.2 Posting a Document

Follow the steps outlined below to post a document to the content library:

1. Click on the Post a Document task under the Library Content Options in the action pane (Figure 8.13, ❶). This opens a dialog box: Post a Document –Step 1 of 5. Select the file you would like to post to the content library from your local computer by clicking on the Browse button (Figure 8.13, ❷). Enter a text description for the document, and click on the green checkmark to continue.

2. In the next dialog box (Post a Document – Step 2 of 5), select the users or teams that should have access to this document (Figure 8.13, ❸). Click on the green checkmark to continue.

3. The next dialog box (Post a Document – Step 3 of 5) allows you to select a subtype for your document. You can post documents to designated locations using this subtype (Figure 8.13, ❹), because they are the equivalent of folders in the content library. Click on the green checkmark to continue.

8 | Essential Tools for Building Applications

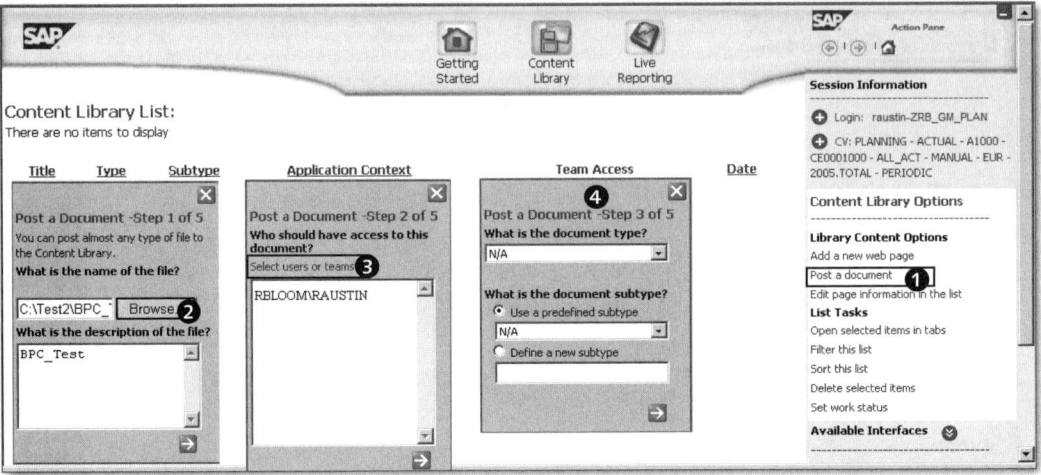

Figure 8.13 Posting a Document— Part A

4. In the next dialog box (Post a Document – Step 4 of 5), you can opt to send an email to users who have access to this document after the document has posted (Figure 8.14, ❺). Click on the green checkmark to continue.

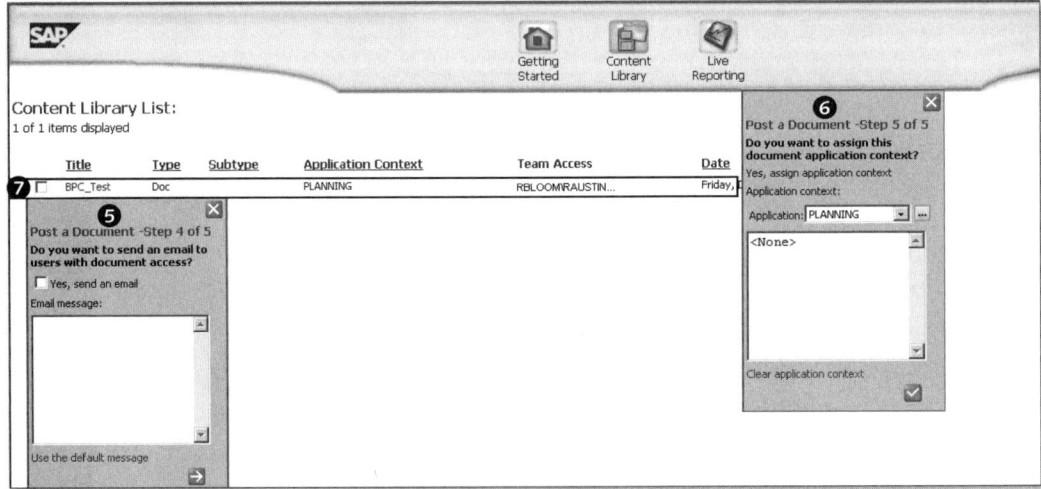

Figure 8.14 Posting a Document- Part B

5. In the resulting dialog box (Post a Document – Step 5 of 5), you can select the application context to which the document belongs (Figure 8.14, ❻). Click on the green checkmark to continue. If you set the application context, you can control the document via work status settings and lock down documents that have the application context specified.

You now know how to post a document to the content library. Next, we will explain how to edit the properties of a document in the content library.

8.6.3 Editing Document Properties

To edit document properties in the content library, click on the Edit Page Information in the List task, which you will find under Content Library Options in the action pane (Figure 8.13). The documents are listed as shown in Figure 8.15. For documents, you can edit the title, type, subtype, application context, and team access. For web pages, you can edit only the Team Access field. After you make changes, confirm them by clicking on the green checkmark under Edit Page Information in the action pane.

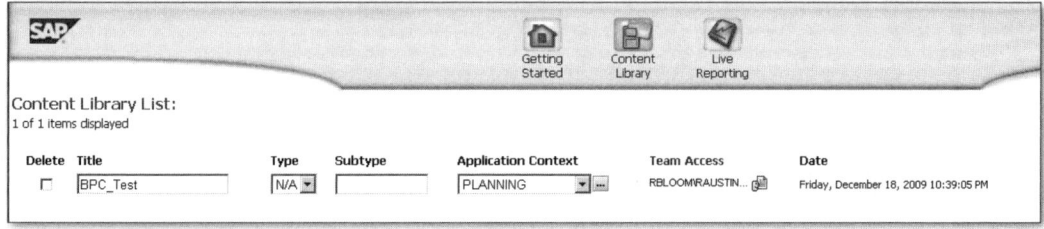

Figure 8.15 Editing a Document

8.6.4 Add Web Page to Content Library

Follow these steps to add a web page to the content library:

1. Click on the Add a New Web Page task under Library Content Options in the action pane (Figure 8.13). The resulting dialog box prompts you to enter the page name (Figure 8.16). After entering a name for the web page, click on the green checkmark to continue.

8 | Essential Tools for Building Applications

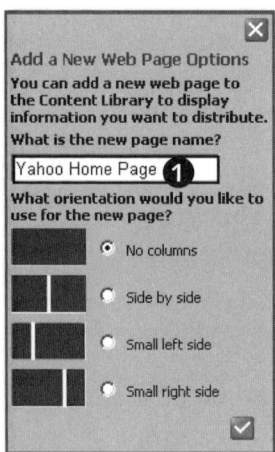

Figure 8.16 Creating a Web Page—Part A

2. In the next screen, you can select one of the following objects to create the web page:

   ▶ Web-Ready File: Lets you select a web-ready file you previously uploaded as the source.

   ▶ Live Reports: Lets you select any live reports you have created for the applications in the application set as the source.

   ▶ Documents: Lets you use the documents you have posted in the content library as the source.

   ▶ Website: Lets you specify a web URL as the source.

   In this example, we will include a link to Yahoo's home page as a web page. Drag the Website object under Available Objects into the Page area (Figure 8.17, ❷). This opens a dialog box titled Website: Step 1 of 2 (Figure 8.17, ❸). Enter the name of the page and specify the pixel height to use to display the web page. Then, click on the green checkmark.

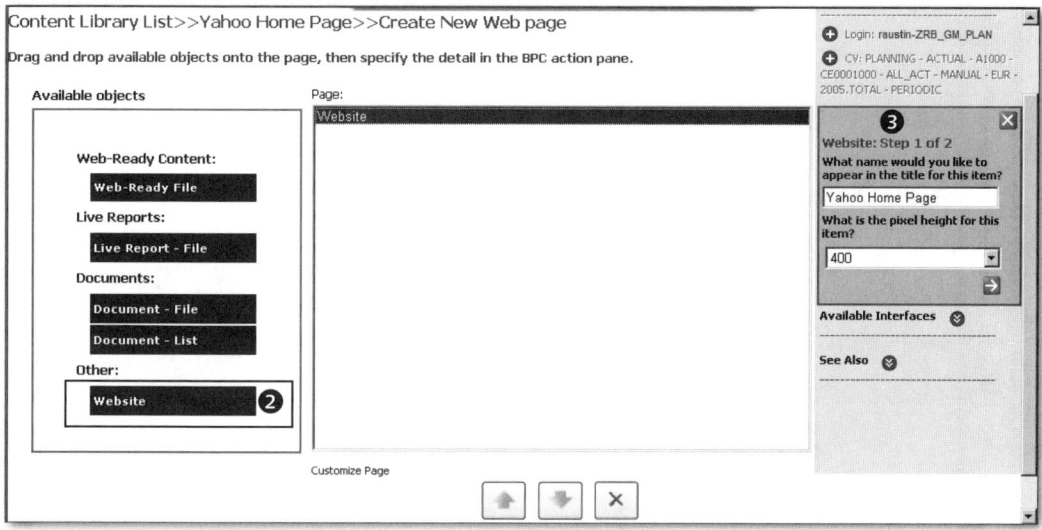

Figure 8.17 Creating a Web Page—Part B

3. In the resulting dialog box (Website: Step 2 of 2), enter the website address and click on the green checkmark (Figure 8.18, ❹).

4. In the resulting dialog box, select the users who can access the web page or make additional modifications to the object (Figure 8.18, ❺). Preview the web page, or click Save to see the finished web page.

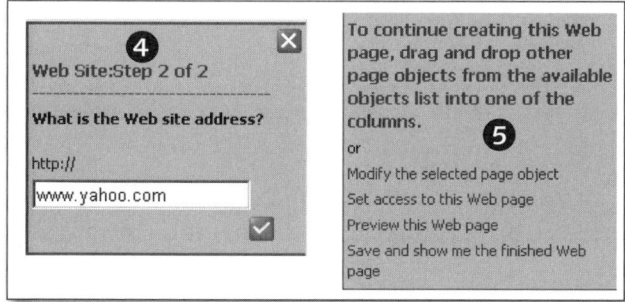

Figure 8.18 Creating a Web Page—Part C

5. After you click on the option to save, the web page is displayed (Figure 8.19).

8 | Essential Tools for Building Applications

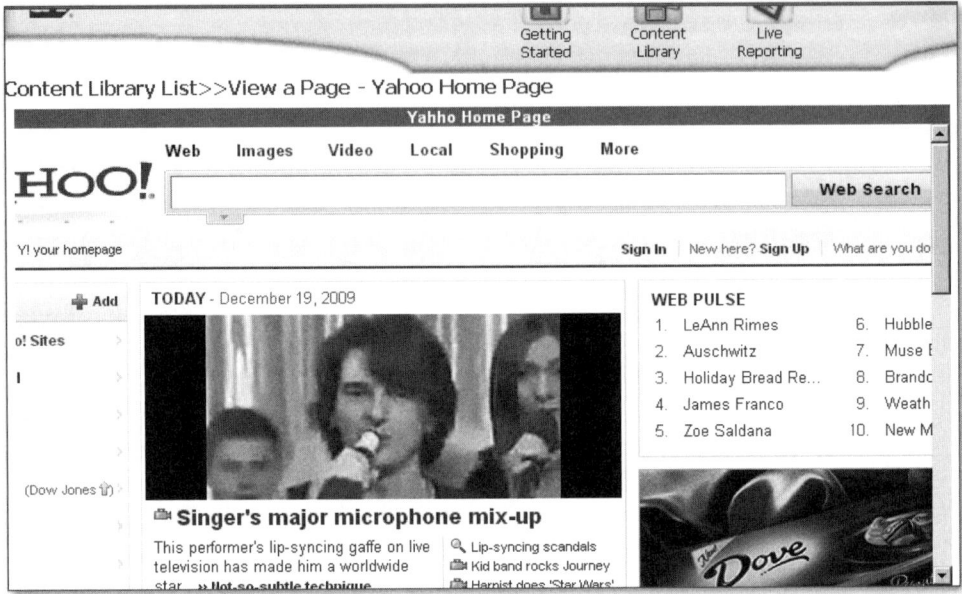

Figure 8.19 Creating a Web Page—Part D

Under the List Tasks, there are additional options viewing and managing the documents in the content library. They are as follows:

▶ **Open Selected Items in Tab**

When this menu task is selected, more than one document can be checked and viewed on a tab.

▶ **Filter This List**

This option lets you select from a variety of options to limit the number of documents displayed.

▶ **Sort This List**

This option lets you sort documents based on the title, type, subtype, application context, and date fields.

▶ **Delete Selected Items**

This option lets you delete one or more selected documents.

▶ **Set Work Status**

This option lets you set the work status for documents that are associated with an application context.

In this section, we explained how to use the content library to post, maintain, and view documents. In the next section, we will review concepts related to managing security within SAP BusinessObjects Planning and Consolidation.

8.7 Security

In this section, we will discuss how users are configured and how their security levels are defined. SAP BusinessObjects Planning and Consolidation provides a simple interface to define task and member access profiles. Task profiles authorize the actions a user can perform, and member profiles define access on dimensions that are marked as secure in an application. SAP BusinessObjects Planning and Consolidation supports the role concept to extend security based on the role of a user in an organization. In this section, we will discuss the terms used in the context of security.

8.7.1 Users

A user should be configured as an active domain user. In addition, in the security folder for an application set, the user should be set as a valid user. If a user is not listed here, the user will not be able to perform any tasks on an application set.

8.7.2 Team

A team is a group of users. An application will be used by multiple users, and each user can play a different role, based on their responsibilities in the organization. A team is helpful when you need to provide the same access to a group of users. When a team is created, a folder to store reports and input schedules for the team is also created. One user in the team can be assigned as a team leader. A team leader has additional access to save reports and input schedules to the team folder.

8.7.3 Task Profile

The types of activities a user can perform in SAP BusinessObjects Planning and Consolidation can be grouped into a task profile. Examples of activities are loading data, entering and maintaining data, executing reports, maintaining comments, creating journals, and so on. Table 8.3 lists administration tasks available in SAP BusinessObjects Planning and Consolidation.

Administration Tasks
Application set management
Define security
Business rules
Application management
Dimension
Locking
Manage audit
Manage comments
Content library
Manage distributor
Manage live report
Manage template
Update to company folder
Web administration
Miscellaneous

Table 8.3 Administration Tasks

With the ApShell application set, there are three types of task profiles provided by default:

- **System admin**
  A system admin user can administer security to other users. The user can create, modify, and delete application sets.

- **Primary admin**
  A primary admin can perform all administration tasks except creating or maintaining application sets.

- **Secondary admin**
  A secondary admin can manage dimension members.

8.7.4 Member Access Profile

When an application is created, the dimensions in the application can be marked as secured. When a dimension is marked as secured, the user needs access to read and write data to the application. The member access profile indicates the dimension data that can be read or written in an application.

8.7.5 Security Model

The option to manage security is available under the task item BPC Administration. The following are the steps to configure security for an application:

1. Assign users to application sets.
2. Create the task profiles based on roles.
3. Create member access profiles based on roles.
4. Create a team.
5. Assign profiles to teams.
6. Assign member profiles to teams.
7. Assign users to teams.

8.8 Summary

In this chapter, you learned several key tools used in managing and maintaining an SAP BusinessObjects Planning and Consolidation application. We started by looking at the steps for moving objects from the development system to the quality assurance and production systems using the transport process. We reviewed how the SAP BusinessObjects Planning and Consolidation system uses concurrency locking to prevent two users from updating the same region of data simultaneously. We also reviewed the parameters that are set at the application set and application levels and how they influence the functionality of SAP BusinessObjects Planning and Consolidation applications. We then studied the process of collecting statistics to assess performance of the system, and activating auditing of data to monitor changes to objects and data in the system. Furthermore, we looked at how to use the content library interface to post, view, and maintain documents in SAP BusinessObjects Planning and Consolidation. Finally, we discussed the concepts to enforce task level and data level security.

In the next chapter, you will be introduced to business rules and how they can be used to support common tasks related to business planning and consolidation. You will also learn how journal templates can be created and used to post adjustments and top side entries. In addition, we will review general tasks that are carried out when consolidating financial data.

9 Consolidation with SAP BusinessObjects Planning and Consolidation

In this chapter, we will review topics related to performing financial consolidation using SAP BusinessObjects Planning and Consolidation.

In Section 9.1, we will introduce you to different types of business rules that can be configured in SAP BusinessObjects Planning and Consolidation. Business rules allow users to set up standard business processes such as currency translation, carry forward balances, and intercompany elimination without having to develop code.

In Section 9.2, we will introduce you to the use of journals in planning and consolidation applications and describe how journals can be configured and used.

In Section 9.3, we will provide an overview of the consolidation logic that is used to consolidate data.

To begin, we will discuss the process of setting up business rules in SAP BusinessObjects Planning and Consolidation and see how they are used to perform business functions without developing custom code.

9.1 Business Rules

Business rules are a key feature of SAP BusinessObjects Planning and Consolidation; they provide an organization setup rules to execute standard business processes without developing custom code. Some of the standard business processes used in planning and consolidation are as follows:

- **Currency translation**
  This is required when an organization does business in more than one country and when multiple currencies are used for transacting business. When multiple currencies are used by an organization, there is a need to convert transactions in the different currencies to one common reporting currency, which is a

requirement for both planning and financial consolidation applications. Currency translation also enables organizations to see the impact of currency fluctuations on the profit of a business, and aids in planning for the future.

- **Carry forward**
  The carry forward of balances is an essential step in the creation of a balance sheet for an organization; it takes place when the closing balance of a balance sheet account for a fiscal period is transferred as the opening balance of a subsequent fiscal period. The setup for this process is taken care of in SAP BusinessObjects Planning and Consolidation by using a business rules table.

- **Account transformation**
  In some scenarios accounts are consolidated or transformed into another account. This is an activity used extensively in cash flow applications. Business rules can be used to perform account transformations.

- **Intercompany elimination**
  This is applicable for an organization that has more than one business unit doing business with each other. In these cases, it is essential to eliminate the intercompany transactions as well as the intercompany profits arising from these transactions.

- **Validation rules**
  Validation rules in SAP BusinessObjects Planning and Consolidation enable an organization to perform checks on accounts. Using the validation rule table, an organization can set up business rules that will validate balances in assets and liabilities/owner's equity accounts for a given period, and report variances for that period. The variances can be posted to an adjustment account, if required.

The advantage of using the business rules table is that it provides out-of-the box functionality to perform the mentioned processes. This helps reduce the TCO of developing and maintaining applications in SAP BusinessObjects Planning and Consolidation.

We will now explore the specific steps for setting up the business rules to carry forward balances and perform intercompany eliminations in SAP BusinessObjects Planning and Consolidation.

9.1.1 Carry Forward

One of the steps in preparing a balance sheet is to take the closing balance of a fiscal period and use it as the opening balance of the subsequent fiscal period. In accounting terminology, this is called *the initialization of balances*.

The process to determine carry forward balances for a new fiscal year is essential for every organization that is required to maintain a balance sheet. To facilitate this process, SAP BusinessObjects Planning and Consolidation lets you automatically generate carry forward balances for the new fiscal period using business rules tables. You can use this procedure to set up the carry forward process for both planning and consolidation applications.

The *Flow* dimension, also called the *Sub-Table* dimension, is a necessary dimension for using the carry forward business rule. Some accounts, such as inventory accounts, have an opening balance at the beginning of a period as well as additions and transfers for the period. The Flow dimension helps with breaking the account into various flow types — such as balances, additions and transfers — for these accounts.

The carry forward process requires the following dimension properties to be included in the Time, DataSource, and Category dimensions:

- **MonthNum in the Time dimension**
  This property indicates the last period of the prior fiscal year and is used internally in the carry forward process to identify the balances used for this calculation.

- **DataSrc_Type in the DataSource dimension**
  The data loaded into SAP BusinessObjects Planning and Consolidation can be classified as input (I), manual (M), and automatic (A). The logic for carry forward in SAP BusinessObjects Planning and Consolidation is set to work only for input and manual DataSource types. Automatic DataSources are generated and addressed during the consolidation process.

- **CopyOpening in the DataSource dimension**
  When this property is set to No, the associated DataSource is excluded from the carry forward process.

- **Category_For_Ope in the Category dimension**
  This setting applies when you want to use actual data as the basis for creating plan balances for carry forward purposes. When the setting is active, the carry forward balance for the specified category uses the category specified in this property for calculating carry forward balances.

- **Opening_Period in the Category dimension**
  The value specified in this property specifies the period to use for creating the carry forward balance. This overrides the MonthNum property in the Time dimension.

- **Opening_Year in the Category dimension**
  The value specified in this property is used as the year for creating the carry forward balance. This overrides the Year property in the Time dimension.

When the setup is complete, the COPYOPENING script is used to execute the logic to create the opening balances for a given period. Add the following logic in your application and call it COPYOPENING.LGF:

```
*RUN_PROGRAM COPYOPENING
CATEGORY = %CATEGORY_SET%
CURRENCY = %GROUPS_SET%
TID_RA = %TIME_SET%
OTHER = [ENTITY=%ENTITY_SET%]
*ENDRUN_PROGRAM
```

In the carry forward balance rules table, you can then specify the settings that should be used for carrying forward balances. The details for setting up the carry forward balance rules table are explained in Table 9.1, which shows an example configuration. More than one record can be entered.

Field Name	Description
Source Account	Specify the source account to use for the carry forward balance. The value specified here can be one of the following: ▸ Base member ▸ Parent member A list of members is defined and filtered using a value of the DIMLIST property in the Account dimension.

Table 9.1 Carry Forward Balance Business Rule

Field Name	Description
Source Flow	Specify the source flow to use for the carry forward balance. The value specified here can be one of the following: ▸ Base member ▸ Parent member A list of members is defined and filtered using a value of the DIMLIST property in the Flow dimension.
Destination Account	Specify a base member as the destination account.
Destination Flow	Specify a base member for the destination flow.
Reverse Sign	Check this option if you want to reverse the sign of the amount when creating the carry forward balance from the source account.
Data Source Type	Specify all the DataSource members you want to use for the conversion. This corresponds to the values set in the Datasource_Type property of the Datasource dimension. You can select from the following choices: Input, Manual, or All. **Note**: DataSources that are of type "E" (eliminations) are not considered for carry forward balance conversions.
Same Period	Check this option when the source time period should be used as the destination time period.
Apply to YTD	Check this option to calculate YTD values for an application that uses periodic measures.
Remark	Specify a brief description for the business rule.

Table 9.1 Carry Forward Balance Business Rule (Cont.)

SAP BusinessObjects Planning and Consolidation includes a data package to execute the carry forward process. When the package is executed, the system prompts the user to enter Category, Entity, Currency, and Time selections for performing the carry forward process.

9 | Consolidation with SAP BusinessObjects Planning and Consolidation

We will now review an example of how to set up carry forward balances in a SAP BusinessObjects Planning and Consolidation application:

1. The dimensions for application ZB2 are shown in Figure 9.1. They include the Flow dimension, because this is a required dimension for executing carry forward balances.

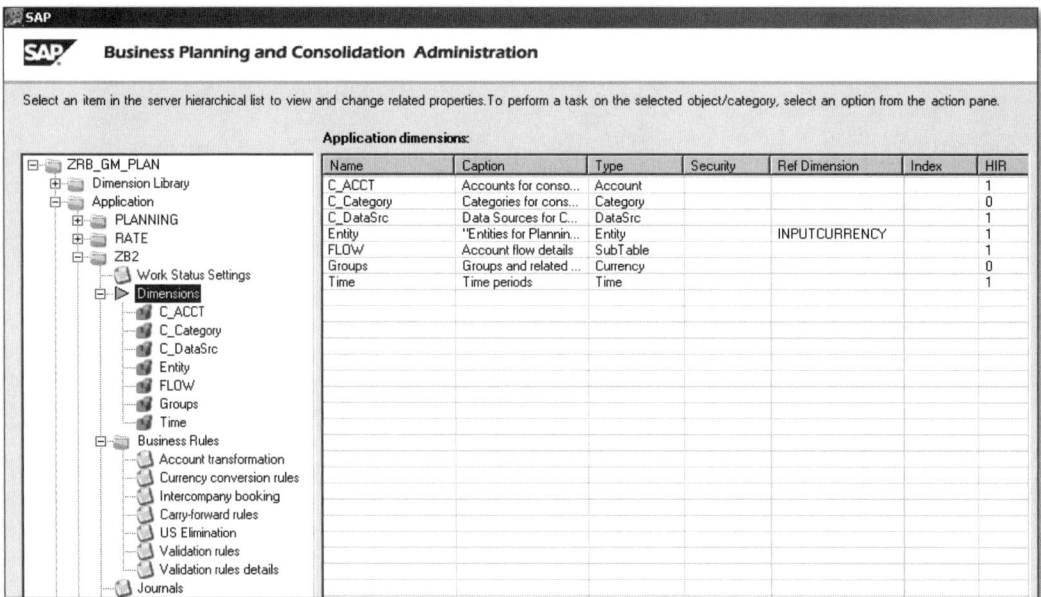

Figure 9.1 Configuring a Carry Forward Balance Business Rule—Part A

2. The members of the Flow dimension are shown in Figure 9.2. The Flow dimension is used to reflect asset movements such as opening inventory, transfers, and closing inventory.

3. Figure 9.3 displays the closing value of the machinery and equipment of entity C3001 for the December 2008 period. The flow F_999 in this example represents the closing balance.

4. Create the standard script logic COPY_OPENING.LGF to execute the copy opening balance business rule, as shown in Figure 9.4.

Business Rules | 9.1

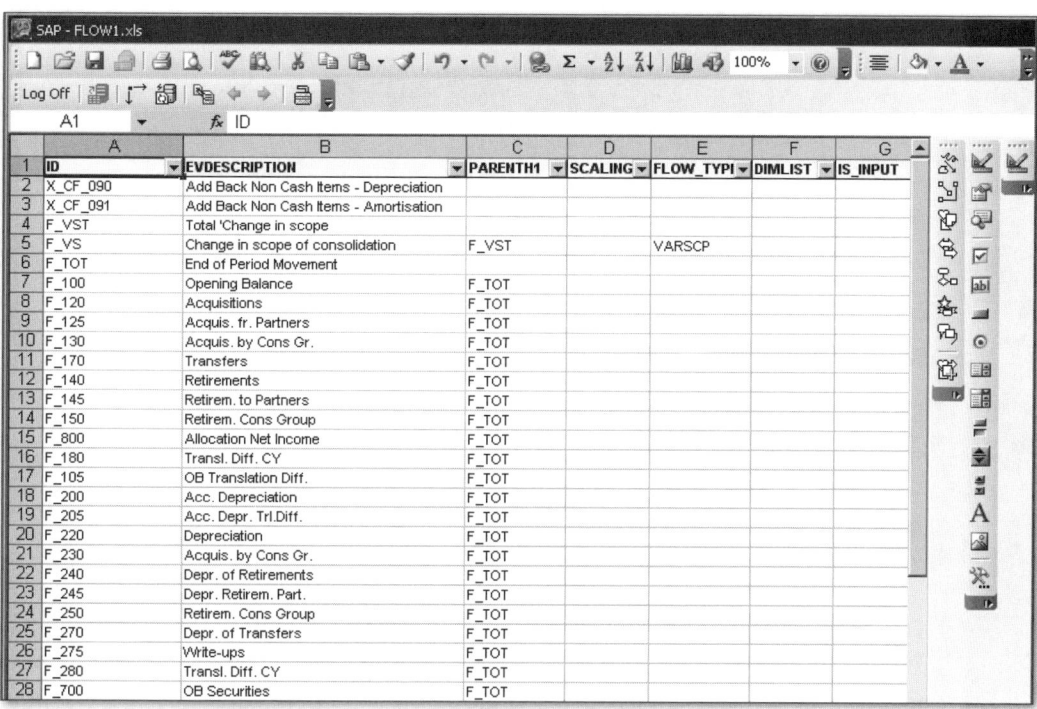

Figure 9.2 Configuring a Carry Forward Balance Business Rule—Part B

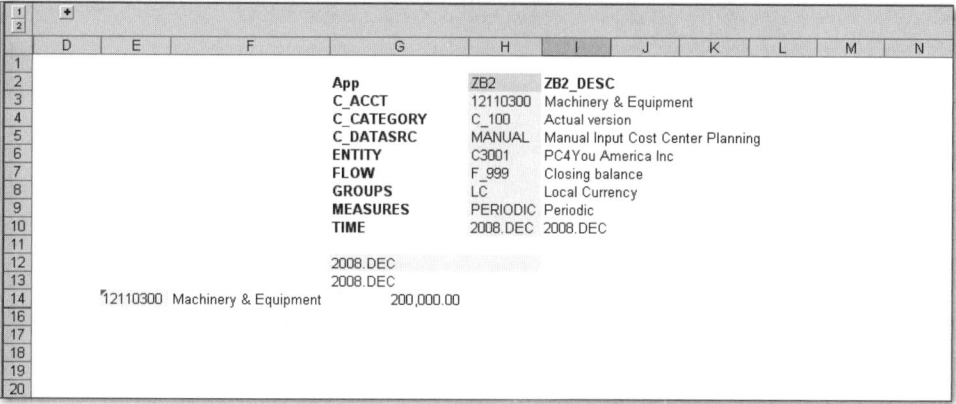

Figure 9.3 Configuring a Carry Forward Balance Business Rule—Part C

9 | Consolidation with SAP BusinessObjects Planning and Consolidation

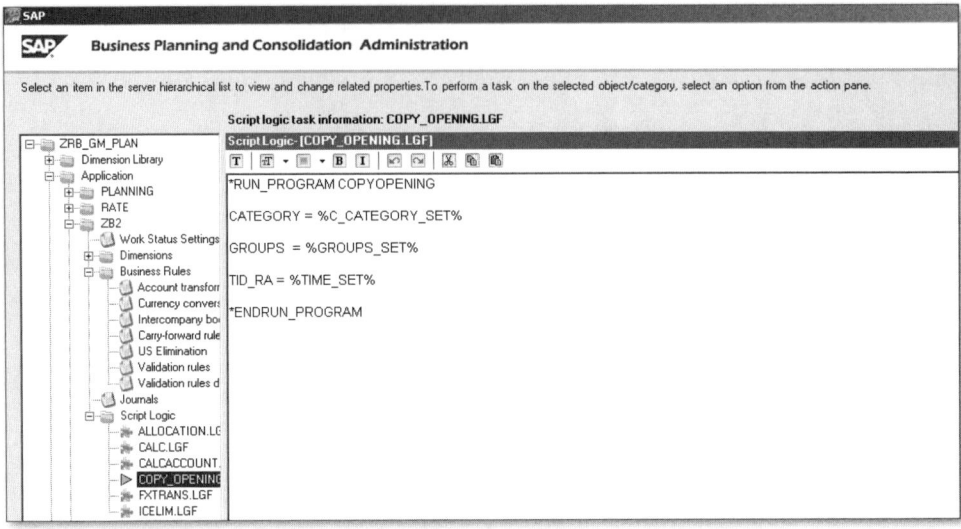

Figure 9.4 Configuring a Carry Forward Balance Business Rule—Part D

5. Define the business rule to configure the carry forward balance of the Machinery & Equipment account, as shown in Figure 9.5. In our example, the closing balance for this account as of December 2008 will be transferred as the opening balance of January 2009 when the carry forward balance script is executed.

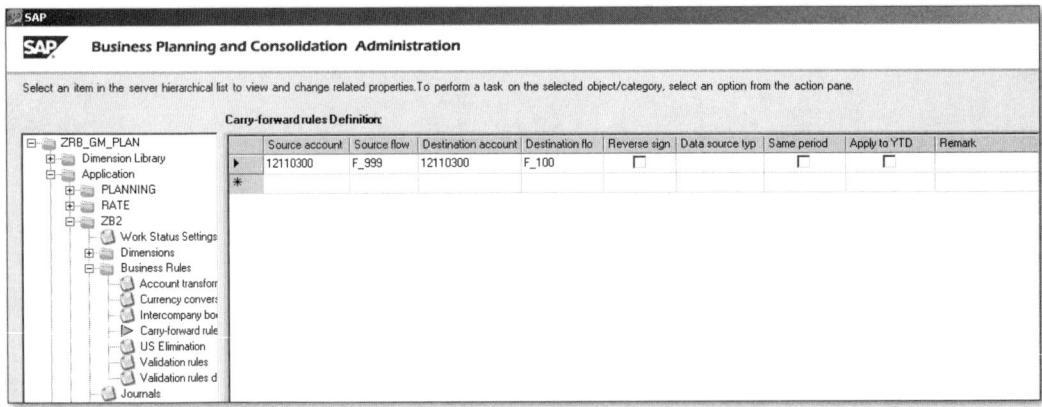

Figure 9.5 Configuring a Carry Forward Balance Business Rule—Part E

6. Run the data package to execute the carry forward balance script, as shown in Figure 9.6. The process chain associated with the carry forward balance is /CPMB/OPENING_BALANCES.

364

Business Rules | **9.1**

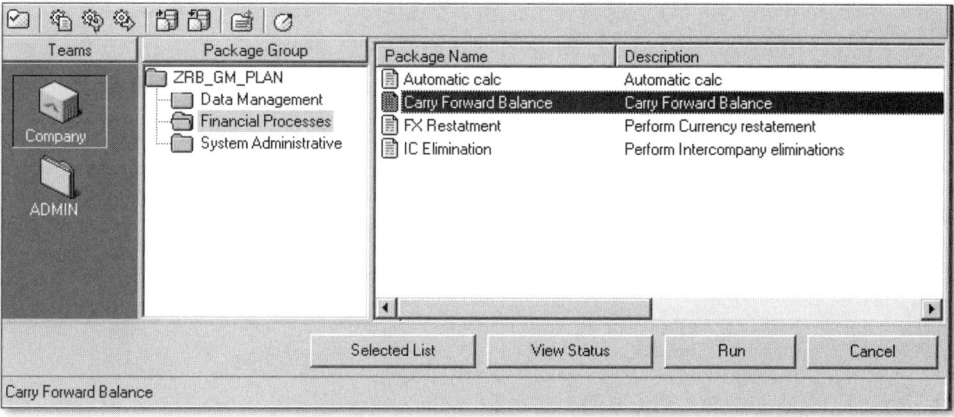

Figure 9.6 Configuring a Carry Forward Balance Business Rule—Part F

7. Make the selections shown in Figure 9.7. We chose the time period January 2009, because we want to create the opening balance for that period.

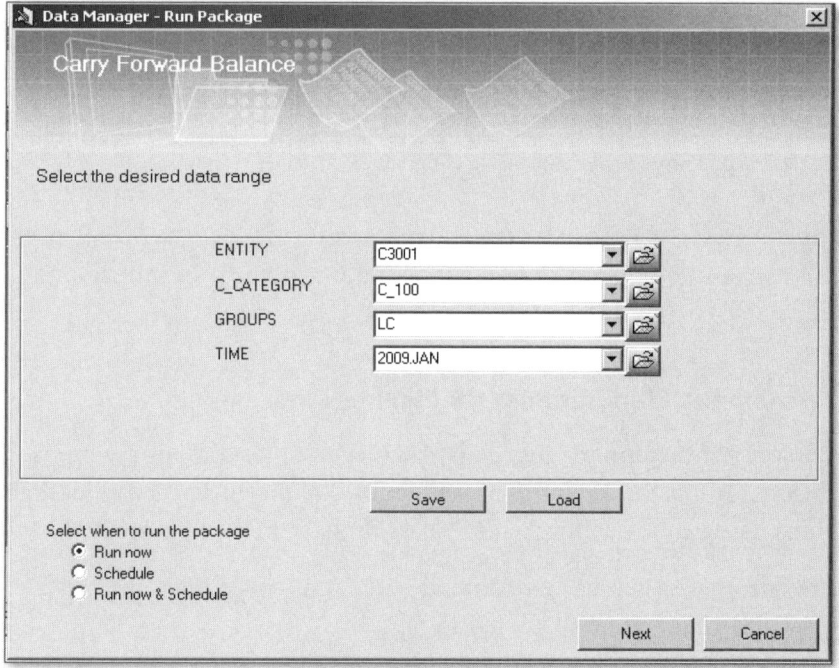

Figure 9.7 Configuring a Carry Forward Balance Business Rule—Part G

365

8. After executing the package, select the January 2009 time period and F_100 (opening balance) for the Machinery & Equipment account. The carry forward balance script has transferred the closing balance of this account from December 2008 to January 2009 (Figure 9.8).

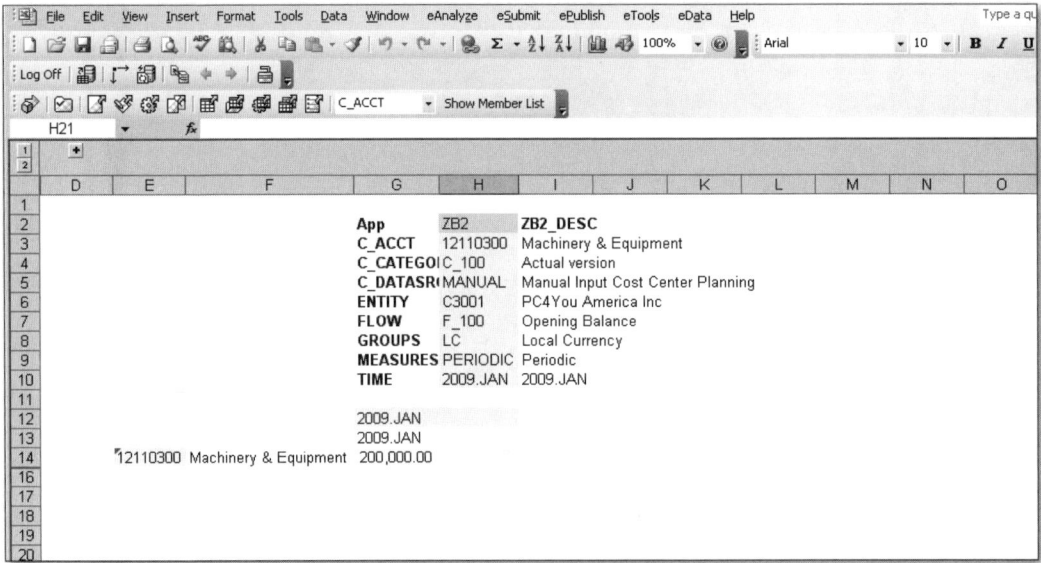

Figure 9.8 Configuring a Carry Forward Balance Business Rule — Part H

You now know how to use business rules to perform carry forward balances. Next, we will explain how to set up the configuration to perform intercompany eliminations.

9.1.2 Intercompany Eliminations (US Eliminations)

The intercompany elimination process is used when an organization is composed of multiple business units that do business with one another. During consolidation, the transactions between the individual business units should be eliminated.

The following are guidelines for performing intercompany elimination in SAP BusinessObjects Planning and Consolidation:

▶ To support intercompany elimination, the SAP BusinessObjects Planning and Consolidation application should include the Intercompany dimension. The dimension type is I.

- The Intercompany dimension should include a property called Entity, and the value in this property should match the member ID of the Entity dimension.
- The Account dimension should include the ELIMACC property, and the value in this property should match the member ID of the Account dimension.
- The Entity property should include an ELIM property, the value of which can be Y or N. The elimination process reads all entries for entities that have the value of this property set to N and then posts eliminations, if applicable, to entities that have the ELIM property set to Y.

The elimination process scans all base level, non-elimination entities. These are entities with the property ELIM <> Y. If the application has a Currency dimension, the elimination process restricts its action to all reporting currencies. These are currencies that have the property REPORTING = Y.

The Account dimension has a property called ELIMACC, which is used in elimination. If the value of this property is blank, the entry associated with this account is not eliminated. If the account has a valid value, and if the system decides that the entry needs to be eliminated, the elimination is posted to the plug account (which is the account specified in the ELIMACC property).

The elimination is posted to the elimination entity below the first common parent. The common parent is derived as follows:

1. The system identifies the two entities for which a common parent must be found. The first entity is the current entity member. The second entity is the entity corresponding to the current intercompany member. The entity of the intercompany member is obtained by reading the content of the ENTITY property of the current intercompany member. The system searches in a selected entity hierarchy for the first member that has both entities as descendants. This is the common parent.
2. Next, the system searches in the immediate descendants of the common parent for a valid elimination entity (an entity that has the property ELIM = Y). This is the entity where the system stores the results of the elimination.
3. The default elimination logic does its searches in the organization hierarchy of the Entity dimension. If no common parent is found, no elimination occurs. If no elimination entity is found below the first common parent, the next common parent is searched.

9 | Consolidation with SAP BusinessObjects Planning and Consolidation

You can also create entries in the business rules table to maintain the source and destination DataSource to use when calling the logic to eliminate intercompany transactions using US Eliminations.

The details for setting up the business table for US Eliminations are explained in Table 9.2.

Field Name	Description
Source DataSource	The source DataSource for which eliminations will apply.
Destination DataSource	The destination DataSource to which eliminations will be applied.
Remark	A brief description of the business rule.

Table 9.2 US Eliminations Business Rules

We will now review an example of how to eliminate intercompany transactions in an SAP BusinessObjects Planning and Consolidation application.

1. The dimensions for application ZB1 are shown in Figure 9.9. You can see that the IntCo dimension is included as a required dimension to post intercompany transactions.

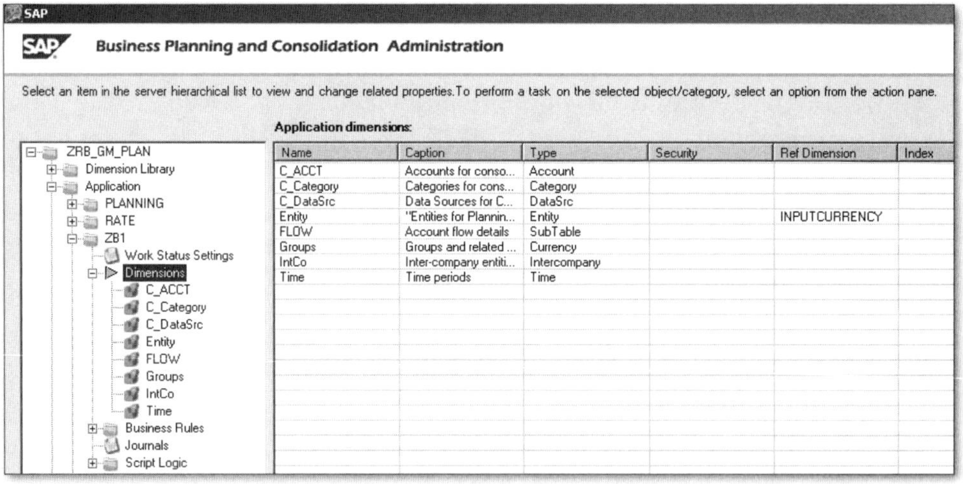

Figure 9.9 Configuring Intercompany Eliminations—Part A

2. The members of the Account dimension are shown in Figure 9.10. The elimination account is a property of the Account dimension; as you can see, the ICSALES and ICCOST members have the elimination account ICDIFF associated with them. When eliminations are carried out, they are posted to the ICDIFF account.

ID	EVDESCRIPTION	PARENTH1	ACCTY	RATETYPE	DIMLIS	DIMLIST	ELIMACC
12110600	Transportation Equipment	1	AST	ENDFLOW			
12311000	Investments in Subsidiaries - Purchase	1	AST	HISTINV			
12710000	Inter-company receivables	1	AST	ENDFLOW	ICEND		21199999
21181600	Other Current Liabilities	1	LEQ	ENDFLOW			
21199999	Cross Company - Clearing Account	1	LEQ	ENDFLOW	ICEND		
25300000	Common Stock	1	LEQ	HISTFLOW		GW	
25711000	Retained Earnings - Prior Years	1	LEQ	HISTFLOW		GW	
25712000	Retained Earnings - Current Year	1	LEQ	AVGFLOW		GW	
2	Profit and Loss Accounts						
33120000	Income Tax Provision - Deferred	2	EXP	AVG			
30527100	Depreciation Expense	2	EXP	AVG			
30527140	Depreciation - Machinery and Equipme	2	EXP	AVG			
32051100	Interest Income	2	INC	AVG			
32051200	Interest Expense	2	INC	AVG			
32091000	Other income	2	INC	AVG			
39000000	Net income/Loss (net earnings)	2	EXP	AVG			
VALIDATIONS	Total Validations		EXP				
VALID_010	Assets - Liabilities	VALIDATIONS	EXP				
VALID_020	Result P&L - BS	VALIDATIONS	EXP				
VALID_030	Depreciation Assets	VALIDATIONS	EXP				
X_CF_090	Add Back Non-Cash Items Depreciation		AST	ENDFLOW			
X_CF_091	Add Back Non-Cash Items Amortisation		AST	ENDFLOW			
ICSALES	ICSALES		INC				ICDIFF
ICCOST	ICCOST		EXP				ICDIFF
ICDIFF	ICDIFF		INC				

Figure 9.10 Configuring Intercompany Eliminations—Part B

3. The members of the Entity dimension, of which ELIM is a property, are shown in Figure 9.11. You will see that some of the entities have the ELIM property set to Y; the elimination process will post elimination entries to these entities. The entity E_CG3 is identified as the elimination entity; for example, eliminations for entities C3000, C3001, and C4000 will be posted to entity E_CG3—this is because they share a common hierarchy, CG3.

9 | Consolidation with SAP BusinessObjects Planning and Consolidation

ID	EVDESCRIPTION	PARENTH1	CURRENCY	ELIM
H1	Investments		EUR	
CG1	PC4You Consolidated	H1	EUR	
C9000	PC4You Holdings Inc	CG1	USD	
CG2	PC4You Europe Consolidated	CG1	EUR	
C1000	PC4You Deutschland Gmbh	CG2	EUR	
C2000	PC4You (UK) Ltd.	CG2	GBP	
E_CG2	PC4You Europe Consolidated	CG2	EUR	Y
CG3	PC4You Americas Consolidated	CG1	EUR	
C3000	PC4You America Inc	CG3	USD	
C3001	PC4You America Inc	CG3	USD	
C4000	PC4You Canada Inc	CG3	USD	
E_CG3	PC4You Americas Consolidated	CG3	USD	Y
CG4	PC4You Asia/Pacific Consolidated	CG1	EUR	
C5000	PC4You Japan Co.Ltd.	CG4	JPY	
C5100	PC4You Australia Pty. Limited	CG4	AUD	
E_CG4	PC4You Asia/Pacific Consolidated	CG4	EUR	Y
E_CG1	PC4You Consolidated	CG1	EUR	Y
H2	Regions		EUR	
CG5	World by Regions	H2	EUR	
CG6	Other regions		CG5	EUR
CG7	PC4You Americas Foreign	CG5	EUR	
H3	Companies		EUR	
CG10	World by Companies	H3	EUR	

Figure 9.11 Configuring Intercompany Eliminations — Part C

4. Figure 9.12 displays the intercompany transactions for entity C3000 for August 2008. You will see the data for ICSALES and ICCOST transactions recorded here.

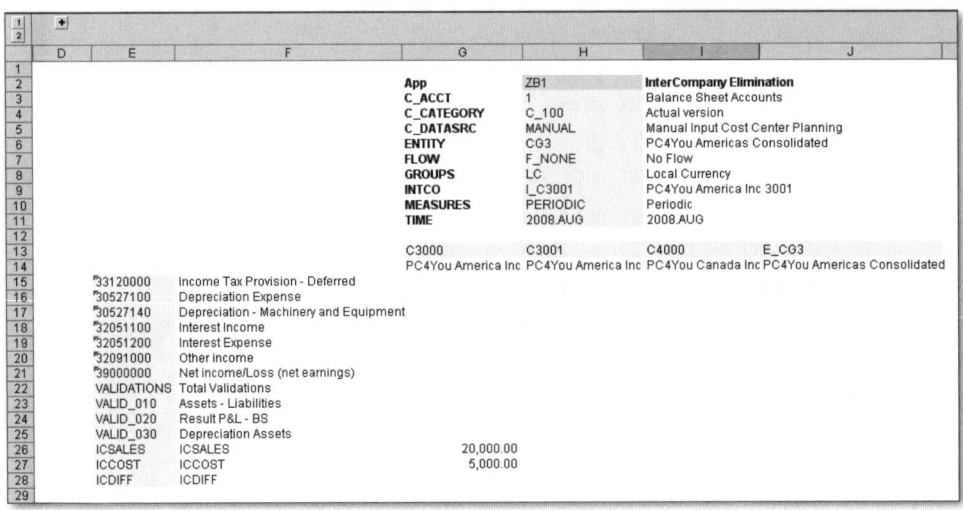

Figure 9.12 Configuring Intercompany Eliminations — Part D

370

5. Create the standard script logic ICELIM.LGF to execute the intercompany eliminations, as shown in Figure 9.13.

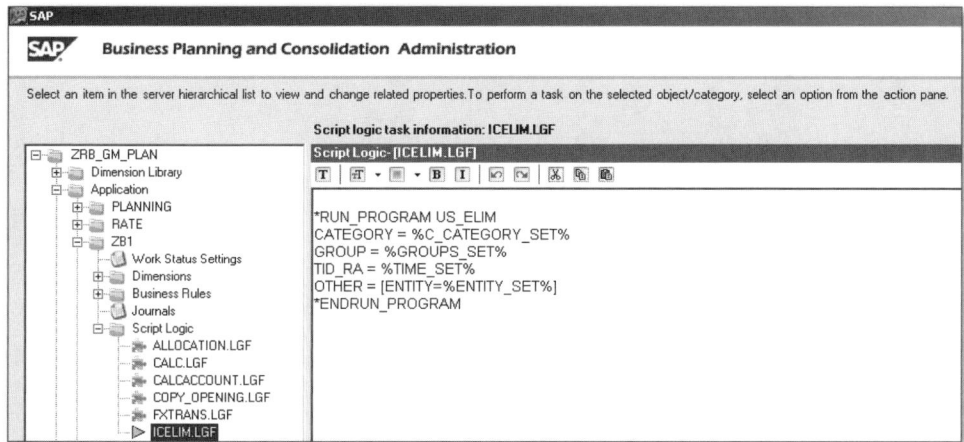

Figure 9.13 Configuring Intercompany Eliminations—Part E

6. Run the data package to execute the IC elimination script, as shown in Figure 9.14. The process chain associated with the elimination process is /CPMB/IC_ELIMINATION.

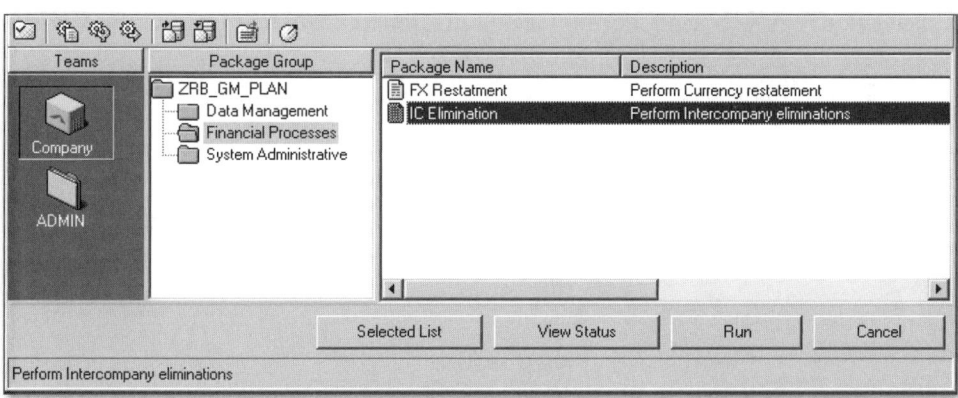

Figure 9.14 Configuring Intercompany Eliminations—Part F

7. Make the selections shown in Figure 9.15. In our example, we chose August 2008.

9 | Consolidation with SAP BusinessObjects Planning and Consolidation

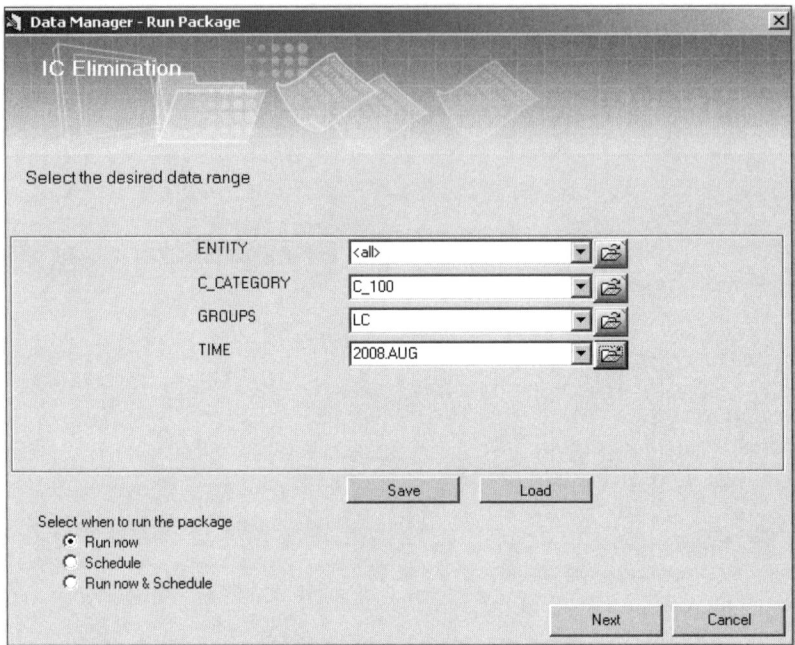

Figure 9.15 Configuring Intercompany Eliminations—Part G

8. After executing the package, select all of the entities for the base members in CG3 to see whether the intercompany transactions were transferred to the elimination entity and whether the difference between the intercompany transactions were posted to the elimination account.

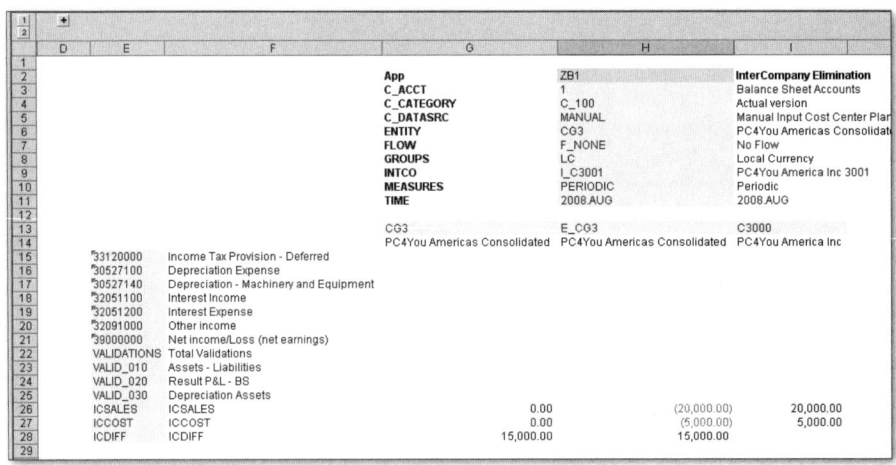

Figure 9.16 Configuring Intercompany Eliminations—Part H

In this section, we discussed using business rules to perform intercompany elimination. In the next section, we will discuss using journals and see how journal templates are created and used in SAP BusinessObjects Planning and Consolidation.

9.2 Journals

Journals are used to make manual adjustments to data in an application; these entries are sometimes referred to as *top-side entries*. During the review and reconciliation of financial data, variances may be detected; to fix these, differences are posted as a journal entry.

A journal template, which is used to create and maintain journals, must be created before a journal entry can be maintained for an application, and you can maintain only one journal template for an application. When a journal template exists for an application, creating a new journal template deletes the existing journal template and also deletes the journal transactions associated with that template.

A user should be granted sufficient authorization to create and post journal entries; we recommend creating a task profile that provides the necessary authorizations for users to perform various journal tasks. You can perform the following types of journal activities if you have the necessary authorization:

- **Create a journal entry**
  When you create a journal entry, a unique journal ID is created.
- **Modify a journal entry**
  You can modify a journal that has not yet been posted.
- **Copy journal entries**
  You can copy existing and create new journal entries.
- **Open one or more entries**
  You can view one or more journal entries. When you select more than one journal to view, you can view each journal entry using the Previous and Next buttons in the Journal Options action pane.
- **Post journals**
  You can post journals to make them active.
- **Unpost journal entries**
  You can unpost a journal entry that was previously posted.

- **Search for journal entries**
  You can search journals to locate and view journal entries previously created and posted.

- **Repost journals**
  You can post a journal that was previously unposted.

- **Lock journal entries**
  A journal entry can be locked, which means that you cannot make changes to it.

- **Reopen journals**
  Reopening a journal is the process of opening a prior journal transaction and posting it to a different set of accounts. To do this, the system should be open for reopening journals at the application level and the source and destination accounts for the reopened journal entries should be defined.

- **Require balanced journal entries**
  The JRN_BALANCE application parameter can be set to Y to require balanced journal entries. When this is set, the debit and credit amounts for the journal entry should match.

- **View report**
  You can generate a report of the journals based on the following criteria:

  - By journal ID: Generates a report based on a single journal entry.
  - By user(s): Generates a report based on a list of users who have created or posted journal entries.
  - By account: Generates a report of journal activity by account type.

  Reports are displayed in the web browser. You can use the available controls to print or export the report.

- **Delete journal entries**
  You can delete journal entries that have not yet been posted.

- **Define journal reopen translation**
  You can define the template and settings for journals that are to be reopened.

9.2.1 Creating a Journal Template

We will now look at an example to show you how to create a journal in SAP BusinessObjects Planning and Consolidation:

1. You can access journals for an application from the Admin Console (Figure 9.17, ❶).
2. Under Journal Tasks, click on Journal Wizard (Figure 9.17, ❷). You are asked to confirm that you want to create a new journal template. If you decide to create a new template, all existing journal data is lost.

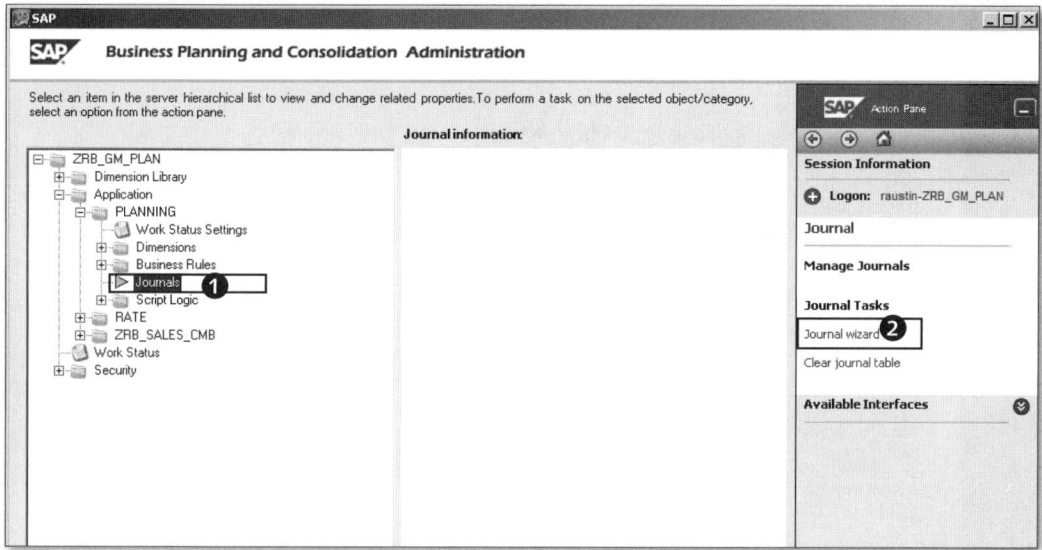

Figure 9.17 Creating a Journal Template—Part A

3. The SAP-Journal Create dialog box is displayed (Figure 9.18). Here, you configure the selections for the journal template, which consists of the following sections:

   ▶ Select Header Dimensions: In this section, specify the dimensions to use in the header section of a journal template. The dimensions you want to use as fixed members when creating the journal entry are specified in the header dimension.

   ▶ Set Header Dimension Order: In this section, set the order in which the dimensions will appear when you create or display a journal template. This applies to the dimensions specified in the Header dimension.

   ▶ Set Detail Dimensions: In this section, specify the dimensions that should be used as line item dimensions in the journal template. More than one line can be created for a journal entry for the dimensions selected as detail dimensions.

- Create Additional Header Items: In this section, you can specify additional items a user should enter when creating a journal entry. This can be used to provide additional information such as a code to indicate why the journal entry was created.
- Summary of Journal: This section summarizes the selections made in the earlier sections. Here, you also confirm the creation of a new journal template.

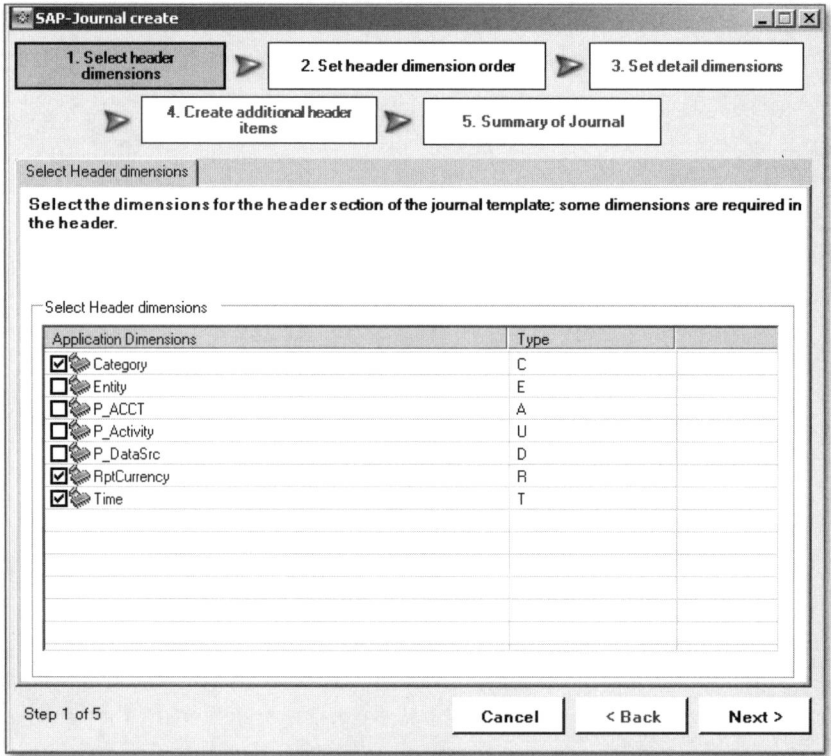

Figure 9.18 Creating a Journal Template—Part B

You now know how to create a journal template. In the next section, we will explain how to manage journals.

9.2.2 Managing Journals

To manage journals, proceed as follows:

1. Log into SAP BusinessObjects Planning and Consolidation for Excel, select your application, and choose the ePublish and Journals menu options to manage journals.

2. Under Journal Options, select the New Journal task to create a new journal entry. Different tasks display, based on the context of your selection (Figure 9.19), which presents the journal entry template for entering the journal transaction. When you click on the Save as Journal task in the action pane, the journal entry is saved. At that time, a unique journal ID is assigned for the journal transaction.

3. To post the journal, click on the Post Journal task in the action pane.

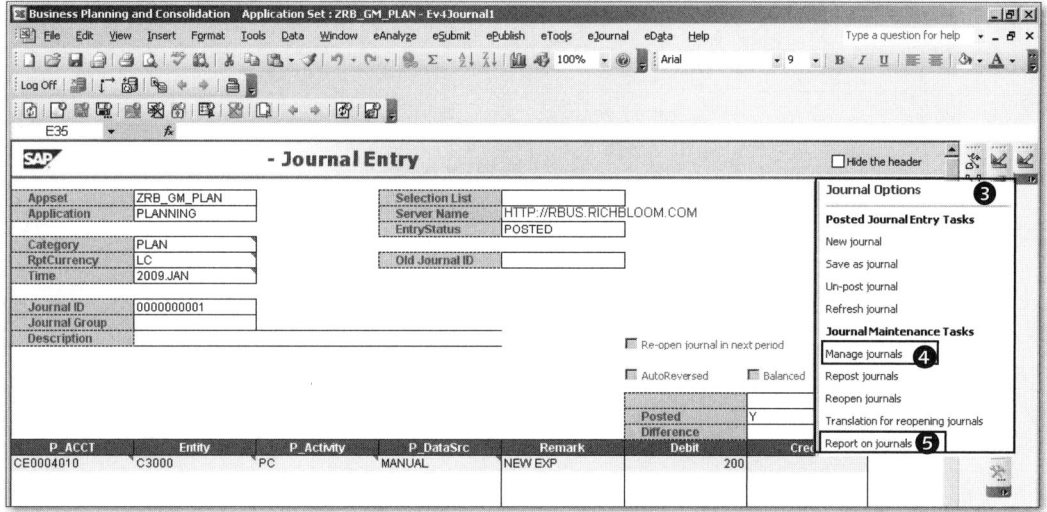

Figure 9.19 Manage Journal Transactions

4. To query journals, click on the Manage Journals task under Journal Maintenance Tasks (Figure 9.19, ❹). This opens the Journal Manager Query dialog box, as shown in Figure 9.20, which lists different parameters for selecting journal transactions. You can also select data based on the status of journals. After making your selections, click on Execute Query.

9 | Consolidation with SAP BusinessObjects Planning and Consolidation

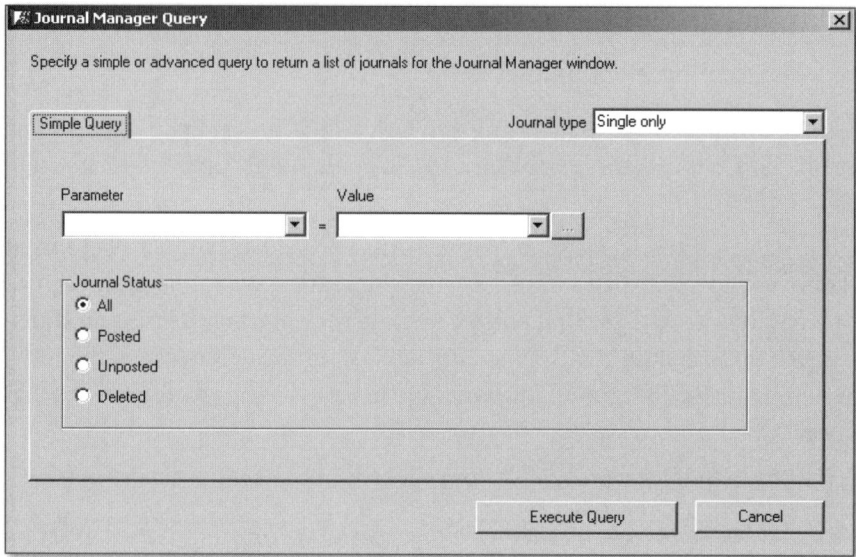

Figure 9.20 Managing Journals—Part A

5. Based on the selections, the journals are listed in a table under the Journal Manager dialog box. After selecting a journal entry, you can perform different actions—post, unpost, copy, and so on, depending on the context of the journal entry selected (Figure 9.21).

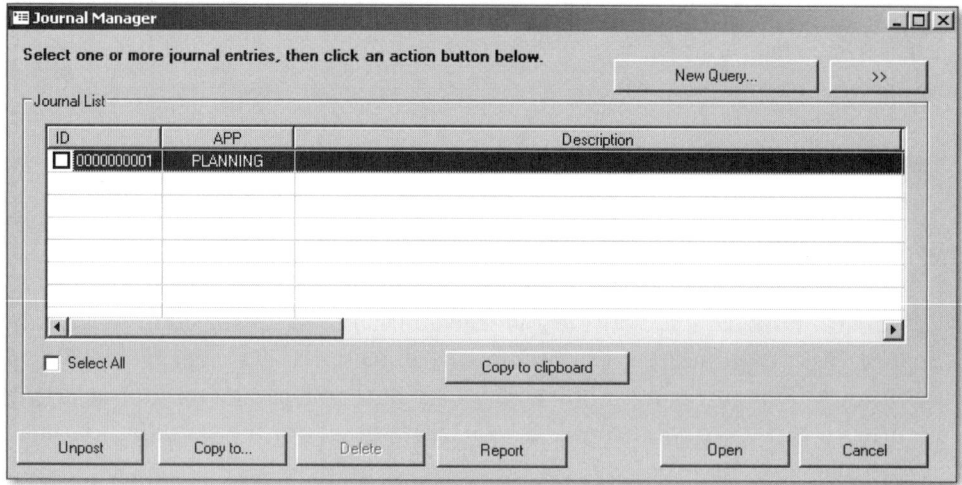

Figure 9.21 Managing Journals—Part B

Next, we will discuss how to report on journals.

9.2.3 Journal Reports

A journal report can be displayed by selecting the Report on Journals task, as shown in ❺ of Figure 9.19. The Journal Report Wizard dialog box includes three options (Figure 9.22). You can generate a report of the journals based on the following criteria:

▸ By Journal ID: Generates a report based on a single journal entry.
▸ By Users: Generates a report based on a list of users who have created or posted journal entries.
▸ By Account: Generates a report of journal activity by account type.

In our example, we have selected the journal ID report format (Figure 9.22, ❻). After selecting the format, click on the Next button.

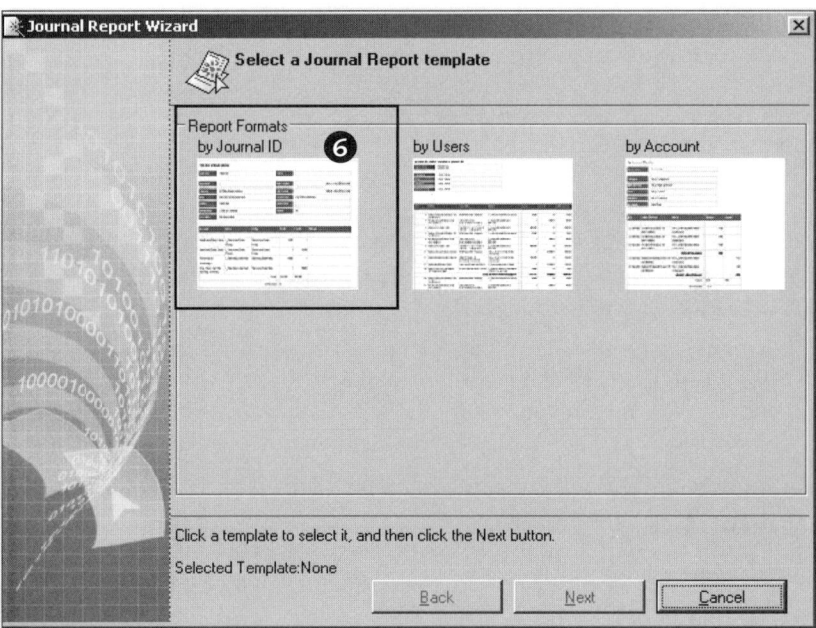

Figure 9.22 Journal Reports—Part A

9 | Consolidation with SAP BusinessObjects Planning and Consolidation

A dialog box displays where you can enter your search criteria (Figure 9.23). After entering your criteria, click on Next to report on the journal entry.

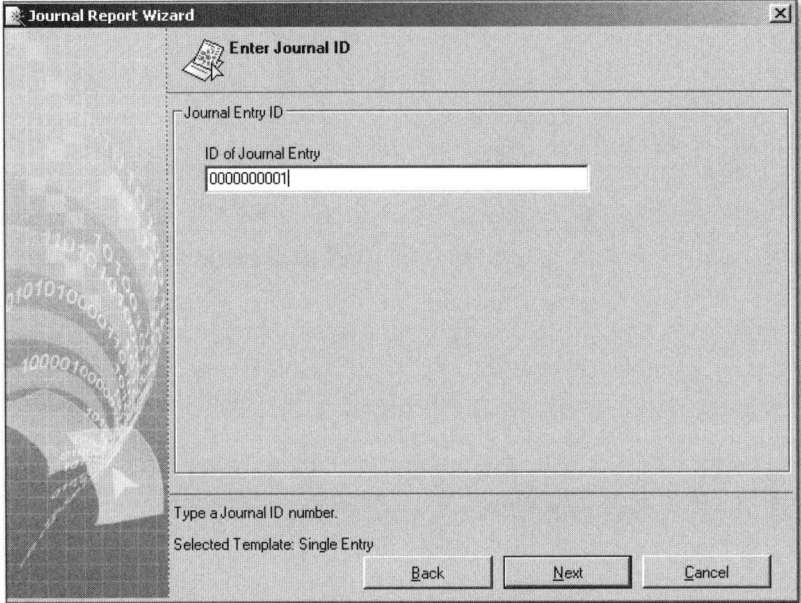

Figure 9.23 Journal Reports—Part B

> **Note**
> Journals do not post delta values. During concurrency locking, the package size for journals is set to 99,999,999, to avoid locking.
>
> The ENABLE_JRN property can be used in any dimension to allow the creation of journals. If the value of this property for a dimension member is set to Y, journal entries can be created based on these dimension members.

In the next section, we will discuss concepts in consolidation and provide an overview of consolidation logic.

9.3 Consolidation Logic

Organizations perform two types of consolidation when reporting financial data, as follows:

- **Legal consolidation**
  This is reporting the financial data of a company for all of the units of the business in one currency. This type of consolidation is required by law and is necessary to meet the statutory requirements of the country where the company is incorporated or headquartered.

- **Management consolidation**
  This type of consolidation is flexible and is governed by how an organization's management wants to consolidate and use this data. Management consolidation can also be used for planning and for understanding the financial state of the company.

The SAP BusinessObjects Planning and Consolidation system can be used for both types of consolidation and provides a robust interface to satisfy requirements. As we have discussed, the process of consolidation is enabled in SAP BusinessObjects Planning and Consolidation using business rules.

To perform consolidation in SAP BusinessObjects Planning and Consolidation, a Consolidation application that includes an Ownership and a Rate application should be created. The Ownership application is used to store the relationship of companies in the group and the investments made by companies among its units; for example, company A may have an equity stake in company B, and both company A and B are individual companies and are part of a parent company C.

The Consolidation application should also include a Group dimension, which is used for consolidating data in the reporting currency of the group company to which the child companies belong. Consolidation is performed using the automatic adjustment process.

The Ownership application is at the heart of consolidation and contains information that is key to the consolidation process—such as the relationship of entities that belong to the group and the percentage interest among the entities in the group. The following types of consolidation methods are used:

- 90: Represents a holding company in a group
- 86: Purchase (global)
- 70: Proportional

Under a Consolidation application, two business tables—Automatic Adjustments and Automatic Adjustments Detail—define the rules for consolidation. The Automatic Adjustments table is a header table, and includes an adjustment ID that uniquely identifies an adjustment. It also includes the source DataSource to which consolidations should be applied. The destination DataSource specified should be a valid member in the DataSource dimension and should have the A Datasrc_Type property (automatic). The consolidation data created during the consolidation process is booked to this DataSource member.

The Automatic Adjustment Detail table references the adjustment ID in the Header table, which is where you can specify the source account and the destination accounts along with a rule ID. The rule ID in the Automatic Adjustment Detail table also refers to the Consolidation table, which defines the formula for how consolidation entries should be generated during the process.

The business library contains the following tables:

- **Consolidation Rules**
  This table contains different rules, which can be referenced in the Rule ID field of the Automatic Adjustment Detail table.

- **Consolidation Methods**
  These refer to different types of consolidation methods available for consolidation.

- **Consolidation Rule Formula**
  Depending on the entries in the Automatic Adjustment tables, a corresponding rule is executed, and the necessary entries are created. Define the formulas to use in calculating the amounts to post.

The automatic adjustment process is handled by a program called CONSOLIDATION. This program is run using the following logic statement in the CONSOLIDATION.LGF script file:

```
*RUN_PROGRAM CONSOLIDATION
CATEGORY = %C_CATEGORY_SET%
GROUP = %GROUPS_SET%
TID_RA = %TIME_SET%
*ENDRUN_PROGRAM
```

9.4 Summary

In this chapter, you learned how business rules are used in SAP BusinessObjects Planning and Consolidation to perform common tasks in a planning and consolidation application. We used a scenario to define the steps for configuring the business rule to perform the carry forward of balances from one accounting period to another. We also discussed the steps to eliminate intercompany transactions and post them to an elimination entity. Next, we discussed the use of journals and the process of setting and using journals in an application. Finally, we discussed the process of consolidating data.

SAP BusinessObjects Planning and Consolidation 7.5 version for NetWeaver is currently in development and includes features such as business process flow, integration with Xcelsius, and a host of new functionalities that give users more power. Chapter 10 discusses these features and explains how you can benefit from the upgrade.

10   Outlook for SAP BusinessObjects Planning and Consolidation

As we write this book, SAP BusinessObjects Planning and Consolidation for NetWeaver 7.5 is in the development phase and is scheduled to be available for general release in June 2010. Several features users have been looking for will be made available in this version, and this chapter previews these new features. The information described is forward-looking, and is thus subject to change by SAP AG.

The release of SAP BusinessObjects Planning and Consolidation 7.5 is focused towards achieving the following main objectives:

- **Harmonization**
  Look, feel, and branding that is compatible to the SAP Enterprise Performance Management (SAP EPM) suite of products.

- **Integration**
  Integration with other SAP products, such as SAP ERP, Xcelsius, SAP BusinessObjects Voyager/Pioneer, WebI, and Crystal Reports.

- **Enhancement**
  Improvement to SAP BusinessObjects Planning and Consolidation product features based on customer feedback.

In the sections that follow, we will take a closer look at these three objectives and examine the specific features within them. Note that the features listed here are specific to the SAP BusinessObjects Planning and Consolidation NetWeaver version.

10.1   Harmonization

SAP BusinessObjects Planning and Consolidation 7.5 for NetWeaver is being enhanced with the goal of providing convergence in user experience for users of all SAP Enterprise Performance Management products. The similarity in look and feel across products makes it easy for users of SAP EPM products to use another product within that suite. This contributes to gains in productivity and ultimately reduces TCO.

10.1.1 Authentication and Single Sign-On

SAP BusinessObjects Planning and Consolidation 7.5 for NetWeaver provides integration with other SAP BusinessObjects applications, including the SAP BusinessObjects Enterprise Central Management Server (CMS). SAP BusinessObjects Enterprise CMS supports authentication mechanism such as LDAP, Active Directory, and the SAP NetWeaver user management engine. In addition, SAP BusinessObjects Enterprise CMS offers the advantage of using the single sign-on feature, which means that users do not need to re-authenticate their credentials when connecting from an SAP BusinessObjects Planning and Consolidation application to other SAP BusinessObjects applications (such as Xcelsius or SAP BusinessObjects Voyager). This also applies to switching between the Admin, Excel, and Web interfaces of SAP BusinessObjects Planning and Consolidation.

10.1.2 Platform Support

SAP BusinessObjects Planning and Consolidation 7.5 for NetWeaver provides a broader choice of open and heterogeneous platform support. The speed and usability of running SAP BusinessObjects Planning and Consolidation on these platforms provides enhanced user experience. The following platforms will be supported:

- **Client support**
  Client support for SAP BusinessObjects Planning and Consolidation has been expanded to include the following:
  - Windows Vista Client (32 and 64 bit), Windows XP (32 bit), and Windows 7 (32 bit and 64 bit)
  - Internet Explorer 6, 7, and 8
  - Microsoft 2003 and 2007
- **Server support**
  Server support has been expanded to include the following:
  - Windows Server 2003 and 2008
  - IIS 6.0 and 7.0 Web Servers

- VMWare-based installation (non-production use only)
- Any database supported by SAP NetWeaver

▶ **Globalization**

The following components of SAP BusinessObjects Planning and Consolidation have been internationalized:

- Software
- Help
- User guides
- Release notes

SAP BusinessObjects Planning and Consolidation will be available in 20 languages.

10.2 Integration

SAP BusinessObjects Planning and Consolidation 7.5 for NetWeaver provides connectivity to non-SAP sources, which removes the need for intermediate flat files or manual rekeying of data, saving time and reducing integration costs. In this section, we will discuss some of the features of enhanced integration that are available in SAP BusinessObjects Planning and Consolidation 7.5 for NetWeaver.

10.2.1 ETL Integration

The following ETL integration features will be made available:

▶ **Reuse process chains**

In SAP BusinessObjects Planning and Consolidation 7.0 for NetWeaver, the process chains used to create data manager packages were unique and not reusable in another data manager package. SAP BusinessObjects Planning and Consolidation 7.5 for NetWeaver provides the ability to reuse process chains across data manager packages.

▶ **Retract master and transaction data from SAP BusinessObjects Planning and Consolidation to SAP NetWeaver BW**

SAP BusinessObjects Planning and Consolidation 7.5 for NetWeaver includes data management packages for BAdI implementation that enable you to transfer master and transaction data from SAP BusinessObjects Planning and

Consolidation dimensions and applications to SAP NetWeaver BW InfoObjects and InfoCubes, respectively.

- **Retract master and transaction data from SAP BusinessObjects Planning and Consolidation to SAP ERP**
BusinessObjects Planning and Consolidation 7.5 for NetWeaver includes data management packages for BAdI implementation that enable you to retract master and transaction data from SAP BusinessObjects Planning and Consolidation dimensions and applications to SAP ERP systems.

10.2.2 Data Replication

In SAP BusinessObjects Planning and Consolidation 7.0 for NetWeaver, transaction data that existed in SAP NetWeaver BW had to be replicated in an SAP BusinessObjects Planning and Consolidation application for it to be used. SAP BusinessObjects Planning and Consolidation 7.5 for NetWeaver enables you to use SAP NetWeaver BW transaction data without replication, through the use of virtual providers.

10.2.3 Drill-Through

The drill-through feature allows SAP BusinessObjects Planning and Consolidation users to directly access information in a source system via a URL. For users who have used the report-to-report (RRI) interface in SAP NetWeaver BW, the drill-through feature in SAP BusinessObjects Planning and Consolidation will be familiar.

A new task, Drill-Through, is available on the action pane when accessing a report via the SAP BusinessObjects Planning and Consolidation for Excel interface. To use it, you first define the drill-through in the Admin Console, and then launch it using the EvMNU function in the SAP BusinessObjects Planning and Consolidation for Excel interface. The syntax for calling a drill-though using EvMNU is as follows:

```
MNU_eTOOLS_DRILLTHROUGH_RUN("drillthrough id")
```

The drill-through is defined as a URL in the Admin Console, and a unique ID is specified when defining a drill-through. In this function, the Drill-Through ID parameter is the ID specified in the Admin Console.

10.2.4 Integration with SAP BusinessObjects Process Control

The SAP BusinessObjects Process Control software is a tool to monitor governance, risk, and compliance (GRC) in an organization. This software can be used with SAP BusinessObjects Planning and Consolidation 7.5 to build manual or automated checks utilizing SAP BusinessObjects Planning and Consolidation data. This increases confidence in the effectiveness of control and compliance for consolidation processes and automates the monitoring process without compromising on compliance.

10.2.5 Integration with Xcelsius

Xcelsius is an SAP BusinessObjects tool used for creating dashboard applications. SAP BusinessObjects Planning and Consolidation 7.5 for NetWeaver is integrated with Xcelsius, which offers the following benefits:

- The data in an SAP BusinessObjects Planning and Consolidation application can be used in Xcelsius for creating dashboards and visually compelling reporting applications.
- The write back feature from Xcelsius to an SAP BusinessObjects Planning and Consolidation application will be available. This will allow data in an SAP BusinessObjects Planning and Consolidation application to be updated using the Xcelsius frontend tool.

The ability to read and write SAP BusinessObjects Planning and Consolidation data using Xcelsius enables users to analyze and write data using an intuitive dashboard application.

10.2.6 Integration with SAP BusinessObjects Voyager

SAP BusinessObjects Voyager is a reporting tool that can be used with SAP BusinessObjects Planning and Consolidation 7.5 for analysis and decision making. With the integration of SAP BusinessObjects with SAP NetWeaver BW, SAP BusinessObjects Voyager can be used for analyzing data in SAP NetWeaver BW. SAP BusinessObjects Voyager will eventually be integrated with the Business Explorer (BEx) reporting tools in the current SAP NetWeaver BW system, and will be called SAP BusinessObjects Pioneer.

10.3 Enhancements

SAP BusinessObjects Planning and Consolidation has been enhanced based on feedback from customers' experiences of the current version of the product. We will discuss some of these enhancements in this section.

10.3.1 Audit Enhancement

Auditing allows an organization to track changes related to activity and data in the SAP BusinessObjects Planning and Consolidation environment. The following auditing features have been introduced:

- Track activity when users enable and disable audit logs.
- Track the original and new value when making a change to data in an SAP BusinessObjects Planning and Consolidation application.
- Trace changes to security settings.
- Record the machine ID and the IP address of the user making changes.
- Audit activities related to business process flow.

10.3.2 SAP BusinessObjects Planning and Consolidation for Excel Enhancement

The SAP BusinessObjects Planning and Consolidation interface for Excel has been enhanced to include the following features:

- The SAP BusinessObjects Planning and Consolidation interface for Excel is officially supported as a Microsoft Excel 2007 Add-in.
- When the SAP BusinessObjects Planning and Consolidation Excel interface is used, several files related to application and dimension data are created on a user's computer. The user will now be able to specify the folder where SAP BusinessObjects Planning and Consolidation-related files will be created.
- The files used in the SAP BusinessObjects Planning and Consolidation for Word and PowerPoint applications can be saved directly on the planning and consolidation server.

10.3.3 Business Process Flow

Business process flow is a feature users have been looking for in SAP BusinessObjects Planning and Consolidation for NetWeaver. It was available in SAP BusinessObjects Planning and Consolidation 5.0 and SAP BusinessObjects Planning and Consolidation 7.0 for Microsoft and drives process consistency by enforcing polices and procedures and tracking status and completion of tasks.

For users who are familiar with the SAP NetWeaver Business Planning and Simulation tool, this feature is similar to the Status and Tracing System (STS) that supports a workflow model for a variety of applications. This is especially relevant in the case of planning and consolidation processes that involve a number of steps and where the process involves a review before the plan data is approved or the consolidated data is considered final.

Business process flow (BPF) is defined as a sequence of steps that correspond to an action. When all of the steps defined in the BPF are completed, the planning or consolidation process is realized. Each BPF is geared towards a particular process; for example, a BPF may be defined for the yearly sales planning process and may consist of steps where data is input, reviewed by management, and approved.

BPF in SAP BusinessObjects Planning and Consolidation 7.5 supports the following features:

- You can use it as a central menu to access the different functions in an application; for example, from a BPF, you can access an input schedule, a report, and so on.
- You can use it as a monitoring tool for multiple levels of review and approval before data is considered final. This is especially helpful in the case of company-wide planning that may go through multiple iterations and approvals.
- You can send email notifications after completion of a task in the process.

Two views are available to monitor the BPF process, the monitor view and the personal (My Activities) view. The former monitors the entire business process flow across the enterprise in one glance; the latter displays the active processes for the user in the process flow as well as the steps that require user action.

Next, we will discuss the steps for configuring a business process flow.

Create Business Process Flow Template

Creating a BPF template is the first step in developing a BPF for your application. BPF templates are created and maintained in the Admin Console. Follow these steps to create a new BPF template (keeping in mind that you first need to obtain the necessary authorization):

1. In the navigation pane, select Business Process Flows and select the Create BPF Template task in the action pane.
2. You will see the Setup BPF screen and are prompted to enter the following information:
    - Define BPF: In this section, you are prompted to enter the name and description for the BPF and select a controlling application.
    - Define Instance Identifiers: In this section, select the dimensions to uniquely identify a BPF instance. A BPF instance is created from a BPF template and more than one BPF instance can be created. The dimension that will be used as the driver dimension is also selected here. By default, the Time dimension is selected in all BPFs.
    - Set Access: In this section, select the users and team who should have access to the BPF.
3. Click on Next to define the steps and substeps for the BPF. On the Define Steps/Sub-Steps screen, click on Add and provide the information outlined in Table 10.1.

Item	Description
Name	Specify a title for the step. This will appear in the BPF.
Instruction	Provide information on what is done in this step.
Enable Reviewers	If a step requires review, select this checkbox.
Allow Reopen	If this checkbox is selected, a step can be reopened by authorized users.
Define Step Region Criteria	Specify the driver dimension, owner, and reviewer property as well as the dimension members for the step. There is a limit of six member definitions per step.

Table 10.1 Business Process Flow—Add Step

Item	Description
Opening Criteria	The setting here determines when a step is open.
	Two options are available for configuring the open criteria: All Step Region or Matched Step Region.
	All Step Region is selected when all of the step regions must be completed before the next step opens. Matched Step Region is selected when it is necessary to open the next step for the same region when the status for a region is complete.
	Note: The first step is always open. It is not possible to define a criterion for opening the first step in a BPF.

Table 10.1 Business Process Flow—Add Step (Cont.)

4. The next step for creating the BPF template is to assign an action to each step or substep. Actions can be assigned to a step or substep as long as there are no further substeps associated with them.
5. Finally, validate the BPF template.

Now that we have explained how to create a BPF template, we will discuss how to create a business process flow instance.

Business Process Flow Instance

A business process flow instance can be created from a BPF template by authorized users, as follows:

1. Select the template and choose the Create BPF Instance action.
2. In the Define Instance Identifiers section of the Setup BPF screen, select the members for the dimensions defined in the template creation interface.
3. Select the instance owner. The list of users specified here is taken from the users and teams you selected in the Set Access section of the Setup BPF screen in the template creation interface.
4. Next, select Create BPF Instance. A preview of the instance is displayed. To generate the instance, click on Finish. Before an instance can be viewed by a user, it must be activated, which is done by clicking on the Manage BPF Instance task in the action pane. After a BPF instance has been created, any changes to the template on which it is based do not affect the instance.

After the business process flow instance has been created, the instance is ready for use.

10.3.4 Enhancements to Consolidations

The consolidation process has been enhanced to better manage the owner calculation logic, as follows:

- A new hierarchy editor is provided to maintain ownership ratios. Earlier, this feature was available only in the Microsoft version of SAP BusinessObjects Planning and Consolidation for NetWeaver 7.0.
- EvDRE reporting using dynamic consolidation hierarchies supports legal consolidation in SAP BusinessObjects Planning and Consolidation for Excel.
- A currency conversion feature that can handle multiple currencies has been made available.

10.3.5 Enhancements to Work Status

As you may recall from earlier in the book, we discussed how SAP BusinessObjects Planning and Consolidation supports setting the work status for a region of data in an application. In SAP BusinessObjects Planning and Consolidation 7.5 for NetWeaver, when the work status for a data region changes, an email notification can be sent to the owners and managers of the corresponding data listed in the owner dimension.

10.3.6 Enhancement to Script Logic

Script logic has been enhanced to include additional keywords, as discussed in this section.

Time Offset

A new keyword, TMVL, is available to calculate offset time values from a given time period. The format for this parameter is as follows:

```
TMVL(offset, base_period)
```

For example, the following statement can be used to offset the time period by four months, starting in January 2010:

```
TMVL(4, 2010.JAN)
```

- Offsets can be either negative or positive.
- The base period can be a hard-coded value, as in the previous example. A time script variable, %TIME_SET%, or a data manager variable prompt variable such as $NEWPER$, can also be used.
- You can use TMVL in:
  - FACTOR/EXPRESSION within REC
  - FOR/NEXT loops
  - IS conditions inside WHEN/ENDWHEN

Nested TMVL parameters such as `TMVL(-1, TMVL(-3, 2009.JAN)) )` are not supported.

Copy Data Across Applications

The keyword DESTINATION_APP is available to copy data from a source application to a destination application. The destination application may not contain all of the dimensions available in the source application. In these cases, you must add the following key word to skip those dimensions:

```
*SKIP_DIM= {dimension name}[,{dimension name},…]
```

If the destination application contains dimensions that are not available in the source application, they can be added by using the ADD_DIM keyword and specifying a dimension name and value.

```
*ADD_DIM {dimension name}={value}[,{dimension name}={value},…]
```

If the dimension names in the destination application are named differently than in the source application, they can be renamed using the RENAME_DIM keyword. The RENAME_DIM key word is used as follows:

```
*RENAME_DIM {dimension name}={value}[,{dimension name}={value},…]
```

Multiple dimension names can be added to the instruction, separated by commas, when using the SKIP_DIM, ADD_DIM, and RENAME_DIM keywords.

When the DESTINATION_APP keyword is defined in a script, all of the subsequent statements used for writing data are directed to the application referenced in the DESTINATION+APP keyword.

The following is an example taken from SAP Help on using the DESTINATION_APP keyword in a script file. To explain `DESTINATION_APP` with `SKIP_DIM`, `ADD_DIM`, and `RENAME_DIM`, say that another application, `DETAIL_PLAN` is created by copying the `PLANNING` application from the delivered `APSHELL`. It is then necessary to do the following:

- Create new dimensions `PRODUCT` and `MARKET`, and add these to the `DETAIL_PLAN` application.
- Replace `P_ACCT` with `P_ACCTDETAIL`.
- Remove the `P_ACTIVITY` dimension from the `DETAIL_PLAN` cube.

The following is the syntax for using the DESTINATION_APP command in your script file:

```
*XDIM_MEMBERSET TIME = 2006.AUG
*XDIM_MEMBERSET CATEGORY=ACTUAL
*DESTINATION_APP=DETAIL_PLAN
*SKIP_DIM = P_ACTIVITY
*ADD_DIM P_DATASRC=INPUT, PRODUCT = NO_PRODUCT, MARKET = NO_MARKET
*RENAME_DIM P_ACCT=P_ACCTDETAIL
*WHEN CATEGORY
*IS "ACTUAL"
*REC(EXPRESSION=%VALUE%)
*ENDWHEN
```

In this example, DETAIL_PLAN is the target application, which has all dimensions of PLANNING except for P_ACCT. This dimension is replaced with P_ACCTDETAIL. Also, DETAIL_PLAN has two additional dimensions: PRODUCT and MARKET. The script logic shown set the values of the target Application DETAIL_PLAN as follows:

- PRODUCT and MARKET are set to blank.
- The value of P_DATASRC is set based on INPUT.
- The value of P_ACCT is copied to P_ACCTDETAIL.

10.4 Summary

The enhancements in SAP BusinessObjects Planning and Consolidation 7.5 for NetWeaver include several features that will not only make it easier for users to navigate inside the tool but will also allow them to use enriched functionality to fulfill their planning and consolidation needs. The software provides extended reporting and analysis via the integration with SAP BusinessObjects Business Intelligence platform. The features provide the same look and feel across products offered by the SAP EPM software suite, and allow organizations to increase productivity and reduce their TCO.

10.5 Conclusion

The contents of this book were distributed into four segments. In the first segment, which included Chapter 1 and Chapter 2, we provided an introduction to financial planning and consolidation. We provided an overview of EPM and discussed the use of the SAP BusinessObjects Planning and Consolidation tool to support the financial planning and consolidation process.

In the second segment, which included Chapter 3, Chapter 4, and Chapter 5, we delved into the concepts and terminologies that are used in the SAP NetWeaver BW and SAP BusinessObjects Planning and Consolidation systems. We presented a case study for a model company, Rich Bloom, Inc., which is a clothing retailer headquartered in the U.S. that has a presence in Germany and England. We discussed the development of data models and the configuration of objects to support the requirements of this model company. We also discussed the configuration of input schedules that are used to allow users to plan, and reports that allow users to view and share information.

In the third segment, which included Chapter 6, Chapter 7, Chapter 8, and Chapter 9, we presented topics on business logic, process management, and collaboration, and supporting tools that can help in configuring the SAP BusinessObjects Planning and Consolidation tool to meet the planning and consolidation requirements of your organization.

In the fourth segment, which included Chapter 10, we looked into the enhancements that will be made available in SAP BusinessObjects Planning and Consolidation 7.5 for NetWeaver.

After reading this book, you should understand how SAP BusinessObjects Planning and Consolidation serves as a complete solution for the planning and consolidating of an organization. The intuitive Excel-based interface used for reporting, coupled with powerful customization features, makes it a sound value proposition for an organization. In addition, the ability of SAP BusinessObjects Planning and Consolidation to integrate with SAP NetWeaver BW in the NetWeaver version provides additional power to leverage the architecture of SAP NetWeaver BW, which is based on a star schema. This architecture not only provides enhanced performance but also a secure environment for managing the planning and consolidation process.

It has been a pleasure to present this book to you. We hope that you have found the information contained within useful and informative, and we look forward to helping you with your training and project implementation needs in the future.

The Authors

Sridhar Srinivasan is a Solution Architect for Zebra Consulting, Inc, Houston, TX. He holds a Bachelor's Degree in Engineering from the College of Engineering in Guindy, Chennai, India. He is a recent graduate of the Master of Business Administration program at Duke University's Fuqua School of Business, with a specialization in Finance.

Sri has over two decades of experience in Information Technology and has been working with SAP products since 1995. He is certified by SAP AG for the SAP Business Intelligence and SAP BusinessObjects Planning and Consolidation products. He has been directly involved with implementations of solutions in these areas for clients in the U.S. and has functioned as a lead consultant in managing the entire life cycle of SAP BPC project implementations, from the project preparation phase through post-implementation support. His expertise is in the functional, technical and project management areas of the implementation.

Sri has lived with his family in the U.S. for the last 20 years and is currently located in Houston, Texas. He can be reached at *sri.srinivasan@rocketmail.com*.

Kumar Srinivasan is a Senior Business Intelligence/SAP Business Planning and Consolidation Consultant for Zebra Consulting Inc., in Houston, TX. He holds a Master's Degree in Finance from Loyola College in Chennai, India. He is also a certified Cost Accountant.

Kumar has almost two decades of experience in Information Technology and has been working with SAP products since 1999. Kumar has expertise providing solutions in the areas of SAP Business Warehouse (BW), SAP Business Planning and Simulation (BPS), SAP BI Integrated Planning (BI-IP) and SAP BusinessObjects Planning and Consolidation (BPC). He provides diverse solutions to clients in areas that cover both back-end configuration and development of front-end user interfaces. His articles on SAP BW have been published in BWExpert.

Before working with Zebra Consulting Inc., Kumar was employed with The World Bank as an Information Officer. During this time, he worked with relational database management systems including Ingress, Informix and Oracle. He also has extensive experience in the development of applications using messaging tools such as Lotus Notes.

Kumar has lived with his family in the United States for the last 17 years and is currently located in Cary, North Carolina. He can be reached at *kshrini77@yahoo.com*.

Sri and Kumar are the authors of *SAP NetWeaver BI Integrated Planning for Finance*, published by SAP PRESS in 2007.

Index

A

ABAP, 45
ABAP, 232
   Application Server, 50
Account transformation, 41, 254, 358
Account Trend, 222
Admin Console, 93
Allocations, 41, 155, 231
Append, 154
Application, 61, 101, 115
Application Optimization, 118
   Full Optimize, 118
   Lite Optimize, 118
Application set, 59, 96
Architecture, 49
Archive audit activity, 156
Archive audit data, 156
Attribute, 63
Attribute change run, 81
Auditing, 323
Authentication, 386
Automatic adjustments, 42, 254
Available interfaces, 184
   BPC Administration, 185
   BPC for Excel, 185
   BPC for Power Point, 185
   BPC for Word, 185
   BPC Web, 185

B

BAdI, 232
Balance sheet, 35
BPC Admin Console, 184
BPC Administration, 185
BPC for Power Point, 185
BPC for Word, 185

BPC — EvDRE Builder, 197
BPC OfficeClient, 184
BPC Web, 185
Budgeting, 19
Business Content, 58
Business logic, 231
Business process flow, 391
   instance, 393
   template, 392
Business rules, 40, 231, 357
BW Accelerator, 45

C

Calculate ownership, 155
Carry forward, 254 , 358
Carry forward opening balances, 41
Cash flow from operation, 35
Characteristics, 52, 71
Clear, 154
   comments, 156
   journal table, 155
Client interface, 50
Collaboration, 39, 277
Collection, 297
Comment, 224, 277
Comparative, 222
Comparison with prior year, 191
Concurrency locking, 331
   Record level, 331
   Sparsity check, 331
Connection Wizard, 93
Consolidating, 191, 222
Consolidation, 19, 45, 155, 357
   logic, 380
Content library, 346
Content management, 324
Control panel, 205

Control panel, 205
Conversion, 143
   Conversion file, 151
Copy, 154
Currency translation, 41, 231, 255, 357
Current view (CV), 181
Current view order of precedence, 210
Custom InfoObject, 70

D

Database Server, 51
Data Manager, 158
Data manager packages, 152
   Financial process packages, 152
   Miscellaneous packages, 152
   System administration packages, 152
Data package, 61, 247
Data replication, 388
DataSource, 55, 128
Data Transfer Process, 56, 135
   DTP, 135
Data Warehousing Workbench, 74, 84, 141
DB Connect, 55
Demand planning, 30
DESTINATION_APP, 395
Development, 325
   System, 325
Dimension
   Copying a dimension, 108
   Hierarchies in dimensions, 105
   Reference dimension, 104
Dimension formula, 231
Dimension logic, 43, 232
Dimension members, 60
Dimensions, 60, 102
Distribution, 297
Distribution and collection, 40
Distribution list, 299
Drag-and-drop, 211

Drill across dimensions, 191
Drill-down, 224
Drill in place, 191
Drill-through, 388
Dynamic templates, 190

E

eAnalyze, 204
Elimination of inter-company transactions, 33
Enhancement, 385
Enterprise performance management, 19
Entity Trend, 222
ETL integration, 387
eTools, 204
Ev, 183, 193
EvAPD, 194
EvAPP, 194
EvASD, 194
EvAST, 194
EvBET, 195
EvCGT, 296
EvCOM, 196
EVCOM, 296
EvCWV, 195
EvDIM, 194
EvDRE, 196
EvEXP, 196
Ev functions, 193, 296
EvGTS, 195
EvHOT, 196
EvMBR, 196
EvMNU, 196
EvPRO, 195
EvSND, 193
EvSVR, 194
EvTIM, 195
EvUSR, 194
Export journal table, 155
External minority interest, 35

Index

Extraction, 55
Extraction, transformation and loading, 55

F

Financial Information Management, 20
Flat files, 55
Flow dimension, 359
Forecasting, 19
Format, 205
Full optimize, 156
FX restatement, 155

G

Grid Design, 198
Gross profit margin planning, 29

H

Harmonization, 385
Hierarchy/Attribute Change, 81

I

IC booking, 155
IC elimination, 155
Import, 153
Import and Send Mail, 157
Import using FTP, 157
Income statement, 35
InfoArea, 63, 83, 84
InfoCube, 84
InfoObject, 52, 63, 72
InfoPackage, 57, 137
InfoProviders, 53, 141
   Logical InfoProviders, 54
   Physical InfoProviders, 53

Input schedules, 183, 222 , 221
Integration, 385
Intercompany booking, 254
Intercompany elimination, 41, 358
Intercompany investments, 34
Intercompany receivables/payables, 34
Intercompany Sales, 34
Investment planning, 29

J

Journals, 357
   Create journal template, 377
   Manage, 377
Journal template, 374

K

K2, 342
K2 logic, 231
Key Figures, 53, 64 , 71, 78

L

Labor planning, 29
Legal consolidation, 48, 381
Light optimize, 156
Live, 229
Loading, 55
Locking, 323
   features, 332
   process, 333
Lock option, 228
Lock status, 225

M

Management consolidation, 48, 381
Mapping, 143

Member access profile, 61
menu, 277
Merge, 170
Modeling, 84, 141
Monitor, 139, 140
Move, 154

N

Nested Row, 191 , 222
.NET Application Server, 50
Non-reporting, 117

O

OfficeClient, 184
Offline, 229
Offline Distribution Wizard, 302
Opening balances, 155
Options, 143, 205
Order of Precedence of the current view, 210

P

Parameter, 205, 323
Park N Go, 228
Periodic, 189
Planning, 19, 29, 45
  Asset planning, 27
  Considerations, 30
  Cost center planning, 27
  Demand, 30
  Finance, 26
  Human resources, 28
  Investment, 29
  Labor, 29
  Liquidity planning, 27
  Long term planning, 24
  Marketing, 28
  Medium term planning, 24
  Methods, 32
  Operative planning, 25
  Planning area, 26
  Planning horizon, 23
  Production, 27
  Profitability, 29
  Profitability planning, 27
  Profit and loss and balance sheet, 29
  Short term planning, 23
  Strategic planning, 25
  Tactical planning, 25
Planning horizon, 23
  Long term planning, 23
  Medium term planning, 23
  Short term Planning, 23
Planning method, 32
  bottom up, 32
  top down, 32
Planning types, 25
  Operative planning, 25
  Strategic planning, 25
  Tactical planning, 25
Platform support, 386
PowerPoint, 277
Process chain, 58, 157
Process dimension, 233
Production, 325
Profitability and Cost Management, 20
Profit and loss and balance sheet planning, 29
Properties, 60
Property, 107
PSA, 56

Q

QTD, 189
Quality assurance, 325
Quarter to date, 183

R

Range, 205
Refresh, 197
Refresh and expansion, 223
Replace, 170
Reporting, 116
Reporting and analysis, 184
Restore journal table, 155
Return on investment, 21
Revalue, 243
Run package, 162

S

Sales planning, 30
SAP BPC for Excel, 184
SAP BPC for Excel, 182
SAP BPC Web, 182
SAP Business Content, 58
SAP BusinessObjects Planning and Consolidation for Excel, 287
SAP BusinessObjects Planning and Consolidation for Power Point, 287
SAP BusinessObjects Planning and Consolidation for Word, 287
SAP BusinessObjects Planning and Consolidation Web, 287
SAP BusinessObjects Process Control, 389
SAP BusinessObjects Voyager, 389
SAP NetWeaver BW, 51
Scheduler, 138
Script logic, 43, 231, 342
Secured dimension, 60
Security
  Member access profile, 353
  Task profile, 353
  Team, 353
  Users, 353
Service API, 55
Shared query engine, 342

SIGNEDDATA, 91
Single Sign-On, 386
SOAP, 55
Solve order, 234
Sort on member, 191
Sort on values, 191
Spend Performance Management, 20
Staging, 65
Standard templates, 222
Star schema, 44
Statistics, 323
Strategy Management, 20
Structures, 214
Supply Chain Performance Management, 20
System reports, 185

T

Task profile, 61
Tasks, 61
Team, 61
Third-party systems, 55
Time characteristics, 53
TMVL, 394
Total cost of ownership, 39, 182
Transformation, 55, 56, 133
Trend, 191

U

Unit characteristics, 53
Universal Data Connect, 55
US Eliminations, 366
User, 61

V

Validate and process transformation file, 160

Validate logic file, 156
Validate transformation file, 156
Validation, 48, 156 , 232
Validation rules, 358
Variance, 191
VB macros, 214

W

Web administration, 337
Web administration parameters
  Application parameters, 337
  Application set parameters, 337
Web application, 55
Word, 277

Work status, 221, 277
Write back, 342

X

XBRL Publishing, 20
Xcelsius, 389

Y

Year to date, 183
YTD, 189

www.sap-press.com

Provides an easy-to-read overview of all Business Objects client tools in an SAP environment

Explains which tools to use for which types of reporting

Offers simple and practical hands-on examples that leve-rage robust sample scenarios and case studies

Ingo Hilgefort

Reporting and Analytics with SAP BusinessObjects

This text provides comprehensive coverage of the major business intelligence tools in the SAP/BO toolset, with a practical focus on the user experience and integration with SAP. Coverage includes detailed application features and functionality, as well as practical, how-to content geared toward end users hoping to maximize the benefits their BI investment by creating actionable, easy to read and disseminate reports, analytics and other business process metrics.

655 pp., 2010, 79,95 Euro / US$ 79.95
ISBN 978-1-59229-310-0

>> www.sap-press.com

Your SAP Library is just a click away

1. Search
2. Buy
3. Read

Try now!

www.sap-press.com

- ✓ Easy and intuitive navigation
- ✓ Bookmarking
- ✓ Searching within the full text of all our books
- ✓ 24/7 access
- ✓ Printing capability

Interested in reading more?

Please visit our Web site for all
new book releases from SAP PRESS.

www.sap-press.com